NOT LIKE A PROPER JOB:
THE STORY OF POP MUSIC IN SHEFFIELD 1955 - 1975
AS TOLD BY THOSE WHO MADE IT

BY JOHN FIRMINGER and MARTIN LILLEKER

Juma

First published in 2001 by
Juma
Trafalgar Works
44 Wellington Street
Sheffield S1 4HD
Tel: 0114 272 0915
Fax: 0114 278 6550
Email: MLacey5816@aol.com

ISBN 1 872204 80 5

Printed by Juma.

PART ONE: THE HISTORY

PART TWO: THE MUSIC MAKERS

FOREWORD

Sheffield has always been a good city for live music, starting with the jazz clubs in the Fifties and rock clubs in the early Sixties. Club 60 was the first rock club although it started by show-casing the country's finest jazz musicians before featuring some of the area's early rock musicians. The Esquire followed suit, featuring legendary blues players as well as top jazz per-formers and many of the rock bands who went on to enjoy international fame and fortune. The enterprising Peter Stringfellow also brought much entertainment to the city with his clubs the Black Cat, Blue Moon and Mojo. It now seems hard to believe that all these venues were popular without the aid of a licensed bar (although there was always a pub next door), serving just coffee and pop, with the music being the attraction. All the venues had their own atmosphere which also made them so pop-ular. For me to visit one of the current Sheffield music venues is not so different today to what was 30 or more years ago. There's often a band playing in an upstairs room to about 20 of their friends while the pub downstairs is packed with drinkers. I have always loved live music so I sup-port the local scene wherever I can but I am sur-prised to see others who can't be bothered to pay a couple of pounds to support a band or venue. Remember, the guy on stage could be next year's big thing.

Having been a product of the local scene I remember with great affection the excitement of those early days when we were starting out. I can recall with fond affectiom making the trip from my home in Beighton into Sheffield, having to take our equipment to the gig by bus - piling it all under the stairs. Any hardship those days was quickly overtaken by the excitement of just going out and playing in a band. Venues like the Gaumont Teenage Shows, Club 60, Esquire, Black Cat etc were very important to us all. Sheffield and the surrounding area was very supportive of myself and the Cruisers and it was this following that helped us to achieve our ini-tial success. I consider myself very fortunate to have enjoyed the success and experiences my career has subsequently brought me. However while me and my colleagues such as Jimmy Crawford, Joe Cocker, Paul Carrack etc were off enjoying the 'big time', I acknowledge the many others who remained keeping the local scene going and active. Many were very popular local-ly and all played a vital role in the city's musical history.

I was pleased to be asked to write the fore-word for this book. John Firminger and I have been good friends since 1961 and was a great support to me and the Cruisers in those early days. Having been a drummer since the Sixties, it was great to have John eventually become a member of the Cruisers in the late Nineties. His interest in music is reflected in his knowledge and impressive archive collection on the local scene as well as popular music in general. Martin Lilleker has also played an important role on the local music scene and continued to do so in his job as music writer for the Sheffield Telegraph and The Star before that. A musician himself, Martin is naturally very sympathetic to the cause and his work for the Telegraph has given great support and encouragement to all the musicians and venues, just as Top Stars Special did for us all that time ago.

This book also recalls people like Chuck Fowler, Roy Barber and Spud West, all of whom helped me in my career and are, sadly, no longer with us. While Sheffield as a city continues to change, some things deserve to be preserved. It has made a valuable contribution to popular music and its musical history is an important one. This book will serve as an excellent docu-ment to Sheffield's place in pop music.

Dave Berry

INTRODUCTIONS

Over the years there has been a wealth of books written about the various aspects of Sheffield's history - industry, wartime, football and transport - but scarcely anything about the local music scene. Sheffield's music scene has of course been briefly covered in the past via booklets and the press, but a proper book would hopefully set the record straight and also give credit to as many people as possible who have contributed towards it through the years. In musical terms Sheffield has got quite an impressive track record. Such names as Dave Berry, Joe Cocker, Def Leppard and Human League, etc have all certainly put the city on the world map. Having become successful international names, they were all products of a very active local music scene that goes back to the late Fifties.

My first glimpse of any local rock'n'roll performers was around the summer of 1958 at the Punch Bowl Hotel, Hurlfield Road. I'd climbed up and peered through a back window of the concert room, I can't remember who was playing but I was riveted. Balancing precariously on the narrow window sill, I was eventually discovered by the landlord and told to get down and clear off, but the vision stayed with me. I later became a follower and friend of Dave Berry and the Cruisers who would subsequently inspire me to becoming a musician myself. My own involvement began in November 1964 when I joined the original Cruisers and made my drumming debut at the Esquire Club on December 13. The audience that night included a number of local musicians who'd come along to see the band play in their own right, after parting company with Dave Berry. Recalling my nervousness, I played right through one number on the on-beat, completely unable to switch to the correct off-beat, much to the horror and embarrassment of the rest of the band.

I eventually decided it was time a proper account of the Sheffield music scene was written. After a number of delays I was encouraged to go ahead with the idea by friends and fellow musicians who also saw the need for such a book. I decided to focus on the period from the mid-Fifties to the mid-Seventies - a period when the local pop music scene thrived, before struggling to survive under the onslaught of discotheques and punk-rock.

It was also very encouraging to learn that Martin Lilleker had had the same idea and in due course we decided to pool our resources and make this a combined effort, in the hope of covering as much ground as possible. While Berry, Cocker and company were off enjoying fame and fortune, there were a lot of local musicians back in Sheffield still making the rounds of pubs, clubs and wherever else they could get a booking. Having been a working musician on the local scene since 1964, I was able to recall many of the bands and venues.

With such an abundance of activity through the years, Sheffield has gone through all the different musical trends and styles. In the early days there was jazz, skiffle and rock'n'roll, then beat music, R&B, country, soul and psychedelic, through to heavy rock. Because the scene was so active, it certainly can be related to by many, many people all round the city. This includes the hundreds of musicians involved as well as all those who used to go and watch (and possibly still do) bands and singers perform. Many people had their own favourites whom they would follow around and their favourite venues where they would meet up and make friends with other music-minded people.

There will be, I'm sure, many musicians, young and old, who can relate back to the book's title, when they were constantly reminded by their parents that playing in a band was "not like a proper job". To them, what was considered a 'proper job' was probably in the steelworks, down the pit or in some other local industry, many of which are now sadly no more than just part of Sheffield's history. Indeed, nowadays being a musician has ironically possibly more stability. There are even student courses now on how to be a working musician or DJ. However, I'm sure that most musicians owe a debt of gratitude to their parents for their initial help in buying instruments and their patience while we learned to play them.

Reflecting back on those earlier times, I've spoken to many people who recall with affection their own involvement and observations. This has been a great help in the attempt give a true picture of what it was like. Some recollections obviously get a bit dimmed by time and also a little exaggerated, whereas some were amazingly accurate, depending, sometimes, on how much had been consumed, but all were valid in putting this book together. It certainly was inspiring to see that so many of the old musicians had kept collections of their old photos, clippings, diaries, etc. Some of these have been used in this book, giving a further insight to those times past. Another great source of information was the Top Stars Special. Published by the Sheffield Star, this supplement started out as a periodical in 1960 and eventually became a monthly before ceasing publication in 1970. It looked at various aspects of entertainment and leisure and was a great voice for the local music scene. This ranged from artists getting major recording deals to group vans running out of petrol on their way back from Worksop. However Top Stars was very encouraging for the local music scene and is fondly remembered by all.

To everybody who has contributed towards this book, I sincerely thank them for their time and their memories. Sadly some of the names included in this book are no longer with us. Needless to say they have all made valid contributions to the local music scene and this book is also dedicated to their memory. Some of the stories and recollections have been both highly humorous and quite sad, but invaluable in recalling some of those rockin' days and I sincerely hope that you will enjoy this return trip to them.

John Firminger

As a journalist on The Star from 1976 to 1986 and the Sheffield Telegraph from 1989 I have been writing about the Sheffield music scene throughout what many people perceive as its heyday, with many bands becoming internationally famous (and many others not even famous in their own households). In the course of that I also became aware of the rich heritage that fostered that scene, going right back to the late Fifties. The first live music I ever saw was the Frank White Band at a small club in Rotherham called the Charade, a few weeks after my 16th birthday in 1969 when I somehow managed to persuade the owner, one Dave Allen, that I was old enough to be allowed in (although he initially turned me away because I didn't have a tie - and I don't think he was particularly enamoured of my 24-inch flare bell-bottomed trousers either). The raunchy rhythm and blues of the three-piece band, Frank's double-necked white Gibson guitar and his huge sideburns, tailcoat, raggy shirt and ripped jeans, topped with a battered top hat and feather, left an indelible mark. Until then the only musicians my friends and I would take seriously were the ones who had records out. And here was a chap living on the doorstep who was as good if not better than all of them. The following week (after persuading Dave Allen that the trouser belt I had knotted round my tie-and-dye shirt collar was really the latest high fashion in ties) the music was supplied by another Sheffield band

McCloskey's Apocalypse. They sounded like The Who meets Frank Zappa and featured a character who ate a light-bulb halfway through the set. Between them, Frank and McCloskey's started an infatuation with local bands that has continued to this day, to the extent that writing about music became my job (praise the lord!). As a singer and cack-handed guitarist with Muckle Flugga (named after the northern-most tip of Great Britain, so there) and then the Wealthy Texans, I even went on to find out what it was like to play at some of the venues that many of the bands in this book played at. Most memorable was the very first one in 1970 with Muckle Flugga, in a church hall somewhere in darkest Rotherham. We arrived there, with our gear, in the drummer's dad's fruit and vegetable van. Halfway through the show, performing a song called Catastrophe if memory serves correctly, the bass player turned round with what looked like blood dripping down his face (for some reason, even though I was the singer, I was right at the back behind the drummer). 'My God,' I thought. 'Somebody has shot him.' It turned out to be a perfectly flighted rotten tomato - and the next one had my name on it. At which point the vicar intervened. I've taken rock'n'roll very seriously ever since.

Martin Lilleker

Remembering the following people:

Eric Ashmore
Roy Barber
Joe Beckett
Mick Bell
Dave Bradley
Mick Brady
Mick 'Flapper' Beaumont
Terry Clayton
Mick Dale
Terry Emory
Reggie Featherstone
Barry Glynn
Ken Griffiths
Fred Guite
Pete Fender
Norman 'Jock' Horan
Pete Jackson (drummer)
Terry Jenkinson
Kenny Pete
Dave 'Cannon' Smith
Ray Stuart
Johnny Tempest
Norman 'Spud' West
Johnny White

And all the other Sheffield rock'n'rollers who are no longer with us.

PART ONE: THE HISTORY

1. NOTHING SHAKIN'

In the early to mid-Fifties Sheffield looked like being the last place on earth to embark on any sort of musical adventure. The city centre, like most in Britain at the time, was drab and dour. The pubs were just drinking holes which didn't sell food and stopped serving at 10pm (it wasn't until February, 1962, that an extra half hour was added, and then only on Fridays and Saturdays). Licensing laws had been introduced during the First World War, aimed specifically at places like Sheffield where manufacturing industries needed to run at maximum efficiency for the war effort, encouraging workers to get to bed early. In surrounding, more rural areas, such as Derbyshire and Barnsley, opening times had been extended to 10.30pm, hence the popularity of pubs such as the Fleur De Lys at Totley and the Old Harrow at Gleadless, both of which were then in Derbyshire, and the Greengate at High Green, then Barnsley. In Sheffield the only music in pubs was usually piano singalongs. In the early Fifties, John Firminger can remember standing outside city pubs like the Brunswick in Haymarket and the old single-storey Black Swan on Snig Hill and hearing intoxicated versions of such hit songs of the day as Mitchell Torok's When Mexico Gave Up The Rhumba (To Do The Rock'n'Roll) and Nat King Cole's Too Young emanating from a smoke-filled bar-room. What live music there was came from big bands in dance halls, one such band featuring local musician Jack Wilcox who was reputedly the first guitarist in Sheffield with an electric guitar. The jukebox revolution, which was to change people's listening habits for all time, had still to take hold. Eating out was considered something of a luxu-

ry and it didn't help that there were less than a handful of restaurants anyway.

Post-war austerity - both moral and financial - was still very much in place and the city centre was struggling to recover from the devastating air-raids which blitzed much of it. Street lights were switched off at midnight, a practice which carried on into the mid-Sixties. British pop at the time revolved mainly around dance bands and crooners. Names like Anne Shelton, Ronnie Hilton, Joan Regan and Dickie Valentine were among the biggest stars. Stage performances and sheet music sales, not record sales, were where the money was and the business was controlled by Tin Pan Alley agents and publishers. The BBC was paid fixed rates by publishers to get songs plugged, a system that wasn't abolished until the mid-Fifties. It was only when rock&roll came along, and a new generation of young hustlers with it, that things were to change. In the meantime most of England, and especially Sheffield, was a musical backwater. Unlike other big northern cities such as Manchester or Liverpool, Sheffield was geographically isolated. Both Lancashire cities were ports, Manchester being linked by the ship canal, and had historic and cultural links with the east coast of North America. They also had huge influxes of Irish immigrants which were to have a strong influence on musical input. It always took Sheffield that bit longer to catch up - but it also led to the city creating its own unique take on musical trends, as well as developing its own.

One of the earliest venues in the Forties/early Fifties was the Cavendish Ballroom on West Street (above what is now the Cavendish Bar) where Constance Grant taught formation dance. But on Saturday nights a jazz band, led by guitarist Ted Needham, played regularly. "It was dark and atmospheric," says sax player Nev Reaney. Ironically, in the late Nineties the ballroom became the centre for a whole different kind of dance and other musics, when it was taken over by Warp Records as the label's centre of operation before moving to London in January, 2000. Needham's band went on to win the prestigious Melody Maker dance band contest in the late Forties. The band then moved to Nether Edge Hall on Fridays and many local musicians sat in with them, including one of Sheffield's most eminent players, Barry Whitworth, who went on to win the prestigious

Advertisement for the first electric guitar in the area

National Jazz Contest in 1961 and played with Maynard Ferguson. "The audience was mostly made up of dance band musicians who wanted to play jazz and they could get up and have a blow," says Reaney. "But some of us were more interested in playing group jazz. My band the Savoy Quintet wanted to play bebop while there was the Black Diamonds who played New Orleans jazz." But there were few, if any, venues for anything resembling new music.

Guitarist Derek Bailey learned the hard way that Sheffield wasn't the ideal place to serve a musical apprenticeship. He was one of only a handful of Sheffield musicians from the decade or so after the war to go on to a worldwide stage. He recalls his first paid job in Sheffield in

Derek Bailey

1950, after returning from being called up. He was in a trumpet, guitar, piano and drums quartet four nights a week at the Pheasant at Sheffield Lane Top. "We played pub music genre. It was just anonymous, playing anything the audience wanted us to play. Requests were the motivation, working your way through a mound of garbage. But I learned to play. I even got made the bandleader. I think that was because I wrote music, which was a bit pointless because nobody could read it. We used to get 10 shillings a night each. But it was a good place to play - the lights would go out at ten past ten, nobody would move, and some of the lights would go back on again at ten-thirty and it would all start up again. This situation went on for a

few months until there was a domestic dispute or whatever and the landlady shopped her husband to the police. We ended up getting fired."

Bailey also got sacked from his next job, after a brief sojourn in Bradford, the first of many trips to other cities to find work. "The trouble with Sheffield was there were only two professional jobs for musicians - in the Green Room restaurant in the Regent Cinema (later the Gaumont) at Barkers Pool, and at the City Hall. I got one of them, with the 15-piece Bernard Taylor and his Broadcasting Band, although nobody could remember when it last did a broadcast, at the City Hall. It was standard big band stuff, six nights a week. I was with them for three months. I think part of the reason I got fired was because during the intervals the band would split into two and we'd do a quickstep medley in which every member of the band took a solo. I stood up and played Ornithology by Charlie Parker. That wasn't the thing to do in a dancehall. But also if there were any economies to be made they always got rid of the guitar player. That's the way it was. But the guitarists struck back in the late Fifties when it was the rest of the band that would get sacked instead."

Bailey headed for Glasgow and other major towns and cities, working in the burgeoning night scene - Sheffield seemingly the only place in the country that closed down at 10pm. The only time he would return to his home city was between music jobs. "I'd end up selling shoes, delivering bread or milk, digging holes, anything to earn some money. I played if anybody offered me a gig." Finally, in 1956, he got Sheffield's 'other job', playing guitar, bass and piano in a trio at the Green Room restaurant working six nights a week. "I couldn't really play the other instruments. It was a terrible band. They used to play in the same key all the time except when I was on the piano. The level of incompetence would not have been tolerated anywhere else other than Sheffield. It did have a reputation

The great Count Basie meets the Savoy Quintet at Sheffield City Hall

among working musicians as being the arsehole of the musical universe. If you got a touring band playing at the City Hall there was nowhere for them to go afterwards. I can remember Count Basie playing in Sheffield and he ended up in the Green Room after the show. I played bass with Basie there - imagine that. And it was the same with Lionel Hampton. The manageress of the restaurant would let them stay on. It was ridiculous because we were the worst band in the world. Glasgow was full of jobs for musicians in the Fifties. Leeds had eight or nine dancehalls, restaurants and clubs to play. I used to play in Leeds more than I did Sheffield and would go there to listen to music, and there was also an after hours thing with many places not really opening until 11. It was a whole different scene. There was a musical community. The key to being a working musician was to get out of Sheffield." Bailey, who also had a short spell playing 'jazz-related music' with the big band at the Locarno on London Road - "I could see the writing was on the wall for that kind of music by then," - finally left Sheffield in early 1957.

Tony Oxley

Bailey was also to go on to have a highly fruitful relationship with another Sheffield musician, jazz drummer Tony Oxley, who also has mixed memories of those early days in Sheffield. Oxley, ten years younger than Bailey, was brought up in Pitsmoor - "We had to change houses a lot because of the blitz" - and his earliest musical memories are of classical music and singing in the Sheffield City Choir at the City Hall. "We were doing one concert and Churchill turned up. I still don't know what he was doing there." He also went with his school to see Sir John Barbirolli conduct the Halle Orchestra at the City Hall.

Oxley started work as an apprentice lathe engineer on £1 13s 6d (£1.67) a week before moving on to Cocker Brothers steelworks on Effingham Road for £7 a week, the wage rise meaning that purchasing a drum kit became a possibility. "All that metallic noise, I don't know if it had some influence on my drumming, if you believe all that stuff of being a victim of your environment. But the smog in Sheffield certainly had an affect on my health. I have had bronchitis ever since. You couldn't see the bottom of the street and the trams had to have their lights on in the day. We always seemed to be fogged in."

One of Oxley's formative experiences as a pre-rock'n'roll adolescent was dancing to big bands. "The resident big band in the local dance hall would play these things - The Hawk Talks, Intermission Riff, Woody Herman's Apple Honey - from the American big bands. When it came to the drum solo, they'd put up Louis Bellson's Skin Deep. We'd dance to it - bebopping we used to call it. Over the shoulders, under the legs, jive - really athletic stuff - and a lot of improvising. There were famous dancers that used to come to our local dance hall. The following was so strong. When rock'n'roll first showed its head, I really thought this can't replace it."

Like Bailey, Oxley took what musical work he could, mostly playing in pubs, often with pianist Fred Boaden. One job he and Boaden had was playing to diners at Atkinson's restaurant on the Moor on Saturday afternoons in the early Sixties. The latter engagement came about thanks to Oxley's stint with the Grand Hotel Society Band led by Winston Lee. "Being the Society Band leader, he knew the right people and he persuaded the Atkinsons to let us play there." Presumably diners were blithely unaware they were listening to Art Blakey-period hard bop. Oxley was another who met many of the visiting American jazz musicians and remembers the difficulty they had in finding entertainment after the show. "Some of them would go back to a house on Machon Bank in Nether Edge where Hayden Cook [local jazz musician] lived. The gas lamp outside became known as the 'Jazz Lamp',

I think because Count Basie had a piss against it." Another visitor to the house, on March 11, 1960, was Ella Fitzgerald who had been at the centre of controversy when she appeared at Sheffield City Hall. The review in the Star the next day carried the headline Ella Was Hustled Off The Stage. "Ella, trying to please fans who were screaming for more, let the show run over time and sang an extra number or two," said the review. "To the amazement of the audience, attendants walked on to the stage, began to tidy up, and practically hustled her off. Possible angry scenes were avoided, the way Ella shook off the incident herself and walked off with a laugh and a smile."

Above: Gavin Bryars with trumpeter Barry Whitworth
Below: Tony Oxley

Bailey and Oxley, particularly, were, unlike many of their colleagues, aiming to be professional musicians. Their contemporaries were not in the same class, as bebop pianist Alex Wyatt admits. "They burned the midnight oil and put in all the hard work. I was scared of Derek. We were just buskers in comparison. He used to look down on us and quite right too. They decided they were going to be musicians full stop, making a living from it. Tony Oxley sat in with my band the Savoy Quintet once and his technique was something else. Our drummer Pete Jackson could only look on in envy." Although Sheffield in those early days was hardly the musical hub of later years, Derek Bailey and Tony Oxley were two of its first musicians who went on to find

acclaim further afield.

Over the next few years Bailey logged up an impressive variety of work - cabaret with Bob Monkhouse, accompanying religious radio broadcasts, performing with The Supremes in a London gambling club, playing on 6.5 Special as well as working with Shirley Bassey and pianist Russ Conway. From 1963 to 1966 he and Oxley, along with Sheffield University philosophy student Gavin Bryars, formed Joseph Holbrooke, a trio which played almost every Saturday lunchtime at the Grapes on Trippet Lane, establishing an improvised music movement that is still a worldwide influence to this day. Bailey is still the movement's leading exponent while Oxley has become a renowned, innovative drummer and band leader and Bryars an award winning composer.

2. THE CHOSEN FEW

For most people in the early Fifties, and teenagers in particular, the main entertainment was still based out in the suburbs, most of which were virtually self-contained 'villages', reinforcing the oft quoted maxim that Sheffield is England's biggest village. What action there was for Sheffield teenagers was at the various Saturday night dances around the city. Music fan Pete Carson recalls some of those early days: "I discovered the music myself through some of my pals who used to go up into the Astoria Ballroom, which was above Burtons on the corner of Staniforth Road, next to the Regal Cinema. They were blokes who were older than me, probably 18 or 19 year olds. I was 15 and they had great ideas where things were heading. Because they frequented some of the US Air Force bases up and down the country, I think they'd got an insight into the American music scene of the day. There were dances at Darnall Labour Hall which was basically nothing more than a shed. One of the instigators was 'old man Dyson' - Alderman Sydney Dyson - one of the politicians of this area. He used to visit when the teenagers were having their dances there." The kinds of sounds that Pete and his friends were jiving to were Tennessee Ernie Ford's hillbilly boogie and the jumpin' R&B of Joe Turner and Joe 'The Honeydripper' Liggins.

Cinema was still the main attraction however. There were almost 50 dotted all over Sheffield, several with their own organist who would play the huge instrument while it rose on a plinth from beneath the screen. Frank White, who grew up in Darnall in the Fifties and was to go on to become one of the city's most revered musicians, recalls that there were seven cinemas within five or ten minutes walking distance from his house in the now demolished Bilton Road - "and they were always full."

Nothing much had changed - except the films had sound - from when possibly the first Sheffield musician to make a national name for himself. Hillsborough-born Reginald Dixon

Reginald Dixon: Sheffield's 'Mr. Blackpool'

served his apprenticeship accompanying silent movies some 30 or so years earlier. In the 1920s he played at cinemas in Stocksbridge and on the Wicker as well as Heeley Palace, where the organ was housed in a tank to prevent it being flooded when the River Sheaf broke its banks, which it did almost every time there was a downpour. Reginald - never Reg - eventually took over the huge Wurlitzer at the Tower Ballroom in Blackpool in 1930. He was told: "If you don't make a success of it you go - and the organ too." He went on to reign supreme for almost 40 years, retiring in 1970, and became known as Mr Blackpool, resplendently dressed in an immaculate white tuxedo. He broadcast more than 3000 performances from the Ballroom on radio - the Queen was a regular listener - and issued countless recordings for his record label, EMI. One collector had two hundred and fifty 78s by him. But Dixon never forgot his home city roots. He was patron of Sheffield Organ Enthusiasts and one of his final concerts was at Sheffield City Hall. "We could have sold it out four times over," said the City Hall manager. Everything from the Big Bands to the Beatles were given the Dixon treatment over the years. "But I won't play punk rock," he said shortly before his death in 1985.

Rock'n'roll had sort of arrived in England in 1954, but the shape of it was the portly figure

of the positively elderly - nigh on 30 - Bill Haley and his Comets. He was a hero to many, but hardly inspired the sort of musical rebellion that Elvis was to cause two years later - although cinema seats were torn up countrywide when Rock Around the Clock was used on the opening credits of controversial juvenile delinquency film, The Blackboard Jungle.

Television didn't really come to Sheffield until 1953 when most people got a TV set to watch the Queen's Coronation. Along with radio, it didn't provide much in the way of inspiration for youngsters. US stars such as Frankie Laine, Johnnie Ray and Guy Mitchell were among the first names to create any kind of teenage hysteria, prior to rock'n'roll. TV producer Jack Good was subsequently one of the few who saw rock-'n'roll's potential beyond just being a short-lived craze. He was to be responsible for such ground-breaking TV rock shows such as 6.5 Special (1957) with Pete Murray, and Oh Boy! (1958), featuring Marty Wilde, Cliff Richard and the Vernon Girls. But even while Elvis was shocking authority with his swivelling hips as Heartbreak Hotel and Blue Suede Shoes hit the top in 1956, much of England was still in the thrall of the skiffle revolution - epitomised by Glaswegian Lonnie Donegan - partly because it didn't take much talent, expensive equipment or command of an instrument.

Requiring a little more musical prowess there was also a jazz boom, with trad and modern jazz fighting it out for pole position. It went on in a bewildering number of rooms in pubs, clubs moving from one venue to another from week to week. One of the first, on a fairly permanent basis, was Club 55 at the Hallamshire Hotel on West Street where the house band was led by

pianist Fred Boaden. "The idea was to be nearer the university," said one of the organisers, Alex Wyatt. "But it didn't work out. It smelled of cat pee." Club 55's successor, billed as Sheffield's first modern jazz venue, was Club Basie on Snig Hill run by Wyatt. This took place

Savoy Quintet at Club 55

Savoy Quintet checking out the tunes at Club Basie

on Tuesday nights at the now demolished former coaching inn, the Black Swan, on the site where one of Sheffield's most revered venues, also named the Black Swan in homage to its predecessor, was to be built in the early Sixties. "We were looking for somewhere to play and the landlord of the Black Swan said we could use one of the old livery rooms above the stables," said Wyatt. "He told us we could do what we wanted with it, 'Burn it down if you want.' We then tried to hump a grand piano up the three flights of stairs but it just wouldn't go. We got an old upright up there in the end. We covered the walls with album sleeves and, I tell you, it was a real thrill playing in front of 60 people." A stage was made out of two tressle tables, drummer

The original Black Swan, home of Club Basie, below

Pete Jackson providing the handiwork. Sax player Nev Reaney: "The temperature in the room went from being really cold to boiling hot, particularly when the open fire was in full flow, so the piano would go out of tune all the time. You could hear the strings pinging, it sounded quite avant-garde. But pianos were only 30 bob each from an auction room and at one point we ended up with three or four of them at the top the stairs. And everybody used to dance, that was the idea."

By 1958 the club, nicknamed Behind the Green Door (after the Frankie Vaughan hit of the time) because of the huge green double door which had to be swung open to get into the stables, had 900 members. The resident band, the Savoy Quintet, was led by Wyatt who "coped remarkably well on an old, sadly out of tune, upright," as The Star reported. The Savoy Quintet also found themselves in demand for various engagements, whether it be on a float at Sheffield Rag Parade or functions. But the most memorable was a wedding reception at the Hallamshire Hotel on West Street. "The room was partitioned into two," says Nev Reaney. "And the family of the bride were in one half and the groom's in the other. We soon realised it was a shot-gun wedding. Nobody was talking to anybody else and everybody totally ignored us. I said to Alex, 'What shall we do?'. Alex said, 'Just keep playing and then get out.'" Wyatt and his fellow beboppers were eventually squeezed out by trad jazzers, the three Bs - Acker Bilk, Kenny Ball and Chris Barber - who reigned supreme at the time, and rock'n'roll. But not before the infamous occasion when the 'dirty boppers' took on the 'Mouldy Figges' - trad musicians - in a musical head-to-head at the City Hall. There was always a big rift between the two jazz factions, to the extent that Humphrey Lyttleton was booed off stage one night at the City Hall because of alto sax player Bruce Turner's modern jazz leanings.

Other, more occasional, jazz nights were held at various venues including the Royal Oak on Cemetery Road. Resident band were the Squires, led by a stalwart of the Savoy Quintet, tenor player Neville Reaney. Club 13, which drew 150 people for Tubby Hayes, started out at the now demolished Blue Boar Hotel before moving to the Brincliffe Oaks in Nether Edge. The Mailcoach Inn on West Street featured the Kay-Em-Uki Stompers (a corruption of Krazy Mixed Up Kids) with clarinetist Trevor Barnes and banjo player Dave Brennan. Then there was Nether Edge Hall, the Fleur De Lys at Totley, Sheffield Training College with the Crescent Jazz Band, and the Darktown Jazz Club at the Haigh Tree Hotel, Bernard Street. But probably the most popular jazz venue was the Old Harrow at Gleadless. Alto sax player Joe Harriott - 'the Ornette Coleman of the Sixties' - with world class drummer Phil Seaman in the band, was a regular visitor as were various Americans including singer Mark Murphy.

Teenagers in the city were excluded from all this because there was no entry for under 18s. Attempts were made to establish clubs in non-licensed premises, such as the now demolished Howard Street Methodist Hall (where Dave Berry saw George Melly perform) and various cafes which hosted Club Chicago and Jazz at the Clef (Kathy Stobart and Don Rendell were among the musicians who appeared at the Clef). Such was the demand that audiences breached the fire regulations and they were soon closed. Terry Wilson, a member of the Nev Reaney Quartet, explained the problem after taking over the Methodist Hall: "It was held on Saturday evenings from 7.30 to 11.30. There was dancing, orange squash, tea and bread rolls. We usually had a real crowd there - between 200 and 300 enthusiasts - and we mixed traditional with modern music. The trouble was that after 10pm all the drunken characters tried to get in and made things a bit rough for us and in the end it was closed down. There have been only about three clubs held on unlicensed premises and all three were closed down."

Between them, trad jazz and skiffle were to play an important role in what was to come. "They were the basis of what rock became - four or five guys who were adequate as musicians but full of energy and ideas. Trad and skiffle musicians didn't have to read the notes like dance band musicians," says Dave Berry. None of the Sheffield contingent in either skiffle or trad made an impact nationally at the time, although several individuals were to make names for themselves later on.

Indeed about the only big success Sheffield could claim credit for was former Bevan Boy, Tony Dalli, below, who came over from Italy in 1952 to work initially in mines at Armthorpe and

Maltby before taking a job at Arthur Lee's steelworks in Sheffield. He was a tenor in the style of Mario Lanza, lived in Heeley, and started out singing in pubs, working men's clubs and cinemas in Sheffield before going on to international success in the mid-Fifties; first of all at the London Palladium, then Hollywood, Las Vegas and Rome - and landing a film contract with 20th Century Fox.

There was also a flurry of excitement when Sheffield United and England footballer Colin Grainger, below - 'the Dickie Valentine of football' - revealed another talent when he sang with American vocal group the Hilltoppers, who had

had a big hit with Only You, at the Sheffield Empire theatre in 1957. He went on to record a handful of singles for the HMV label. He released This I Know in 1958. Disc magazine said: "A useful debut. The boy's got a warm ballad style and a lot of strength which is firmly controlled here. With a little more experience I can see Mr Grainger scoring a lot of goals in his new field." During the football close season he toured the country in variety shows, earning £100 a week. His football earnings were just £17 a week, having moved to Sunderland, and this was for a player who had scored two goals on his England debut against Brazil at Wembley. And, on a personal note (writes Martin Lilleker), his brother Jack Grainger, who played for my team, the wholly unfashionable Rotherham United, was a much better player but couldn't sing.

One Sheffielder who made a name for himself, but not in a musical way, was prominent classical musician, Herman Landers. He was the founder and one of the conductors of Sheffield Philharmonic Orchestra. He also invented a robot 'spanking machine' in 1958. It was designed to administer corporal punishment "under continuous and precise medical control" so prison staffs would be relieved of applying corporal punishment by hand, and that the machine would provide punishment to suit the medical condition of the prisoner. Mr Landers, also a Sheffield magistrate, eventually relented, saying: "The machine was designed for flogging in prisons and, as the Home Secretary is now to reintroduce the cat, it should now be forgotten." Beat that.

3. ROCK ME DADDY-O

It was the skiffle boom which inspired teenagers across Britain to take up music. Leading the way was the 'King Of Skiffle' Lonnie Donegan, long-time banjoist with Chris Barber's trad jazz band. There were also the Vipers, the Worried Men (with Terry Nelhams - soon to be Adam Faith) and the Chas McDevitt Group including Nancy Whisky. Roy Barber recalls: "Lonnie was a big influence. My mother got me out of bed one night - it was probably only about quarter-to-eight - to come watch this guy. It was the wildest thing I'd ever seen and skiffle got a lot of people playing."

The essence of skiffle was the simplicity, energy and the fact that it was easy to play. All that was needed was an assortment of home-made or cheap instruments - guitars, banjos,

mandolins, washboard, dustbin lids for cymbals, tin pans, paper and combs plus the obligatory one-string tea-chest bass and somebody with a passable voice. Bands could set up on street corners, in back gardens, front rooms, almost anywhere. Roger Harrison of the Sapphires: "We had about six rhythm guitar players - all without amplifiers - a tea-chest bass and that sort of thing." Some inherited their instruments, like Alan Wood: "My grandfather had this ukulele. I thought it was a guitar. I cleaned it up and scrubbed it. I took it to school in 1958 where they had a guitar class only to be told I couldn't stay, as it was not a guitar with four strings, it was a ukelele." Mick Hallam, of one of Sheffield's earliest skiffle groups the Mainliners, was luckier: "My guitar was my dad's. He had a group at the Norton Hotel in the wartime."

An early starter was Neil Bridges of the Blue Diamonds. "From being 12 years old, I had music lessons off a black guitar player who used to play with the Earl Of Wharncliffe. He was

Musical youth: the Blue Diamonds skiffle group, and below, their first record

a mechanic at TC Harrisons. He was from Burma and lived about five doors away. I got special permission to play in pubs. They shut at 10 o'clock in those days and kids didn't go in pubs. I played at the Greengate Hotel and Sicey Hotel two or three nights every week. I'd be 13 and my brother used to go and see jazz bands in Grimsby. He came back with a Chris Barber LP and there were two tracks on it by Lonnie Donegan, one of which was Rock Island Line, and that started me playing. I was playing them two songs before skiffle came out." The Blue Diamonds Rhythm Group were possibly the first young band to make a record. The 8" shellac acetate, recorded in 1957 in a small studio above Curtis's Record shop at the bottom of London Road, features a couple of popular skiffle numbers, Worried Man and Greenback Dollar. Although the performance is pretty basic, it demonstrates the typical exuberance of many of the young skiffle outfits.

Most of the young skifflers, such as Pete Wardlow, were still at school - "I had a skiffle band when I was 12 in 1956." Another school skiffle group was the Andy Capps from the Ecclesfield/Parson Cross area that included Pete Jackson. "It was all basically lads who were in your class, 'cos they were handy. It wasn't whether you could play owt, it was just case of wanting to be in. There was Ray Hines, me, Richard Holroyd and Frank Stewart."

It wasn't long before there was plenty of competition in and around the city with skiffle

SKIFFLE WINNERS GET CASH

THE LUMBERJACKS, a young skiffle group who won a special award for junior entrants in a skiffle contest staged last Tuesday night by the Sheffield Association of Mixed Clubs and Girls' Clubs, received their prize of a cheque at St. Mary's Community Centre, Bramall Lane, Sheffield, last night.

It was received on behalf of other members of the group by 14-year-old Edward Sayles, of Merlin Way, Firth Park.

The presentation was made by Mrs. Madeleine Smith, chairman of the association.

The group all of whom are aged 14 and attend Hatfield House Lane Secondary School, Shiregreen, Sheffield, intend to use the money to buy themselves a drum.

During the evening, St. Mary's Youth Club presented a one-act play. They are affiliated to the association.

groups like the Delta Four, RAF Skiffle Group, Sapphires Rhythm Group from Walkley, Lumberjacks from Shiregreen, Checkers from the Darnall/Manor area, Cross Rhythm Group and Devils Skiffle Group, both from Parson Cross, the Four Imps, Zodiacs with Frank White, Headlanders (formed by washboard player Vic Cocker and occasionally featuring

younger brother Joe), the Sundown skiffle group, with future Rotherham MP Stan Crowther and comedian Duggie Brown, also from Rotherham the Downtown Rhythm Group, the Devil Chasers (a trio made up of three vicars from Thurnscoe), The Mainliners, the Border River Scuffle (sic) Combo (which included vocalist Johnny Tempest from Frecheville) and the Frantic Four with Brian

Holy skiffle, The Devil Chasers

'Chuck' Fowler from Beighton.

Cinemas in and around the city would frequently feature skiffle groups just playing through the house PA. Frank White: "I can still hear the sound of my guitar through the PA now." Jim Greaves of skiffle group the Checkers recalls one memorable performance at a cinema. "A character who's still knocking about Darnall, Dennis Needham - a right hard-case - used to follow us about and shout requests. He'd gone to see us at the Lyric and the audience was noisy. He went, 'Owd on lads when you've done that one,' and he got up and turned and faced the audience. 'Listen you shower of fuckers. I've come to see these lads and I want to hear 'em an'all so shurrup.' It was brilliant. The only noise I heard after that was the clapping at the end of every song!" Frank Peach, lead singer with Ricky and the Rebels: "I played many of the cinemas around Attercliffe - the Regal, Plaza, Adelphi, Globe, etc. On Sunday nights they used to have groups on. We used to do anything that came along. People would book you for wedding receptions, private functions. I became known for singing He's Got The Whole World In His Hands, the Laurie London number. It was very popular at that time and I'd got that sort of voice that hadn't quite broke." One of Frank's biggest 'engagements', as they were called, was a rare spot of rock'n'roll at the City Hall - "I got up and did a spot with Ted Heath's

The Black Cats

Orchestra. He asked me if I'd like to do it. That was one of my biggest thrills." One of Dave Hawley of the Black Cats' biggest thrills came when he played at the old Trades Club at the top of the Moor in 1956: "I was 14, all the top acts came on all in one night, that's where I first saw Ronnie Dukes and Rickie Lee. But what I remember best was when a prostitute came into the dressing room, put her hands straight down my trousers and said, 'That'll make you play better.' I was shell-shocked."

Along with the skiffle craze were numerous competitions. In one at St Mary's Youth Club, Bramall Lane, the Lumberjacks won the cash prize with which they said they intended to buy a drum. At another the Blue Diamonds won the princely sum of £15 which they used to record themselves. The biggest competition was the National Skiffle Contest organised by London promoter Stanley Dale (who later became the manager of Johnny Kidd). This ran throughout the summer of 1957 and, for a week starting on

September 23, came to the Empire Theatre on Charles Street. Established stars Jim Dale, who was compere, and the Vipers, fronted by future TV and radio personality Wally Whyton, headlined the shows, with the remaining entertainment being provided by the battle between the local skiffle outfits. With the average group consisting of about six members there would easily be about 300 skifflers appearing during the week's contest. Jim Greaves of the Checkers: "Jim Dale was good at organising it. He was the first person in showbusiness we'd ever heard swear. He told us we'd got to come on at exactly the right time and stand in exactly the right place or we'd get a 'bollocking'. As 16-year-old lads it sort of shocked us that these people used this sort of language." Another participant was Chuck Fowler and his Frantic Four: "We were obviously the best that night but there was this other group on with a tea-chest bass. This lad was skiffling away and he jumped on the tea-chest and it folded into a great big heap into the drum-kit and they won because of their exhibitionism." Vic Cocker's group the Headlanders also took part but brother Joe had to be content watching from the audience. The Sheffield finals involved six local outfits - the Checkers, Greycats, Mainline Rhythm Group, Mike Jackson, Twin Cities and winners the Moonshiners from Barnsley. The winners were nearly always chosen by audience reaction so if a group had taken a large following success was virtually guaranteed. The promoters would be too intimidated to go against such powerful support even if the group was not up to scratch. Jim Greaves and the Checkers were runners-up: "The Moonshiners brought about seven coachloads from Barnsley. We didn't mind 'em doing that but we wished we'd thought of it first because it more or less went on the amount of

Barnsley winners, The Moonshiners

applause." The Moonshiners were good at that sort of thing, as Dave Hawley recalls: "There was a skiffle competition somewhere off Chapel Walk and the first prize was a record maker. It looked like a Dansette and it made a brown disc. The Moonshiners won that, they won everything. They were older than us and they had six strings on their guitars. We used to say, 'No wonder he can play, he's got six strings on his guitar.' That was your way out - 'If I had got one I could play like that.' We could all play three chords and word got out that somebody knew four. It really meant something in those days, having a little advantage. We were jealous." Winners of another skiffle contest in Rosehill Park, Rotherham, were the Stop Press skiffle group which included future comedian Duggie Brown: "When we won the contest, the local newspaper asked us how we felt about it and we said we were 'dead chuffed' which they interpreted in print as 'shocked, surprised and wonderfully pleased!'" Duggie later became a member of the Four Imps, another Rotherham skiffle combo. Representing the Regal Cinema ar Attercliffe, they took part in the 6.5 Rhythm Contest organised by Star Cinemas. Aided by three coach-loads of followers, they won the finals at Worksop on May 18, 1958, and went on to be seen on national television - "We appeared on 6.5 Special from Kingston upon Hull singing Be Bop A Lula, taking over from Bob Cort who sang the signature tune," said Duggie. The Mainline Group, from Low Edges, had only been together for six weeks when they came third at the Empire Theatre contest. They went on to become one of the most predominant of the early Sheffield skiffle outfits. They got together when guitarist Hayden Percival met up with fellow guitarist Mick 'Fritz' Hallam: "It started with Hank Williams. We used to go to Hayden's house and listen to some of his old

Hank Williams records and try to work the chords out." They managed to put a few songs together and would perform at Heeley Teen Bar. From there they became part of a roadshow with different acts, performing at places like Middlewood Hospital. They were also regulars at the popular skiffle and folk club at St George's Hall, Brook Hill. By now they joined by Tony Gilbert on the obligatory tea-chest bass: "We were into Lonnie Donegan and played for his local fan club which we ended up running. We had a trip to Blackpool to see Lonnie. We took our instruments and we met him afterwards. He played backstage with us. He was very good to us, really helpful and encouraging. Not at all stuck up. He'd show you a few chords on the banjo." The Mainliners subsequently expanded to a four-piece with Gilbert on upright bass and Mickey Beaumont joining on drums and appeared at the Gaumont and Woodseats cinemas.

One of the biggest annual events for Sheffielders was the fair held every year at Farm Grounds on Granville Road. Waltzers would spin, dodgems would bump and the huge swing-boats would have everybody screaming and laughing while the smell of hot-dogs and onions, candy-floss and toffee-apples permeated the air. The sound of the latest hits would blast out in unison with the continuous chugging of diesel engines. For young and old it was a very atmospheric place. At the side of the fairground a talent show was organised by the Sheffield Star with young performers having a crack at singing alongside featured acts. An appearance by the Checkers led to them playing with Lonnie Donegan at the Empire Theatre. Jim Greaves: "We'd entered the talent contest at the fair on the first night and they invited us to play for the week for money. It coincided with Donegan being on at the Empire. He turned up one day and sat

The Mainliners Rhythm Group

The Chequers on stage at Farm Grounds

on stage while we performed. He invited us to the gig that night at the Empire and we sat backstage and had a jam session afterwards. Then he took us to the Howard Street Jazz Club. He was a smashing bloke Lonnie."

By mid to late 1958 most of the skiffle groups had started changing over to playing rock'n'roll. Trevor Woodcock: "Rock'n'roll was coming in at the same time as skiffle was still going. I can remember we did a skiffly type number followed by a Buddy Holly number." Chuck Fowler: "Skiffle and rock'n'roll were sort of crossing and the Everly Brothers were becoming popular." Pete Jackson: "You could do skiffle without drums but we wanted to go a bit further. So I asked my brother Roger, 'Do you want to be in a group?' He hadn't got any drums so he bought a snare and a cymbal. At that time, with Cliff Richard and the Drifters, Terry Smart played with one snare and a cymbal and that's where Roger got it from." Duggie Brown's band, the Imps, also changed: "We became the Kool Katz and then I went on my own as Douglas Brown."

For many young musicians their first ever appearances were at school concerts. Alan Wood: "Bob Grundy knocked on my door out of the blue and said 'You've got a guitar, fancy going on the school concert?' So we learnt a couple of songs - Jesse James and Tom Dooley. It was in the first year." Pete Jackson also recalls the admiration from schoolmates: "There were only like two or three lads out of about 600 pupils who could play guitar. Kids used to say, 'I didn't know you could play.' There were three lasses who formed a Ponytails type of group and they wanted us to back them as well on concerts." Other early gigs were at youth clubs around the city, Twilights' guitarist Dave Hopper: "The very first gig we ever did was at Littledale Youth Club and they had a collection for us after. We got about three shillings and six pennies between us. All the kids put their pennies in the hat."

4. C'MON EVERYBODY

One of Sheffield's earliest rock&rollers came in the unlikely form of Alan James Montague Stuart Wortley Mackenzie, better known as the Earl of Wharncliffe or Lord Rock'n'Roll as he was dubbed by the newspapers at the time. The Eton-educated Earl, an ex-Royal Navy seaman and stock car driver, announced his intention of "livening up the aristocracy" on his 21st birthday in 1956 when he was given a set of drums.

He became a member of the Musicians' Union and joined the Johnnie Lenniz rock'n'roll group from Chesterfield. He started out drumming at weekly dances in Bolsover, "cheered on by stamping youngsters." In December the band was banned from playing at Swanwick Memorial Hall, Old Whittington, with the chairman of the governors, Michael Swanwick, saying: "We did not want any more trouble for fear of losing our licence for music and dancing." The Earl declared: "We consider the cancellation rather a compliment. It shows what our music does to these teenagers. We knew we were good, but not so good as to be dangerous." In April, 1957, he played in variety with the band at the Empire Theatre in Sheffield and in September they appeared on a stage once graced by Marlene Dietrich, Noel Coward, Tallulah Bankhead, Liberace, and more recently, the 'wonder boy' of British rock'n'roll Tommy Steele, at the Cafe De

The Rockin' Earl of Wharncliffe

Paris in London. The Earl was featured on a special number The Lenniz Jump on which he was let loose on his drums for four minutes. A year later his rock'n'roll career was over, saying he wanted to concentrate on modern jazz: "I don't want to knock the rock but I am considering forming my own group."

Nobody was going to make a name for themselves while the only outlets in the late Fifties where bands might get noticed by a wider audience were the occasional talent contests. The Carroll Levis' Search For Stars was at the Empire on Charles Street in the spring of 1959, shortly before the theatre was demolished. It was compered by authoress-to-be and sister of Joan, Jackie Collins. One entrant was Pete Jackson and his group the Andy Capps. "There were loads of bands and single acts. We didn't get through, it was sort of, 'We'll let you know, don't ring us, we'll ring you.' 'Well, I'm not on the phone.' 'Well tough shit then.'" Other entrants included the Debonairs with singing drummer Bob Vickers and guitarist Charlie 'Wag' Collier who got so hot, according to the press, he had to wear dark glasses to stop the sweat from running in his eyes. Cool man! Also participating were another local band calling themselves the Rolling Stones. Not the Rolling Stones. While Mick Jagger and Keith Richards were just finishing at school in London, a bunch of teenage Sheffield schoolboys - Jimmy Fletcher, Tony Lewis, Roger Garratt, and twins Geoff and Mike Robins - formed a band, called themselves the Rolling Stones, and reached the finals of the Carroll Levis show against tough opposition from semi-professional groups. Magazine Disc reported in its April 25, 1959, issue that, "throughout their act guitarist Tony Lewis carried on like a real trouper after he had dislocated his arm." Another participant was Pat Leslie who had been singing with Mickey and Johnnie, fellow former students at Sheffield College of Arts and Crafts. The two boys decided to enter the contest as a duo. Pat: "They said they wanted to go and be like the Everly Brothers, so that left me out. I went on on my own and sang Ann Shelton's My Happiness and came second. Mickey and Johnnie came nowhere." The winner of the contest was 13-year-old rock 'n' roller Mel Dean - "I think he won because he was young and everybody said, 'Isn't he good for his age'." Pop weekly Disc reported: "The youngster plays the guitar and rocks to any sort of rhythm." The teenybopper was part of a family tradition. His mother and father appeared with many top name acts and were known as the Dixie Dandies. Mel's grandfather Fred Brand was 'the famous' Chocolate Drop. And his other grandfather Daniel Gibbons was an Irishman who wrote plays and songs and was described as "a sort of Dublin Irving Berlin without a fortune."

Then there was the Locarno on London Road which had rock'n'roll nights on Sundays and Thursday and also hosted heats of the National Singing In Harmony contest for young singing groups, one heat in 1958 being won by guitarist Malcolm Green and - singing in public for the first time - David Holgate Grundy, soon to be Dave Berry, doing an Everly Brothers type song. One reporter of a certain age from the Sheffield Star braved one of the teenage rock'n'roll nights, paying his 1s 6d to get into the Locarno: "While I suffer rock singers fairly gladly, my musical penchants might conceivably be regarded as four-sided. One quick glance at the pulsating, gyrating phalanx which confronted me, with its kaleidoscope of multi-coloured jeans, sweaters and socks, however, soon assured me

The Dominos: David Grundy and Malcolm Green

that I wasn't going to hear Handel's Largo tonight. It was Record Request time when I got there, and after hearing five consecutive opii of the elastic Mr Presley I thought it was fair to assume they were partial to him." Live rock-'n'roll followed from Laurie Gold and his Pieces of Eight. Then there was the talent contest. Andre Lorenz, 'chocolate-coloured' Lloyd Thompson and Ernie Andy were pipped at the post by a joiner from Rotherham, Dennis Cox, who sang Paul Anka's You Are My Destiny. He won £1, which was fortuitous because he hadn't got his bus fare home.

Meanwhile, out at the Embassy Ballroom on Mansfield Road which opened in 1956, proprietor Ron Storey had banned rock'n'roll types and 'eccentrics' on Saturdays, the busiest night of the week. "I want to see a return of the prewar manners and dress in the dance halls," said Mr Storey. "Rock'n'roll has driven the select type of dancers away. The youngsters go out and get a few penny'oth of wine gums and when they come back they're noisy and in high spirits all evening. I predict that rock'n'roll will be dead within a year." The reporter, the same one that had gone to the Locarno, added his own two penny'oth: "Many of us, I'm sure, will join with Ron in wishing a speedy grave to the rock bug. If only more of us were in a position, like Mr S, to add more nails to the coffin. Since it was imported from America three years ago we have had to suffer not only the alleged music, but also the corruptive by-products of this crazy cult. As well as encouraging a distorted dress sense among the youngsters, the cancerous claws of rock'n'roll have spread confusion, crime and promiscuity."

Thankfully, the dance halls were not the only centres of entertainment. There was also what was to become the mainstay of local talent in the early Sixties, youth clubs and church halls. It took pubs a while to pick up on the possibilities. It was also to take a little while before rock'n'roll would have an impact on live music in Sheffield. "The fact that rock'n'roll was huge in the States didn't make any difference to the provinces. It was as though it hadn't happened over here," recalls Dave Berry who was a teenager living at Woodhouse in the late Fifties. There were Saturday night dance bands - Ted Heath, Stan Kenton, Humphrey Lyttleton and the like - at the City Hall. More relevant were visits to Sheffield by Buddy Holly, Eddie Cochran, Jerry Lee Lewis and blues singer Big Bill Broonzy, but they were few and far between.

"There were weekly variety shows at the Empire with the likes of Tommy Steele, Terry Dene, Vince Eager and Johnny Gentle, but they were just variety acts, English versions of what the promoters thought would pass for Elvis," says Dave Berry. The man behind virtually all of those acts was manager Larry Parnes, but he did get it right when he turned Liverpudlian Ronald Wycherley into Billy Fury, since it was Fury, along with Adam Faith and Cliff Richard, who were to dominate British pop until the Beatles came along in 1962. Cliff was one of the first to visit Sheffield in October, 1958 when the 17-year-old appeared at the City Hall. With his band the Drifters he was bottom of a bill headed by US stars the Kalin Twins, and had just released his first single Move It. By 1958, thanks to Elvis, Eddie, Buddy, Jerry and, to a degree, Cliff, Billy and Adam, Sheffield had finally caught up, and local bands started playing all over the city.

One of Sheffield's first proper rock'n'roll bands was the Blue Harmony Boys, which evolved from the RAF Skiffle Group, and eventually became the Twin City Beat Boys. The members were from Sheffield and Manchester, hence the name. The original line-up was Jimmy Holden on guitar, Geoff Morton, piano, Biddy Bidwell, bass, Dave Fish, baritone sax, and Pete Wardlow on drums. They were later joined by two tenor sax players - Jerry Gilmore and Jock 'Scotty' Adler (Norman Horan) - and did Little Richard style music.

The Frantic Four with pianist Chuck Fowler was already leaning towards rock'n'roll and whose style owed a lot to his heroes Jerry Lee Lewis and Chuck Berry. It was that, and the

Jerry Lee to be, Chuck Fowler with unusual mike stand

band's 'proper' rock'n'roll drummer, which attracted the young Dave Berry to sing with them.

The Mainline Skiffle Group also turned to rock'n'roll, becoming the Mainliners, and featured a full drum kit and electric guitars. They were fronted briefly by singer Danny Harman, a good-looking Canadian formerly known as Danny

Rivers. Roger Harrison: "He'd taken his name from the Harman Mountains in Canada, or so he said. He turned out to be a bit of a liar." In fact it was the Sheffield Star Teenage Club which had ran a competition to help the singer come up with the name. Harman went on to join the Sapphires who became the Cherokees. Roger Harrison: "He was a good singer but eventually ran off with the guitar player's wife so that was the end of that. I never saw him after that." Harman was also at the centre of a riot at Hillsborough Memorial Hall. Keith Linaker: "He came on with all the make-up on and gold lame suit and they started throwing pennies at him. Next thing they're all throwing things at us. My brother-in-law worked at Brown Baileys and he fetched three vans full of lads who'd just come off afternoons still with their sweat-towels and boots. There was a big battle over this kid's

From Canada, Danny Harman

WHY THEY CALL HER THE GARTER GIRL...

MEET Sheffield's music-making Main-Liners ... and their glamorous girl vocalist "The Garter Girl" (pictured above).

Blonde, petite Sylvia Dale got her title through the coloured garter she always wears (below the knee) when she sings with the group.

A shop assistant, she lives in Norton Lees Crescent, Sheffield.

And, oh yes, she's engaged to a marine.

Leader of The Main Liners is six-footer Ray Stewart, who first formed a group when he was with the Army in Germany. The group? The North West Ramblers.

With his latest rhythm group he builds his music, somewhat bravely, around a bass electric guitar.

Numbers

The experiment seems to have paid dividends too for The Main Liners are another group that has been promised a chance at the Shepherd's Bush Gaumont.

Incidentally the group—and the "Garter Girl"—will be on stage at next week's Teenage Show at the Gaumont.

Together with Ray, who plays electric guitar, will be guitarist Mick "Fritz" Allen, an 18-year-old apprentice electrician, "Manx" Green, a 19-year-old clerk and electric bass expert, and Dennis Dryden on drums.

One of the numbers they hope to try out is their new beat version of the oldie, "Ghost Riders in the Sky."

singing, an absolute riot. It was on the front page of The Star." The Memorial Hall, more commonly known as the Memo, was a popular venue for young talent. One of the bands that appeared regularly was the Sapphires whose drummer was Roger Harrison: "We played there for about two or three years, every Tuesday night. We used to get a pound between us, four bob [20p] each." Pete Wardlow of the Twin City Beat Boys: "I remember playing the Memo and doing rock'n'roll - Gene Vincent, Elvis and all that stuff."

The Mainliners expanded their line-up to include singer/manager Ray Stuart. Also in the line-up was singer Sylvia Dale, known as the 'garter girl': "I used to wear my skirts quite short years before the miniskirt 'cos I'm only very small. So I thought, 'I'll wear a garter and that's how I'll be known.' It was really a bit of a gimmick. I think we went down well in most places because it was rare to have a girl singer. There were only us and the Greycats at the time with a girl singer. There were very few girl singers around - Connie Francis, Brenda Lee and Helen Shapiro." The group made regular appearances on the Saturday Morning Teenage Shows at the Gaumont and also began getting bookings outside Sheffield. Eventually Sylvia and Mick Hallam became husband and wife but, because of Mick's job, they left the group and moved out of Sheffield. Hallam: "I wasn't popular at work. I had to make a choice, either to do the job or go skiffling. Whether it was jealousy or what they didn't like it." Ray Stuart recruited new blood including Tom Rattigan: "Ray asked me to join the band on guitar. The trouble was I could-n't play a note. I had-n't got a clue. So Ray sat behind a curtain strumming away while I mimed. I could see the rest of the band didn't like this idea at all." Other early rock'n'roll outfits included the Greycats, with singer Jenni Lee who was later replaced by powerful female vocalist Pat Leslie. Then there was the Debonairs with singer Bob Vickers, the Harlequins with singing drummer Paul Denton and the Miami Five which featured accordionist Eunice, and the Sonnets with guitarist Keith Chalmers and drummer Gerry Wigley.

The equipment was often quite primitive. Pete Wardlow: "We got one of those big old fashioned curved radios with valves in and it'd got a dial on the front. You could plug into the back and we used that as an amplifier." Roger Harrison: "Pete Wardlow's band used to practise down at the dancehall at the top of Wood Street off Langsett Road. They hadn't got an amplifier between them so they used to hire one from an electrical shop at Crookes, up Matlock Road. It was like a big old radio/amplifier. They used to get ten bob [50p] for playing down at this dance-hall and it used to cost them nine shillings and six pennies to hire this thing. They used to fetch it in a wheelbarrow and they all used to plug into it." Frank Miles recalls how his band, the Frantic Four, would all share the same amplifier. "Chuck [Fowler] made this amplifier with one 12-inch speaker and we put the lead guitar, the rhythm guitar, the bass and all the vocals all through it." With everbody sharing the same amp it would naturally sooner or later overload as experienced by Pete Wardlow: "I'd go on singing Sea Of Love and they're at the back - John Dance on piano, Benji on drums, Linfitt on lead guitar, and no bass, just Otter on rhythm guitar. All of sudden I smelt smoke and Linfit's wireless had caught fire and there's blokes running on putting sand on. He carried on and there's smoke and flames coming out." That wasn't the most dangerous incident. Roger Harrison: "Benji played guitar but he hadn't got an amplifier when he bought his first electric guitar. Because it was an electric guitar, he just thought you plugged it into the mains and it became louder. And that's what he did. He put a plug on the end of the lead and plugged it into the mains and got a right belt off it, burnt all his fingers. He could have been killed."

Pete Wardlow also explains how they also tried to improve the sound of the piano: "We put drawing pins in to get that jangly sound like Jerry Lee Lewis." Drummer with the Sapphires, Roger Harrison recalls his first kit: "A snare drum and a cymbal that's all I used to have. I used to stand up and play. Eventually I bought an Ajax bass drum from Willgooses but I hadn't enough money to buy a pedal as well. I used to carry it every Tuesday night right down to the Memo and back at the end of the night. I'd set it up on the stage, sit behind it but not play it 'cos I had no pedal. Even if I'd got a pedal I wouldn't have known how to play it. Just for show that's all it was. I did that for at least 12 months, carrying it up and down Walkley Lane." With Roger's limited playing skills, the prospect of playing on a full set of drums was intimidating: "The Greycats came with all this equipment - proper amplifiers, full drumkit. Dennis, the drummer, said to me, 'Use my drums if you like.' I said, 'Oh no, no, it's all right Dennis,' purely because I was frightened I wouldn't have known how to play it. I'd have been totally lost."

Chuck Fowler: "I had a pal called Lewis Edwards who was a hero of mine. He used to be tinkering all the time with radios. He made us our first amplifier, a 12-inch speaker not in a box

but on a baffle board. That's all we had. Sometimes we'd use the club's PA system with those great big silly old microphones that sound like you're singing down a grate. We didn't know anything about microphones. I was buying all sorts of mikes. Cheap Japanese crystal mikes had a very thin sound and tended to feedback easy. Gradually the old Reslos and the Shures came." Frank White: "We had a 15-inch speaker for the PA. It was heavy duty stuff then. I remember doing the Gaumont with 15-watt amplifiers but you could hear it." Jim Greaves remembers how his group the Checkers came off worst when they traded one of their instruments: "Slats, our bass player, had got this second-hand bass and it was a snip. It was obviously worth some money. But we wanted a bass with an orchestra spike on it so he could spin it, so he swapped it for a bass from the Vipers. We were doing the picture-house circuit and we'd got two bookings at the Regal on Staniforth Road so we left the instruments there. When we come to play the following time the bass was in two pieces. It had folded. We'd only had it two weeks so the Vipers got the best of the bargain on that." Black Cats guitarist Dave Hawley: "We had a gut bass string on our tea-chest bass. We played the Parson Cross Hotel and they had a beautiful double bass standing up in the corner, so we pinched the string off that and put it on our tea-chest bass." Alan Wood: "The tremelo-arm modification on our Lucky-7 was the opener from a sardine tin."

The lack of musical ability held back many young aspiring musicians. Most simply taught themselves through trial and error. Dave Hopper: "I'd had an acoustic guitar for two years and I didn't know which way the strings should go. I'd not been able to fathom out how to play anything on it and there was nobody to teach me. Sometimes I'd mime to Ricky Nelson records. My hands would be going and I thought it sounded great. As the record faded away there'd be this horrible discordant sound - me still playing."

When it came to records, the place to go was Philip Cann's Record Shop at the top of Dixon Lane. Walking past the awesome sight of 'Big Ada' on her fruit and veg stall, the stairs led down to the rows of LPs displayed on the wall, by names such as Chuck Berry, Lena Horne, Faron Young, the Champs and Perry Como. In the listening booths you could spend hours listening to the new releases and sometimes even buy one! Roger Harrison: "I used to go down to Cann's every Saturday with my spending money and buy a record. I had a wind-up gramophone and I used to put it on. Little Richard or Jerry Lee or Chuck Berry. And my dad would always say after it had finished, 'Huh, I can't recommend that.' Every week he used to say that." Rock'n'roll music seemed alien to many of our elders as Roger recalls his dad opinion of it, "'Tang-tang, yah-yah, all bloody night, folks go out to enjoy thi'sens, not listen to that row!'" Stu Moseley: "The best thing for me was when my dad took a job on the Morning Telegraph at nights. He'd go out at six at night and not come back till four in the morning. I had one LP, Elvis's first album, and my mother loved Elvis, and I played it back to front all day for months and I didn't get another record until Elvis Two came out." Stu also recalls: "Joe [Cocker] was able to play his records at night as his dad would go to bed early and he was a bit deaf which was a bit handy for Joe. There was also his Auntie Eva who used to live in the attic, she used to drift through. She was Joe's dad's sister, very timid, and didn't like the outside world at all. We used to be sat there at four in the morning and she used to come down, drift through, like a ghost. She only came out at night."

Philip Cann's also had a musical instrument department with an eye-catching selection of guitars hung on the wall. These ranged from expensive looking semi-acoustics like Hofners to Rosetti Lucky 7s that were cheap in both price and design. Nevertheless, these green or red instruments of torture (for the player) got many a young guitarist off and rollin'. Milners on Howard Street was another supplier of guitars where young musicians like Mick Hallam would go: "We used to congregate in there after the Gaumont." It was there that John Firminger first caught sight of a Hofner Futurama. "Sunburst in colour and looking magnificent, I thought that this was just like the one Buddy Holly played and was subsequently purchased by Cruiser Frank Miles." Frank White: "Wilson Peck's, that was the best shop in town. I remember going in when

I was at school just round the corner. I can still see me going in there and listening to Bill Haley and to Perkins' Your True Love." Fashion-wise a lot of Sheffield's teenagers of the Fifties would gravitate to Winstons on Snig Hill, where all the self-respecting Teddy boys and Teddy girls could purchase the latest fashions such as drape jackets, brothel creepers and bootlace ties. Sheffield's youngsters were now getting hip.

5. TEENAGE KICKS

Unsung hero, Harry Murray

The major showcase and the real starting point for most Sheffield rock'n'rollers in the late Fifties was the Saturday morning Teenage Shows at the Gaumont Cinema in Barker's Pool which began in late 1959 and attracted audiences of up to 1,600 teenagers. Dave Berry: "One of the unsung heroes was Harry Murray the manager. He seemed ancient to us. Looking back he was probably only about 29 or 30 [45-plus it turned out]. But he ran a whole series of concerts over a period of about two years which featured every band in Sheffield that was any good." Jimmy Crawford: "We used to go along to the Gaumont to watch the acts. Harry Murray was a good bloke, he was one for the kids and there was a queue of bands to get on, but it was done properly that was the nice thing. Big stage, lighting, and proper announcing on and off, it was a real plus to us, the best chance we could have to start us off really." Frank White: "I can't recall going to the Gaumont and not hearing guitar players. It was always very competitive. We were always watching what equipment the others were using." The shows always featured

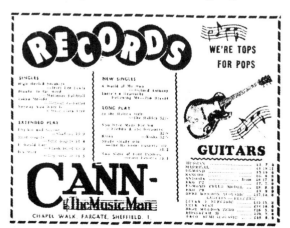

many other young up and coming groups and singers, plus a feature film - "Those shows were brilliant," says Black Cats guitarist Dave Hawley. "I can remember standing behind the screen and watching the film Rock! Rock! Rock! backwards."

Rock'n'roll duo Mickey and Johnnie made several appearances. Trevor Woodcock was Mickey: "The first time we worked there was with the one guitar, just stumbling through. Then we'd find ourselves doing vocal backing for other acts, then they'd give us backing." Jimmy Crawford: "Everybody had their favourites. It was good and it was friendly." Other acts included Ray Stuart and the Mainliners, Johnny and the Nightriders, Johnny Tempest and the Mariners, Ricky and the Rebels, Johnny Tombstone and the Deadbeats, Danny Harman and his band the Vulcans, Bob Vickers and his Debonairs (described as the "dandies" of the rock'n'roll scene), and 13-year-old Mel Dean who appeared on television and was on the same bill as Adam Faith. Another star group to emerge from these shows was Shane Fenton and the Beat Boys from Mansfield whose singer died suddenly. It was the group's friend Bernard Jewry who then, with the blessing of the dead singer's parents, took on the name of Shane Fenton and changed the band's name to the Fentones.

The youngsters also got to meet the stars at the Teenage Shows with the Star newspaper and its Teenage Club which had started in March, 1959. The club held teenage parties in the Green Room above the Gaumont where they could "meet their favourite pop stars, talk with them, have a cup of tea with them and get their autographs." Guests at the inaugural party were Marty Wilde and Russ Conway. Other visitors included Cliff Richard, Adam Faith, Anthony Newley, Johnny Preston, Conway Twitty, Freddie Cannon and Billy Fury. It was the success of these parties and the establishing of the Teenage Shows later in the year which led, in 1960, to the Saturday night Star including a Teenage Page. This would subsequently lead The Star to publish the pop supplement, Top Stars Special, which was to go on to chronicle the next decade of pop music in Sheffield. One of the magazine's earliest reports was from the

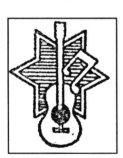

Star Teenage Club badge

Gaumont: "The young performers rapidly gained experience and turned out more and more polished numbers as they competed for popularity with an equally young and critical audience." It also reported that it was the very first club of its kind outside London: "It came into being long before Liverpool had caught on to the idea."

For the performers the Teenage Shows were quite nerve-racking as Dave Hopper of the Twilights recalls: "It was our very first band. We'd all only been playing about three or four months and we'd had an argument with the drummer during the week. He refused to do it so we had to play without a drummer. We did Kon-Tiki by the Shadows without a drummer. It'd only been out about three or four days and we'd just learned it. It was so nerve-racking to be doing a real gig instead of a youth club - and not have a drummer." Some never made it to the Gaumont as guitarist Alan Wood remembers: "We were in Milners music shop one day and Ray Stuart heard us strumming and singing and asked us if

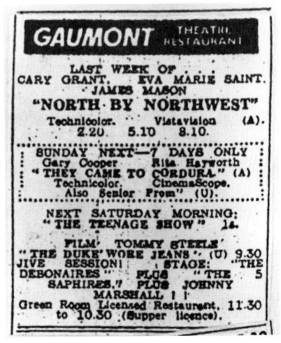

we'd do the Gaumont. We needed electric guitars so we had to buy a pick-up. My family had a whip-round and I bought one. Then on the morning before the show singer Bob Grundy lost his voice completely, he'd been practising so hard. So we never did it." Roy Ledger never made it either - for simpler reasons: "It was too early for me - 10 o'clock." Ricky and the Rebels singer Frank Peach: "Working as a hairdresser on Saturdays it was hard but my boss used to let me take my lunch-break at the appropriate time. Luckily I was working in town at that time so I

On stage at the Gaumont Teenage Show, Dave Berry and The Cruisers

used to be able to go and do my spot on the Gaumont and then go back to work."

The shows also helped put the focus on the city centre for the first time. "Before the Saturday shows began teenagers were thronging to see groups play in all the outlying districts of Sheffield," said Top Stars. "Places like Dinnington and Beighton were the strongholds of top groups such as Jimmy Crawford's and Dave Berry's and playing at Lathkilldale was just about the pinnacle of success to be reached in those days. The centre of Sheffield remained a desert as far as rock and jazz were concerned. There was just no interest whatever and the performers went out of the district to give shows. They had to and yet in the little villages the enthusiasm was tremendous."

In March, 1960, Harry Murray organised a coach trip to the 'Teenage Talent House' at the Gaumont Theatre in Shepherd's Bush, London, to showcase some of Sheffield's rock'n'roll talent, including Dave Berry and the Cruisers, Twin Cities Rhythm Group, Mickey and Johnnie and Ron Lindsay and the Coasters. It turned into a riot with London youngsters among the audience of 500 (of whom about 80 were from Sheffield) fighting and throwing objects. The Star reported the story under the headline, 'Londoners Fight In Bid To Smash City Show': "Mr Ron Evans, manager of the theatre, said: 'It was a deliberate outburst. The London boys came to the show determined to prove to the Sheffielders that they were tough.' Catcalls and crushed cartons greeted 22-year-old compere Jeff Garb when he faced the 'fans' in his black shirt and lemon sweater. The Twin Cities Rhythm Group was immediately welcomed by hisses, boos and a shower of pennies, lighted matches and ciga-

rette ends. Worst affected of the Sheffield party was 19-year-old Dave Berry who had just begun his act when violence broke out in the stalls beneath him. Plucky Dave, who sang on throughout the trouble, said: 'No one listened to me. They were too busy fighting.' When the Sheffield rock'n'roll stars left the theatre, they found that scores of the London youngsters had stayed behind to boo, sneer and hurl abuse after their coach. A huge banner, which boldly advertised 'The Teenage Show from Sheffield, the City Of Steel' was ripped to shreds by the mob." Guitarist Jim Holden, who played with a fractured thumb, was quoted as saying: "They were a shower of hooligans," while his girlfriend Lily Slim added, "They were not even civilised. They called us foreigners." Trevor Woodcock of Mickey and Johnnie remembers the cold reception: "We were warned before we got there that the London kids weren't going to take to us that easily. The thing that sticks out in my mind was when Berry was up there singing and the first three rows just stood up and turned their backs on him." Frank White: "It wasn't because we were bad. It was because we were from the north." Jimmy Crawford: "They threw money at us and I picked it up and threw it back at the bastards. They couldn't believe it. Cliff's agent turned up, but the local kids didn't want to know us good or bad, but we did the show." The riotous concert, all eight minutes of it, was filmed on 35m. It was called Fury Unleashed and had a special showing at one of the Saturday morning shows.

Another memorable incident at the Teenage Shows involved Johnnie of the singing duo Mickey and Johnnie. Pete Wardlow: "I remember one morning somebody threw something at him

Mickey and Johnnie: Sheffield's answer to
The Everly Brothers

the shock of the incident made me forget my guitar and amplifier. We went back and it was still sat there." Frank Peach recalls more wildness from the young audience: "The young girls used to go mad. I've had my clothes ripped many a time, which was very nice. Did your ego the world of good." Sylvia Dale: "They were wonderful, we never had any trouble. The kids would stand at the stage-door asking for autographs. We thought that was absolutely brilliant." But as the audiences became more and more boisterous, the Saturday morning shows came to an end. Pete Wardlow: "The kids were getting carried away and throwing too many things. Ice cream cartons weren't hurting enough, so they were throwing heavier things. But at least they'd let you know if they liked you and they used to fetch 'em off as well if they didn't like them." Terry Roe: "What it was was the Teds coming more and more to the fore, trying to show their authority."

The Gaumont started to put on big names opening with Gene Vincent and Eddie Cochran in February 1960, two months before the car crash that killed Cochran and injured Vincent. Pete Wardlow: "The first time I ever heard anybody put instruments through a PA system was with Eddie Cochran's guitar." Also sat on the front row awe-struck with Cochran's act were Phil Crookes and his pal Joe Cocker, "As we watched Cochran moving around the stage and looking down into the audience, Joe kept saying, 'He keeps looking at thee.'" Not so impressed was the Sheffield Star which gave British teen-idol Vince Eager a better write-up than Cochran: "American rock star Eddie Cochran's harsh singing voice and jogging movements were a little wearing to both the ear and eye. Vince Eager gave a first class performance and held his own with the more famous American stars." The Star held a press reception for the two Americans on behalf of the newspaper's Teenage Club where

and it cut over the top of his eye. It could've had his eye out. He carried on singing with blood running down his face." Roger Harrison: "That's something that always sticks in my mind. I remember thinking at the time, 'That's tremendous that to keep going like that.'" Jimmy Crawford: "Harry Murray read the riot act after things got thrown. The audiences got really rowdy and it was packed." Trevor 'Johnnie' Woodcock: "The Gaumont manager came on stage and gave everybody a good talking to. But

Rock'n'Roll stars Vince Eager, Eddie Cochran and Gene Vincent meet fans at the Star Teenage Club party in the Green Room of the Gaumont Cinema, January 1960.

they also noted another celebrity: "Sheffield's Elvis Presley, lanky Dave Berry, was examining the stars closely." Shortly after that the Duane Eddy/ Clyde McPhatter/ Bobby Darin package played to a packed Gaumont, although Darin's

> CITY HALL, SHEFFIELD
> ENORMOUS ATTRACTION
> TONIGHT AT 6.30 and 8.50.
> Arthur Howes presents (by arrangement with Lew and Leslie Grade Ltd)
> The great American Recording Stars
> BUDDY HOLLY
> and the
> CRICKETS
> Gary Miller
> The Tanner Sisters   Des O'Connor
> Ronnie Keene and his Orchestra
> Seats: 10/6, 8/6, 7/6, 6/-, 5/-.
> Platform 3/6.
> Wilson Peck Ltd., Fargate (27074).
> And a' the Hall from 6 p.m.

Sinatra-orientated performance left fans somewhat disappointed. Dave Berry recalls: "Bobby Darin was the first performer I saw to throw a wobbler when he started shouting at the lighting man at the Gaumont." Another Teenage Club event was at the Locarno Ballroom on July 5, 1960. This was a fund-raiser in aid of children's entertainer Mr Pastry's idea of a heated swimming pool for Yorkshire spastics. Appearing were regulars Ron Lindsay and the Coasters, Tony Cooper and the Harlequins, Mickey and Johnnie and Dave Berry and the Cruisers.

It was at the Gaumont and across the road at the City Hall that fans got to see some of their rock'n'roll idols in person for the first time. In May '57 Frankie Lymon and the Teenagers had appeared at the City Hall, followed a year later by Buddy Holly and the Crickets. Woodhouse fan Cliff Hircock was there and even got to meet the legendary Texan: "I found him very nice to talk to, despite being a big star, a very ordinary man. He was interested - I thought impressed - that we'd stayed around so long after the show [1.30am] to meet him and he was quite willing to stay and talk to us as long as we wanted. We chatted for about 20 minutes or so about guitars and the chord-work in the various songs." Mickey and Johnnie's biggest influence was the Everly Brothers. Trevor Woodcock: "We did an audition at the City Hall for this show with the Everly Brothers. Jimmy Crawford had organised it in the afternoon and Dave and myself did an Everly Brothers number. Then Jimmy did two numbers with us backing him. One was Running Bear with us doing this 'oom-pa oom-pa oom-pa'

backing. The thing that sticks in my mind more than the audition itself was - I could not believe it - the Everlys came in while we were on stage waiting for our chance to audition. They'd got these tailed coats on so we took the programme to a tailor in town and said, 'We want some jackets like these.'"

The City Hall saw more highly memorable concerts during the early Sixties featuring the likes of Gene Vincent, Jerry Lee Lewis, Sam Cooke, Little Richard, Chuck Berry and Carl Perkins. Roger Harrison remembers Little Richard's performance vividly: "He was dancing about on the piano and he slipped and fell off and laid on the floor. It was all planned I'm sure, but we didn't know that at the time. He laid on the floor groaning with the mic close to his mouth. The band all stopped playing and you could've heard a pin drop. Everybody's thinking, 'What's the matter?' - a real electric atmosphere, everybody wanting to know if he was all right. And then suddenly, 'Awopbopaloobop alopbamboom!' and he was off again. And that really impressed me at the time, a real bit of showmanship."

One first-time visitor to the city, Chuck Berry, who played at the City Hall in May, 1964, made a surprise after-show appearance at the Ajanta Restaurant on Carver Street. He joined in at a session with Los Caribos who had a two-night a week residency at what was one of the first Indian restaurants in Sheffield. "He played a bit of hip guitar," said band leader Trinidadian Ziggy Hosein. Los Caribos, who had first got together in 1960, played a style which one reporter dubbed Caribbeat, a mixture of bluebeat, bossa nova and latin rhythms. The rest of the line-up included vocals, two guitars, harmonica, trumpet and various bits of percussion - maraccas, risso-risso, conga, bongos and gourd. Top Stars Special said of Los Caribos's music: "It is lilting,

Los Caribos

melodic, yet meaty enough to satisfy the most beat crazy teenager, and folksy enough for the most way out Leadbelly fan." Other visitors who got up and joined in with Los Caribos included Danny Williams and David Whitfield. Los Caribos went on to make a self-financed record for Sheffield Arts Festival, organised by Sheffield University, in June, 1964, featuring a Spanish folk song from Trinidad, Tabaquite, a version of Summertime, Mexican Merengue, Peanut Vendor and calypso A Russian Satellite.

The jukebox had become a popular attraction and, according to DJ John Peel, the first pub in Britain to have one installed was the Barleycorn on Cambridge Street in 1957 (however, this is open to conjecture). This resulted in the ousting of pub entertainers Sam and Lil who, unfortunately, suffered the same fate a few weeks later when a jukebox also replaced them in the Lady's Bridge Hotel. By the mid-Sixties jukeboxes were commonplace in pubs. Some pubs, as Stu Moseley remembers, were particularly popular because of the jukebox selection: "We used to go to pubs like the Minerva and the Albert and monopolise the jukebox." Gaspin' Gus: "We used to go to the Albert because the jukebox had one of Jerry Lee Lewis's Sun singles on it." Another popular teenage and student pub was the Raven on Fitzwilliam Street, also a haunt for musicians. Sheffield University student and future TV newsreader Carol Barnes has happy memories of it: "Thursday night was our main night - you got free cheese and onion sandwiches and black pudding which they brought round on trays. I also remember the landlord trying to stop me dancing to the jukebox, doing the Shake or something, saying he didn't have a licence." She also admits to singing a "hideous rendition" of Mike Sarne's Come Outside with "the university's first ever rock band" The Dynamics at Graves Hall.

A favourite location for Sheffield teenagers in the late Fifties and early Sixties was the coffee bar. Here they could meet up, listen to the jukebox and make one cup of coffee last all night. There were a number of these teenage hangouts around the city. The Disc Jockey at the bottom of London Road was the first place John Firminger heard That'll Be The Day by the Crickets and another haunt was the Octopus at Handsworth. Marsden's Milk Bar, opposite the Peace Gardens, converted its downstairs area into the Teenage Tavern and was opened by Dickie Valentine. The pop balladeer was greatly surprised when Marsden's manager Horace Lyles asked him to autograph a five pound note (prob-

ably worth about £100 today). John Firminger can remember one Saturday morning there, looking at the jukebox in sheer wonderment as it throbbed out Duane Eddy's Cannonball. He and his school mates used to frequent the Zodiac at Park Hill on weekday nights and it seemed like Cliff Richard's High Class Baby was the most played side on the jukebox. Another favourite in the city centre was the Sidewalk Cafe, opposite Philip Cann's records and instrument shop on Chapel Walk, and La Strada on Ecclesall Road. On Saturday afternoons musicians could be seen in regular haunts like the Sidewalk, always a good place to meet up, have a laugh and pose. Dave Berry and Johnny Tempest frequented there although the waitresses didn't seem to keen on them sitting there for an hour with just one cup of coffee!

The El Mambo, located next to the stage-door of the Empire Theatre on Union Street, was more notorious. Peering in through the glass doors, it seemed like some sort of wild den of iniquity with Teds and dubious looking women - a place your parents would warn you against entering. "That's where the teddy boys used to hang out. We didn't go there because we thought it was a bit dangerous," says Frank White. Stu Moseley: "When I was a teenager in the early Sixties I used to go the El Mambo and you could get a reefer for £1, that was a horrendous price." Terry Roe: "Some people would go in there just to show how brave they were and go and stare at somebody." One person who did go in the El Mambo regularly was Jim Greaves of the Checkers: "We were the resident band. It was a good place, I enjoyed it and the people used to flock in. Inside, it was called Heaven and Hell, upstairs was 'Heaven' and downstairs was 'Hell' and that's where we used to play - in Hell. Some people said that's where we belonged. Acts from the Empire used to go in there and have a jam with us, people like Marty Wilde, Colin Hicks and the Most Brothers." The Del Vikings also played at the El Mambo. Teenage guitarist Dave Hawley: "We played downstairs, it was deadly dangerous. We loved it, you got your todger felt whether you liked it or not." Back in those days being a teenager certainly seemed like a lot of fun!

As the scene began to develop, so the groups started obtaining better equipment. Pete Wardlow: "The Sapphires had (Hofner) Club 60s and they were the first band I ever saw to get a Futurama. They played at the Memo and came on with the Futuramas and they both had these blue and white Watkins V-shaped amps." Pete

The Frantic Four: written on back of photo - "Don't worry about the two men at the front, they're squares."

6. DADDY, YOU'RE A SQUARE

Youngsters becoming musicians was something parents found hard to accept and the more time spent pursuing this, the more they frowned upon it, claiming music was taking over when more time should be spent concentrating on work or studying towards a career. At first Joe Cocker described his dad as, "Very Victorian minded and thinks I'm an idiot." However as Joe became successful his father's attitude changed, saying, "I'm glad he's got to the top, he's tried hard and long enough." Mal Hooley: "I remember telling my father, 'Look we've got all these gigs and I'm now grossing about £9, so I'm thinking of doing this full time.' He didn't like it." Working as a full-time musician was seen as a very precarious occupation. John Firminger told one foreman he was going leave the job to go full-time with a band, at which he asked somewhat bemusedly, "But you can't make a living doing that can you?" Unsympathetic parents was an ongoing problem as Dave Hopper found out: "I always used to be getting some stick

Jackson: "The first amplifier I bought was about nine inches by a foot, a little Elpico, a green amp with an oval speaker, just like a little radio. I used to think, 'This is loud!' Six watts of undistorted sound." What did Pete put through it? "I put my foot through it first one night when it didn't work. It was then I bought a Watkins Copycat - one of the first ones - to put through that little amp." Roy Ledger: "I bought my first guitar and my mother bought the amp, a Watkins. It blew up at the Lyric at Dinnington. I was with the Strollers with this little Watkins amp and then one day I turned up with a Vox AC-30. That meant we'd got three on stage then, that was a super band!" Alan Wood: "My first proper band that had electric guitars and electric amplifiers and proper drums was Big Tony Laurie [real name Barry Carr] and the Classics." Another revolutionary instrument was the electric bass. Chuck Fowler: "Pete 'Pop' Taylor went and bought the first bass guitar that came out. I think it was a Hofner and I'm sure it was the first electric one in Sheffield. But we hadn't got an amp to plug it in 'cos when he plugged it into ours it just farted away. So he mimed with the bloody thing, he was that proud of it. We entered this competition and Pop insisted on using this bass guitar. You couldn't hear it. Pop's dad was right upset about it and said, 'You've lost 'em that competition playing that bloody thing.'" Mick Hallam: "We had one of the first echo units, based on a revolving tape, and it kept busting. So I had to keep nipping behind the curtain to mend it with Sellotape."

Joe Cocker with his ever-supportive mother, Madge

about not having a proper job, even when I was with Joe [Cocker]. I was always playing guitar four, five, six hours a day. Sometimes even when I'd come in from playing - it might be about three o'clock in the morning - I couldn't resist having a play that would turn into about three hours. On several occasions I just realised in time that my dad would be coming in from work on the night shift. I'd put the guitar down, switch the light off and get into bed. A few minutes later there'd be footsteps coming upstairs. He'd come into my room, touch the light bulb and say, 'Ah, that's only just been turned off hasn't it. I wish you would stop wasting all this electricity!'"

A lot of our elders really did have our interests

at heart as Pete Jackson recalls: "We heard a lot of years later that on all them nights that we went out gigging me mother never slept a wink until she heard the door shut and we - me and Rog - were in. And that was like two and three in the morning coming back from wherever." Trevor Woodcock: "Suddenly coming in at three o'clock in the morning with my mom or my dad waiting just to see everything was all right, I think they understood that it went with the rock'n'roll. I used to sit in front of the record player, play about a line of music, take it off and try to find it on the guitar. And then the next line. They'd probably sat through many hours of that 'cos they'd bought me the guitar and they'd bought me the record player. So they weren't going to blow it all by saying I couldn't get in late."

Although parents did probably feel that the preoccupation with music was the end of civilisation as they knew it, some, like Pete Wardlow's parents, were encouraging: "We used to practice in our front-room. My dad used to say, 'Come on Elizabeth, them lads and lasses will be here soon, get them sandwiches made.' All the kids in the street would congregate outside our house on Sundays and they would be bopping in the street and all the neighbours would be stood in the yard with cups of tea. And they thought it was marvellous." It was also generally their parents that young musicians turned to when they needed the money for new instruments, etc. One example was Pete Jackson's dad Harry who was the guarantor for a new Antoria guitar, bought from Milner's Music shop on Howard Street on August 27, 1960. "It was a Guyatone solid, Hank Marvin had one like it. Twenty-six quid at £2 a month. In them days me father must've thought, 'It's crippling me this, I can't pay this.' And then, when we went for the Fenders and the Voxs, my dad really

Out all night: Dean Marshall and the Deputies

Small Goods A/c No. 11/18/1
Mr H. JACKSON
9, TURIE CRES.
SHEFFIELD 5.

MEMORANDUM ONLY
1o ANTORIA SERIES ELECTRIC GUITAR
supplied under Hire Purchase Agreement dated
27TH AUG, 1960.

Monthly Hire of £ 2   payable on the
27TH   day of each month

SPECIAL NOTE
Please bring this card with you or send it with each payment. A 3d. stamp should be enclosed for the return of the card and the receipt when payments are made through the post.
SAFETY FIRST
When sending Treasury Notes, Postal Orders or Cash through the post, the letter should be registered to guard against loss as Wilson Peck Ltd. take no responsibility for lost remittances.
No receipt recognised other than our official printed form.

Pete Jackson's dad signs for new guitar from Milners.

flipped." John Firminger can also recall his dad reluctantly paying the deposit of £20 (about two weeks' wages) for a second-hand Premier drum kit from Bradley's Music. Another one was Mal Hooley's dad: "I'd also got equipment on hire purchase. I was paying for my Fender bass which was £135 and my father signed for it and I suppose that spooked him a little bit."

But for many young musicians getting together to play in a band was a lot more important than any parental advice, even though they wanted to pack their jobs in and put their parents in debt at the same time. Roger Harrison: "I worked in the civil service at the official receiver's office. I was also playing with the Kenny Pete Five and getting home at four and five in the morning. I did it for a few months and then one of them had to go, it either had to be the music or the civil service. My parents weren't too happy about that. They thought I was stupid packing in a secure job with a pension, but rock'n'roll won. It wasn't much of a contest, I didn't like the civil service anyway. I was very bored in an office all day, looking through the window and wishing I was out there. The other civil servants all frowned upon me leaving, saying, 'You're stupid.' But there was

one guy who was my immediate boss and he used to write plays for radio. Nobody knew that, he never told anybody down there. He encouraged me. He said, 'Look, do you want to finish up like me when you're 50 years old? If you've got a chance of going out and doing something you enjoy, take my advice, go and do it,' which was great."

Being a musician and having a day job was hard work, thanks to the long and unsociable hours involved. Graham Oliver: "We'd got a drummer from Chesterfield so we had to set off for a gig first by driving from Swinton to Chesterfield to pick him up, go and do the gig at the back of beyond and then take him back to Chesterfield. I'd get in at about five in the morning and then go to work at Morphy Richards making washing machines." Ernie Booth, motor mechanic by day, bass player by night, recalled going to work straight from the previous night's booking. "I went to work in my red band suit. I walked into the garage and the foreman looked at me and I said, 'Good morning.' He said, 'Good mornin'? Tha'll get good mornin' coming in at this time.' It was half-past nine and I started at eight. I put my overalls on over the top of the red suit." Johnny Tempest and Tom Rattigan also found a day-job hard going. "We both started work on a building site and we turned up with make-up still on from the night before and our white stage-shoes. The saw us coming and they hammered us, they made John walk up this hill

carrying a big hammer then had us carry bags of cement on our backs up the hill. We found it very hard and he's down this hole digging away like mad with this foreman standing over him shouting ' c'mon, c'mon, don't stop, keep digging' and poor old John's face... he looked terrible, it was really killing him. When we'd finished we felt like we'd been hit with cricket bats, we didn't go back after that!"

Ernie Booth's dad was a veteran club act himself and encouraged him to pack in his job: "My dad pushed me into it. He said. 'Do a comedy act and play the guitar, play the Shadows and Bert Weedon. Stop chuffin' about with motorcars and get on the clubs.'" Dave Berry's parents were also very understanding: "I think I had a bit of an advantage as my dad had played. We had holidays every year in England, even though I was only from a working class background, and he paid for them every year with the money from his band. Otherwise he'd never have made enough money to take five people - I had two sisters - away on holidays. Also they'd been involved in it with us at the beginning, doing the residencies of four or five shows each week. So they knew that I was earning the money. But they still asked why I couldn't still work and there was also that feeling of how long it would last. When you're 19 or 20 you're not really bothered about what's going to happen in five years and I'd got no future planned anyway. At that time, we forget that there were only about 480,000 people unemployed, so you could always go back and get another job." Roy Ledger, with his mother also being a musician, never had any problem: "She never stopped me 'cos she's always played herself but she always said it was my downfall 'cos I learnt too much, too young, about the world. I went the wicked way as a young grouper did in those days." Paul Carrack: "I became a bit of a hippy which horrified my Mum. She always hoped that I'd come home in the middle of the night so that the neighbours wouldn't see me. But despite what

Dave Berry and his mother

she thought of my and the band's appearance, she always looked after us when we came home and made sure we were all fed."

Another son of a musician was Glyn Owen: "My father was a guitar player. He played six-string, what they called orchestra type stuff, and he also played lap-steel. He was a big fan of Hawaiian guitar and he taught me to play. When we had whatever success we did have he was amazed." Chuck Fowler's father was also a musician but didn't really approve of his son's musical preoccupation: "He'd been brought up in a different era altogether. Churches were all the thing and he was a church organist and he did it extremely well. He just couldn't get to grips with what I was doing, just couldn't understand it." When Roy Barber packed his job in to join

Paul Carrack: hippy

Dave Berry's Cruisers his parents saw it as a career-move: "They were all right actually. I think probably they were impressed because it was Berry."

Some later on found their wives or girlfriends didn't like the idea of them being musicians either. One was Keith Linaker: "We won the club-land award and an offer to go professional working at a big hotel in Jersey for six months." Susan Linaker gave her husband-to-be an ultimatum: "She said, if you go to Jersey you don't come back here." Keith: "So that was the end of my career playing guitar, finished." Barry Marshall: "Many a good man has gone down that path."

7. MAKIN' THE SCENE: CLUB 60

The emerging local music scene was all a bit rough and ready and there was still no venue that was devoted to live music, somewhere that could act as a meeting ground for Sheffield's young musicians. The problem was to be a recurring one over the next 40 years - a lack of venues, never mind the paucity of night-life generally. Even as late as 1960 one teddy boy, asked by the Sheffield Star what he was going to do that night, said: "I just don't know man. What is there to do in Sheffield? It's a real dump of a place. There's just nowhere to go apart from the pictures or a coffee bar. There's just no night life here at all." Although rock'n'roll was regularly played in clubs, pubs and dance halls in Sheffield in the late Fifties, there were no venues that teenagers could call their own. And it wasn't until 1960 that that began to change.

An early venue was a 'rock cellar' on City Road, where Danny Harman and the Vulcans and Ron Lindsay would play on Saturday nights. It was in the basement of St Aidan's Church Hall, and would later, as the Black Cat Club,

Is this pop group poster really necessary?

"'PERVERSION," "Fetishism," "Knickers," "Kinky" and "Thank Christ for the Bomb" are words and a phrase not normally associated with that distant relation of the squirrel, family, the American groundhog.

But they are words and a phrase incorporated in a poster now prominently pasted-up outside Sheffield's City Hall to publi-

Letter

cise the one night stand to be staged there next Monday by those very distant relations of the entertainer family, The Groundhogs.

This group's pictorial poster is made up of its members' faces drawn against a background of jumbled words and phrases — some of them listed in my opening paragraph — and sketches, which include those of nude and near-nude female figures.

It is a great pity that such a poster is deemed necessary by this pop group to persuade young people to part with the 60p necessary to secure admittance to a concert of music and song.

My strongest objection, however, is to a couple of crude caricatures appearing in the poster's background which should never be permitted to share a pop group's publicity sheet with "knickers," "perversion," "thank Christ for the Bomb" and nudes.

The first caricature is that of a man who was one of the world's greatest entertainers, an artiste whose inimitable interpretations of songs gave — and on disc and film still give — immeasurable pleasure to people throughout the world; a performer whose name and voice will surely never be forgotten: Al Jolson.

The subject of the second caricature is comedy actor Richard Hearne in his "Mr. Pastry" make-up. This brilliant artiste's work in all entertainment mediums, and his

The Groundhogs' poster outside the City Hall.

unselfish and untiring efforts at raising money to provide swimming-pools for spastic children, have earned him universal admiration and loc.

The Groundhogs will presumably enter the City Hall through the doorway with the illuminated sign over it which reads "Artistes Entrance." When the group can pass beneath that sign without feeling the acute embarrassment of impudent imposters their front-of-hall publicity will no longer need to feature "perversion," "Fetishism," "knickers," "thank Christ for the Bomb," nude and semi-nude girls and, above all, caricatures of artistes of the calibre of Richard Hearne and Al Jolson.

Alan Goode, Psalter Lane, Sheffield, 11.

Different attitudes, as this Star letter shows

become a popular live music venue in the hands of Pete and Geoff Stringfellow. One of the early rock group residencies featured Ron Lindsay and the Coasters in a room above the Foresters on Division Street: "We called it Club Torrid. It was hot. We played there every week in 1960 or so, but it wasn't big enough," said Jimmy Crawford. Dave Berry also had a go later on, starting Bluesville at the Albert just down the road. His irreverant humour was already showing through - his advert in the Star said: "The Kroosers, Albit O'tel, Next Munday, Blewsvile Klub."

However, the first real venue devoted to live music for teenagers was Club 60. Terry Thornton, a regular visitor to Club Basie at the Black Swan, had been impressed by the atmosphere created in the room above the livery stables. He looked for something similar and found it in the damp, 'haunted' beer cellars of the old disused Acorn pub on Shalesmoor. He and Danny Harman spent five weeks clearing the 1,566 square feet area and then cleaning everything up. "It was really tough work," said Harman. "It took us hours and hours until our backs were almost at breaking point. But I think it was all worth it... At least as the appearance of the club goes. We shall just have to wait and see whether it is successful or not." The Star described what the cellar was like before the work started: "The jagged stone walls and low curving roof were cracked with age, and oak beams, bricks, mortar and ancient relics of the past were scattered over the uneven floor. The smell of wine and hops still lingered like sea mist in the alcoves. Spiders' webs hung like lace on the walls. It looked for all the world like an Egyptian tomb buried in the earth." Thornton and Harman painted the walls and built a bar out of huge varnished oak beams, with 18-gallon beer barrels converted into tables. Behind the bar was an old clock. "It was my grandfather's," said Terry. "It strikes 57 times on the half hour." There was half an old cartwheel on the bar, with a ship's fender and a case full of stuffed animals nearby. On the walls there were colourful murals painted by local art students. It was billed as Sheffield's first Teen and Twenty beat club, serving soft drinks and coffee. It had no pretensions to being smart and was dimly-lit. By the time Club 60 opened on October 5, 1960, Harman was no longer on the scene and it was run by Terry and his wife Audrey. Membership was one shilling with an additional fee on club nights.

Terry, a draughtsman, had worked in the same drawing office as Ron Lindsay (Jimmy

Terry Thornton (right), pianist with Ron Lindsay and the Coasters

Crawford) and another wannabe musician Tony Cooper in the late Fifties at steelworks Davy United. He played piano with Cooper's band the Harlequins and Ron Lindsay's first band the Coasters but he made his mark with Club 60. Jimmy Crawford: "I think for atmosphere, to say it wasn't London, it was absolutely unique. Terry created an atmosphere that was absolutely suited for youngsters loving rock music in those days. We went over to Manchester me and him before he opened Club 60 and had a look at the students clubs, but they were mostly like political clubs, meeting and drinking places, but mostly basement establishments and Terry thought that would lend itself to rock music."

It was playing piano in the Coasters, in 1958, which initially inspired Thornton to open a club. Jimmy Crawford: "The last gig he did with the Coasters was in a pub in Rotherham on New Year's Eve. Somebody poured beer into the piano and he couldn't play so he walked out halfway through the gig. He threw a wobbler and left. And that was the last time we were on stage together." He was also fed up of the tiresome chore of carrying equipment round to bookings. Club 60 started as a jazz venue with top names such as Tubby Hayes, Johnny Dankworth, Bill Le Sage and Don Rendell along with local musicians like Tony Oxley, Nev Reaney and Barry Whitworth. Nev Reaney: "Club 60 had tremendous atmosphere. We were used to jazz being played in places like Nether Edge Hall which had absolutely no atmosphere at all. Most places were like that, built for ballroom dancing. Nether Edge Hall was a place that you might expect to run into your mum and dad but you wouldn't bump into them in Club 60. Kids felt like it was their own place." But Club 60 didn't really begin to take off until it also took in beat music and rock'n'roll. "We started by putting on modern jazz and for the first six months we had

The dirt, the cold, the dark..." The only ventilation was when the door at the top of the stairs was opened. "Lumps of blue smoke would blow out," said Terry. "It was a great atmosphere though and people loved it." "As it was subterranean it had sort of an illicit atmosphere," says John Firminger. "There was a smell of paraffin and it was pretty cramped." It drew groups and punters from all over the country - according to one report, among old membership records for the club was the signature of a Liverpool member, one John Lennon.

Even if it was, "the dampest dive east of the Don," according to the same reporter, musicians such as Berry and Frank White remember it as the best club in Sheffield, " Dave Berry: "It was excellent, and it had a proprietor who was into music and was a musician." Terry Thornton returned the compliment: "I knew Dave Berry would make it big one day and I asked him to become resident at Club 60 on Saturday nights. He did it for the record-breaking fee of £6."

Among the regular rock bands that appeared there, Jimmy Crawford and the Ravens and Dave Berry and the Cruisers were the biggest draws. Other oufits who played regularly included Ricky and the Rebels, Johnny Tempest and the Mariners, Bobby Dawn and the Twilights, Pete Fender and the Strollers and Ray Stuart and the Drifters. Guitarist Roy Ledger first played the club as a 13-year-old with the Twilights: "It was just so different, the concept of it, going into a cellar." Pete Jackson: "We did it with the Deputies, it was a brilliant venue. I thought it was the best venue for atmosphere, for audiences and bands. You were that cramped on the little stage, it was a bit like prohibition, although there was only pop to drink - prohibition lime and lemon!" Roy Ledger: "It just proves you could enjoy yourself without drink." However Club 60 goers would invariably go a few yards down

a very thin time," Terry told Top Stars. "But when Saturday night became pop night the people started coming and the club started to make money." It was dubbed Sheffield's answer to the Cavern in Liverpool - "a grotty little hole with just enough room to swing your hep cat in," as one Sheffield journalist put it at the time. "Club 60 had everything - atmosphere, talent, it was the stomping ground for some of the best outfits in the area," said Thornton. "It made names of people like Jimmy Crawford and Dave Berry. In fact it started the whole beat cult round here. We didn't need gimmicks to draw the teenagers. The place flooded, it froze up, and the kids loved it. Every natural disadvantage attracted them.

Subterranean rock: Ricky and the Rebels and The Ravens on stage at Club 60

More underground sounds: Don Rendell Quintet and Johnny Dark and the Midnighters

Shalesmoor to the Ship, where the landlord had cashed-in on this by painting his back room in an assortment of wild colours and calling it the 'Zen Den'.

Club 60's stage, in the largest of the three rooms in the cellar, was a wooden platform only about six inches high. With a capacity of 250, those stood at the front were virtually nose to nose with the bands and, although it was often cramped, this was also part of its appeal. Jimmy Crawford: "If someone hit a note on a guitar somebody's wig would blow off. Fantastic atmosphere, you felt like you were a group member."

However, Thunderbird Ernie Booth remembers one drawback: "When it was raining, it used to drip from the ceiling. Sometimes we'd be playing and we'd get wet through." It was also believed Club 60 had a ghost, allegedly one of the victims of the Great Sheffield Flood of March 11, 1864, which claimed two lives at the nearby Ship Inn. Jimmy Crawford: "Johnny Tempest spent a night at Club 60 there to disprove it was haunted. It didn't put anybody off from going there." A Sheffield Star photographer who accompanied Tempest tried to take a picture but on each of his six attempts the flash failed to go off. Dave Hopper, also of the

Twilights, remembers the venue had unusual pass-outs: "Potato stamps. They'd say, 'Let's have a look at your hand. You haven't got a stamp on it. You can't come in here.' But once inside, the music was loud, the lighting was dim and it was great." Another regular performer was Frank White: "Club 60 was probably the best rock'n'roll club ever, anywhere. If I could open that place again I would."

The Acorn building seen today with the old Club 60 door at left

8. EVERYBODY'S ROCKIN'

A number of ballrooms left-over from the danceband era started putting on rock'n'roll nights. These included the City Hall Ballroom and the ornate surroundings (not to mention cavernous sound) of the Cutlers Hall, both ruled by jobsworthies. Stu Moseley recalls: "When we played the Cutlers Hall this guy came striding towards the piano, and he says, 'How long are you going to be?'." The Central Ballroom in Attercliffe, converted from an ice-rink, had weekly 'twist' sessions, and another popular place was the Locarno on London Road. Out of town there were similar goings on at the Empress Ballroom, Mexborough, Goldthorpe Astoria,

Club 60 members sat round the coffee bar

Monaco Ballroom, Worksop, St Joseph's Hall, Thorne, and in Chesterfield there was the Victoria Ballroom and St James' Hall, the latter known as Jimmy's. Dave Berry played them all: "The Vic was a very good venue. Bob Sole was the manager, he was very, very good. At the

time I was doing Georgia On My Mind and Come Rain And Come Shine and Bob said, 'Why don't you come down?' I went down on one of the band nights and I actually sang with the big band. I remember that was my first experience, very unusual at the time. Jimmy's was a really wild place, it was a place you didn't actually go into the audience. We were always backstage." Other regular band gigs were places like the Gainsborough, Lincoln and Scunthorpe drill halls. But Jimmy's wasn't the only place outsiders needed to tread carefully. At the Empress at Mexborough there was an incident involving people waving live wires about to fend off a mob. And the venues weren't always ideal. At the Mart in Sleaford, the stage was up in the rafters and to get to it the band had to climb a ladder. Dave Berry: "We were so high up our drummer Kenny couldn't see the audience and thought we weren't playing to anybody."

As well as playing in various church halls and dance halls, bands began finding a regular source of work around pubs and clubs in the area. Pete Wardlow of the Twin Cities: "We started off at the Cannon Hall, Fleur De Lys, Greengate, Blue Bell, Sicey Hotel, Arbourthorne Hotel and Woodthorpe Hotel. We were the first band to go in virtually." Pete recalls why some

pubs were more popular back in the Sixties: "The Fleur De Lys at Totley, the Old Harrow at Gleadless and the Greengate at High Green did so well because they were then outside Sheffield. The Sheffield licensing laws were different because the pubs stopped serving at 10 o'clock in the week. The Fleur was in Derbyshire then and it was a half-past ten bar, same at the Greengate, which is why people used to flock out there." Stu Moseley remembers how you could have a night out, all on the equivalent of 50p: "We'd have enough for our bus fare to town, ten pints, a packet of cigarettes and bus fare back, all for a ten bob note." Singer Pat Leslie and guitarist George Gill were the first live act to perform on Sundays with their spot at the John O'Gaunt. Many pubs had their own concert or music room, complete with one or two dressing rooms. With one on either side of the stage, these would be used and abused by many of the Sheffield groups. Many people also had their favorite pub or pubs where they'd go and see the bands in action. From one side of Sheffield to the other, pubs large and small aimed to fill their concert rooms by booking groups two or three nights a week. Linda Harvey: "It wasn't a case of, where is there to go? It was, which one shall we go and see?"

The Greengate Inn had weekly residencies featuring Dean Marshall and the Deputies, Vance Arnold and the Avengers, the Scott William Combo and the Hillbilly Cats. Other pubs on the north side of the city were the Sicey Hotel at Shiregreen, Shiregreen Hotel, the Wharncliffe Hotel at Firth Park and Parson Cross Hotel. The latter had a massive concert room, and played host to a national beat group competition, the Mackeson Rhythm Group Contest, with top EMI record producer Norrie Paramor among the judges. The event was featured in New Record Mirror showing Dave West and the Cherokees, Peter York and the Pontiacs and Johnny Tempest and the Cadillacs (the winners), in action. At the other end of town, there was the Magpie at Lowedges, Centre Spot at Base Green, Birley Hotel, Frecheville, and the Blue Bell, Hackenthorpe. The latter was dubbed the Palladium of the North and was one of the first local pubs to start booking local name bands and bands from out of town with the likes of Doncaster's Lee Walker and the Travellers and the Cresters from Bradford, a great band that featured brilliant guitarist Richard Harding and superb singer Mal Clarke. Also from Donny were the completely nutty Alex Winston and the Flinstones, and there was Me and Them from Barnsley. The latter caused controversy with their first record for Pye. It was called I Think I'm Gonna Kill Myself. They played it safe with the follow-up, a cover of Lennon and McCartney's Tell Me Why.

SHEFFIELD BEAT COMP RESULTS

The Mackeson Rhythm Group Contest, held throughout the Sheffield area, came to an exciting climax on Thursday, October 31. The six finalists fought a close battle and the judging panel had a more than usually difficult job deciding the winners.

According to all reports the eliminating heats had been just as close so the conclusion can be drawn that the beat scene in Sheffield is of the highest standard.

The groups taking part in the final were Johnny and the Cadillacs, the Lincons, the Cherokees featuring Dave West, the Kenny Pete Four, the Whirlwinds with Sandra and Ray Verne and the Chequers.

Each group played a fifteen-minute programme and the proportion of originality was high. No one attempted to copy the established groups of today which was a strong point in favour all round.

Some good original material was heard, especially from the Cadillacs.

First prize of 100 guineas went to Johnny and the Cadillacs, while the runners-up, the Cherokees, featuring Dave West, collected 50 guineas.

Recording tests were also offered by Columbia Records and top recording manager Norrie Paramor invited all the contestants to submit tapes for consideration.

The judging panel comprised Miss Myrna Malinsky, ABC-TV; Norrie Paramor, Columbia A&R Manager; Barney Colehan, BBC-TV, and Jimmy Watson, editor NRM.

Following suit was the Abourthorne Hotel where landlord Alf Pickering was a popular figure with both punters and bands alike. As well as booking bands, he'd sometimes help out by running them to gigs if need be. Johnny Tempest and the Cadillacs were firm favourites there as were other outfits like the Sheffields, the Originals (ex-Cadillacs) and Joe Cocker's Big Blues. Alf also had a couple of American acts play at the 'Arber' with Johnny Duncan and the Bluegrass Boys (Last Train To San Fernando) and, believe it or not, the Platters (or at least a version of them). These were thriving times for Sheffield pubs. The Dog and Partridge at Attercliffe was a regular place to see live bands although it wasn't one of the most salubrious of places to spend a night out. Frank White had the unfortunate task of playing noon and night there once as Dave Hopper recalls: "Frank was playing there a lot at that time, so he got talked into doing a noon and night. It wasn't very good as there was often nobody in at all and when there was nobody in, it was worse than if it was full of idiots!" Just down the road was the Broughton Inn where, as Pete Wardlow recalls, the drums had to be set up in an unusual way: "You used to have to put them on the top of the grand piano." In the city centre, there was Minerva (now the Yorkshire Grey) on Charles Street where the first band led by Joe Cocker, Vance Arnold and the Avengers, made their first public appearance in 1961.

Outside Sheffield, too, nearby village pubs also featured bands. There were the Lordens and the Squirrel in Dinnington, the Saxon in Kiveton Park, while out in the Derbyshire Peaks there were the Lathkilldale Hotel and Monsal Head Hotel. Near Chesterfield, the Barrow Hill Hotel featured live bands four nights a week with regular appearances by Frank White and Joe Cocker. Some of the pubs could be quite volatile. The Ball Inn at Bramley was infamous and the Fighting Cocks at Rawmarsh lived up to its name. Jimmy Crawford recalls one wild night playing at Thurnscoe: "Between sets Frank White came in salivating and looking rough. Some lads had asked to look at his guitar and had beaten him up. So we climbed into the van and went for these lads. They were too big and too many of them to fight so I just drove straight at them. Didn't stop to find out what happened but I think we flattened a couple of them against a wall. We were always a bit aggressive in those days. You had to be at Goldthorpe and places like that." Glyn Owen recalls one close shave at the Queens, Maltby: "In the early days we had a couple of Marshall two-twelves and one fell off

the stool on to this woman's head. The 12-inch speaker fitted right on to her head as it fell on her and this enormous bloke got up and said, 'Are tha gunna get this speaker off me mother?' To which we said, 'Certainly sir!"

It was a boom time for local musicians exemplified by Dave Berry and the Cruisers who, in December 1960, turned professional. "We were earning enough money and we only played the gigs we wanted to. We were getting probably twice what you would get in a normal day job," said Berry. John Firminger: "The pubs proved to be ideal for the group scene. Some of the groups had a big following so people would go everywhere they played, from Hackenthorpe to High Green. It wasn't just a case of entertaining people in the area. I think the pubs cashed in on what was happening. Some of the pubs were real shit-holes. But as long as the beer was all right, the band and the audience didn't care. And there was no chance of the bands getting a soundcheck. It was more of a tune-up."

The only trouble with the pub scene was that it excluded teenagers from getting a taste for live music, which is where Club 60 really came into its own. It was not a club as we understand them now. It was more like a glorified youth club but in a dank cellar. The success of Club 60 was to pave the way for the likes of the Stringfellows to come along and take the live scene by the scruff of the neck. But that wasn't to be for another two years.

9. CALL UP THE GROUPS

Jimmy Crawford became Sheffield's first chart star in 1961 when I Love How You Love Me went to number 18 in November, 1961, five months after reaching number 49 with Love Or Money. There was to be nothing else until Dave Berry and the Cruisers had a hit with Memphis Tennessee almost two years later but it wasn't for the want of trying.

As the number of young musicians getting involved in local bands grew in the early Sixties, so did their aspirations. The May, 1962, issue of Top Stars ran a four-page feature spotlighting some of the local bands, proclaiming: "Never before in the history of 'pop' music, has the Sheffield district produced so many talented groups as there are at the moment... all seeking stardom and several likely to find it." Rock and rhythm groups were springing up from one end of the city to the other. From the Ecclesfield/ Parson Cross area were bands such as Dean Marshall and the Deputies, Peter York and the

Pontiacs and the Dave Graham Four. From Crookes there were Ray Stuart and the Tremors, Vance Arnold and the Avengers, Johnny Hawk and the Falcons, Vince Young and the Vantennas and the Cherokees with Dave West. Over at the other side of town there were Frecheville's

The Classics

Johnny Hawk and the Falcons

Johnny Tempest and the Mariners, and later the Cadillacs and Danny Russell and the Demons. From the Norton/ Gleadless/ Manor area were the Wildcats Rhythm Group, Bobby Dene and the Twilights, Big Tony Laurie and the Classics and Jess Hunter and the Trekkers. Darnall also had its share of young rock'n'rollers like Johnny and the Nightriders, along with guitarists Frank White and Dave Hawley, and the Riley brothers, drummer John and Ozzie on bass. Other Sheffield combos included Shaun Dean and the Ramblers, Pete Emmett and the Skyliners, Dave Clifford and the Orpheons, Bobby Dean and the Vulcans, Mark Stone and the Questers, Tony Gale and the Stormers, Pete Lloyd and the Strangers, Barry Laine and the Sound Barriers,

Steve Allen and the Vikings and Terry and the Bluestars, etc.

In early 1962 Colin Arnold, the manager of the Plaza Cinema at Handsworth, organised a marathon rhythm group contest that proved very popular with young beat music fans. The venue also put on a series of Sunday rock'n'beat concerts billed as Bringing Them To You - Stars of TV, Disc and Tape. Big names such as Screaming Lord Sutch, Johnny Kidd and the Pirates, Gene Vincent, Shane Fenton and the Fentones starred alongside up and coming names from around the country and top local bands. Trevor Woodcock of the Originals recalls

Peter York and the Pontiacs with singer Ronny Coy (left)

appearing with rock'n'roll legend Gene Vincent: "We were chatting to him at the side of the stage. All I can remember is there was something weird about him, he was a real oddball but great on stage." Linda Harvey went to all the shows: "My mum used to iron a lot of the stage suits. They all knew my mum who was known as Max. She always used to have everybody back for coffee and sandwiches. Lord Sutch always used to come back to my mum's and floor my dad with politics."

Early on many of the groups would model themselves on Cliff Richard and the Shadows, with a lead singer fronting a four-piece band with lead and rhythm guitars, bass and drums. The rhythm guitarist was there not to sing and play, but simply to fill out the sound. Roy Barber: "If you were the rhythm guitarist you got stuck with that label. If you tried to bemoan that, you were trying to show off I suppose." Neil Bridges: "This kid came up to me and said, 'Would you play lead guitar in our new group?' I said, 'I don't play lead, I play rhythm.'" Alan Wood: "It became embarrassing to be called a rhythm guitar player - 'What d'you mean, y'don't play lead?' But at the time Bruce Welch and others were proper rhythm guitarists with a phenomenal knowledge of chords and timings and that's what we tried to do." Dave Hopper re-evaluates this function: "There's certain things on those old rock'n'roll songs, if you've got a rhythm guitarist you'd improve your sound no end 'cos it filled it out. The only thing about playing rhythm is not to be too loud." However, sometimes the rhythm tended to be louder than anybody else.

Being a musician though did make you seem special as Roy Ledger explains: "If you walked in with a guitar, you were God. There was this bird at school that I used to fancy like mad and she didn't want to know. I actually chatted her up to come to the Locarno and I couldn't get rid of her when she realised I was in a group." The comedian Bobby Knutt joined a group by accident: "I used to go up and see Mark Stone and the Questers. I went up one Saturday afternoon and they were rehearsing all these Shadows instrumentals. I said, 'What's up?' 'We're at Shiregreen Community Centre tonight and Stoneys not coming, he can't get back in time from his holidays,' and they had only found out because Roger had got a phone. Not many people had phones in those days. So I said, 'I can sing, I'll get up with you.' They said, 'You can't sing.' 'Give me that microphone, I'll show you.' I learned four songs that afternoon, Be Bop A Lula, Mean Woman Blues and two Joe Brown songs, Layabout's Lament and What A Crazy

Mark Stone and the Questers

World, and I did them in a Cockney accent. I ran home and told me mother I was on stage tonight at Shiregreen. She bought me a new V-neck jumper and a little dickie bow with a pearl on the front that sat underneath your collar. I thought I was Jack the lad. I went on that night and just as I was finishing my last song Mark Stone arrived and threw a wobbler because I was using his microphone. And old Kenny Timms had a barney with him and then came out and asked me if I wanted to join the group for good because they'd just sacked Stoney. From then on it was Bob Andrews and the Questers [Bobby Knutt's real name is Robert Andrew Wass]. But I could never do the rock 'n' roll stuff like Joe Cocker, Pete Fender and Berry. I couldn't sing it. I was more ballads, I had a pretty nice voice. So I used to do comedy and piss about."

There was a lot of friendly rivalry between bands and they would often pick up ideas from each other. Ernie Booth: "In those days we had a bit of competition with bass players. There'd be Mal [Hooley], Fleety [John Fleet] and one or two others. We'd all nick parts off each other." Roy Ledger: "I remember seeing Frank Miles in Cranes Music Shop and asking him to show me how he played that two tunes at once thing that he could do on Yankee Doodle Dixie." Alan Wood recalls how his band the Classics concentrated more on image than playing: "We used to support all the guest bands at the Azena Ballroom and we were immaculately turned out with mohair grey suits, little black dickie-bows, pointed handkerchiefs, all the same shoes, Vox amplifiers, Trixon drums, Fender guitars, etc. What surprised us was when bands like Dave Berry and the Cruisers came, they'd arrive at the last minute looking a bit dishevelled, their gear tatty and guitars with no cases. And I could never understand why a band as smart as us could sound so shite and they sounded phenomenal. That was my first eye-opener - that there was more to rock'n'roll than just looking good."

Getting to the gig was often a problem. Dave Hopper: "My first band took everything on the train to Chesterfield. When we came out we'd missed the train shortly after 11 o'clock so we had to wait with all the tackle 'til about 1.30 in the morning for the next train." Hopper later solved his transport problems by utilising his baby's pram. "We'd got a young un who was less than a year old. Nobody could pick me up. Where I lived then on the Wybourn it was only a mile and half to the gig at the Staniforth Arms. So I thought there's only one thing I could do and that's put my gear on the pram and push it there, and fortunately the weather was OK. It wasn't easy. I'd got to be careful on the pavements so the gear wouldn't drop off. It took about 30 minutes longer than to walk there normally. When I got there, instead of going straight inside, I took the pram round into the car park and parked it between two cars and went in and asked if somebody would come and give me a hand in with my gear. After the show I'd got to take it all back." Pete Wardlow: "When I played at the youth club I would carry my drums in a twin pram and walking up the street I would often get stopped by old women wanting to look at my babies. We used to take all our gear on the bus - drums, guitars, amps, the lot, and shove it all under the stairs." Some were more fortunate like Jim Greaves of the Checkers: "Harry Driver - he was our driver - had got an old Studebaker. There was enough room for three groups in that and that's how we got about. It was only when we'd fallen out that we bought an ambulance. Then we sold it back when we made pals with Harry again."

Dave Berry: "We didn't have a van till later and I will never forget having to play at the Butchers Arms at Thurnscoe on Christmas Day lunchtime and at night. We had a driver with an Austin A40 van who took us to Thurnscoe. He then went home for his Christmas dinner. The pub closed at 2pm and we ended up walking the streets of Thurnscoe until the pub opened again in the evening." Roy Barber recalls a trip to Maltby at the other side of Rotherham: "We got a Saturday night and the Sunday in Maltby which to us was a 'tour'. So we stayed over, got bed and breakfast. It seemed a long way in those days." Ernie Booth: "There were no motorways and vehicles weren't like they are now. They were always breaking down." Dave Robinson: "The M1 used to finish at Derby and we had a puncture at Clay Cross. We came all the way back from Clay Cross with a flat tyre and kept filling the tyre with straw!" Stu Moseley: "We had a Vauxhall van with no petrol gauge. We went to play a few dates in Wales. The last gig was in Newport and we had to drive back the

Baby you can drive my car: The Whirlwinds travel in style

Always available, group van driver, Reg
Featherstone, left, with Dave Hawley

same night. We had no money, we'd been ripped
off by the agents - and no petrol gauge. It was a
fantastic gig though, all we had to do was get
home. We just managed to get back to
Handsworth and all we had left was nine pennies [about 4p]." Sometimes musicians had to
be resourceful as Brian Watson recalls: "We got
the singer from one of the soul bands and when
we went to pick him up in Havelock Square we'd
got no money. He said, 'Hold on a minute, I'll
just go and get some money.' Then he comes
out with all these shillings. He'd robbed the gas-
meter for petrol money so we could go on this
gig!" The unsung hero for a number of bands
was little Reggie Featherstone who could always
be called upon to get a band to the gig in his
trusty Ford Thames - by whatever means. Dave
Hawley recalls one occasion when Reggie's girlfriend came to the rescue: "Reggie said to
Maureen, 'Get upstairs and get your tights off.'
'Oh Reggie, are we going to have a night of pas-
sion?' 'No, the fan belt's gone on the van.'"

Jimmy Crawford, of course, had his own van
and he remembers how Frank White's then girlfriend, always used to leave her shoes in the
van with the gear: "And after a while I would
have 18 pairs of different shoes in the van. I
said to Frank, 'If she doesn't get her shoes out
while we are on stage, I'm throwing them out.'
He said he'd tell her. He never believed I would
and neither did she. So we stopped in Fitzalan
Square with the van - Saturday night, all the
drunks around, taxis, trams and buses - I
opened the back doors and threw them into the
street and drove off. She said, 'Frank, he's
thrown me shoes out.'"

Whether it was a case of honour among
thieves or some kind of naive trust among musicians, sometimes the dealings within bands

took some swallowing as Dave Hopper found
when he put in his notice to leave one band.
"During my six-weeks notice the cheeky sods
said, 'Look, we're gonna have to get a new van
so can you give us your share?' So I said, 'Hang
on a bit. I'm leaving as soon as you get another
guitar player.' So they then said, 'Well what we'll
do is, give us your share and whoever comes in,
we'll get it off him and give it back to you. But if
we don't get this van we're out of work.' So, like
a muggins, I said, 'Okay.' I'd done half of my six
weeks notice. I said, 'Right, but don't forget I
want this money back.' So I get dropped off and
I didn't see them for months!"

A regular port of call for both musicians and
fans alike was Violet May's record shop in the
city centre. Former store detective Violet May
Barkworth (cousin of film/TV actor Peter
Barkworth) started out by selling second hand
clothes and through her interests in music
moved on to selling second hand records.
Having had premises on Duke Street, the

Vinyl goddess,
Violet May

Pavement on Park
Hill, South Street
and Broad Street,
her final location
was at the top of
Matilda Street,
just off the Moor. Among the thousands
of records in stock - jazz, folk, country, classical
and rock'n'roll - collectors could always find
something of interest. John Firminger used to
spend many hours down at her Broad Street
shop sifting through the various boxes of LPs,
EPs and singles. Violet's shop somehow lost
some of its charm when it moved to Matilda
Street. Jenny Colley: "It was never the same
when she moved, it didn't have the same atmosphere." The disorganisation of her previous
shops was often part of the appeal, rummaging

through the hundreds of records to find a rare single or album. She sold the shop and retired in 1978. Ten years later, after being reported dead by the Star, Violet proved otherwise by announcing in the newspaper that she was to make a comeback at the age of 78 with premises in London Road. However, due to her health, she was advised not to go back into business and remains another figure local music fans remember with affection. Another place for record hunters was Ken's Records stall down in the old Rag Market. Here one could find plenty of promotional copies of new releases, many of which have since proved to be quite collectable.

The Stone House pub in Church Street was another regular meeting place for musicians. Saturday afternoons would see members of various bands getting together and swapping stories about gigs, girls, instruments and other musicians. At first the landlord, a large Dutchman by the name of Hoffman, didn't seem too happy about having a bunch of long-haired musicians in the place and served them under sufferance. But gradually, when he realised that here was a regular bunch of drinkers patronising his pub every Saturday afternoon, he became more friendly. It also acted as something of a labour exchange. Roy Ledger: "You used to go in and say, 'Anybody want a guitarist tonight lads?'" Whether it be for Joe Cocker or Stu Moseley or Chuck Fowler, there'd usually be a bass player, drummer or guitarist to cover the job. If Phil Crookes couldn't play with Joe, Dave Hopper would stand in without thinking about it. One of the musicians available was Pete Jackson: "We used to use the Stone House just like the Trades Club was used. If you weren't working at the weekend, you would pile in. You could go in many a Saturday afternoon and not be working and end up with a job. You all used to sit near the phone. When it went someone would ask, 'Is so-and-so in?' and you'd say, 'No', even when whoever they were asking for was sitting opposite you. You'd say, 'No he's not, but I'm not working tonight,' and get the job!' Dave Hawley: "You'd go in with one band and come out with a different one." Barry Marshall: "The Stone House was a buzzing place on a Saturday afternoon. You could just join a band for the night." There was also one bass player who was always up for the best offer as Hopper explains: "Dave Green was the only one who was up for bids on a Saturday afternoon. He was the only one who could be in three or four bands on a Saturday at once. You'd say, 'Greeny can you do us a job on Tuesday for two quid?' Someone else would say, 'We're

stuck on Tuesday, we'll pay you £2.50,' and then he'd say 'Any advancement on £2.50?'" Dave Hawley: "He got known as 'Two in the arse Green' because he would always get £2 more in his back (arse) pocket and join a different band." However, after an afternoon drinking session, some of the musicians were hardly in a fit state to do a night's gig anyway! Changes in the various band line-ups would be frequent. The same faces would turn up in different bands weekly and it was hard to keep up with sometimes. However, as Dave Hopper remembers, there was one performer whom everybody seemed reluctant to play for: "If Ray Stuart came in, everybody would disappear to the toilet!"

10. BLACK CATS AND BEATLES

In late 1962 the live scene was transformed by the opening of two new clubs, the Esquire and the Black Cat - and the arrival of the flamboyant Peter Stringfellow and brother Geoff, born and bred in Pitsmoor. Peter had already had a number of jobs, leaving Central Technical School at 15. One of his first jobs was at the Regal Cinema in Attercliffe where Duggie Brown also appeared: "John Baldwin was the manager and I used to compere the shows. Pete Stringfellow, who was the projectionist in the week, would do the lighting for the Sunday shows and shine the light down on me." Pete Stringfellow: "I had my 16th birthday at the Regal. I used to play records between the films and I got told off for doing that. I used to play

Starting out: where Pete Stringfellow began his career. Ad also shows Dougie Brown's first group, The Four Imps

Green Door by Frankie Vaughan. We used to have parties on the stage after everyone left." Peter went on to work as an apprentice turner with the English Steel Corporation where one of his fellow workers, "who made my life hell in my final weeks at the steelworks," was one Johnny Greaves. Peter left the steelworks to join the Merchant Navy before returning to Sheffield and doing various jobs including setting up a photography business in Newcastle. Back in Sheffield he worked for Darnall retail company Dobson's which sold goods door to door. He ended up being accused of theft and was jailed for three months, serving a month in July, 1962, at Armley in Leeds. It was that experience which prompted him to start his life anew.

Back home he answered an advert in the newspaper for a driver with his own van to take a band to gigs for £3 10s a night. He went to the address in Frecheville and the door was answered by Johnny Greaves, except he was now calling himself Johnny Tempest, singing with his band the Cadillacs, and wearing stage makeup. Tempest recognised his former workmate and told him he couldn't have the job and gave it instead to Peter's friend Billy Oldham. Billy told Peter how the Cadillacs earned £13 a night for going on stage three times at venues such as St James's (Jimmy's) in Chesterfield which held 800 people paying 2s 6d to get in. Peter soon worked out that that meant that the venue was clearing anything up to £85 a night. He went to see Dave Berry and the Cruisers at Jimmy's and was knocked out by one of his first experience of live music, even more so by the possibilities of earning money by promoting bands. He tried to hire the venue but had to look elsewhere as it was booked up. Younger brother Geoff took him to a couple of venues in

THE BLACK CAT CLUB

ST. AIDAN'S, CITY RD.
TUESDAY, 1st OCTOBER
Frankenstein and The Monsters
PLUS The Newtones.
7.30-11.0   3/-.   Guest 3/6.
FRIDAY, 4th OCTOBER
DAVE BERRY & The Cruisers
Coming This Month
THE MERSEYBEATS, THE BIG THREE
WAYNE FONTANA
and THE MINDBENDERS.
Yet another great show coming to the
CITY HALL, SHEFFIELD.
WEDNESDAY, 17th NOVEMBER
THE STRINGFELLOW BROS. present
THE ROLLING STONES
with DAVE BERRY and
THE CRUISERS.
WAYNE FONTANA and
THE MINDBENDERS.
Vance Arnold and The Avengers
Johnny Tempest and The Cadillacs
Karen Young AND The Vampires
(now Pye Recording Artists).
TICKETS AVAILABLE SHORTLY.

Sheffield including Club 60. Peter: "I was impressed but not impressed. I was like a townie kid in those days. It was the definitive club in a basement which is what I thought clubs were. At least it stood up to that. The only thing was that there was no excitement to it. It was very jazzy. It was Terry Thornton's and he was a jazz man." It made him all the more determined to find his own venue. "I went out as far as Bradfield and the Rivelin area, looking at barns, thinking kids would go anywhere, just like rave culture now. I was convinced if I could get a barn, knowing nothing about licences or acoustics, I could open a club out there." Peter told Top Stars Special at the time: "There is not enough room in some pubs for a really swinging session, and a lot of young people do not like going into pubs anyway. And if we make any money my idea is to get a hall of our own which we can decorate as we like and have rock and twist sessions every day of the week."

One venue they looked at was St Aidan's Church Hall in City Road located on the border of two housing estates, the Manor and Arbourthorne. It already had dances on Friday nights and on March 23, 1962, Beat

Geoff and Pete Stringfellow

Promotions, had started 'The Beat Scene', a weekly beat night, starting with Mike Berry and the Outlaws, followed by Danny Carson (March 30) and Dave Berry (April 6). But it didn't take off until Stringfellow took over. He hired the hall for £2 10s a week and on Friday, August 17, 1962, Pete and Geoff started their own twist sessions for teenagers at the hall. The club sported a sign saying, "Dig this daddy'o," in big black letters with a drawing of Andy Capp dancing in one corner. Also shown was a cloud with the number '7' written on it. "It was supposed to be Cloud 9 but I'm a bit dyslexic and it ended up as a '7'," admits Peter who still has the original sign hung up in his office at the world famous Stringfellow's club in London.

Providing the music that first night was Rotherham band Stewart Raven and the Pursuers whom Peter had seen at the Cannon Hall pub at Firvale. They had two drummers,

St Aidan's Church Hall, with Pete's original poster, right

played Buddy Holly numbers and featured Jill 'the living, twisting doll'. Despite the band not being particularly well known, there was a queue outside. Peter still had a lot to learn. When the band took a break after the first of their three 20-minute slots things went dead. Peter ended up fetching his mother's radiogram and his cousin's collection of six records to keep the audience entertained. "In mum's living room the radiogram was loud," said Peter. "In St Aidan's church hall it was barely audible." He and Geoff lost £25 on that first night and didn't do much better the following week when the Pursuers were on again. "Against all the odds and with everybody screaming at me I persevered for one more week," says Peter. "I had Dave Berry next and I knew that he was bound to pull a large crowd. I was convinced it would

The Brook Brothers at the Black Cat

work, but just to be sure I took out a big £6 advert in the Sheffield Star.". This time the brothers cleared £65 for themselves, and did the same the following week with Johnny Tempest, by now a friend of Peter's. The club also became the Black Cat, with a new sign, when Tempest played. Stringfellow was on his way. "Geoff gave me the idea for a venue," said Peter. "He's a more steady character than me. It started off as a money venture. I didn't know the difference between a jazz group and a rock group at first. But soon few knew as much as I did." It was a family venture with Geoff helping with the booking of the band, their mum was cashier and dad doorman. Not everybody has great memories of the Black Cat however. "I used to work there regularly," says singer Karen Young, "It was a horrible, dingy place."

Up and coming names from around the country followed including Frank Kelly and the Hunters, Ian Crawford and the Boomerangs and hit parade stars the Brook Brothers. But the first real crowd-puller, at a fee of £50, was Screaming Lord Sutch and his band the Savages which included future Fleetwood Mac legend Peter Green on guitar. Many of the emerging Merseybeat groups played there, such as the Searchers, Undertakers, Big Three, Rory Storm and the Hurricanes, Freddie Starr and the Midnighters and Faron's Flamingos. Stringfellow: "After the Beatles I booked everything from Liverpool - the Spiders, Undertakers etc. I told Freddie Starr to stop telling jokes. It killed the atmosphere. I stopped booking him." There were also bands from Manchester - Hollies, Wayne Fontana and the Mindbenders and the club's most popular act, Freddie and the Dreamers. Whether planned or otherwise, the brothers' timing when booking some of these bands was fortuitous, as with the Searchers who were at number one with Sweets For My Sweet when they played at the Black Cat. Probably the most illustrious visitor was Gene

Vincent but Stringfellow lost money on the 27-year-old rock & roller. Peter: "Gene Vincent was a booking for myself, I was slightly older than my crowd who were teenagers. I remember Be Bop A Lula which was Fifties, my era, I had to book him. But he had gone, it was over for him, not for me. He turned up and backstage and he was in a straight black suit, I said, 'Where's your leathers?' He said, 'I don't wear that stuff anymore man'. But it is still one of my highlights." Peter also learned how to entertain the crowd, whether it was through the antics of horror acts Ray 'Frankenstein' Stuart or Count Lindsay, both of whom Stringfellow claims to have invented after having seen Lord Sutch, or by holding 'silly games'. "When the bands stopped playing the crowd would start fighting. The only way to stop it was to entertain them. I'd get up with the microphone and organise silly games. I'd have piccalilli sandwich-eating competitions and give the winner ten shillings. The sandwiches were totally lethal but it kept everyone amused until the band came back on." The Stringfellows were also DJs at the club. Alan Wood: "Peter used to live across from me on Lamb Hill Close at Richmond and I'd often have to knock him up and say, 'Your car's been broken into again.' He used to have Triumph Heralds with soft-tops and people would cut through the top and take out the record collection. So then he would swop cars to try to fool people."

But even by 1962 most people in Sheffield were probably still not fully aware of what was going on in their own city, still a passing fad for most of them who were probably too busy trying to get to grips with the latest dance craze, the Twist. The September 1962 issue of Top Stars was almost wholly devoted to the craze with twist star Chubby Checker on the cover. The rise to fame of the Beatles changed all that and it was the Stringfellows who brought them to Sheffield. In October 1962 the Liverpool group, who had spent more time on stage in Hamburg than they had in Britain, made their first entry into the charts with Love Me Do. Nobody took that much notice until their second single, Please Please Me, went to number two, just missing out on top spot thanks to a combination of the Shadows, Jet Harris and Tony Meehan and Frank Ifield. Mop-top hysteria and the Merseybeat sound was about take over the pop world. And on Saturday, February 12, 1963, the Beatles played Sheffield for the first time.

Pete Stringfellow has made much, may be even a whole career, out of his coup of being the first promoter to put the Beatles on in Sheffield. But the fact is that the group were playing

Chubby Checker's new version

Chubby Checker and his partner perform the latest version of the dance — the Popeye.

It goes like this: 'Give at the knees, swivel in the middle, clap those hands, go man go.'

absolutely everywhere that year, doing anything up to three shows a day in venues in different towns. Their first album, Please Please Me, was out in April, as was a new single, From Me To You, and manager Brian Epstein was making sure everybody knew who they were. Peter Stringfellow originally booked them for the Black Cat for an £85 fee, negotiating with Epstein from a telephone box, but soon realised he would have to find somewhere bigger as the Beatles' second record began to take off. After being turned down by various venues he found the Azena Ballroom, a posh dancehall on the outskirts of the city at Gleadless Townend. He managed to persuade the owner, funeral director Arnold Fiddler, who had built the dancehall for his ballroom dancer wife, Zena, to let him hire it for £29. He went on to sell 2,000 tickets. Hundreds more turned up on the night. Windows were smashed and the fire doors mysteriously opened. Keith 'Mo' Linaker: "We'd never seen anything like it, it was Beatlemania in Sheffield for the first time." Terry Roe: "You couldn't hear them for all the screaming and what I could hear, I didn't reckon much to. I thought the Sheffield bands had a better sound at the time." Terry also made an impression himself that night: "I got my foot in the wires and pulled the main plug out just before they went on. I got out of the way when that happened!" Pete Jackson had met the Beatles a few months earlier: "I

The Beatles on stage at the Azena Ballroom

said, 'You're in Sheffield in so many months aren't you at Pete Stringfellow's thing?' And they said, 'Yeah, are you coming to that one? Well come backstage you'll be all right.' I went to the Azena and I'm trying to get through and this bouncer says, 'Nobody's coming backstage, sorry.' The dressing room door opens and Lennon saw me and I said, 'Remember me?' and he said, 'Go on let him in'. I swopped plectrums with Lennon."

That wasn't the only concert - all 40 minutes of it - that the Beatles played that day. They had just driven over the Pennines from a matinee at the Astoria Ballroom in Oldham. The day before

they had been in a studio in London recording the ten tracks that would complete the Please Please Me debut album, John Lennon putting down the final vocals to Twist And Shout at 10.45pm, sucking fruit gums to stop his voice packing in altogether. It must almost have been a relief for Lennon, who could barely sing the following night, when the screaming drowned the band out at the Azena.

The Beatles were to play Sheffield four more times that year, all at the City Hall. Less than a month later - March 2 - they were fourth on the bill to Kenny Lynch, Danny Williams and headliner Helen Shapiro. They were then part of the Chris Montez/ Tommy Roe tour and on May 25 appeared with Roy Orbison who started out as the headliner but by the time the tour reached Sheffield the Beatles were headlining (also on the bill were Gerry and the Pacemakers). They finally headlined in their own right on November 2, a concert that Peter Stringfellow can take credit for arranging having personally persuaded Brian Epstein to add an extra date on a tour which originally by-passed Sheffield. The Star reported that ticket touts were out in force, offering 8s 6d tickets for £3 and that the queue to get in started with two Sheffield girls, Betty Nixon and Molly Haslam, aged 13 and 14, getting first in line at 7.30am.

One recipient of the people who couldn't get in at the Azena on that night in February was the R&B Club at Frecheville Community Centre, just a mile away, where the Cresters were playing. But for organiser Tony Smith that was not much compensation. He had spurned the Beatles for that same night at Frecheville Community Centre. "I was offered the Beatles for £65 by their tour agency. I turned them down because I had seen them on Scene at 6.30 on the television and I didn't like the look of them, sitting there in their leathers. I do regret that now. It looked like being a bad night for us until the Azena overflow people turned up. Stringy was always coming to our club to see what we were

Once The Azena, now a supermarket

doing. He came up once wanting to know how on earth we had managed to get the Byrds. He thought it was the American lot but this was the Birds from London [featuring future Face/ Rolling Stone, Ronnie Wood]."

The club, which started out as the Rock Club, ran from 1962 to '67. It was run by a handful of 20-year-olds headed by salesman Smith and opened in December, 1962, with Freddie and the Dreamers, becoming the R&B Club on October 1, 1963 with a double bill of Dave Berry and the Cruisers and The Big Three. "The whole idea was just to raise money for the community

Frecheville Community Centre, once home of the R'n'B Club

centre," says Smith. "We got ten per cent of the takings to buy records and for expenses, and the rest would go to organise pantomimes and for outings for the pensioners." Top admission price was around 6/6d (32p). Changing to the R&B Club it was held on Saturdays and Tuesdays, and saw regular visits from the likes of the Spencer Davis Group featuring Stevie Winwood (Smith collared Spencer Davis in the Howard Hotel on Howard Street between sets at the Esquire to book the band for Frecheville), Long John Baldry, including Rod Stewart who later appeared with his own band the Soul Agents, Wayne Fontana and the Mindbenders, the Pretty Things, Screaming Lord Sutch, the Big

Three, John Mayall's Bluesbreakers, Barron Knights, Nashville Teens, Hollies, Alex Harvey's Soul Band and Germany's number one group the Rattles, as well as regular appearances by Berry, Cocker, Tempest and Crawford. The Rattles, who went on to have a British hit with The Witch in 1970, were one of the most expensive to book at £100, Cocker or Tempest between £12 and £15.

The club's estimated 800 membership boasted more female members than males at a ratio of about 60/40. Tony Smith: "There was a pond behind the centre and some of the musicians would go out there with a guitar and serenade the girls as they were going into the club. We never had any complaints about the venue from the bands, although Rod Stewart did insist on having a separate dressing room from the rest of his band. And the committee were not too pleased when Screaming Lord Sutch almost set the curtains alight. We also used to go to Liverpool to check out the bands there. We'd go to the Cavern at lunchtime when Cilla [Black] worked in the cloakroom, and there would be six bands playing. We would then book some of them for the R&B Club. We also had an arrangement with other venues such as the Lyric in Dinnington and Rawmarsh Baths. Bands would do the first spot at one of the venues and then head off to the next venue. It cut our costs down."

Just a few hundred yards along the road was the Church Hall on Smalldale Road where the Zodiac Club operated. This ran every fortnight with mainly local bands and occasional out of town such as the Barron Knights and Jackie Lynton and the Jury. This later led to organisers Alan Penny and Martin Hill running their own group agency Lane Enterprises. There was also Frecheville Co-op Hall which featured Dave Berry and the Cruisers regularly on Wednesdays, with bands like Johnny Tempest and the Mariners, the Cadillacs and Doncaster's Lee Walker and the Travellers standing in when Berry and co were elsewhere.

For Stringfellow, the Beatles' date was a defining moment: "I was totally blown away by the glamour and the excitement. That night changed my life. I knew that one Black Cat Club wasn't enough. I wanted more; I wanted what I'd had that night, every night." The Stringfellows also impressed Brian Epstein who offered to take them on but they didn't want to leave Sheffield. "We were really mixed up in the local Sheffield scene so we decided against it," said Pete.

11. MONSTER MASH

In the summer of 1962 Screaming Lord Sutch and the Savages, with a totally outrageous act and a fantastic backing band, had blown a storm through South Yorkshire with some incredible gigs in Rotherham, Doncaster and Sheffield. It was to spark off a brief but memorable spate of Sheffield horror-rock bands.

It was Darnall teenager Terry Roe who started the local horror trend as the ghoulish figure of Count Lindsay III. Terry had originally fronted a rock'n'roll band as Vince Rogers and the Sabres which included schoolboy musicians Alan Wood and Bob Grundy. Roe: "I was a wanderer and I went working down London and finished up in Watford. I used to follow Screaming Lord Sutch round, not for Sutch but the band. I was an avid Chuck Berry fan and when they were tuning up they used to go through a lot of his stuff before they went on to the crap with him. The horror thing started for me at the Black Cat. It was Elvis Presley's birthday so Stringfellow had got all these Elvis impersonators on - he also had a pie-eating competition, owt to draw the crowd in. I got up and did I'm A Hog For You Baby and started jumping all over the place and going berserk. Then Stringfellow got me getting up with different bands like the Cruisers, who didn't like it, and one thing led to another."

Roe became Count Lindsay, taking the name from Jimmy Crawford's former stage-name Ron Lindsay, although he was often billed as Count Linsey (sic). The Citadels were his backing band, renamed the Skeletons. Keith 'Mo' Linaker: "We copied Screaming Lord Sutch. We used to wear masks and bandages covered in blood that was a red dye." The Count soon found he had a challenger: "Ray Stuart came along and said, 'I can do that better than he can.' Pete Stringfellow thought that sounded good and organised a contest - Count Lindsay against Frankenstein." Stuart backed out.

Of all the horror acts the Count's was the most chilling and probably the most mad - and things didn't always go according to plan. The act climaxed with him swinging across the stage with a noose round his neck. Keith Linaker: "He'd put his hand through the rope and when the chair was moved it was his strength that kept the rope off his throat. At Catcliffe his hand slipped out and he nearly strangled himself." Terry Roe: "That day the noose was a bit too tight and I couldn't get out of it. They had to let me down." Later on the Count also came a crop-

per on ice at the Silver Blades ice rink. Roe: "They'd put the coffin right in the centre of the ice-rink with the band spread round. I got out of the coffin with a piece of meat that was about three weeks old. It stunk horrible. That was supposed to be my heart. When I got out all I did was slip and slide, falling about on the ice!"

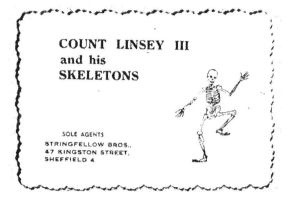

COUNT LINSEY III
and his
SKELETONS

SOLE AGENTS
STRINGFELLOW BROS.,
47 KINGSTON STREET,
SHEFFIELD 4

There was also a particularly painful gig at Bradford: "There was this bloke following me. He was doing everything to me, nutting me, kicking me, putting his fingers in my eyes. I just pretended I wasn't feeling anything, like it was just bouncing off. Afterwards he came in the dressing room and we had a set-to." Terry was often a target: "Especially at Chesterfield, at Jimmy's. Our drummer ended up hitting somebody with a cymbal."

Under Stringfellow's management the Count and the Skeletons were booked to support to the Beatles at the Azena. Keith Linaker: "We couldn't believe it - on the same stage as the Beatles. John was very offish, a bit, 'I am a Beatle,' but the rest of the lads were smashing. They used our amps together with their amps, joined-up for sound." Terry Roe: "Probably because I'd buggered theirs up." Linaker: "When the Beatles' show was over they went in our van and we went in theirs because of the fans who ran after us. We then met up outside Sheffield and switched vans back." Count Lindsay and the Skeletons also played a gig on the Beatles' home-ground at the Cavern. Terry Roe: "Stringfellow got us there, it was supposed to be a swop, or as he termed it, 'the Aidan's Shake for the Cavern Stomp.'" However, on the night a stand-in guitarist had to be found, as Keith Linaker remembers: "We'd all arranged to go but our guitarist Ray was a draughtsman at Davy United's and his dad said, 'There's no way our Raymond is going to the Cavern Club and leaving that job.' So we were in trouble with no lead guitarist." The stand-in was Joe Cocker's then Big Blues guitarist Dave Hopper: "Just by chance we hadn't got a gig with Joe. I wasn't

HORROR

How the girls love it!

EVER since Eve met the Serpent in the Garden of Eden, man (and woman) has been fascinated by the horrific.

[remaining body text illegible]

● Frankenstein *[caption partly illegible]* ... with the aid of The Monsters. Below, screaming Lord Sutch is one of his primate incarnats.

One of the Sleepwalkers.

● Howling Dark Dave in full cry — dressed as a Viking invader.

Neil Coates

● Firm favourite at St Aidan's Sheffield, is Count Looey III (front row, right), who poses with fellow ghouls, Count Dracula and The Skeletons.

really bothered how much we were getting paid, it was just the experience of playing at the Cavern. I had a skeleton mask on though so I don't think anybody recognised me!" Keith Linaker: "They'd never seen a horror act. They'd never seen Screaming Lord Sutch, so we went better than a normal group." Terry Roe: "I was stood backstage in the dressing room while the Big Three were on and I was rocking. By the time I went on I'd lost all my inhibitions and I just flew off the stage at them. I cleared about four rows of chairs. Hopper was there and he played out of his skin, a brilliant night."

They also went to Germany. Terry Roe: "We left Stringfellow to go to Germany. He'd got these bookings for us that were really good but we wanted to go abroad. Fraser Hines' brother was in charge as the go-between for the Top Ten Club in Hamburg and he'd been after us for a while. We didn't need to audition really." The band were a big hit as Keith Linaker recalls: "At the Top Ten Club they used to shout, 'We want the man with the white face.' That was Terry with his top hat and white face and he used to go down a bomb." Other acts at the Top Ten Club at the same time included the Alex Harvey Soul Band, the Giants (including one Kenny Slade), Freddie Starr and the Midnighters and Rory Storm and the Hurricanes although Terry Roe found himself becoming disillusioned: "When I got there I wasn't bothered, I'd had enough of it. I was more interested in what others were doing than what I was doing, it was just a load of rubbish really." He split with the Citadels and worked briefly as Count Lindsay with the Daizies: "I stood in with them, but my heart wasn't really into it anymore. I didn't like what they were doing. It was all pop - Beatles and Foundations, all that type of stuff. I used to run Dave Hopper about and that's all I wanted to do really, just get involved with a band."

The ghoulish goings-on were always popular in Sheffield and they were matched by imaginative adverts in the Star for the shows. One for the Central Ballroom in Attercliffe stated that there was a Count Dracula and Count Lindsay III in the city and the management wanted them to prove their worth 'DEAD OR ALIVE' and their fees would be One Pint Of Maiden's Blood Each! Another advert said Count Lindsay and the Skeletons had just returned from Outer Mongolia to play at St Aidan's. Terry Roe: "It was Pete Stringfellow. He'd say, 'Go down to Top Stars Special and give 'em a load of bollocks!' We just played 'em along. When they said, 'Where are you from?' I just said Outer Mongolia."

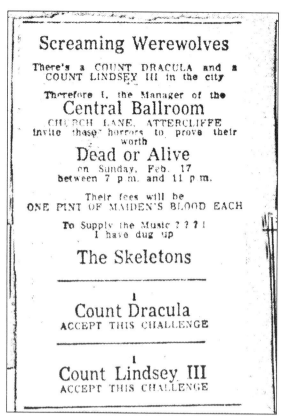

Another horror-rocker was singer/musician Dave Poole whose creation was the fearsome-looking Howlin' Dook Dave. He would dress up in full Viking chieftain garb. Terry Roe: "He was another musician from Darnall who jumped on the bandwagon." The Dook's band also included members of the Citadels, Dave Cannon and Bob Grundy. There was also Quasimodo "Hunchback of Notre Dame," whose appearance at the Cutlers Hall in April, 1964, carried the warning, "Give it a miss girls, if you're a bit squeamish. It's horrific, it's horrific." But probably the best remembered (usually for all the wrong reasons) of all the horror acts was Frankenstein and the Monsters featuring veteran rock'n'roller Ray Stuart (See The Music Makers: Chapter 7).

12. BOOM, BOOM, BOOM: THE ESQUIRE

Following Club 60, Terry Thornton's next venture was the Esquire in Leadmill Road, in the building now occupied by the Leadmill, converted at a cost of £1,000 from a disused Victorian three-storey flour mill. Terry had been reluctantly forced to give up Club 60 when it was revealed planners wanted to demolish the old Acorn building. The opening weekend - October 5, 6 and 7 in 1962 - featured a mixture of trad jazz from local outfits, modern jazz from Johnny

Dankworth and Cleo Laine, Tubby Hayes, Ronnie Ross and Don Rendall, plus beat music from Dave Berry and Shane Fenton. "Within hours of opening the doors, the club was under siege. All three floors were packed with bearded and long-haired jazz fans and beatniks," said the Morning Telegraph.

While Stringfellow's Black Cat catered for fairly straightforward pop and beat bands, the Esquire was more jazz, r'n'b and blues. On Friday and Sunday nights it was jazz while groups were featured on Saturdays and Mondays. It was a huge success from the word go and another highly atmospheric place. And whereas the Black Cat was only one night a week - Fridays - and, whichever way you looked at it, was still a church hall, the Esquire was open four nights of the week and had more of the feel of a proper club, despite the lack of any alcohol for sale. The membership fee was half a crown [12p] a year. The three-storey building was divided into a first floor reception area with cloakroom, changing and ladies rooms. On the second floor was the dance floor and stage area, and looking down on that through a large hole cut into the thick wooden floor was a balcony coffee bar from where members could watch the dancers and performers. Thornton, who was an accomplished artist, decorated the walls with paintings, album sleeves, strange bits of sculpture, a wooden skeleton and even the odd pair of ox horns, 7ft alligator and a crocodile. Screaming Lord Sutch told Top Stars it was the only place he felt at home - apart from a graveyard. And Johnny Dankworth said it reminded him of a Roman Arena.

The Esquire was to become a mecca for rhythm and blues fans with American blues singers such as John Lee Hooker (whose song Boom, Boom, Boom was played by nearly every band that appeared at the club), Jimmy Witherspoon, Little Walter (backed by Frank White's band), Sonny Boy Williamson II, Screaming Jay Hawkins and Memphis Slim playing there. The influence of the Esquire's music

John Lee Hooker at the Esquire Club

policy was also reflected in some of the concerts at the City Hall, particularly The Blues and Gospel Caravan which played there in May, 1964. It was reviewed the following day in the Star under the headline Magnificent Concert By Negro Group. It read: "Muddy Waters, Sonny Terry and Brownie McGhee are to pop what Michelangelo and Raphael are to pop art - old masters of an expression which transcends the barriers of colour and creed. As founder members of a negro musical tradition which, in its hybrid modern form has become a commercialised cult, they were given an ovation rarely accorded by teenage audiences these days." Also on the bill were Sister Rosetta Tharpe and Cousin Joe Pleasants.

The Esquire also hosted many up and coming British r'n'b acts - Long John Baldry, the Kinks, Animals, Spencer Davis, Pretty Things, Manfred Mann, Alex Harvey, Jimmy Powell, Georgie Fame and the Blue Flames, Alexis Korner, Merseybeats, Small Faces, Graham Bond (with the likes of Ginger Baker, Doncaster-born John McLaughlin and Jack Bruce in the band) etc. Chuck Fowler: "I played there once when Graham Bond was on. He was strange. He threatened to kick my speakers out of the window if I didn't shift them." Thornton would sometimes sit in on piano with visiting stars.

However, it was an awkward place for bands to get in as there were two flights of narrow stairs. Roy Ledger explains: "It was like, let's go up these stairs, and then, let's go up some

Present
America's Great Blues Artist
SONNY BOY WILLIAMSON
Backed by the
LEN STUART QUARTET
Plus the areas Leading Blues Combo
VANCE ARNOLD and the AVENGERS
Thursday, 13th. February, 1964.

This Ticket Admits One Person Only   TICKET 5/6

Georgie Fame and the Blue Flames climb the stairs
at The Esquire

more stairs. Everything's upstairs, man. Then you finish up at the top and look down and there's a big hole in the floor - oh there's the stage, I missed that on the way up!" It was a great view from the balcony although the stage wasn't very big and couldn't take much gear. Ernie Booth remembers: "Whoever got there first, you would use their gear. Mal Hooley was playing with Pete Fender and he used my amp. I said to him, 'What's it sound like?' and he said, 'It sounds like a saxophone.'" Bang in the middle of the stage was a pole which supported the floor above. While it got in the way for most bands, Dave Berry made it part of his stage act. "I used to use things like that, creeping round it and developed it later on for TV shows." Roy Ledger: "You were all right if you weren't a guitar/vocalist 'cos you'd got to put the mike stand somewhere. Berry had got the mike in his hand so he could lean round the pole and everything."

Some of the Esquire's most popular events were the occasional all-night gigs. The Christmas All-Nighter on Saturday, December 21, 1963, featured Dave Berry and the Cruisers, Vance Arnold and the Avengers, the Liverbirds and Scott William Combo, running from midnight until the next morning. Ernie Booth: "We used to do a gig somewhere else

and go and play there after." Terry Thornton briefly reopened Club 60 in November, 1963, after discovering that the old Acorn pub had been saved from demolition. The Debonairs, credited as the first of the Sheffield beat groups to release a record, played on the opening night. The Esquire was the subject of a BBC TV documentary, Alienation Of The Young, intended as a follow up to a similar programme on Liverpool's famous Cavern Club. BBC officials had visited the club several times and after questioning local fans decided it was a suitable location. The club's top attraction, Dave Berry and the Cruisers, provided the live music in front of a packed house. The Esquire was also used for another television production in 1964 as background for a play about a girl on the run. "BBC film cameras whirred as powder-pale-faced girls in distinctly Mary Quant-inspired fashions whirled with their equally long-haired partners to the throbbing rhythm of the Cruisers," said one report. Another memorable night at the Esquire was in February 1965 when, following the demise of the jazz sessions, the club went more over to pop with a new DJ record bar, launched with an appearance by Jimmy Savile who did the honours for a fee of £100. To make way for the new record bar a concert grand piano had to be dispensed with and literally came under the

Upstairs, downstairs: on the upper floor the coffee
bar while The Fentones play on the stage below
with the pole

hammer as Frankenstein (Ray Stuart) reduced the instrument to little pieces with a sledge-hammer. Two weeks later, following a successful late Saturday night jazz session with Tony Oxley, Terry Thornton had to get another piano for monthly all-night jazz spots. In June, 1965, the Walker Brothers were almost dismembered by hysterical screaming girls. Their performance ended after only four minutes, with Scott Walker taken to the dressing room with a cut lip. When they returned to the stage a group of "hefty male members formed a barrier round the stage

John Walker of the Walker Brothers besieged by fans at The Esquire

and there were no further incidents." Still, they got off lightly. At Birmingham Scott had his trousers torn off while at Bath Gary lost six shirts when fans invaded the dressing room. By the summer of 1966 the Esquire was featuring film shows among its attractions with a series of Batman films from the 1940s. There was also "Sheffield's most famous Shakespeare fanatic." He was simply known as Hamlet and first came to 'fame' when he was filmed by Granada Television's Scene at 6.30 at the Esquire. He was already well known locally on building sites and beat club stages for his spontaneous recitations of Shakespeare. Terry Thornton hired a film crew to film him in action. "It's amazing how the kids just stop and listen to him reciting passages from Shakespeare," said Terry. "He's appeared here several times and always manages to hold everybody spellbound."

Author JP Bean recalls an 'expensive' night at the club: "I went home and my dad said, 'Where y'been?' I said, 'To the Esquire to see Little Walter.' He said, 'How much is it to go in there?' I said, 'Five bob.' He said, 'Five bob? I should want t'bloody drum kit for five bob.' I only ever went there to see 'names'. I saw Jimmy Reed there and I think Zoot Money's band supported

The Four Corners

him with Paul Williams. I saw Spencer Davis a couple of times." John Crookes: "The Esquire was my favourite club because it featured more of my kind of music - R&B and blues." The DJ from the Twisted Wheel in Manchester, Roger Eagle, was impressed by the Esquire's music: "The Esquire is great. On a visit there a few weeks ago we heard a very good selection of records. Indeed here's one club where the mod influence has not ruined the appreciation of R&B." And one of northern soul's best known DJs, John Vincent, who became a resident at Wigan Casino, started his career deejaying at the Esquire. Kenny Slade: "I don't think I've played in a better club, it was a great atmosphere."

13. THE BEAT GOES ON

By early '63 many local groups had started to take in the sounds of Merseybeat, spearheaded by the Beatles, Gerry and the Pacemakers, Searchers, etc. Groups would now be seen in

The Rotherbirds

leather stage outfits, Beatle boots and longer hair. Johnny and the Cadillacs became the Texans, the Falcons became the Four Corners, who boasted, "a brand new sound for beat fans," the Questers became the Four Blades, Pete Emmett and the Skyliners became the Beat Squad, Dean Marshall and the Deputies became the Lizards and the Citadels became the Sharks. Woodseats boasted the Deccas, one of the few all-girl groups in South Yorkshire, while Rotherham also had its own version with the Rotherbirds who had obviously taken the idea for their name from the similarly tagged Merseybeat group the Liverbirds. The Nocturnes, on finding out there was already a Liverpool band of the same name, became Who? Their guitarist Zeke Fisher then sat in the window of Bradley's music shop on Fargate hold-

Passers-by were puzzled recently when they saw Zeke Fisher, rhythm guitarist with the Nocturnes, sitting in a music shop window. And that was the idea, for the group have taken the new name of WHO?.

ing a placard asking 'Who?' until the police came and fished him out. The band later repeated their mistake by becoming The Who, eventually settling on Who's Who.

One side effect of the success of the Beatles was that by the beginning of 1963 every record company, talent scout, promoter etc headed for Liverpool, with maybe a glance in at Manchester while they were passing. Sheffield didn't get a look in. The city and its host of bands was in danger of getting left behind. Liverpool could boast success with Frankie Vaughan in the Fifties, Billy Fury in the early Sixties, and now the Beatles, Gerry and the Pacemakers, the Searchers, Billy J Kramer and many others, Manchester had the Hollies, Freddie and the Dreamers and Wayne Fontana and the Mindbenders. All Sheffield had to show for itself was a minor hit for Jimmy Crawford.

"We built up an incredible following in Sheffield," says Dave Berry. "But once bands like the Beatles were successful, expectations were different. I can remember sitting in pubs and people asking what was happening with my career. I think now that if I hadn't happened in 1963 that would have been it for me. And for a lot of bands in Sheffield that didn't happen and after 18 months, they and their fans got disillusioned. Even Joe Cocker was on the verge of packing it in." John Hall, drummer/ manager of Johnny Tempest and the Cadillacs, expressed those frustrations in The Star: "We've just about saturated Sheffield. We get good bookings all over the South Yorkshire area and we've a great reputation and hundreds of fans. But there's no-one left to impress here any more. We want to travel outside Sheffield - build a bigger reputation, get to London and Manchester and the rest of the provinces. But we just can't afford to give our jobs up and turn fully professional. It's a risk you can only take if you have a record deal." Soon it was obvious something needed to be done if Sheffield was going to compete.

Reflecting this, Top Stars Special wrote in May, 1963: "Entertainment-wise, Sheffield just doesn't appear to be on the map. The plain fact is that young people in this city just don't seem to get any encouragement. There's no doubt that a few more clubs like the Esquire and the Black Cat would be welcomed by the teenagers who have been used to spending their spare time either at the cinema or coffee bars. Take a walk round any back street in Manchester and there are cellar clubs like the Oasis and the Three Coins where kids can jive, twist and generally let their hair down." Indeed Manchester could boast almost 30 successful clubs in the centre of the city alone. The report went on: "Yet for some strange reason, Sheffielders, especially the powers that be, are suspicious of these clubs. The few who have opened clubs find themselves haunted by the police, who seem to expect trouble. And those who have tried to open likely-looking premises find a curious difficulty in getting permission from the authorities. Maybe half the trouble is the lack of suitable premises near to the city centre, yet there is no doubt that there are disused warehouses and cellars which could be converted at very little cost. But people who try to open them up meet with a blank wall of disapproval. The dimly-lit cave-type premises so common on the continent fascinate teenagers - it's a way to get away from the rather humdrum routine of everyday life - somewhere you can go and dress like an Eskimo and no one would care tuppence."

If clubs in Sheffield were not threatened by demolition, they seemed to be under threat from the police. The Esquire was subject to a heavy-handed raid in August 1963 while Vance Arnold and co were on the stage. All 500 teenagers - the majority of whom were not, as required by law, members of the club - had to give their names and addresses which the police then checked against a street directory. "A police officer came in and told us to close the bar," said owner Terry Thornton. "It was only selling orange juice. I think they had all been reading too many detective stories." The headline in The Star the following day read, Chicago-Style Raid On Jazz Club. Dave Berry, as ever ahead of the game after playing in Hamburg, added: "After being on the Continent I am amazed that people put up with such a dull night life here. We need more clubs where people can combine eating and dancing."

The Stringfellows continued to do their bit and their next venture in 1963, was regular Sunday night sessions at the Blue Moon Club located in an old church school, turned warehouse, in Johnson Street, off Nursery Street. Peter carried on with Friday nights at the Black Cat before passing the venue on to 22-year-old Tony Wainwright. The Blue Moon opened in May,

1963. One of the venue's most memorable nights was when the Kinks, riding high in the charts with You Really Got Me, played on September 20, 1964. It was yet another indication of how the Stringfellows had a nose for booking bands at just the right time. Peter told Top Stars: "It's really planning in advance, plus good luck. It shows we are on the ball. We have had a few artists here just before they went to

The Blue Moon as it is now

number one or just after and this has worked out perfectly."

The Stringfellows also organised a trip in April, 1963, to the famous Cavern Club. However, the night ended in trouble as Terry Roe (Count Lindsay) recalls: "We got there on a Friday night and they let us in while all the regulars were outside in a line waiting to go in. There were that many of us, most of them didn't get in. They waited for us coming out and we had to run through a hail of bottles. There were bottles flying all over the place, at the coach and everything. They hated us for it."

Other Stringfellow promotions included shows at Sheffield City Hall, a venue which was still virtually out of bounds, other than as a punter, for local musicians. That year the likes of Ella Fitzgerald, Oscar Peterson, Brenda Lee, Mantovani, Shirley Bassey, Matt Monro and Frankie Ifield, not to mention the Beatles, were the staple fare at the venue, while the Gaumont Cinema was only a little more adventurous with Joe Brown and the Bruvvers, the Tornadoes, Shane Fenton and, er, Rolf Harris on one bill, the Everly Brothers and Bo Diddley on another and the return of Little Richard. The two Everly Brothers/ Bo Diddley shows at the Gaumont on October 22, 1963, were not particularly eventful but it was for support act the Rolling Stones who were about to release their second single, I Wanna Be Your Man, as Bill Wyman recalls in his book Stone Alone: "After the show we went on the town and suddenly realised how vulnerable we had become. We began talking to two local lads in a coffee bar when out of nowhere a crowd formed outside the windows. The old guy in the cafe didn't know who we were and didn't want any trouble so he threw us out. We survived a bit of a scramble back to the hotel where Brian and I met two girls, later nicknamed the Pifco twins, and spent the night with them. The Stones were to go on to play in Sheffield another five times. At the City Hall they topped the bill

on November 13, 1963, played two shows with joint headliner John Leyton on February 27, 1964, another two shows on May 29, and also joined the Hollies for two shows on March 11, 1965, which also included Dave Berry and the Cruisers. One ten-year-old from Mexborough, Graham Oliver, later of rock band Saxon, was in the audience: "My brother was at Mexborough Youth Club and they had a trendy vicar who took all the lads to see the Rolling Stones. There was a spare ticket so they took me. I was only ten, but I did notice Frank White's double-neck guitar with the Cruisers. I'd never been to a concert before. I can remember all the girls' stocking tops and everything because they were like writhing about on the floor and their skirts were riding up. I was too young to think anything other than it was just odd. The Stones came on and Charlie Watts was drumming away on Last Time and this guy gets on stage and shoves an autograph book under his nose. This bouncer grabs him and this kid in turn grabs Charlie Watts round his head while he's still trying to drum.

> 7" EP to be played at 33 megacycles per hour (uphill) —, playing time — 7·26 x 10³ feet (at the speed of sound)
>
> Yes! It's here, folks! The very first Sheffield Rag Record, presenting for your entertainment four well-known sound of Sheffield.....
>
> LOS CARIBOS — purveyors of West Indian Carribeat music. The University is fortunate in possessing such an outstanding example of this genre.
>
> THE ADDY STREET 5 — the University Jazz Band — the only traditional band to reach the finals of the Inter-University Jazz Competition.
>
> THE VANTENNAS—extremely popular beat group, both in the University and the City.
>
> DAVE ALLEN BIG BAND—regular performers in the University Union. Well-known throughout Sheffield.
>
> N.B. Label incorrect—read as above.
>
> WARNING. Please do not use worn nails or pins as this will irreparably damage the trailer pin
>
> Sleeve designer by courtesy of the ...... oo.

That's the image I have of that concert, that and Brian Jones wearing a white suit. The lad next to me said he'd rather see Herman's Hermits. My next gig was Jimi Hendrix two years later." In that same year the Stones also played two shows with Spencer Davis at the Gaumont on October 10. They were not to play Sheffield again for 30 years, when they appeared at the Don Valley Stadium. They also played at Doncaster Gaumont on October 12, 1963, Doncaster Baths on December 4, 1963, another two shows at Doncaster Gaumont on September 24, 1964, and again on October 11.

The R&B tones of the Rolling Stones along with the Kinks, Manfred Mann, etc, were also having an influence on the Sheffield scene which now boasted bands like the Smokestacks, Detroits, Krawdaddies, Green Onions, Gaelic Blues, the Kegs, Cobwebs and, from Chesterfield, the Deens.

Stringfellow tried to put the focus on Sheffield groups and organised a huge showcase for local bands at the City Hall. On September 16, 1963, ten local bands played at the showcase, the biggest so far for local bands who would also be performing in front of record companies. And Top Stars asked, 'Can Sheffield beat Liverpool in the Battle of the Beat?' On the bill were head-liners Dave 'the Baron of the Beat' Berry and the Cruisers (three days later their first single, a cover of Chuck Berry's Memphis Tennessee, entered the charts); Karen Young and the Cadillacs (Top Stars Special reported that Young was "a girl singer with a bright future in show business,"); veterans the Debonairs (their first single for Parlophone, When True Love Comes Your Way, was about to come out); Vance Arnold and the Avengers (finally making inroads with a 'new' rhythm and blues style); Dean Marshall and the Deputies ("much improved"); Frankenstein and the Monsters (Ray

The Debonairs

'Frankenstein' Stuart had recently broken two fingers - while being dragged on stage in chains at Morecambe); the Vantennas ("rockers, bal-lads, twist and rhythm and blues"); the Greycats (one of Sheffield's oldest and best known groups, fronted by singer Pat Leslie, played Top 20 covers "as if they made every record in it"); Ray du Verne and the Chequers (Pete Stringfellow's latest discoveries, fronted by the lively Jerry Lee Lewis-like Ray); and the Vampires (contrary to their name, they were billed as, "four of the nicest chaps one would wish to meet"). The show was a highlight for many as Pat Leslie remembers: "It was a big night for

The Vantennas

local musicians and everybody did it for nothing and it helped to set Pete Stringfellow up."

It was a sell-out, reflecting the support for local talent. Roy Shepherd of The Star wrote: "I've never seen so much enthusiasm packed into the City Hall both from the performers and the youngsters in the audience. It was a most exciting experience. All the groups deserve praise for their efforts." Tony Hatch from Pye Records said: "It was a very good show indeed. I have never seen another one quite like this. It was great. We have never seen anyone so enthusiastic, or so many local artists all togeth-er." The judges - record company representa-tives - chose the Vampires as the winners, part-ly thanks to a virtuoso performance on harmon-ica by singer, songwriter and organ player John E Alexander, previously with Jimmy Crawford's Messengers, who also contributed original songs and strong arrangements. "You'll Hear More About This Man," ran the headline in the September issue of Top Stars. The line-up also featured Don Allison and Brian Cooke on gui-

The Sheffields' original line-up: Dave Fawcett, John Alexander, Richard Smith, Don Allison

tars, Dave Fawcett, bass, and Richard Smith on drums. One of the judges Tony Hatch, later to be better known as a songwriter, took them under his wing, renaming them the Sheffields. They went on to make three singles for Pye with Hatch as producer. But even before the first single was released Cooke left, opting for a 'proper job': "It was a difficult decision. I had to choose between the rather hazardous life of show business and a steady career. I chose to stick to my insurance job - it has great prospects and I don't want to risk losing it."

The first single featured two original songs written by Alexander, It Must Be Love and Say Girl. Heralding its release was a four-page promotional supplement, It's History, put out by Kennedy Street, the top Manchester agency with whom the band had signed. Disc, in February 1, '64, noted: "Special point to listen for is John Alexander's first class r'n'b mouth organ noise." Don Allison left the band soon afterwards. He suffered from asthma and found the workload heavy going. They advertised in London for a replacement, finding one in Sheffield in Roy Ledger of the Chevrons. The next record was to have been another Alexander original, Steel Drivin' Man, about Sheffield steelworkers. Hatch said he had never heard anything like it before from an English group and was sure that it would be a hit. But the track, along with the proposed B-side, Plenty Of Love, didn't get released for unknown reasons. Instead the second single was a real up-tempo commercial version of Muddy Waters' Got My Mojo Working, on which the Disc review (April 4, '64) once again noted, "Best thing about this group's version is the harmonica interjections of John Alexander." The B-side featured another original, Hey, Hey Lover Boy, with a distinct Bo Diddley arrangement. Roy Ledger recalls the preparation behind their recordings: "We'd rehearse it for three days on the trot, six hour rehearsals every day. Then when we went in to do a record they'd do it in two takes and the first take was always the best one anyway." Developing from straight R&B, the Sheffields' music took in elements of jazz as Roy explains: "All the jazz came when I played with the Sheffields 'cos we were playing blues which is the next thing to jazz. You move on to swing and then jazz. And of course there was all the knocking about with the lads down London. Cliff Barton, bass player with Long John Baldry, took me to his house in Islington and said, 'This is jazz,' and started playing Roland Kirk and Charlie Mingus and actually explained to me what they were playing. I thought, 'This is amazing - eureka!'" This influence showed on

the Sheffield's final single, an excellent adaptation of vibraphonist Milt Jackson's Bags' Groove re-named Skatwalking, featuring a wordless duet between Alexander and guitarist Ledger. They toured to promote the record but were unable to appear on television's Ready Steady Go after Ledger managed to drop a piano on to his foot and hand, leaving him virtually unable to walk. The record failed to chart.

Despite the Sheffields' lack of chart success they had become a respected live act, mixing rhythm and blues covers with blues and, ahead of their time, a touch of jazz-rock. They knew their chops sufficiently to back Memphis Slim and Champion Jack Dupree on British tours and found themselves joined on stage one night in London by T-Bone Walker, the American blues guitarist whose knowledge of the blues guitar was reckoned to be second to none. Memphis

Slim said of them: "The Sheffields are a group worth watching. They have wonderful arrangements and a full and close sound which shows that they work in harmony and, more important, think in harmony." They also topped the bill at the Marquee in London, with one Rod Stewart as support act. Skatwalking was the last to be heard of one of the city's most original outfits of the time. Nowadays, their records are regarded as serious collectors' items and worth in the region of £60 apiece. John Alexander was also one of the first British musicians to play the electric piano but that came to an end when he, and the piano, fell off the stage at Norwich. He used an amplified ordinary piano after that. Strangely enough, he quit a promising career in the business as Roy Ledger recalls: "A talented lad, a shame 'cos he's never done anything since. The last time I saw him, about 15 years ago, he was working at what was Walsh's [House Of Fraser and now TJ Hughes] selling

The Sheffields, left to right: Roy Ledger, John Alexander, Dave Fawcett, Richard Smith

TVs."

Stringfellow's next promotion at the City Hall was another marathon bill, headed by the Rolling Stones, on November 13, 1963, with support acts including Wayne Fontana and the Mindbenders and Vance Arnold and the Avengers who were on second. The Sheffield Morning Telegraph review the following day described the Stones as, "Five raving beat boys from London who look like Neanderthal men," while Vance Arnold was acclaimed as, "Surely a star of the future," exposure that finally began

Karen Young and Jimmy Savile

to alert record companies that Sheffield may have a new star. Singer Karen Young, who was also on the bill with the Cadillacs, has vivid memories of the Rolling Stones who had just broken into the charts with Come On and I Wanna Be Your Man. "The Stones were sat on a circular seat back stage with totally expressionless faces. They ignored everybody and didn't speak to anybody." In late January, 1964, Wayne Fontana was back at the City Hall again, at another Stringfellow promotion, this time with Dave Berry and the Cruisers, the Hollies and, once again, Vance Arnold and the Avengers. Two months later Berry and Vance Arnold also featured at the Tops Stars Ball at the Locarno on London Road, another showcase for local talent with teenagers displaying their mod fashions as they did the Shake. Also appearing were regular favourites the Sheffields, the Texans and special guest Janice Nichols, the 'Oi'll Give It Foive' girl from ITV's Thank Your Lucky Stars.

Sheffield bands began to play all over the country as well as on the Continent. Groups were much better equipped with line-ups featuring Fender, Gibson and Gretsch guitars coupled up with Vox AC30 amplifiers and decent PA systems and even some with their own vans. Cranes Music on Lady's Bridge was a regular Saturday morning hang-out for musicians who would easily spend two or three hours trying out some of the various guitars that were on display, much to the frustration of the manager as invariably most musicians would simply try out the instruments and not buy one. Up town, Wilson Peck's at Barkers Pool, had a long history in Sheffield for selling fine musical instruments, mainly pianos. Over the road Bradley's Music set up premises at the top of Fargate and included a wide selection of instruments both cheap and expensive.

While most bands were looking for work around the city, the Jetblacks were the exception, often playing abroad. Originally a five-piece country and western band they were lead singer Ricky Everett, guitarist Steve Wondaer, bass player Rick Summers, Alan Marshall, drummer, and lead guitarist Martin Scott. Although they rarely played Sheffield, in October, '65, fans voted them the top group in Top Stars. In June, following a tour of France, they became a four-piece when Everett left due to, "contrasted musical interests." In January, 1967, they embarked on what should have been a two-month tour of Germany and Switzerland but ended up spending almost 12 months away, playing US airforce bases, as reported in Top Stars. However the band usually spent enough

The original Jetblacks

time in Sheffield to have their pictures taken dressed in their trendy Guardsmen's tunics (a la Sgt Pepper). Wondaer and Summers collaborated as songwriters (under their proper names of Alcock and Crane) and claimed to have written more than 300 songs. Two of them, What Have I Been Doing and Everyone Makes A Mistake, were recorded by Chris Farlowe as B-sides to Handbags and Gladrags and Moanin'. The Jetblacks might not have been one of Sheffield's best known groups but they were certainly the most travelled.

One of Sheffield's first black rock'n'rollers was Vic Lynch, vocalist with the Cortinas. He was a talented singer, bass player and pianist, and loved singing country and western. The Cortinas, which included 15-year-old drummer Derek Lunn, were mobbed when they played at the Beat Sounds 64 Festival in Cleethorpes, fans letting down the van's tyres to stop them leaving and they also won the Big Beat 64 competition at the Black Cat, first prize £100. Dave Robinson of the Cortinas: "We were playing at the Minerva Tavern in Charles Street. Vic asked

The Cortinas, left to right: Spud West, Derek Lunn, Dave Robinson, Vic Lynch

us if he could get up and he got up and sang Ramblin' Cowboy and probably Blue Suede Shoes and so we integrated him into the band. He even agreed to play bass. It was a nice little band." The band eventually split due to the usual group arguments - "Material, money, venues, rehearsals, etc." Vic went on to front his own band the Lynch Mob while Lunn, whose talents had been noted by orchestra leader Cyril Stapleton, went on to further his career as a jazz drummer.

One of Sheffield's more eclectic bands in the mid-Sixties were the Kozaks who claimed to serve up ballroom dance music, r'n'b, country and western, ballads, beat, pop and Polish folk music. They were Zygmunt Szewczyk on drums, brother Zdzislaw, bass/ vocals, organist Andrzej Jagiellowicz, and guitarist Robert Thompson. The Wee 3 caught the eye in 1964 by wearing scarlet suits and white polo necks. They also played a bewildering array of instruments. Big Three fan Ray Ashton, played guitar, bass, drums, sax and harmonica, drummer Bob Smith played guitar, harmonica and piano while bass player Neil 'Bonga' Powell was also proficient on

The Wee 3

guitar, harmonica and bagpipes.

This leads us to Rob Roy and the Rebels who wore full Scottish regalia on stage. And not forgetting The Cobwebs who had a sax player called Ivor Willy? Small Paul and the Young Ones appeared on the same bill as Little Richard, Gene Vincent, the Applejacks and the Fourmost in 1964. "The young perishers almost stole the show from Little Richard," said one large Midlands booking agency. They wrote their own songs but were unable to take up an invitation to tour Spain and Germany because they were not 18. Small Paul was all of 13. One oddity on the Sheffield group scene in the mid-Sixties were the Surfriders, a Hawaiian-style group that included 18-year-old dancer Penny Evans. Performing her hula dance, complete with grass skirt, she shared vocals with the group's accomplished Hawaiian guitarist John Marsden, a world authority on Hawaiian music who called himself Johnny Tradewinds. They specialised in Hawaiian songs such as Blue Hawaii and Luau Song but also included pop songs and standards such as Sweet Georgia Brown.

While many Sheffield bands sought the fame

The Surfriders

and fortune of being hit parade stars one band who didn't were the Originals. Made up of former members of the Cadillacs - Barry Brumpton, Mick Beaumont, Tom Rattigan, John Wilson and Barry Glynn - they told Top Stars: "Showbiz is a rat race. We shall play for the fun of it and for pocket money. We just want to entertain and enjoy ourselves." It would seem that this would be the continuing theme for most Sheffield combos.

14. GOT MY MOJO WORKING

Possibly the most famous venue Sheffield has produced, the Mojo [it was later renamed King Mojo and finally the Beautiful Mojo], opened in March, 1964. The Stringfellows had taken over an almost derelict Victorian house which had previously been Dey's Ballroom premises at the junction of Burngreave Road and Barnsley Road at Pitsmoor. They rented it for £30 a week from local businessman Ruben Wallis, with the stipulation that the pictures of

Pete with the Mojo sign

the Queen and Duke of Edinburgh were kept on the wall.

They gave the place a new coat of paint, including paintings of African warriors with bits of mirrors for eyes, and built a small coffee bar at one end of the dance floor. Peter Stringfellow asked punters to the inaugural Mojo Dance to bring along "their idea of what a mojo is". The back of the stage ended up decorated with puppets, golliwogs, walking sticks, umbrellas and even dustbin lids. "This is the kind of club where everyone can let their hair down and enjoy themselves," said Peter. "And I find that a quiet appeal for good behaviour does more than strong-arm tactics." Once again it was a family enterprise with Pete's mum taking the money on the door and his cousin worked in the cafe bar. Geoff managed the business side of the partnership leaving the more extrovert salesmanship side to Peter. "Although Peter has never had a steady job, he makes a marvellous salesman," said Geoff. "He's got the technique." The capacity was about 200 but many more crammed in for some of the live shows. The Mojo, named after the song, I Got My Mojo Working, was to make an immediate, if short-lived, impact. It got off to a shaky start when the opening night featured Buddy Britten and the

Mojo Menn: Manfred Mann at the Mojo with golliwogs decorating the back of the stage

Pete with original Drifter Clyde McPhatter

Turner with the Ikettes and a 13-piece band (crammed on to the 25ft by 6ft stage - "I've never seen so many people in one small area," said Stu Moseley who was in support band the Reflections), Procol Harum, Pink Floyd, Alan Bown Set, Wilson Pickett, Garnet Mimms, Jimi Hendrix, Stevie Wonder, John Lee Hooker and Inez and Charlie Foxx. Eric Burdon and the Animals played with the stage strewn with bottles of Newcastle Brown while the Move had a bank of working televisions on the stage which they then smashed up with axes, and also chopped up an effigy of Hitler. There were also a number of names that were to go on to be famous, including one Reg Dwight who played organ with Bluesology and Wilson Pickett. The

Regents, who had just missed out on the charts when their version of If You Gotta To Make A Fool Of Somebody was eclipsed by that of Freddie and the Dreamers. Peter: "The Mojo opened up as a blues club because the blues was cool, very cool and you could just paint it black with red lights, except that I opened up with Buddy Britten and the Regents, who were a Buddy Holly band. I had this cool club with a Buddy Holly band opening it. He was the wrong act." But with the emphasis on rhythm and blues and bands such as Long John Baldry, Alexis Korner, Alex Harvey's Soul Band, Animals and Wayne Fontana and the Mindbenders the Mojo soon took off. After two months the club had more than 800 members and was "the talk of the town", according to Top Stars Special. Peter: "I was lucky. Like the Black Cat we were on another major bus route. I used to stand outside and you could tell from the first two buses how full you were going to be. If the first bus was empty I knew I was going to have a bad night."

There were to be many memorable shows featuring top English and American names. These included Ben E King, Sonny Boy Williamson, Manfred Mann, Rod Stewart, Ike and Tina

STAFF			
E. STRINGFELLOW	1	0	0
D. KNOWLES	1	10	0
J. WILSON		10	0
K. WILLIAMS		10	0
LADIES		15	0
GENTS		15	0
	5	0	0
SHOTGUN EXPRESS	50	0	0
COFFEE BAR	13	2	5
MEMBERSHIP	2	7	6 (19)

The account card for Shotgun Express who featured Rod Stewart

Pete Stringfellow, second right, seen here with John Hall, Malc Towndrow, a Soul Sister, Gillian Hodge, Coral Browne (the future Mrs. Stringfellow), and another Soul Sister

ARTISTES and FEES			STAFF WAGES	
			BRIAN TURNER	£1
£	s.	d.	JIM STRINGFELLOW	£1
			C.J. STRINGFELLOW	£1
			MELVIN	£1
£	s.	d.	BARBARA HILL	10/-
			LADIES	£1
£	s.	d.		
Small Faces			GENTS	£1
£ 80 s. 0 d. 0				
£ 80 - 0 - 0			£ 6 - 10 - 0	

FLOATS					
DOOR	£	s.	d		
Coffee Bar	£	s.	d.	MEMBERS	6/- 825
CLOAKROOM LADIES	£	s.	d	GUESTS	6/- 330
CLOAKROOM GENTS	£	s.	d	CROWD	6d 1155
TOTAL	£				

Account card for Small Faces at the Mojo

Yardbirds included Eric Clapton before he left to join John Mayall while Steampacket/ Shotgun Express featured Rod Stewart, Peter Green, Mick Fleetwood, Julie Driscoll and Brian Auger. Andy Summers of the Police was guitarist with Zoot Money and his Big Roll Band.

Few local bands played the Mojo, but when they did, it was memorable as Barry Marshall of The Lizards recalls: "It was one of the first gigs at the Mojo and we supported the Who. It was such a small stage that when their roadies turned up they said we could use their gear. So we said fine - and blew it up. It was just one of those things. Pete Stringfellow had told us that we had to do a 45 minute set, but we barely had enough material and one of the songs was Can't Explain. That was the only hit the Who had had at that stage. The band turns up and we told Pete Townshend our problem and he says, 'Fuckin' hell, I'm sick of it already. You do it.' So we played it and they didn't. And they came for a drink at the Gate with us afterwards."

The Mojo - and the audience - soon got a reputation for good music. Edwin Starr, born appropriately enough in Sheffield (Alabama, that is), played his first UK gig at the Mojo in 1966: "I felt comfortable because everybody was so receptive, knowledgeable. They knew all my records, they knew all about the record company and other artists on the label, it was aston-

ishing." Inez and Charles Foxx were another act who appreciated the welcome they got. "It is a joy to work here, it really is. Everyone enjoys themselves and are never afraid to show their appreciation," said Inez after a show at the University followed by an all-nighter at the Mojo. "In London, and in some places in America, the audiences are very blase. They take you for granted because they are used to seeing nationally-known artists every week. In the provinces it's a different atmosphere altogether, and especially we find this in Sheffield. They seem to be really glad that you're paying them a visit." The same article also said: "Yet no-one can deny that as a music or pop-minded place Sheffield must be bottom of the league."

But some of the acts Stringfellow booked were not what they seemed. The 'fabulous' Temptations, the Fabulous Four Tops and the Irresistible Isley Brothers were the acts they purported to be by name only. He was quoted in Top Stars in September, 1967, after booking what he thought was the original Temptations: "I can hardly believe we've actually got them. It seems to good to be true." And so it proved. He soon learned from that and the Mojo became a mecca for northern soul fans who flocked to the dusk-to-dawn all-nighters. Peter was establishing a name for himself as a DJ, playing obscure soul records from the States: "I got records that never got played on the radio. I used to go down to a little cellar on Wardour Street in London every other Saturday. You didn't get a chance to listen to them. You'd pick a box and buy whatever he'd got. I was playing that stuff a long time before Wigan Casino and before it was called northern soul." He was also willing to experiment and one night played Tchaikovsky's 1812 Overture. Everyone stopped dancing and talking and listened to the classical sound booming around them. "It was a bit of gamble," said Pete, "But it paid off. As the piece drew to a close the applause was as deafening as the music had been." The decor also changed with the times, with the African warriors being replaced by PopArt black and white stripes, which also adorned Ruben Wallis's grand piano which he had left in the club's care. Then it was on to a Thirties theme with murals of American cars and gangsters, and regulars turned up in three-piece pinstripe suits and trilby hats.

Peter Stringfellow also surpassed himself with the adverts for the Mojo which were placed in the Star. The descriptions were entertaining, if often unintelligible. For instance, on May 30, 1964, the following wording appeared: "Mojo

Pete and Geoff singing to teenagers from the Mojo, as seen in the film *Girl With A Gun*

members now have exclusive rights to call themselves The Jomos (a new name for peaceful and sensible moderns). Boy members known as Hoochies and girls Koochies. This is exclusive to the Mojo Club and anyone using it fraudulently will have the wrath of the almighty Dr Kimbo Joe Minga Mo." The same advert included a plug for a performance by "the great R'n'B preacher himself, Vance Arnold and the Avengers - The Screamingist, Shoutingist, Fattest Raver in the Whole Wide World." Other venues rose to the challenge. The Cutlers' Hall advertised concerts with: "It's a gas, it's a gas, it's frantic lass. So hobble along to the fashionable beat centre, tonight, yes, tonight, twitch, twist and shake to the vibrant beat of Lee Roy and the Avengers." And an advert for Club 60, by now billed as Subterranean Club 60, proclaimed: "Get your kicks on Route 82," and billed Chuck Fowler and the Trekkers as: "Really R n B tonight. Weird guitar, rocking piano, raising the rumpus. Way out Modybodys welcome. Can your Monkey do the Dog?" And over at the Esquire Pete Fender was advertised as: "The longest, thinnest, most controversial odd bod in the biz, with crew cut and ten gallon hat." The Blue Moon advert was restrained by comparison: "Sunday! Sunday! Sunday! You'll laugh so much you'll want to cry at the crazy antics of the King Goon, Rockin' Henry and the Hayseeds." By the middle of 1965 Pete Stringfellow was able to claim that the Mojo had become one of the top four clubs in Britain and quoted Zoot Money, Spencer Davis, Long John Baldry and Goldie and the

Gingerbreads as backing him up. "The one thing that makes the Mojo stand out is that it is run as an entertainment. It is a happy club and it is organised," he said in July, 1965. "I don't allow long hair or things like combat jackets in my club. I go for the smart teenager and I want a check on who comes in."

The Esquire had a much more relaxed approach to what people wore and how long their hair was but Stringfellow was wary of the problems of "immorality and drug taking" - purple hearts and other pills had started to infiltrate the club scene nationwide - which had besmirched clubs in the Manchester area and had given ammunition to critics in Sheffield who were too ready to accuse the Mojo of being a centre for such activities. The clean-cut image was to save him for a while but it was to catch up with his club and all the other teen clubs all too soon.

But whatever the music the Stringfellows kept up with the trends and for many young Sheffielders they could do no wrong, although local bands virtually didn't get a look-in, thanks to Stringfellow's decision to concentrate on bigger, out-of-town names. The brothers also had their failures. Ventures with clubs at Wakefield and Featherstone had to be abandoned because of difficulties in booking the halls at the right times. The brothers also landed a small part in a film, Girl With A Gun, starring Monica Vitti, Stanley Baker and Cherie Blair's dad Anthony Booth. Peter and Geoff were filmed strumming guitars with teenagers from the Mojo outside Hyde Park flats.

Within weeks of the Mojo opening a big rivalry had developed between Stringfellow and Terry Thornton. The BBC TV cameras came to Sheffield shortly after the opening of the Mojo, to film a documentary, The Long Journey, depicting modern youth on the move in Sheffield and four other cities. Stringfellow wasn't impressed: "I was horrified with the beatniks and scruffy teenagers who were selected for interview from coffee bars and clubs in Sheffield. The producers of the film seemed to have deliberately chosen the worst types and painted the worst possible picture of Sheffield teenagers." He issued an invitation to parents to attend an open night at his clubs so they could see for themselves that "everything is above board". Thornton, whose Esquire was one of the clubs featured, said he had no intention of doing the same. "They just wouldn't understand the way kids let off steam. I agree that the film painted a pretty dismal picture of the city and that some of my club members said some pretty outrageous things. They just put on one big act for the benefit of the BBC. But underneath they are all decent kids. Personally I think the Esquire was the only bright spark on the programme." The Mojo and the Esquire also traded insults via their adverts in the Star.

Peter Stringfellow: "Of course there was rivalry between me and Terry Thornton. He was literally the first with the club scene and he was what you would call today cool. He was cool, laidback. The Mojo was anything but cool, Mojo was wild, crazy, noisy, jump on any fashion that was going. The Esquire opened and closed as the Esquire, never changed a damn thing. What really got Terry going was when a German band came over, the Rattles, and I heard they were packing his club out so I sent word down to the group and paid them more money than he was paying them and got the next two bookings from them, and he went beserk. The crown on the Mojo logo, I nicked that off the Esquire. He had it over the 'E' in Esquire, so when it became the King Mojo I put an advert saying I now reclaim the Crown. He didn't like it. My adverts were like poster boxes for what I was thinking. It was a very personal club."

Dave Berry recalled allegiance of groups between the different venues: "If you played the Esquire, you were an Esquire man. The Mojo was not a club I played regularly. I think I only played there about twice. But I did play at his [Pete Stringfellow's] other clubs, the Black Cat and Blue Moon." Jimmy Crawford: "Thornton and Stringfellow were bitter rivals, it was like daggers drawn. Stringfellow used to tell Terry that he was going to be big, very big. And he'd leave Terry for dead, that he'd be a millionaire before Terry had even got his first £30 in the bank. But the Esquire was fantastic. I never worked the Mojo because Terry was a mate and my pianist but I never came into contact with Stringfellow although I heard the stories about

him and Terry having their head-on clashes. If you worked for Terry down at the Esquire you wouldn't work at the Mojo." Dave Manvell: "They used to send gangs of youths up from the Esquire to do raids on the Mojo. Brian the doorman would say, 'Right, I want everybody inside, I've had word that they are coming up from the Esquire.' Whether any of these gangs appeared or not I don't know because we were all inside by that time but there was this big rivalry. The Esquire people were older than our group and the bands that played there didn't appeal to the Mojo crowd. At one bit the Mojo crowd used to dress in blue pinstripe suits and carry those blue plastic macs, that was one of the uniforms when it was decorated with gangsters on the wall. From there it progressed to hippie types and Stringfellow painted the club to suit. It was much more fashion orientated."

Stringfellow continued to keep the Mojo ahead of the game, Top Stars Special reporting in September, 1966, that the club was, "booming because it has consciously joined in the mod-setting trends associated with London." The report continued: "Meanwhile its hitherto lone rival, the Esquire, seems to be wallowing without an image. Whereas the policy of the Mojo is unashamedly not to promote local talent, the Esquire seems neither to promote local talent or any trends, or provide national artists." Peter Stringfellow also got involved in managing local bands. One was harmony group the Citadels as Keith Linaker recalls: "The name was from St Aidan's Church. Over the door was 'Citadel' and Stringfellow picked it for us. He did nothing financially for us but he pushed us and made us rehearse very, very hard." Terry Roe: "He said he was going to make us big-time, cut corners for us. We were going up to Sunderland doing big gigs when we could've been at the Centre Spot or somewhere like that." Guitarist Roy Ledger of the Sheffields: "Pete Stringfellow was brilliant. He listened to what people said and he wasn't afraid to pick the phone up and say, 'I've got a great band here, are you going to book em?' He got us the record deal, he got us in all the London clubs and he got us on tours with the Animals and Long John Baldry." Eventually Peter had to drop some of the groups in order to develop his own career as Roy Ledger explains: "He wanted a new club in Leeds, so he sold the Texans and us to raise the money. After that it all went downwards because the new people didn't know how to manage us. We signed up with this agency in Stoke-on-Trent that thought, 'This is the pop world, let's get into it,' but they hadn't got a clue what they were doing basically and within nine months the band had disbanded. The drummer Richard Smith's dad said, 'You're going to go to music college,' after which the band split up and I went with Dave Berry." And so another Sheffield band bit the dust, but the Stringfellows went from strength to strength.

15. CENTRE OF ATTRACTION

With Dave Berry finally getting recognition and the Esquire and Mojo flourishing, 1964 saw an explosion in the number of bands. Top Stars Special reported that there were more than 300 in the city, with many others in Chesterfield, Rotherham, Doncaster and Barnsley. By this time things had also gravitated towards the city centre. Much of the disruption caused by the rebuilding of the city centre after the war had been completed, with the city council and developers instigating their own version of the blitz as many fine old buildings were torn down to make way for the ring road, and new thoroughfares built such as Arundel Gate which cut a swathe through the city centre. There were new department stores, office blocks and multi-storey car parks. There were even a few more places to eat, Dave Berry remembering that the opening of a Berni Inn steak house on Orchard Street was something of an event. Sheffield city centre was no longer dull and dour, just plain ugly. The Clean Air Act had made the city centre a more agreeable place, buildings were sandblasted of years of soot and grime. There were also huge

slum clearances in the central areas of Sheffield with Darnall, Attercliffe and other east end areas to follow over the next decade. These were to destroy close-knit communities, although there were attempts to re-house people close to each other and, in the long run, were also to signal the end for much of the entertainment in the suburbs. For instance, Banners Corner in Attercliffe, was once a shopping and entertainment area to rival the city centre itself. New houses on vast estates had been built at Gleadless, Stannington, Bradway and Totley and, most significantly for the city centre, 'the streets in the sky,' as envisaged by Corbusier, the reinforced concrete blocks of Park Hill and then Hyde Park, towering over the city centre on land that had once been the medieval deer park of the lord of the manor. The new tower blocks prompted one visitor to Sheffield in November, 1964, Inez Foxx, who along with partner Charlie Foxx played at the Mojo, to say they reminded her of New York.

A lot of people suddenly found themselves living almost a stone's throw away from the city centre and that is where they looked for their entertainment. It was also easier to get about, although many still bemoaned the passing of the trams in October, 1960. Even the cinema, which had managed to survive the advent of television in Sheffield in 1954, was beginning to lose its all-encompassing lure. City centre pubs had simply become more amenable, even serving a cheese sandwich if asked nicely. And jukeboxes took over from pianos. For instance, there was the new Black Swan on Snig Hill. A new building arose from the rubble of the blitz in the

The Cherokees at the Saints Club

The Saints Club

BELLHOUSE RD.

ST CHRISTOPHER'S CHURCH HALL

Tonight—from Liverpool

Derrie Wilkie & the Others

Also

DAVE WEST and the CHEROKEES

Admission 3/6

early Sixties, and the Black Swan, with a staff, mostly part-time, of 51, opened in 1963. Entertainment was provided by organ and drums. The arrival of Terry Steeples, a former cinema manager from Rotherham, in 1964 changed all that and he was to go on to establish the Black Swan as one of Sheffield's most famous venues over the next decade or so.

Lots more clubs opened. Just round the corner from the Mojo was the Saints, at St Christopher's Church Hall in Bellhouse Road, Shiregreen. This had started out, much like the R&B Club at Frecheville, to raise funds for the church but the organisers, Wilfred Smith and George Lidster, turned it into a commercial venture with Dave Berry playing on the opening night. Other visitors included Dave Powell and the Five Dimensions, the Merseybeats and Liverpool-based Irish band, the Wheels, a line-up which included a name which was to become well known in Sheffield 30 years later, guitarist Herbie Armstrong. Smith and Lidster also opened the Kinky Club in Wincobank, but their biggest success was promoting the Fortunes at Tinsley Working Men's Club where 500 people were turned away.

Other church hall/ youth club venues, where the occasional name band played as well as local bands, included St Columba at Crosspool, Dobcroft at Millhouses, Norton Church Hall, Dore Church Hall, St Mary's on St Mary's Gate and St Oswalds at Bannerdale, and there were also the Ace of Clubs at Darnall public hall, the Pyramid Club behind St Mary's Church, Handsworth, and the Buccaneer Club at Greenhill Church Hall. The Mad Hatter Club, at the junction of Broadfield Road and London Road in Heeley, also put on bands, including Jimmy Crawford and Rockin' Henry and the Hayseeds.

To give some idea of what was available, the following is a list of visitors in November/ December, 1964. At the Esquire you could see Sister Rosetta Tharpe, Alexis Korner, Jimmy Reed, London City Stompers (and various other jazz bands), the Fairies, Screaming Lord Sutch, the Vigilantes, Jimmy Powell and the Five Dimensions, the Original Cruisers, Crawdaddies, the Raves, an all-nighter with Frankenstein and the Monsters, Dave Berry, Joe Cocker, Scott William and Dave Hawley. Over at Stringfellow's Blue Moon Club there were the Four Pennies, Pretty Things, Yardbirds, the Boys and Applejacks (a line-up which included female bass player from Sheffield, Megan Davies). The Mojo had blues legends Sonny Boy Williamson and Howlin' Wolf as well as the Soul Sisters, Spencer Davis All Stars, Johnny Kidd and the Pirates, Joe Cocker's Big Blues, Downliners Sect, the Ricky Ticks and Chris Barber's Jazz Band. The Raves played at the Cutlers' Hall, Sheffield University Students Union and Club 60 where there was also a midnight till dawn session with the Frank White Combo, the Mindreaders, Scott William Combo, Nomads, Loiterers and John Conqueroo in aid of Judd's Mates - described in Top Stars as "that wailing threesome that packs 'em in with musical entertainment of the wildest type," - who had been involved in a car crash.

The Saints Club featured the Mighty Avengers, Zoot Money's Big Roll Band, Wayne Fontana and the Mindbenders, the Crestas, Shavells and Dennisons. Wayne Fontana also played at Frecheville R&B Club just as the band had reached number five in the charts with Um Um Um Um Um Um, and there was also a date for the Spencer Davis Group. One of the more memorable visits was that of Sonny Boy Williamson. The 64-year-old who stood 6ft 2 inches, had quite a reputation but his career had been revived by the interest in Britain. He had been supported by Vance Arnold and the Avengers in February at the Esquire and returned to play at the Mojo. He was dressed in his own version of British haberdashery - a two-tone pinstripe suit with a bowler hat at a rakish tilt. He usually played drunk and had cemented his reputation in Birmingham, setting fire to his hotel room when trying to stew a rabbit in a coffee percolator. He died less than a year later. Guitarist Dave Hawley also had good reason to remember Williamson when he played at the Esquire: "I went into the dressing room and Sonny Boy was having a piss in the sink, although there was a toilet next door. He then put his harmonica into the sink and soaked it in the piss. I asked him what he was doing and he said, 'I'm just softening up the reed to make it sound better.'" The 19-year-old Rod Stewart was also a regular visitor to Sheffield in 1964 with Long John Baldry's Hoochie Coochie Men. Newsreader Carol Barnes, who was a student at Sheffield University from 1962 to '65, recalls an appearance at the Students Union, then closed

THE LYRIC

DINNINGTON.

Wednesday, May 20

The Scoop of the Year

Personal Appearance of America's

No. 1 Pop Star

LITTLE RICHARD.

Admission 8/-.

LAST BUS FROM DINNINGTON TO SHEFFIELD 11.50 p.m. Token tickets to get you into this show will be given out on SATURDAY, MAY 16, at the usual Beat Night.

For advance tickets send S.A.E. and Postal Order to Mr. Canwell, 54, Walesmoor Ave., Kiveton Park.

Bama-lama Bama-loo: The Quasar of rock'n'roll hits Dinnington

to outsiders. "Long John was the main singer but on this occasion he had a scrawny, ugly bloke with a mod haircut who liked a drink. He came into the union bar afterwards and sank a few. Some of the rugger types took exception to him, with his weird clothes and hair and gave him a bit of verbal abuse. He gave as good as he got."

There were also venues in Rotherham. The Twist Club - 'the largest beat club in town' - was held in the Assembly Rooms and then Rotherham Baths, ending up at Clifton Hall. Local groups were booked along with well known national names. However, this didn't always go down well, as club manager Wilf Wake told Top Stars: "Nationally known recording groups are not attracting the audiences they should. Their performances are not up to the high standard that their booking fees would indicate and lesser known groups are doing just as well and sometimes even better." There was also the Lyric Ballroom at Dinnington which regularly had bands on a Saturday night, including a real scoop, a visit by Little Richard on May 20, 1964 for the admission price of 8 shillings. The more usual fare featured the Applejacks, Wayne Fontana and the Mindbenders and other beat groups.

There was also in 1965 the Mod Club in Rotherham, attracting the likes of Joe Cocker, the Fenmen, Them and the Manish Boys, the latter one of the first bands to feature David Jones, later to change his name to David Bowie. And there was the 21 Club at a church hall on Moorgate, which was superceded by the Pendulum Club, but after losing money on Cliff Bennett and the Rebel Rousers, Tony Rivers and the Castaways and the Fenmen the policy by 1966 was just to play records and have the occasional local groups. It was to become a major northern soul venue.

Other popular venues for teenagers in the early Sixties were swimming baths. At night they would be converted from swimming to dancing with wooden floors that slid over the bath, with a large stage at one end. This didn't happen in Sheffield, although Glossop Road Baths used to host rock'n'roll dances in the late Fifties, but swimming baths became popular live music venues in Rotherham, Barnsley, Rawmarsh and Doncaster, featuring many of the big names with local combos as support. Rawmarsh Baths first started putting bands on in 1961 when the resident band was the Pete Chester Group, which included young pianist Chris Andrews, later to find fame and fortune in his own right with Yesterday Man and as a songwriter. Promoter Les Slater, one of the unsung heroes of the beat revolution in the area, made one mistake, turning down the Beatles in 1963 - for £50. Other bands that played included Billy J Kramer and the Dakotas, Cliff Bennett and the Rebel Rousers, one-hit wonder Ricky Valance, the Roulettes and Pretty Things. Dave Hopper played there with the Strollers, supporting Gerry and the Pacemakers: "They'd just got to number one and they'd got to do this gig because they were contracted to do it. Here they were at number one playing at Rawmarsh Baths. We knew they were coming up but we didn't know who they were to look at and Pete Fender went and sat on Gerry Marsden accidentally." Rotherham's Johnny Silver and the Thunderbirds were regulars at Rawmarsh Baths as bass player Ernie Booth recalls: "That was the first place I ever heard an electric trumpet, a plugged-in trumpet, and that was with Tom Jones. What used to get me about that place was, it used to finish at half past ten and at quarter to 11 everybody had gone. Because they didn't have cars, they'd gone to catch the last bus."

The Beatles did play at Doncaster Baths and Roy Ledger was in support band the Thunderbirds: "I just thought they were so professional, miles in front of everybody. John would walk up and thank 'em for clapping while Paul would turn round, look on the list for the next number, and as John was saying thanks, he'd be coming back to the mike and saying, 'The next number is so and so,' and one-two-three and straight in. There'd be none of this pausing and, 'What are we gonna do?' They could all play and they could all sing." Also there that night was Cruiser Roy Barber who remembers speaking to them: "It was just before we went to Germany and we were asking them what Germany was all about, playing at the Star Club. They said, 'Watch you don't get pox.' I also remember they said they'd heard us do Memphis Tennessee on one of these Saturday radio programmes, and it'd pissed them off a bit because they thought that they were the only ones who knew that song. Which shows how scarce that material was." Neil Bridges also remembers meeting the Beatles just as they were emerging: "We did an audition in Manchester at the Hume Theatre and the Beatles were there. John Lennon was sat next to me with his feet over the back of the seats and Paul McCartney was sat next to him. That's the audition that got them on to that teatime show, People and Places."

And over in Chesterfield, Cruisers' bass player John Fleet and David McPhie, drummer with Chesterfield band the Blueberries, opened the Smokestack Club every Thursday in the now-demolished Queen's Park Hotel, the Scott William Combo playing on the opening night. There was also a new lease of life for Hillsborough Memorial 'Memo' Hall with a Friday night beat club while another Friday night spot, the Sheffield Scene Club, opened in nearby Upperthorpe at Eversley House. Sheffield was now buzzing, but read on...

16. READY, STEADY, GOING...

The first cracks began to appear in the beat boom, with small audiences for the Animals, Nashville Teens and Searchers at the City Hall. Until then the 2,300-capacity City Hall, which would hold two shows each night, had virtually been guaranteed full houses. One theory was that teenagers could see the established pop stars on TV pop programmes such as Top of the Pops, Ready Steady Go and Thank Your Lucky Stars, and saw no point in seeing them live. "It could mean that the youth of the country have grown tired of the stereotyped line-up of the pop group," said one reporter. "Maybe they have grown tired of the fantastic proliferation of groups and the Tower of Babel of their many names."

Terry Thornton: "The Sheffield kids are having too much of a good thing. Sheffield's been knocked sideways with all sorts of shows. We have the lot already. It's reached saturation point. If we put on a big name there is not the response there was a year ago. Sheffield is a little different from elsewhere. Sheffield audiences have always been more critical. Three years ago we were ignored. Now promoters put on a glut of shows."

Pete Stringfellow: "The impresarios say the stars are demanding too much money but I don't see that since often the impresarios have a hand in the management of the groups themselves. I remember the days of the 2s 6d seats. Nowadays it's hard to get five bob ones. Every teenager still wants to see the groups but they are just not prepared to go on paying out the prices. Some promoters even brag about the money they earn. No wonder the kids are disgusted."

There was also the relative lack of national success for local bands. Only Dave Berry had really hit the big time in Britain but over in the States the British invasion of the American market was in full swing and Sheffield didn't get a sniff. The Beatles had already managed to achieve the amazing feat of having the top five singles in one week in 1964 and a year later the US charts were dominated by them along with the Rolling Stones, Dave Clark Five, Kinks, Herman's Hermits, Wayne Fontana and the Mindbenders and even Freddie and the Dreamers while outfits such as Them, Yardbirds and Pretty Things were hugely influential. American bands pretended to be British, dressing up in regency costume and giving themselves names such as the Sir Douglas Quintet, the Palace Guard and Richard and the Young Lions.

There was also the advent of the pirate radio stations which played music that teenagers wanted to hear, unlike the staid old BBC which wasn't to respond for another two years with the setting up of Radio 1, staffed almost wholly by former pirate station jocks. Another factor was the state of the charts which saw Ken Dodd, the Seekers, Barry McGuire, Petula Clarke and various Tamla Motown acts battling it out with the remnants of the beat groups for chart superiority. It was all a bit of a jumble.

Terry Thornton had no doubts what the problem was in Sheffield - a lack of originality. "Only one, yes, one, just one lad emerged from the hundreds in the city - only because of one fact, not his size 13 shoes or his good looks - but because he has a different style. It is as simple as that, he is different, not a cardboard copy. I mean Dave Berry," said Thornton in June, 1965. "We must have originality, anyone who copies ideas doesn't rate with me at all, and there's plenty of them - groups, songwriters and club owners - all cashing in on someone's hard thought out ideas. For example the multitude of groups who copied the Beatles and Stones in both their music and appearance - hey look, there's Ringo Starr - oh no it's Bill Bloggs from Barnsley. On the subject of originality I must compliment our local groups whose main influence in appearance and line-up is still Cliff Richard, but sound like a watered down Beatle or Stone with ambitions to work at the Dog and Flea or the Bull and Duck. In fact, apart from Joe Cocker, Frankenstein and Scott William, you could band them all together and there would still be nothing much new to emerge from them. How many local groups play out of town teen clubs? Not many - they aren't good enough and these are the only places where groups can establish themselves and become national names - not in the usual haunts of pub and beer clubs. It's a vicious circle and most of our local groups are that far behind and are without one good idea between them that they can't get work in teen clubs anyway."

Top Stars Special laid the blame firmly at the doors of the working men's club circuit and the teenage clubs themselves: "Rightly or wrongly, the teenage clubs tend to go for the outside product and are hardly nurseries of home talent in the way that the Cavern was. The danger is that in the present situation too many groups are shying away from the music they really like and which they excel at, and are being forced against their tastes into the cosy world of the working men's club. The group rat race in the Sheffield area is too great for them to survive in any other way. It is difficult to see a group with the talent of the Beatles, Rolling Stones, Manfred Mann or the Animals ever arising on a Sheffield circuit composed of the WMC. And there is precious little elsewhere for a group of this type to develop their talents." Even orchestra leader Cyril Stapleton chipped in when he came to Sheffield to oversee auditions at the Helen Wilson Settlement, Neepsend, for his Radio Luxemburg-sponsored Search For A Star which was visiting every major city in the country. "Some of these here may be technically better than groups in the charts. But it's originality plus personality that makes the difference." The two-day event attracted groups from all over the region including local bands Vic Lynch and the Cortinas, the Vantennas and folk group the New Foresters. There was also the Mansfields, from Mansfield, with future Ten Years After drummer Ric Lee.

Peter Stringfellow had a go at the attitude of Sheffield at large: "All Sheffield people want out of life is long, steady drinking, and then they criticise the kids who come along to my club. There's nothing else in Sheffield for people but drinking. There is nowhere else more beer conscious. In London and other big cities, they find other things to do in life. I give my club members first-rate artists. But the rest of Sheffield does not want to bring international artists to the city. All they want is fifth-rate pub entertainment. That is why we never get any top-rate artists coming out of Sheffield. Because local artists are reared on pub entertainment. Part of our failure is to establish ourselves is lack of pride in the town. Other towns, Liverpool for instance, have a fierce pride in their town. Sheffield has nothing like that and it holds us back in everything. And attitudes here are just the same as they were 20 years ago."

Indeed Stringfellow virtually abandoned putting on local bands in favour of playing records. "People are beginning to dance again, usually in circles of half a dozen or more, each doing individual movements to the the Dog or the Monkey. They no longer want to listen to groups," he said. "We would like to help little local groups and we have been trying to give younger ones a chance but we are in business, and when we have done this we have had so many complaints that we just can't take the risk any longer."

Drug and "immorality" allegations had already surfaced at the Mojo as early as May, 1965. The first came when Rochdale pop group David John and the Mood made allegations on television about drug-taking in northern clubs, only days before they were due to play the Mojo. They later told Top Stars reporter Richard Redden that their remarks were made about northern clubs generally because they were not allowed to mention names on the television, and they were referring to certain clubs in the Manchester area. It was an unfortunate coincidence that their next club appearance was to be at the Mojo. Stringfellow only allowed them to play when they made their position clear and publicly upheld the name of the Mojo. But the damage was done. Worse was to follow however and the unlikely scenario was a run of the mill election meeting for the Burngreave Ward. Two residents stood up and made serious allegations against the conduct of club members, accusing teenagers of using gardens by the club for immoral purposes and "wickedness". Redden spoke up for the Mojo in Top Stars: "In the many times I have been to the Mojo I have never seen any act of immorality either in the club or the grounds. My job also takes me into Sheffield Juvenile Court frequently. Only once had any case of misbehaviour at the Mojo ever been brought before the court during my experience. When you consider what happens when mods and rockers go crazy in the South, parents in Sheffield should be thankful that there are music clubs to give their children something to occupy their time. Through no fault of his own, Peter Stringfellow has become involved in a series of misfortunes. If you want to convince your parents that clubs are worthwhile places to go to ask them to go with you and see for yourselves." Unfortunately it would be magistrates, rather than parents, that Stringfellow was going to have to convince.

Another problem with Sheffield - the lack of any real nightlife - was highlighted by a visit to Sheffield City Hall in November, 1965, by American close harmony folk trio Peter, Paul and Mary. After the show they asked Richard Redden where they could spend the rest of the evening. "The time was 10.30pm and the answer horribly apparent," reported Redden. "This was one of the few cities - and there must be very few indeed - with half a million people and no night life. The trio looked dismayed, as all the South Americans and other overseas visitors are going to be when they come to Sheffield for the World Cup. So I had to explain that Sheffield's smaller neighbours were much more enterprising and suggested the Sidesaddle Club at Doncaster and the Carlton Club, Chesterfield." Paul and Mary opted for the Carlton, simply because it was nearer. Peter Yarrow decided he'd rather

meet some people, preferably students, and went to a student flat in Endcliffe Crescent, Broomhall, the home of John Rawlins, ex-treasurer of Sheffield University Folk Club. He ended up arguing the finer points of the record industry and life itself with a crowd of 20 students. They then headed "in a fleet of jalopies" to a late night Chinese restaurant in the city centre, the conversation carrying on until late into the night after Yarrow led the bunch past "startled" porters to his rooms in the Grand Hotel.

Among other visitors to Sheffield in 1965, the most notable was Bob Dylan who played at the City Hall in June. Dylan was in a reticent mood after the concert. Asked about about what he was going to do in the future his reply was "sleep". And his answer to the connection between the names Bob Dylan and Dylan Thomas was, "Aw, none". He returned on May 14, 1966, by which time he had become one of the most revered songwriters in the world. This was his infamous 'electric' tour backed by The Band. The venue was the Gaumont Cinema and manager Harry Murray reported that the tickets sold out even faster than for Beatles' shows. Dylan wasn't to play Sheffield again for 32 years. December 8, 1965. saw The Beatles' last visit to Sheffield when they play at the Gaumont. The somewhat frantic show was compered by Sheffield singer and comedian Jerry Stevens. His real name was Gerard Pinder, he was from Gleadless, and had played football for Sheffield United and Notts County reserves, before being spotted by Del Shannon singing at a club in Manchester and went on to make several appearances on TV.

The nearest the area had to a nightclub was Greasbrough Social Club, in Rotherham, which for a time rivalled Batley Variety Club as the north's top night spot. The 800-seat concert room, added in 1964 to the former United Army, Navy and Airmen's Servicemen's Club, was opened by singer Ann Shelton. In its short life, just five years, it attracted the stars including Dusty Springfield, Kathy Kirby, Karl Denver, the Tornados, Lonnie Donegan, Freddie and the Dreamers, Vera Lynn, Johnnie Ray, PJ Proby, Duane Eddy, Cat Stevens, the Bonzo Dog Doo-Dah Band, Bobby Vee and even - 'direct from America - Jayne Mansfield. The building eventually became a supermarket but now lies derelict and vandalised.

The World Cup finally hit Sheffield in the summer of 1966, with matches being played at Hillsborough. There was a huge influx of fans from West Germany, Argentina, Spain, Switzerland and, in the quarter finals, Uruguay.

Magistrates didn't look on the licensing situation anymore kindly. Terry Steeples at the Black Swan somehow managed to achieve what had previously been impossible and got longer opening hours. But Dave Berry, in the process of having his first hit for 15 months with Mama and on tour with the Small Faces which called in at the Gaumont in August, was incensed by the rejection by Sheffield Licensing Magistrates of a beer garden for the World Cup. "This really disgusts me. It is so narrow-minded. Far smaller towns like Darlington and Stockton have night clubs and better entertainment facilities than Sheffield."

Nationally there was a bigger threat looming, especially for the virtually unregulated clubs such as the Mojo and Esquire, when a Bill was put before Parliament in early 1966. The Bill, sponsored by Mr R Gresham Cooke, MP, was motivated by the goings-on at certain clubs, mainly in the Manchester area. The Private Places of Entertainment (Licensing) Act intended to regulate teenage clubs which, because they sold no alcohol, had managed to escape the strictures on other licensed premises. Numbers admitted, fire exits, toilet facilities and other areas of concern would come under its aegis, forcing club owners to apply for a music and dancing licence. To give some idea of the draconian measures, the capacity of venues was to be based on the room needed for ballroom dancers. The Bill wasn't to become law until October, 1967, but the writing was on the wall.

Top Stars Special welcomed the bill but had reservations: "What we dislike is not so much the bill itself, as certain sections of the community who are backing it. These are the people who assume that immorality and drug-taking will take place wherever several hundred young people gather together without the guidance of an attendant parson. In short, these are the people who are always running down young people and their tastes. We would hate to see them get a grip on the clubs for it would mean supression."

A visit by the Spencer Davis Group to the Mojo in February, 1966, just after hitting number one with Keep On Running, illustrated perhaps why the Bill was necessary. The venue was so crowded that Davis was driven to comment: "When you play at a club that gets so jammed as this, it is impossible for the kids and for the group. The PA system was poor because the speakers were covered in bodies. Some poor kids fainted." Peter Stringfellow: "There was no such thing as capacity in those days. We'd just cram them in. Never saw a policeman in the Mojo. We knew we were really full when the Spencer Davis Group played and the coffee bar floor collapsed. People used to stand on these barrels and it collapsed, went down three feet, God knows what would have happened if it had gone through." It was a warning he should have heeded.

There was one boost for Sheffield however with the opening of the city's first independent recording studio, Unit 19. It opened in April, 1966, after much delay. According to director John Williamson, it was, "the first time facilities like this have been available outside London". Unit 19, built at a total cost, including state of the art recording gear, for £20,000, was housed beneath the Penny Farthing in Furnival House on Eyre Street and was opened with a champagne reception and guest of honour, Lord Mayor, Alderman Jack Worrall. The studio also signed a contract with EMI to give them first choice of records made by the studio for national release. One of Unit 19's first moves was to hold a talent contest at the Esquire, one heat being won by 14-year-old Paul Carrack's band the Saville Row Rhythm Unit. Four months later £9,000 worth of damage was caused when water flooded through the ceiling, closing the studio for two months. Among musicians who recorded there were the Saville Row Rhythm Unit, Frank White's Katters, the Mod-S-T, Stampedes, Westernaires and Bob Davis Four.

17. I GOT SOUL

Soul music had begun to take over in early 1966 as records by the likes of Otis Redding, Sam and Dave, Arthur Conley, Wilson Pickett, Eddie Floyd and Joe Tex became all the rage. And visitors to Sheffield, particularly to the Mojo, included big US names such as Rufus Thomas, Solomon Burke, Edwin Starr, Garnett Mimms, Oscar Toney Jr, Stevie Wonder and Ike and Tina Turner. Their influence soon saw a crop of soul bands emerge from Sheffield. These included Delroy's Good Good Band, Lubi Souls, DD Whatson and the Big Crowd, the Reflections (one of the first bands to get sax and trumpets in 1965), Tom Brown's Schooldays, Bloos Express, Bitter Suite, CG Morris and the Reaction (which included a young Paul Carrack), Chicago Line (whose record Shimmy Shimmy Koko-Bop was produced by Peter Stringfellow) and, leading the way, O'Hara's Playboys, a band of Scottish musicians who moved to Sheffield in 1966. Most of the bands featured big line-ups of at least six members with brass sections, organs and, in some cases, dancers and backing singers. Chesterfield DJ David McPhie kept readers up with developments in his column in Top Stars as tastes moved from the soul sounds of Memphis to the underground sounds of the West Coast.

One of the earliest venues for black music was Eversley House on Upperthorpe Road which became the Caribbean Club in 1964, a regular Saturday night spot for West Indians, the first alternative to the shebeens held in the cellars of various houses across the city. Jimmy Cliff, Jimmy James, the King Coles, the Esso Steel band and My Boy Lollipop hitmaker, Millie, were among the live performers who appeared there. "There is not a lot going on in Sheffield," said organiser, driving school owner Edgar Brown. "There are only parties but you don't want just

Travellers Express

Lubi Souls with Pete Gill, back right

that. There should be a place somewhere a man can go along to any time to take his wife out for an evening." Millie now lives in Walkley, apparently.

The seven-strong Travellers Express featured young Jamaican musicians and they made an impressive appearance on ITV's Opportunity Knocks in May 1968. They occasionally played in Sheffield, including a regular Sunday lunchtime session at the Cavendish Club on Bank Street, but most of their work was out of town and in Europe. The band was fronted by singer Dave Sweater, with Capone on guitar, Smokey on drums, saxophonists Skippy and

Tich, Lolly on the organ and Baby Face Lenny on bass. The Pitiful Souls, later to become the Pitiful, were the second of two all-black Sheffield combos. They originally started out as pop band the King Coles, with brothers Leroy and Ted Walcott on bass and drums, Lloyd Williams on organ and vocals, Noel 'Mr Pitiful' Lindsay on sax, and Ben 'Junior' Brown on lead guitar, and were a popular act on the clubs and pubs circuit. When soul music started getting big with younger audiences they made the switch to soul at the beginning of 1967. At first bookings were scarce but gradually they became popular on the local scene. They were one of the few local bands to play at the Mojo, and can be heard with the track Never Like This Before on the Rag Goes Mad at the Mojo EP, recorded at the venue on June 29, 1967. This was helped by an appearance in a talent contest at the Silver Blades ice rink that resulted in a spot in the finals at Streatham Ice Rink where they came third, winning £50. Back at the Silver Blades, the Pitifuls made an appearance performing on the canopy over the front entrance to the building, heralding the arrival of former Tornado, Heinz and his band the Wild Boys. Leroy and Ted had previously met Heinz two years previously at a show at the Gaumont and had asked him for advice on forming a group and promised that they would have a group to show him on his next

Pitiful Souls

Up on the roof: The Pitiful Souls welcome Heinz and The Wild Boys to Sheffield Silver Blades ice rink

visit. Hauling their gear on to the roof of the foyer might have been taking it a little far but Heinz was impressed: "I thought they would forget all about that promise. But there they were waiting for us to arrive. I think it was marvellous." They went on to become probably Sheffield's most successful soul band, heading out on various tours to Europe, the Middle East, North Africa and the Far East. They eventually relocated to Singapore where at least one of them remains.

Following in their footsteps were CG Morris And The Reaction. They were led by Clive Morris, a former choirboy at All Saints School, Burngreave. He had previously sang Elvis-type rock'n'roll in a local band. He then joined the Saville Row Rhythm Unit which included young drummer Paul Carrack. Clive went on to front Reaction, following the departure of original vocalist Steve 'SR' Walker. The band expanded to an 11-piece show, including a four-piece dancing troupe called the Marvels. Glyn Owen recalls their visual impact: "They had polka-dot shirts with big collars, the brass section were in purple and the rhythm section were in pink. There was a lot of rehearsing done for this synchronised moving - the sax and the trumpet were up and down with the guitars. We did songs like Willy Nilly and it would involve a lot of this gyrating and so, to add a group like the Marvels to the Reaction, made it a whole moving experience."

Burngreave, home of most of Sheffield's immigrant population, was the hotbed of soul talent and living across the road from Clive Morris was one of Sheffield's most dynamic soul performers, Delroy Palmer. A former member of the King Coles, he went on to form the Delroy Soul Federation with bass player Barry Watson who told Top Stars, March, '65: "We wanted Delroy because coloured singers are the only ones who put all their heart into this kind of music." He went on to front the Delroy Good Good Band (replacing DD Whatson as singer) who were more popular outside Sheffield which never really had a huge soul following. Their first appearance in London was at the famous Tiles Club in Oxford Street on April 6, 1967, which was followed later in the year by a six-week residency at the La Plata Club in Rome. Glyn Owen: "He was a phenomenal act. As soon as we went on the Midlands circuit we were having people like Jeff Lynne who was with the Uglys, supporting us." Delroy relied on some stage props as

C.G. Morris and The Reaction

The all-singing and all-dancing Delroy Palmer

Glyn recalls: "He wore a pair of raspberry-stained plimsolls, which were his dancing shoes. He also had a hair-straightening kit, acquired to emulate James Brown who by then was straightening his hair. We were coming back from the Midlands and the van was wobbling about so we stopped to have a look and the inside back tyre had a puncture. So we opened the back doors to get the spare out and the main thing that fell out was Delroy's suitcase that contained his shoes, his hair-straightening kit and a crumpled stage shirt. The roadie then booted it under the van saying, 'Good heavens, that's our singer's suitcase.' We went to the gig the following day and we couldn't break it to him that we'd lost it. We went on and opened up with something like Night Train before we gave Del the big build-up, and someone said he's not coming on. He wouldn't put in appearance for about five songs because he hadn't got his hair-straightening gear or his shirt and his dancing plimsolls. A lot of what Delroy did wasn't the singing, it was the dancing and the visuals that went with it. The undoing of Delroy was when we got in the studio to do a Les Reed number. It became evident that Delroy did this type of singing which ultimately wasn't very intelligible when it came to a recording studio. It fell flat. They wouldn't take it because of the vocals yet the band played very well." The only known recording of Delroy and the band is his contribution to the Rag Goes Mad at the Mojo EP, a pulsating version of Arthur Conley's Sweet Soul Music. Returning to what he did best, Delroy went on to front the nine-strong Delroy and the Detroit Soul Sound. Not much more was heard from him until he was charged with the murder of Terence 'Popeye' Modest in an attack with a sabre at a blues party at his house in Havelock Square, Broomhall, in 1978. He was found guilty of manslaughter and sentenced to seven years in prison. Six years later he was jailed again for living off the immoral earnings of his common-law wife. He went on to run an all-night cafe, Pinky's, at Spital Hill, which became notorious after two shooting incidents in the late Eighties. The cafe closed in 1990 and Palmer was declared bankrupt.

By day Graham Hudson worked downstairs at Wilson Pecks in the sheet music department. But soul fans knew him as DD Whatson. John Crookes recalls: "He wanted to be Sheffield's answer to James Brown. The album James Brown At The Apollo was what started the band off. We did it as it came out and because a lot of the stuff was in the charts we became a chart band." The band became DD Whatson and the Big Crowd with a line-up of two saxes, bass, drums, rhythm and lead guitars and vocals. For a while the band included two black girl backing singers Rose Blake and Eda Bonney who also featured in the band's 'snazzy dance routines'. Image-conscious DD had definite ideas about how he wanted to look. John Crookes: "He was a snappy dresser and wore all the latest gear. He actually went with his own drawing of how he wanted his hair and took it to this old barber in Stocksbridge and said, 'Can you cut my hair like this?' The barber got it something like and afterwards kids were going to his shop and asking for a DD Whatson." Whatson later worked at Harry Fenton's men's outfitters in Chapel Walk and would often be seen in Top Stars modelling the latest men's gear. Along with Crookes on bass and later sax, the band included another colourful character, saxist and ex-Territorial Army musician Johnny Edge. He was ten years

D.D. Whatson and the Big Crowd

older than the rest of the band so he was something of a father figure. He was known to the police, thanks to a 'chequered past'. He was also the band's van driver but because he was banned had to be careful where he drove. "We could never go through Rotherham," says Crookes. "We had the band's name painted on the side of the van so we always made sure we drove round Rotherham rather than through it." But one night they risked it. Sure enough they were stopped by the police and Edge was subsequently prosecuted. The case was reported in the Star under the heading, 'Group Had No Ticket To Ride'. A split came when Whatson wanted to go professional and most of the band didn't. He put together a new line-up featuring two members of the Big Crowd and Dave Slade Four, plus experienced London saxophonist Tommy Tuft. They became DD Whatson's Good Good Band, taking the name from Hog Snort Rupert's Good Good Band, a London soul band they had seen at the Esquire. Manager Philip Duffield was able to find them work further afield only for DD to get into personal problems, quitting the band and moving to Scotland. On the lookout for a new singer, the band was introduced to 19-year-old Delroy Palmer who took over as frontman on Christmas Eve, 1966. The premier venue for soul and R&B acts, not just in Sheffield but in the north of England, was the Mojo. "It was always an aspiration to play the Mojo," says Glyn Owen. "Particularly as they had a policy that they didn't book local bands. They wanted touring bands that were well

known." There were plenty of other venues that featured soul music both live and on disc including Shades, situated in the basement of the old Greystones Cinema, on Ecclesall Road. It opened on October 7, 1967. It was a first venture for a man who was to become a familiar name on the local club scene for the next 30 or so years, Markson 'Max' Omare who had originally come to Sheffield from Nigeria. The club was intended as a multi-racial social centre and was opened with a steel band, African food and a speech from the Lord Mayor of Sheffield, Ald Harold Lambert. There was live music at least once a week, usually soul from out of town bands. Junior Walker and the All-Stars, Hot Chocolate and Desmond Dekker were among stars who played there. Joe Cocker had a Tuesday night residency at the venue but, as Dave Manvell recalls, it wasn't very popular. "Sometimes there would only be a handful of people there. Tuesday night wasn't a busy night anyway but at that time Joe Cocker wasn't a big draw either. He was seen as being a bit of a has-been. Sometimes we would go there and he would just be standing around waiting to see if anybody turned up and pack up the gear and go home without playing." Steve Dawson: "We did Shades and it was the same for us, nobody in, absolutely nobody." Max would feature bands somewhat reluctantly. Glyn Owen: "He wanted to use bands like us because it was the flavour of the month, but he always felt it was a bit of an intrusion into his club. He didn't want it affronting the customers and the speakers were always in the wrong place." Clive Morris: "I got fed up with the place. Max could have made a mint if he had kept his head. He kept changing his criteria with signs saying 'No sexy dancing here please,' and he messed the bands about a lot of the time." Keith Riley of Shape Of The Rain: "Shape played at Shades and after we'd played our set, he came on and said, 'now for some good music'." Busiest nights of the week were Wednesday which was Students and Nurses night with the entertainment including a trio of go-go dancers, and Saturday night, more of a multi-cultural affair with Afro-Caribbean families joining in, along with teenagers, to see the soul bands that played. Omare then opened Genevieve in Charter Square in April 1972 and continued his policy of presenting the best in black music with the likes of Arthur Conley, the Elgins and Inez Foxx.

The Silhouette Club opened above shops on the corner of London Road and Broadfield Road at Heeley Bottom on December 10, 1966,

Reflections with Stu Moseley, second left

financed by a local businessman. The premises, in what was formerly the Mad Hatter Club, had a stairway from London Road into a hall-like room with, at one end, a glass-enclosed disc jockey booth and stage, with a large coffee and snack bar at the other end. It opened four nights a week with regular live music. The prospects were not too good from the word go, with early attendances disappointing, despite its position on a major road and bus routes. Then there was the problem with local bands: "It is chaotic try-ing to get hold of them. A lot don't even know each other's surnames. I cannot understand how they organise themselves," said organiser and booking agent Maureen Prendergast. Inevitably it was not to last for long and became soul club Highway 61 (well London Road is the A61) a year later, taken over by partners Dave and Sylvia Dickson, who also managed Travellers Express. It too was also short-lived. The stage is still there to this day, now used as a photographer's prop by the business that took over the premises in early Eighties, model agency Style. The Ark Club operated every Friday night in St Nathanael's Church Hall, Crookesmoor, from October, 1967, and became successful enough to open on Saturday nights

as well. "I don't mind admitting we've gained a few decor ideas from the Mojo," said organiser Michael Jackson. "When that club closed there were obviously a lot of young people from Crookesmoor who missed the dancing." Any profits went towards buying carpets for the church. One regular was Dave Manvell: "It didn't last very long because there always fights out-side." Another soul club was held at the Funky-Butt, named after part of the blurb on a Geno Washington album sleeve. It was held at St Aidan's Church Hall, once the home of the Black Cat, and was run by the former disc jockey at the Silhouette Club, Marvin Blue (real name John Leneghan). Just out of town there was the Road Runner at Aston cricket pavilion. For more discerning tastes in soul was the Boardwalk Club that operated inside the Sheffield Industries Exhibition Centre on Carver Street. Organiser 'Hank' Hancock explained in Top Stars: "The Stringfellows are catering for the majority who like fast soul and Tamla stuff, but we want to cater for the minority who like slow soul." Membership was 2/6d (12.5p).

Many of Sheffield's soul exponents travelled out of town to Hull where the music was also enjoying a healthy following, although according to Clive Morris there was no rivalry as the bands all had their own patches. "We knew that in Mansfield Pitiful Souls had a following, in Hull Travellers Express had a following, and in York CG Morris had the following. So we all had our own little areas where we played." Life on the road was still hard as Glyn Owen testifies: "Everyone had to have a degree in siphoning petrol and stealing milk bottles in the morning for your breakfast. I was quite well off when I joined. I was smoking Benson and Hedges and drinking rum and coke. We used to drink at that time in soul clubs. We'd have some money to spend at La Favorita - La Fav - the famous coffee bar on Division Street."

Although a lot of the audiences were white there was seemingly no racism with soul music being the common ground. Clive Morris: "It wasn't the thing then, I found more racism when we went to Scotland. And that was against the white members. I was welcomed. That was a shock to me when I found out they didn't like English people. It used to be difficult talking to young girls as a black guy because of the stigma around at the time but I did quite well." John Crookes: "There was rivalry between the white soul bands and respect towards the black groups because they were black and we thought they must be better, whether they were or not." By the spring of 1967 soul music was losing some of its popularity in the city, according to some of the bands. Good Good Band manager Peter Duffield told Top Stars in September '67: "Sheffield is soul-destroying - in more ways than one. Sheffield is just not interested." Stu Moseley: "When Traffic came along I didn't want to do the soul thing anymore. I just turned round and told the sax and trumpet players, that was it. They said 'soul will never die'. But it did for them."

The Mod sound was also becoming popular thanks to bands like the Small Faces, who made their debut in the provinces at Club 60 in 1965, and the Who. Maurice Green, manager of the Locarno on London Road, planned to put on all-nighter sessions featuring mod bands, including the Alan Price Set and the Graham Bond Organisation, after having successful try-outs with Lee Dorsey and the Easybeats. The idea was that on Saturday nights the usual ballroom dancing would run until 11.30pm as usual, with the mod sessions taking over from midnight until 6am. Sheffield had its own mod-style bands, moving on from the influence of the Beatles, Rolling Stones, Kinks, etc. These included Jigsaw (previously the Lizards), Square Circles, Who's Who, Mickey's Monkeys (led by the late Mick Dale), Us Peeple, Darley Craw's Amblers, Chicago Line, Bob Davis Mood and the Male Set who added a violin to their line-up in the hope of achieving a sound "no other group has got". Another band striving for their own musical identity were The Mind Of Adam, who included singer Hughie "Jock" Lightbody who later followed in the footsteps of Alf Pickering and Terry Steeples providing a stronghold for live bands via his two pubs, the Wetherby at Swallownest and subsequently the Midland in Killamarsh.

18. FLOWER CHILDREN

In 1967 psychedelic rock began to take over, thanks to the influence of the hippie movement in the States and the mind-warping effects of LSD. The Beatles released Strawberry Fields in February (kept off the top spot by Petula Clark's This Is My Song and Release Me by Engelbert Humperdinck) whle the summer was dominated by Whiter Shade Of Pale, All You Need Is Love and San Francisco (Be Sure To Wear Some Flowers In Your Hair). And sure enough, Sheffield took the hint. Everybody from Peter Stringfellow and Joe Cocker to Dave Berry and Frank White were sporting long hair and hippy garb. The Mojo declared, "Beautiful People Love The Mojo," and adorned the club with flowers. Friday nights became a Love In session with regulars wearing flowers in their hair. Adverts appeared in the Star's Jazz And Beat column as, "Peace And Love In A Colourful World Of Happiness. PS: The Dandelions In Our Garden Are Free. Don't Rush, Plenty For All." And in order to create a friendly and happy image for the Mojo and its patrons, Pete and Geoff made

The Male Set

Flower joy for Pete and Coral Stringfellow at their Sheffield Register Office wedding, August 1967

a presentation of flowers to a group of OAPs. Peter Stringfellow: "I saw the San Francisco flower power thing and it blew me away, the way they were looking, the kaftans, flowers, so I introduced it into Sheffield in that wonderful summer of 1967. We used to buy boxes and boxes of flowers, and send them round to old people and the hospitals, we wanted to be loving at that point. I loved it all." The club was repainted with flower designs and members started wearing kaftans, beads and even cow bells. The musical emphasis also mixed the serious soul of the Northern soul scene with the hippie music of San Francisco. Stringfellow took to wearing a kaftan and would often stop records halfway through to philosophise on whatever took his fancy. And the now Beautiful Mojo put on gigs that people still talk about today.

Sunday, January 8, saw one of the first glimpses in the provinces of the Jimi Hendrix Experience or, as the Mojo advert at the time put it, "Roaring into 1967 with the new weirdo trio, Jimi Hendrick's Experience (disc Hey Joe, Hey Joe)." It was to be a controversial night. The day before playing the Mojo, Hendrix had played at the New Century Hall in Manchester. After the gig the band borrowed the tour van and Noel Redding drove them to the Twisted Wheel where they were refused entry and the plainclothes police turned up. Noel Redding: "I was nervous because of driving without proper insurance. They started searching me and found an anti-smoking pill in my wallet. I tried to tell them what it was, but they were looking for the bust

of the century so they hit me in the face and knocked my glasses off. They left Jimi alone because he was a foreigner and, in those days, exempt from police harrassment." The Manchester police then tipped off their Sheffield counterparts about what had gone on. Farcical events followed. Sure enough, the authorities turned up at the Mojo but as was customary whenever there was a problem at the Mojo, it was the fire brigade that rolled up, not

SUNDAY: JAN: 8th 1967.

DOOR — MEMBS. 5/- GUESTS 6/-

£5			
£	70	0	0
10/-	30	0	0
SILVER	11	3	6
𝑑	4	6	6
MISCELL			
TOTAL CASH	115	10	0
FLOAT	9	0	0
DOOR	106	10	0
CASHIER	E. Stringfellow		
	MEMBS	368	
	GUESTS	48	
	TOTAL	416	

Account card for Jimi Hendrix at the Mojo

the police. Dave Manvell was among the audience that eventful night: "They used to come in on the excuse that they were doing a numbers check for the fire regulations. There was supposedly all that aggro with drugs and things but I never saw the police there." Pete Stringfellow: "Two burly firemen turned up and demanded to see the black guy with the drugs. They walked into the dressing room and said. 'Come on blackie, where's these drugs?' Hendrix said: 'No drugs in here man.' The firemen had a look around and as they were leaving I asked them to apologise to Mr Hendrix. They said, 'Sorry about that laddie,' and Hendrix looked up from what appeared to be a six-inch joint and said 'Hey, cool man'."

After having a pint of bitter down at the Sportsman on Barnsley Road, Hendrix went on to do a blistering show at The Mojo including Purple Haze which he recorded three days later and Star Spangled Banner but to the tune of the British national anthem. He played the guitar with his teeth and behind his head, and smashed a guitar (but not the Strat he usually played). He also played a few tracks off the Are You Experienced album which came out in May 1967, including a version of Machine Gun, renamed The Blitz, with, as Dave Manvell remembers, "wailing sirens and explosions all generated by guitar and amplifier." Dave Manvell had other reasons to remember that gig: "During the show I stood at the side of the stage right next to Jimi and when he got off stage after the first set he asked me the way to the toilets so I took him there. We stood in the stalls together and he asked me how he could get some drugs. I told him to hang around the toilet and somebody was bound to sell him something." The city proved to be eventful for Hendrix who returned to Sheffield on November 17, 1967, to perform two shows at the City Hall, with support acts including Pink Floyd, The Move, The Nice, Amen Corner, Eire Apparent and Grapefruit, plus compere Pete Drummond. Hendrix's bass player Noel Redding

has vivid memories of the concert: "Sheffield was terribly enthusiastic and we got torn apart coming out of the hall, losing clothes, glasses, hair, I always wondered what would happen if the detachables and semi-detachables (like hair) ran out." In the audience for the first show was future Saxon guitarist Graham Oliver, then 14, who had bunked off school for the day. "Everybody was just sitting there open mouthed when Hendrix started to play. Nobody had seen anything like it before. One minute there was Amen Corner playing Bend Me Shape Me and the next there was this guy having sex with his guitar. I've never been the same since. It was one of those events you never forget."

Other memorable shows at the Mojo that year included an all-day event featuring Pink Floyd and on Sunday, October 8, it was the turn of Stevie Wonder. He was just 17 and making an impact in the charts with I Was Made To Love Her. He performed at an all-day session from 1 to 11.30pm. It was one of the highlights of the venue's short reign and also turned out to be one of the very last sessions.

Stringfellow also hosted the Mojo Show at the City Hall, featuring the Drifters, Alan Bown Set, Amboy Dukes, Ronnie Jones and the Q Set and local band the Pitiful. "Flowers were in buttonholes, pinned to guitars, strewn about the stage," reported Top Stars Special. "And as the Alan Bown Set won louder and louder applause, teenagers from the circle and the gods sent flowers cascading on to the stage and the stalls." Shops opened such as Lift Up Your Skirt And Fly on Norfolk Street which sold "the latest Chelsea clothes, black velvet dresses and black crepe trousers with 30ins bottoms". Chapel Walk became Sheffield's answer to Carnaby Street, with Harry Fenton's the trendy place for clothes. Aspiring young pop stars would hang out there, leaning against the wall trying to look cool, much as Dave Berry and Johnny Tempest had done in an earlier era. Then there was Sexy Rexy's clothes shop on Charles

Street. The Locarno on London Road started the Carnaby Club, in homage to Carnaby Street, one of the attractions being a contest to find Mr and Mrs Carnaby with a £10 cash prize for the winners.

Drugs, which were normally restricted to Purple Hearts, pep pills and reefers, and previously associated more with the jazz fraternity, became more available in rock circles. Pubs such as the old Minerva, once a beatnik hangout, and cafes, particularly La Favorita, were alledgedly at the centre of it. One frequenter of La Fav can remember regular visits by a chap in a taxi who used to sell cannabis, and even roll a joint if the buyer didn't know how to do it, for 1s 6d. One rock veteran recalls an experience at a gig at Lady Mabel College, near Rotherham: "There were a lot of bands on. We all had a couple of heavyweight tranquillisers on the way there. We were sat on the front row and we couldn't stay awake. They were so powerful but in those days they used to give things like that to little old ladies." The more common form of 'pleasure' was smoking pot. Stu Moseley: "In the Sixties, everybody was smoking. Henry McCullough's [Joe Cocker's Grease Band] trick was to ask a policeman the way with a joint in his hand. And that was on High Street."

Dave Berry, who had gone for the full long-hair and beard look, spoke out in the April, 1967,

Dave Berry

edition of Top Stars: "I'm not afraid to say that I know people who have taken this kind of thing. They have a 'smoke' like you or I would have a drink. There has been far too much publicity about it. This has created a curiosity among youngsters. The more people say about it the worse the problem will become." He also expressed a penchant for psychedelic music: "I should certainly like to see something really big come of it. There is no end to the way it can be adapted by a good producer. I have seen it done on stage a couple of times and it's far more interesting to watch a group playing in that setting than just seeing four or five lads with instruments." Even Frankenstein moved into psychedelia although Ray Stuart declared he had always been in that vein: "I was using flashing lights and bombs and smashing things up before anybody even thought of the word."

But it was also all about to go horribly wrong.

19. THE SHAKEDOWN

By the end of 1967 the Mojo, the Esquire, Club 60 (or the Six O Club as it had become), Blue Moon, the R&B Club at Frecheville, many of the pubs, not to mention the various swimming baths, church halls and other temporary venues, were virtually all to be gone as venues.

It was the new Entertainment Licensing Act which was to finally close the Mojo which had been dogged by controversy throughout its short life. It found itself tainted with drug allegations and, in an effort to clean up the club's image, Peter Stringfellow had halted the popular all-nighters which were deemed to be at the centre of the scandal. He had already had one close call in early 1966 when he was taken to court under the Public Health Act. Spinster Grace Birch complained that she was woken up at 2am by Charles and Inez Foxx singing 'Georgie Porgie don't you love me anymore'. Miss Birch's brother Douglas said: "I had to give up my job as a long-distance lorry driver because I couldn't get enough sleep. When there are all night sessions my wife and I stay up all night, there's no point in going to bed." On that occasion Stringfellow managed to persuade the magistrates that he would improve the soundproofing. But the complaints continued and on April 15, 1967, there was a final dusk-to-dawn rave with Geno Washington and the Ram Jam Band. Residents had complained about the noise; teenagers having sex in the car park and in gardens; drugs; and then there was the budgie breeder who claimed his birds didn't hatch an egg for four years because of the noise. Social workers spoke up for the Mojo and there was even a visit by the Lord Mayor. But to no avail. The budgies came home to roost, so to speak, in October, 1967, when the Mojo had to apply for a licence under the new act. A local drug dealer was produced as a witness by the police, saying he had sold pep pills at Mojo all-nighters. The licence was refused, an appeal failed, and everything the Stringfellows had done lay in tatters, the doors of the Mojo finally closing in December.

The fact that the club had become internationally famous and attracted a galaxy of international as well as up and coming stars counted for nothing in the end. And it appeared it wasn't taken into account that the Mojo could boast a membership of almost 5000 teenagers and attracted punters from all over the country as well as France and America.

One lasting momento of the Mojo was the 1967 Rag Goes Mad At The Mojo EP. The

University Rag Week disc was recorded live at the venue, hosted by Peter, and featured club favourites the Tangerine Ayre Band, Pitiful Souls, Delroy Good Good Band and Joe Cocker's Blues Band. Not that Stringfellow was a man to give up easily. Within weeks of the closure of the Mojo, he and Geoff had organised the first "Mojo reunion show" at the City Hall Ballroom, featuring Junior Walker and the All Stars - "It's gonna be a scene, baby," said the advert. The band had originally been booked for the Mojo on that date. Pete was also mooted to take over from Cathy McGowan as host on the popular TV pop show Ready, Steady, Go, but this fell through when the show was axed by ITV. He then did a four-week tour as compere with Georgie Fame and Geno Washington. But as Pete told Top Stars, it proved too much: "It wore me down. I enjoyed it but decided I wouldn't want to do any more tours."

The Esquire had given up the ghost in early 1967, before the new act even became law. Terry Thornton saw the writing on the wall and he started to concentrate on his other businesses, including antiques and property dealing. When the lease came up for renewal, Thornton didn't take it up, saying: "We couldn't do anything big anymore," and, rather mysteriously: "The Esquire is owned by a Manchester firm. I only work here. It was not my idea to close the club. I only play a very minor part in the operations. There hasn't been very much movement recently and I don't think our scene has been replaced by anything in Sheffield. There is nothing happening." In July, 1967, some of the mystery was unravelled when Glossop DJ Peter 'Pedro' Birchall announced that a new club, the Stiles, would emerge from the old Esquire, managed by a committee of eight people from Sheffield and Manchester. His idea was to bring to Sheffield a club which is run on the lines of those in Manchester. "There's nothing like it here at all," he said. "The main idea is that we keep people dancing the whole night. We hardly play any pop records. That hurts a bit at first because teenagers like to hear Hit Parade records, but we shall play mainly music on the Tamla Motown and Atlantic labels. Clubs in Manchester are just regarded as ordinary business. But in Sheffield they are looked upon in a different light, probably because there are so few." The Stiles did indeed open - and closed shortly afterwards. One of the few bands to apperar there were Shape of the Rain in September, 1967. Terry Thornton faded away from the scene, leaving behind a rich legacy but not much to show in terms of national success. Little more was to be heard of him until the mid-Nineties when he was jailed for plotting to kill his ex-lover Eileen Caulton. In court he denied the offence and continues to do so to this day. He was also accused of being a satanist and an active member of the National Front. He was released in 1999. Jimmy Crawford: "Terry was well-heeled through antiques, not the music business, but he earned his start. Terry was a quiet bloke, although he did show later that still waters run deep, with his prison thing. His father was chief engineer at Davy United and was very highly thought of. Funny little guy with a smile and a laugh but you wouldn't know Terry was his son. Without Terry the bands like Dave Berry and myself and Chuck Fowler, would have had a lot longer haul to get it off the ground. Terry approached it properly. He tried and was very helpful." The Esquire itself was abandoned and the building had sporadic use, latterly as a car repair workshop, before the premises became the Leadmill in 1980.

The R&B Club at Frecheville had also stopped putting bands on, with out of town groups becoming too expensive and the new law restricting the size of audiences making it hard

Reactivated: Club 60 becomes the 6-0 club with organisers David Staniforth and Bob Davis

to make a profit. "There were only local groups left really and they were playing all the local pubs anyway," said organiser Tony Smith. "And the capacity of venues was based on ballroom dancing. We couldn't make it pay anymore." It became the JB Club for a short while before closing once again. September, 1966, had also seen Club 60 reactivated this time as the Six-O Club by David Staniforth and singer Bob Davis whose band the Bob Davis Mood was resident. It only operated for a few months and in the January '67 edition of Top Stars Mary Murphy and Helen Miles bemoaned its closure, asking: "Why close the only cellar club when everyone's taste doesn't run to such clubs as the Esquire or Mojo? Why should Sheffield be so far behind the times, lacking what nearly every city has - a cellar club?" The cellar occupied by Club 60 is still on Shalesmoor but little is left of it. It turned out that one of the main drainage channels in Sheffield ran directly alongside it which was why it regularly flooded. It was used to store baths and sinks until recently but the final straw came in the mid-Nineties when a particularly bad flood washed away the last vestiges of Club 60.

Stringfellow also inspired others to follow his lead, not always with great success. In Rotherham, there was the short-lived Lemon B Jefferson club at Columba Hall, College Road, Masbrough, started in August 1967 by Mojo regular Dinky Dawson - who went on to be a sound engineer with Fleetwood Mac, the Byrds and Steely Dan - along with fellow Mojo dancers Arthur Clover and David Growns. Live bands included the Herd featuring Peter Frampton, but most of the time it was the DJing talents of the threesome, Clover playing the likes of the Byrds, Doors and Seeds, Dawson going for Motown and soul while Growns was more of a rock&roll man. A police raid which revealed that there were 200 more people than the 500 legal capacity led to its premature demise. Dawson was also the DJ at Clifton Hall in Rotherham. Graham Oliver: "He was one of the big names in the area that you had to get on with to get anywhere but we weren't quite proficient enough at that time early on so we never really got on with him but we went there all the time and saw loads of bands."

Stringfellow went on to open a new club, Down Broadway (the original intention was to call it Sock It To Me One More Time And Shout Hallelujah), in a cellar beneath the Stylo shoe shop on High Street, in May 1968. During the day Down Broadway was a "bistrotheque", where you could listen to blue-eyed soul over pie and chips and a cup of tea, while four nights a week it was a 'go-go' room with live music. Soul singers Arthur Conley and Percy Sledge played there as well as up and coming psychedelic/prog rockers such as Jethro Tull. The tenure was short, little more than six months, as Stringfellow started looking for new premises when the profits from Down Broadway turned out to be minimal. He found what he was looking for on Dixon Lane, by Sheffield markets, seven floors above Burton's the tailors. It became the Penthouse and Stringfellow spent £12,500 developing it. He also, much to his surprise, got a drinks licence. He soon acquired

Pete Stringfellow as depicted in Viz magazine cartoon

the trappings - a Bentley car and a house in "upmarket" Meersbrook (he had lived in the flat above the Mojo until its demise) - of his latest success but, despite putting on bands such as Yes, Stringfellow was uncomfortable with the violence that went with the hardened beer drinkers who were attracted to the Penthouse. He, Geoff and others ended up in court after a confrontation with some drinkers from Rotherham. Peter was fined £100 for possessing an offensive weapon - a truncheon - and Geoff £200 for possessing a gas pistol. The Penthouse was put up for sale a year later. A new owner took over and it continued as a disco with the occasional live music. Steve Dawson of Sob: "We did it loads of times but we didn't like it because it was up about 50 flights of stairs. When I was driving for other bands I particularly hated taking McCloskey's Apocalypse to the Penthouse because they had a Hammond organ and you can't tip them on their sides because they go out of tune so it was all hands to the pump to try and get this thing up the stairs."

Stringfellow left for friendlier climes - first Leeds and Manchester and then international fame with the Hippodrome and Stringfellows in London - but Sheffield never really gave him the appreciation he deserved, although Mojo reunions still continue to this day. The Mojo helped put Sheffield on the pop map and it was as popular with the musicians who played there as with the punters. Barry Marshall: "It was a great atmosphere. But then everywhere was full at that time. People had a few bob in their pocket, there was full employment. It was one of those times. They say it was the swinging Sixties and it was." Geno Washington, who played regularly with his soul revue Ram Jam Band, still fondly recalls the place more than 30 years after it closed: "Even now when I meet up with musicians from that era we talk about the Mojo. It was probably the best club in the country at the time because the audience were there for the music. And Pete Stringfellow was a good DJ, he would play the right records to get the audience in the mood. There were other good clubs such as the Twisted Wheel in Manchester and Club A-Go-Go in Newcastle but we all loved the Mojo. I still see Pete occasionally. He invites me to events he has but I don't see him so often since he opened the table dancing club. My wife would whup my ass if I went there." And in the year 2000 when The Who played at Sheffield Arena, Pete Townshend remembered the Mojo as "an amazing club" and praised Sheffield as a centre for mod bands.

When the Mojo was finally demolished in

1982 to make way for housing, the developers wanted to call the new development Mojo Mews. The residents - and the budgies - got their final revenge. They objected, saying the name would immediately send the area downmarket. It became Firshill Mews.

The roller-coaster ride started by the beat boom was well and truly finished with not a lot, apart from memories, to show for it. Dave Berry: "It was a healthy scene but probably no healthier than Birmingham, Newcastle or Manchester. To be honest I think the scene is much more vibrant now. In the Sixties everything was very spaced out, with clubs scattered across the city. Stringfellow's clubs were all out of town, there was only really Friday nights at the Esquire in the city centre. People tend to look at it through rose-tinted glasses." Karen Young, on a rare visit home to Dronfield in the summer of '67, bemoaned the state of music in Sheffield: "It's not a bit like it used to be. Sheffield used to have a really good scene going. Now there's nothing." Mick Wilson of McCloskey's Apocalypse: "The best years were '62 and '63. You could buy the Star to see who was on. You would be spoilt for choice. If you wanted to see Joe Cocker you would just look to see where he was playing that night. Every pub that had a concert room had a band playing every night. Sheffield was absolutely crawling with live music, just as much as Liverpool or anywhere else. By 1964 gigs were much harder to come by. It was a craze like hula-hoops. It was just flavour of the month for two years. Everybody was in a beat group. The market was flooded and people got fed up of it."

20. ROUTE 61: THE CHESTERFIELD CONNECTION

In Chesterfield however, things were still pretty active although getting very strange indeed, thanks in both contexts to DJ Dave McPhie. He was the former drummer with the Blueberries who had released their version of Ike and Tina Turner's It's Gonna Work Out Fine on Mercury Records in 1965. Always enthusiastic, he turned out to be a bit of a musicologist especially when it came to American West Coast bands. He opened a record shop, Some Kinda Mushroom, in Chesterfield, later opening a branch in Sheffield. He also had his own independent studio at home used primarily to record

Chesterfield band Shape Of The Rain whom he managed. He had started DJing at the Victoria Ballroom, formerly the Top Rank, in late 1966. He went on to book bands at the Odeon Ballroom in Chesterfield, calling it the Grand Black Daffodil Club. Bookings included John Mayall's Bluesbreakers with Eric Clapton, but the venue was short-lived. The Victoria, however, was to become a centre for music that was not available anywhere else, attracting a lot of people from Sheffield once the likes of the Mojo and Esquire had gone.

Dave Berry, Shane Fenton and Jimmy Crawford, as well as the Hollies, Crusaders, Small Faces, the Who and Moody Blues had played at the Vic while it was still the Top Rank. One particular vivid memory for McPhie was a show by Little Richard. "I got on stage to introduce Little Richard only to find myself being pushed off by this fellow who turned out to be Little Richard's own personal introducer." There was also an unforgettable appearance, for the few who were there, by the Jimi Hendrix Experience at the ABC Cinema on April 8, 1967. The ABC also saw visits by the likes of the Everly Brothers, the Walker Brothers and the Ronettes. When McPhie initially took over at the Vic, it became "Britain's only Yum-Yum Centre - new thing from Bwanee Junction, Darkest Africa, with

Chesterfield r'n'b band the Blueberries in front of crooked spire

The Blueberries with Dave McPhie seen at front

an easy place to negotiate if you had long hair and loon pants. DJ Ken Blair recalls having to wear cycle clips on the bus to disguise the flare in his trousers and avoid getting beaten up. Few of these bands played Sheffield in their early days. Sheffield University was about the only venue that catered for such tastes and in 1968/69 was putting on the likes of Jethro Tull, the Nice and Family. Barry Smith, manager of

Shape of the Rain members, above, Len Riley and Brian Wood and, below, Ian "Tag" Waggett

discs by Hoots Mon McPhie", which was possibly inspired by some of Stringfellow's wacky press adverts. Eventually he ran it as a club, initially as the Velvet Underground, in June, 1968, and then the Gallery, from July, 1969. The first four acts to be booked in at the Velvet Underground - blues singer Champion Jack Dupree, psychedelic Londoners Blossom Toes, Chesterfield's own West Coast aficionados Shape of the Rain, and revered American guitarist Stefan Grossman - were typical of the eclectic music that was to follow. McPhie was one of the first promoters in the north to latch on to the new progressive rock movement which had grown out of the R&B and soul scene, combined with psychedelia.

The Vic was where people would go, including many from Sheffield who had previously been regulars at the Mojo or Esquire, in the late Sixties to see the likes of Jethro Tull, King Crimson, Family, Stone The Crows, Yes, Genesis, Tyrannosaurus Rex, Fairport Convention, Battered Ornaments, the Edgar Broughton Band, Roy Harper, East Of Eden etc. McPhie also promoted concerts elsewhere, including Pink Floyd at the notorious St James Hall (Jimmy's) in Chesterfield. The town was not

Shape of things to come, the Gear

Bradleys record shop on Fargate, was impressed: "We knew the name Jethro Tull - before he ever hit the charts." The university also put on the Moody Blues, Brian Auger and Julie Driscoll, Fairport Convention, the Hollies and, er, Adge Cutler and the Wurzels, at the annual Union Ball. It was open to students only. Some of the new bands went on to play at the

Shape of the Rain on stage: left to right Keith Riley, Tag Waggett and Brian Wood and right, supporting Fleetwood Mac

QUEEN MARY COLLEGE,
MILE END ROAD.

'Marys'

Fleetwood Mac
Plus
SHAPE OF THE RAIN
Plus
Disco

on **FRIDAY, NOVEMBER** 27, 7.30-11.30 p.m.
Admission 12/6
Tubes: Stepney Green, Mile End.
Inquiries: 980-1240, 980-5303.

City Hall, but only once they became major names.

McPhie also took Chesterfield band Shape of the Rain under his wing. They went on to gain a national profile and record a major label album. They were also typical of acts of the time. Everybody was trying to do something different and Shape of the Rain, a band which dated back to the early Sixties as soul/ Tamla outfits the Gear and the Reaction (not the Sheffield band), had their own one-off approach. While there was still a welter of soul outfits around, Shape of the Rain, thanks to the influence of McPhie, they had embraced psychedelic rock, particularly the West Coast sounds of the likes of Love, Byrds, HP Lovecraft and Jefferson Airplane. "Dave McPhie was the West Coast sound expert," says guitarist Brian Wood, "There were few people doing that sort of thing at the time." The Shape line-up was completed by brothers Keith and Len Riley on guitars and bass respectively, and eccentric drummer Ian 'Tag' Waggett, who was from the Keith Moon/ Kenny Slade school of drummers. He was just as likely to be found swinging from the stage curtains as playing the drums and also supplied an element of danger. Shape, as they were known to their fans, wore a bit of make-up, used oil lamps to form a psychedelic backdrop to the live performance, a primitive smoke machine, utilised backing tapes and would cover the amplification with flowers. They also employed unusual instruments - 12-string guitars, bits of percussion such as bongos and pedal steel. Keith Riley: "We'd use slide and steel guitars when other bands had never heard of them."

They were virtually resident at the Velvet Underground and were regularly called upon to support acts at Sheffield University, including Pink Floyd, Free and, on a rare visit to the UK, American band Love. Other regular venues included the Black Swan, Shades and they were also one of the featured bands at open-air concerts in the bandstand at Weston Park, which became a regular occurance in the early Seventies. The band also went down a storm in London, especially at the Marquee and the Speakeasy, and eventually recorded an album, Riley, Riley, Wood and Waggett, for RCA subsiduary Neon. This came about through Dave McPhie's connection with London publisher/producer Tony Hall, much in the same way that McPhie had done previously for Joe Cocker. Unfortunately the album didn't quite catch the full Shape of the Rain sound but is still a highly collectable item. After the album, things began to fall apart with Len Riley leaving to be replaced by guitarist Pete Dolan, Tag concentrated on percussion while Nip Healey and then Pete Wright came in on drums, and another addition was keyboard player Stu Moseley: "We were then the band most likely to do something and we recorded a couple of things." A&R man and former student at Sheffield University Dave Bates (he later went on to sign Def Leppard and ABC) attempted to get the band with Phonogram. One of the demos they made was a great cut of one of Shape's bluesy/rock pieces I Need Somebody. They were offered a £30,000 deal but by this time the band was in such a state of flux they didn't take it up. Keith recalls another session: "We did a session at Pathway Studios in London with Keith Relf producing, it was probably his last session as he died shortly after." The band continued through until 1976 when it became another casualty of the disco boom.

Another venue McPhie supplied bands for was the Barrow Hill Hotel at Staveley, an off-the-beaten track pub which had long-standing residencies for the likes of Frank White and Joe Cocker, as well as regular appearances by other local bands. The only problem was the power supply in the hotel was on a different cycle to that necessary for the bands' gear. "They used to run the power from the public toilets just outside," admits McPhie. Yes, the Chesterfield scene was quite strange.

21. HALLS OF FAME

Ironically, while Sheffield bands had virtually no platform, apart from pub gigs and the occasional support to out of town names passing through, visiting live music acts in the city was probably more in abundance than at any time before or since.

The City Hall, in particular, came into its own from 1968 onwards with top name acts such as Pink Floyd, Black Sabbath, Free, Deep Purple, Led Zeppelin, Jethro Tull, Stevie Wonder, Mott the Hoople, as well as more obscure acts such as Quintessence, the Incredible String Band, Heads Hands and Feet, Van Der Graaf Generator (on the same bill as the then unknown Genesis and Lindisfarne for all of six shillings for any seat) and a similar package featuring Jackson Heights, Every Which Way and Audience. Typically, Peter Stringfellow, now running the Penthouse, was not impressed with the venue: "It's more suitable for a United Nations discussion. The seating is uncomfortable and acoustically it's an echo chamber." Then again he had just lost £350 on a promotion featuring Fleetwood Mac shortly after they hit number one with Albatross. "People in Sheffield are not pre-pared to spend over 10s (50p) for a pop concert, even if they are number one." The new 'progressive' music also didn't go down too well with the old guard at newspapers like The Star. Keith Strong reviewed Jethro Tull at the City Hall in November 1969 with the words: "Not a satisfactory concert. It is to be hoped that, if a 1969 time capsule were to be buried for our descendents to dig up, we would not be judged by the contortions of a frock-coated, one-legged flute-player."

The Lower Refectory at Sheffield University hosted a lot of the new bands as well and occasionally went one better. There was an appearance for Leon Russell, after the Mad Dogs tour with Joe Cocker, which was noticeably snubbed by Cocker who was in Sheffield at the time. And in February 1972 Paul McCartney unveiled Wings at the venue which had been booked only six hours earlier, a condition of the appearance being that there would be no publicity and no entry for the media. Almost 1300 students paid 50p to get in with hundreds more seeing the performance from outside as the curtains of the hall were drawn back. The main problem at the university was still that non-students found it difficult to get in. The Star reported: "For most people it is a case of pressing their noses against the window and looking longingly in, since they are for members only."

One of the university's earlier attempts at letting in the great unwashed had been a failure. The annual Sheffield University Festival in June/July, 1966, was, for the first time, open to the general public. The week-long festival, at the students union, was headed by the Who, plus the Moody Blues, Jimmy Witherspoon, Alexis Korner and Victor Brox. It was the first sign that the university realised that perhaps the general public might appreciate the occasional invite. In the event it proved to be a bit of a disaster, particularly when the Who were to play. Roger Daltrey, John Entwistle and Keith Moon turned up but there was no sign of Pete Townshend. Support band Tony Rivers and the Castaways kept on playing, then records were put on but still no Townshend. Eventually the three-quarters of the band left, heading off to Stringfellow's flat at the Mojo, and the audience were informed of their departure 20 minutes after they had gone. Townshend turned up hours later - his car had come off the M1. As a PR exercise it was dismal. The Who promised to come again but next time it would almost certainly be a normal student dance - outsiders barred.

It was a situation that was not to be resolved

until as late as March 23, 1993, although a blind eye appeared to be turned well before that, when the licence at the Western Bank site of the University of Sheffield Union of Students was finally changed to allow non-students into gigs. The venues, now the Foundry (formerly the Lower Refectory), the Park and the Octagon, became separate entities, thus getting round the law that still prevails today and has led to difficulties for the the likes of Crookes Working Men's Club, Ecclesall Non-Political and the shortlived Speakeasy on Abbeydale Road, all of which were used as venues only to fall foul of the Private Members rules.

And it was not surprising that there was some resentment against Sheffield University from the Sheffield public who would not only complain that they were paying for the students and the facilities anyway but that the university tried to remain aloof from the rest of the city.

Martin Lilleker had first hand experience of the difficulties of getting into the venue on more than one occasion. "Buying tickets was not a problem but actually getting in was. You'd get as far as the porter who would then ask to see your Students Union card. If you hadn't got one you then had to persuade a student to sign you in. Seeing as this meant that the student would then be legally responsible for anything this complete stranger might do in terms of damage or mayhem, it wasn't surprising many were reluctant to say yes. Which is why I ended up listening to half of Focus's set outside, along with my mate from Rotherham. I must admit, I was tempted to lob a brick through the window but luckily some kind-hearted student eventually helped us out."

Dave Manvell was another who had to rely on being signed in: "I used to go down really early, 6 o'clock, to get in." That had its advantages: "I went in once and Traffic and Tim Rose were just knocking a ball about and they asked me if I wanted to play baseball with them which I did. John Bonham played drums with Tim Rose that night. On another occasion I ended up drinking rough cider at 1s 2d a pint at the bar with Jimmy Page and Robert Plant when Led Zeppelin were playing. And Keith Emerson of the Nice used my comb to jam the keys together on his keyboard." He also remembers the Who playing excerpts from Tommy and indulging in showmanship, Keith Moon throwing his drums around, with the roadies conveniently placed to catch them, and smashing mock amplifiers. And there was also the occasion Cat Stevens played an acoustic version of For Your Love with the Yardbirds.

22. COME TO THE CABARET: TONY CHRISTIE

THE NEW CARLTON CABARET CLUB
WHITTINGTON MOOR.   Phone 5745 CHESTERFIELD
Voted by the Stars as probably the most lavish Night Club in the whole country.
★ Superb Dining Facilities ★ Fully Licensed to 2 a.m.
★ Continental Casino Room ★ Star Cabarets featured every night.
ALL THIS WEEK — THE COUNTRY'S TOP VOCAL GROUP
★ THE DALLAS BOYS ★
May 3rd Week — YANA. May 10th Week — THE KING BROTHERS.
May 17th Week — SUSAN MAUGHAN.
May 24th Week — THE CHARIOTS.
Subsequent weekly Floor Shows feature the following Stars:—
ANNE SHELTON   BOB MONKHOUSE   JILL DAY
RAY ELLINGTON QUARTET   MIKI & GRIFF   RONNIE CARROLL
JIMMY YOUNG   RONNIE HILTON   BILL MAYNARD
Membership invited.   Send S.A.E. for full details.

Following the closure of the Mojo and the other teen clubs, night clubs and cabaret finally began to take hold in the city centre in the late Sixties. Until then anyone wanting to go to a nightclub in the area had to travel to the Carlton at Whittington Moor, Chesterfield, which was established in the early Sixties, the Sidesaddle at Doncaster, or Greasbrough Club in Rotherham. Sheffield's first club was the Cavendish on Bank Street which opened in 1967 and featured acts such as Jackie Trent, Scott Walker, Sandie Shaw, Billy Eckstine, Bob Monkhouse and the Bachelors. It later became part of the Bailey circuit and went through various changes - Romeo's and Juliet's, Cairo Jack's and, most recent incarnation, rock club the Corporation. A year later, in early 1968, the 2,000-capacity Fiesta opened in the new Pond Street development. Reputed to be the largest nightclub in Europe, membership was one guinea for men and 10s 6d for women. It was featured the very top names in showbusiness. Ella Fitzgerald, the Beach Boys, Roger Miller, Matt Monro, Roy Orbison, Tommy Cooper, Ray

Fiesta house band The Ricky Day Four with, left to right, Dave Allen, Ricky Day, John Fleet and Terry Clayton

Charles, Morecambe and Wise, Jerry Lee Lewis, the Four Seasons are just a few of the stars who appeared. It also hosted in March, 1971, a Festival of Pop, featuring the Kinks, Equals, Blue Mink, T Rex, Curved Air, Wild Angels and Southern Comfort on consecutive nights. It was owned by the Lipthorpes, two enterprising brothers who even made Colonel Tom Parker a serious offer to bring Elvis Presley to Sheffield. However, one can only imagine the kind of chaos such an event would have brought to Sheffield's city centre. Resident musicians who worked at the Fiesta included ex-Cruiser John Fleet on bass, Val Talbot on guitar and keyboards and band leader, the late Terry Clayton on drums. Two of the last stars to appear there were rock-'n'roll legends Bill Haley and Chuck Berry. And next to the Fiesta, the Top Rank Suite opened and was soon to become a valuable addition to venues in the city. Other clubs and discos included the Penny Farthing on Eyre Street, Tiffany's in the old Locarno which was decked out in

South Sea island-type decor and you could dance to the resident band, the Top Rank Suite that became Roxy's, and the Heart Beat at the Queen's Road Mecca complex which also included a casino, a bingo hall and the Silver Blades ice rink. The Silver Blades became a short-lived venue itself for bands. Stu Moseley: "It was the worst gig in the world. They would skate while you were playing. There were two stages, one at each side. Everything was soaking and salt everywhere." At Hillsborough football ground there was the Ozzie Owl Club. Stu Moseley's band the Reflections played there: "We arrived early and we're not on until late so we started on the large brandies. During our first spot on the second number - the curtains were pulled. That was embarrassing." In Barnsley there was the Club Ba-Ba, Bailey's at Monk Bretton and the Bird Cage at Hoyland. In Chesterfield there was also the Aquarius. Not that they all prospered. Howard Brecknall of the Heart Beat was quoted in Top Stars in April 1967 as saying: "People in Sheffield need educating. Many of them can't get used to the idea of being able to go out at nine or ten in the evening. It could because of the steelworker element which is very strong here. If they get up very early they don't want to be staying out until the small hours."

Over in Rotherham, Dave Allen was joining the nightclub business and set up the Charade at the Stag roundabout. Live music was one of the attractions and the Strawbs (featuring Rick Wakeman), Keef Hartley Band, as well as McCloskeys Apocalypse and Frank White, played there. Allen went on to open Josephine's nightclub at Barker's Pool, which has continued to flourish to the present day. Other Rotherham nightclubs at the beginning of the Seventies was the Oasis at Kimberworth and the Windmill at Rotherham United's football gound at Masbrough.

It was all a bit of a turn round for teenagers in the city who, until late 1967, had had the choice of several unlicensed clubs, including the Mojo and the Esquire, to which 14 to 17-year-olds could go. The story has remained the same virtually ever since. No wonder a lot of people who were in their teens in the period covering Club 60 in 1960 through to the Mojo closing in 1967, recall it as nothing less than a golden age. The situation was summed up by 'Depressed Teenager' who wrote to Top Stars Special: "When pubs are turning into discotheque clubs with groups and jukeboxes and places like the Mojo are turned into bingo halls, we are being driven to drink. You may say, 'Why

Tony Christie

don't teenagers go to youth clubs which are provided for them?' Well someone who is used to going to somewhere like the Mojo just doesn't fit in at a youth club of teenyboppers and three to four-year-old records. We want more entertaining places to go. It is not such a great thing to ask in a city the size of Sheffield. After all the Cavendish and Tiffanys have been made for older people, why not just one decent place for us."

One of the major benefactors of the cabaret boom was Tony Christie, who was to go on to become one of the biggest international stars Sheffield has ever produced, the first since Joe Cocker's success in 1968 with A Little Help From My Friends. He was already beginning to make an impact that year. After five years learning to cope with the demands of the give-us-our-money's-worth-or-else circuit of working men's clubs and cabaret across the country, both as a solo artist and with bands such as the Trackers and the Counterbeats, he had finally landed a recording contract at the ripe old age of 23.

His first record, in 1968, was the ballad Turn Around, a minor hit but enough to show that he could follow in the footsteps of fellow big-voiced balladeers such as Tom Jones and Engelbert Humperdinck who had already broken through. He might have lacked the former's on-stage oomph perhaps and the latter's good looks, but he had what it takes. Tony, a smooth-cut, smart-suited singer, fitted the bill perfectly, despite the flower power boom. "I don't go along with this psychedelic scene at all," said Tony at the time. He resisted the lure of Las Vegas - despite that being the title of his first hit - but he ended up with all the trappings. There was the Rolls Royce Silver Phantom, number plate TON 10, his own nightclub, Christie's, the pilot's licence so he could fly himself to watch his then team Leeds United, the nose job, the big house in Sheffield...

Christie was born Anthony Fitzgerald on April 25, 1944, at Conisbrough. He started his singing career at the age of 15, first with a close harmony duo, the Grant Brothers, then solo under his own name, Tony Fitzgerald - he later changed it after seeing Julie Christie in the film Darling - combining singing in the clubs with a daytime job in the stores of British Oxygen in Rotherham. He then became lead singer in the Counterbeats, replacing Karen Young, becoming first Tony Christie and the Counterbeats, the Tony Christie Show before going solo again and then fronting Tony Christie and the Trackers. But it was with his band the Pen Men, that he signed to MCA and hooked up with two of Britain's most prolific songwriters, Mitch Murray and Tony Callender. Success had to wait until 1971, first with Las Vegas which reached number 11 and then I Did What I Did For Maria, the latter remaining his biggest hit in Britain, reaching number two.

It was the famous US songwriting team of Howard Greenfield and Neil Sedaka who provided him with the song which was to make him internationally famous. Is This The Way To Amarillo?, a driving up-tempo number which utilised the full power of Christie's voice, went on to sell more than a million copies, reaching number one in Germany, Spain, Austria, Belgium, Switzerland and Sweden and the top 20 in six other countries. He was in demand worldwide. There were other hits - Don't Go Down To Reno, Avenues And Alleyways in 1973 and Drive Safely Darlin' in '76 in Britain.

Even when the hits dried up, Christie was still in big demand on the cabaret circuit until that too slowly dwindled. Or, as Jarvis Cocker put it in the lyrics for Stars On Sunday, a song he was to write about Christie in 1998, "The chicken has flown the basket..." By the early Eighties Christie's career in England, with the decline of

the cabaret circuit seemed to be virtually over. He said at the time: "There isn't much call for my sort of work in England. It's abroad where all the work - and money - is. I could earn twice as much in Germany as I do here." That was in 1983 but he couldn't possibly have envisaged how he would end up making money in Germany.

By the mid-Nineties he was virtually forgotten in his home city, having moved to Spain in 1991, and appeared to have turned his back on a singing career that had started in the late Fifties. Little did we know that Christie's career was not only flourishing but he was selling more records than ever - recording German schlager music, better known as thigh-slapping oompah, synonymous with lederhosen and steins of beer. "I would never dream of playing it to any of my English friends," says Christie who had agreed to record a single, Kiss In The Night, after he bumped into a successful schlager music producer at a charity gala in Munich. "I thought it was awful. I just expected it to disappear. It went to number one." Being back in the limelight, albeit with schlager music, also enabled him to get back on the road and he regularly tours with a German band, playing city hall-size venues, performing his hits and classic songs such as Solitaire in a two-hour show.

Little did he know in 1998 that he was also in demand back in Sheffield, thanks to a combination of the All Seeing I - who had just had a hit

with Beat Goes On and were looking for a singer for the follow-up - and Pulp's Jarvis Cocker who was writing lyrics for the band. When Cocker was but a slip of a lad growing up in Intake, the only Sheffield singer to make any sort of an impact on the national scene, apart from his namesake Joe, was Christie. So to Jarvis, Christie wasn't just any old singer, he was a star and he was local. He had no-one else to measure against Christie. The subsequent single, Walk Like A Panther, named after the title of Christie's first album, was released in January 1999 and hit the top ten. A video to accompany the record was filmed in Sheffield's Castle Market, just round the corner from where Jarvis used to work in the fish market, scrubbing crabs. Christie was back on Top of the Pops for the first time in more than 20 years. The following week Jarvis Cocker replaced him as the singer on Top of the Pops - Tony was unavailable as he was committed to his annual tour of Germany.

Christie, whose teenage idols were Frank Sinatra, Buddy Greco and Sammy Davis Jr, was suddenly back in the limelight in England, thanks to Sheffield musicians' almost uncanny knack of doing things rather differently to those of anywhere else. The new found success in the UK was short-lived, although he contributed vocals to four songs on the All Seeing I debut album, Pickled Eggs and Sherbet, sharing the honours with some of Sheffield's biggest names of later generations Phil Oakey, Jarvis Cocker and Stephen Jones. Tony turned out to be one of the few Sheffield musicians to span the generations.

23. ACID, ROCK AND BLUES

Psychedelic rock and the blues boom, epitomised by bands like Fleetwood Mac, Chicken Shack and Groundhogs continued to influence bands in Sheffield in the late Sixties/ early Seventies.

Bands with suitably enigmatic names began to emerge including McCloskey's Apocalypse, Laughing Gravy, Shape of the Rain, Acid, Newton Zapple, Greensleeper, Sob, Lazy Jake, Red Hot Property (or Red Hot Proper Tea as the band insisted), George Gill's Farm, Le Trombone Noir and the Pharmaseutrical Earth Mover. The latter couldn't spell pharmaceutical and gave their explanation for the name as: "Well pharmaceutical has something to do with drugs and hearing us play is like taking a drug which moves the earth," said singer Steve Walker. "It was a choice between that and the Articulated Jam

The Pharmaseutrical Earth Remover

Jar." They described themselves as a 'dedicated blues band' but created a psychedelic effect by featuring a light show and films of such things as blood plasma projected over the band while they performed.

Bands were beginning to experiment with their sound. The combination of blues and rock that had become popular with bands like Cream, Jimi Hendrix, Traffic, Jethro Tull and Deep Purple was also beginning to influence Sheffield's bands. The Frank White Band veered in that direction while three-piece band Panic (formerly known as Sounds Of Mephistopheles) were becoming a leading name locally with their brand of 'heavy' bluesy rock. Tom Brown Schooldays mixed soul with the sounds of Hendrix. Another outfit in the same frame of mind was Aston band Euphoria Blues and Progressive Group. Then there was Sheffield's first jazz/ folk group, Infinity Promenade, featuring 37-year-old Eddie Baxter on sax and flute. Another band, Acid - the colloquial name for LSD - included 16-year-old guitarist Cary Baylis, a pupil at King Ecgbert School, later to become a songwriter for Take

The Panic

That and top session player. They played "progressive blues" and the line-up was completed by drummer Ian White, bass player David Hobson and singer/ organist Paul Heatley. Another band moving in a 'progressive' direction were Titus Groan, influenced by Jethro Tull and Traffic, and fronted by Stu Moseley on flute and vocals. "We had Freddie Guite, an excellent drummer, and steady Pete Jackson on bass. And young Glen Turner," says Stu. "This young kid turned up in a cab for the audition with two women, one's his mum, the other his grandma. It was Glen and he was 15. He was spot on, knew every Beatles song and he could play Eric Clapton style. Glen went on to work with Chris Stainton in Tundra. I went to see him London and he was living in a one room flat. It was a room that was divided into two. The other bloke had the half with the window." There was also Manic Depression (Top Stars managed to rename them Maniac Depression) after the track of that name on Jimi Hendrix's first album.

Love Or Confusion, also named after a Hendrix song, featured 16-year-old guitarist and vocalist Phil Brodie and were credited as Sheffield's first 'rave' band. With regular publicity via Top Stars they became popular locally after just nine months. "That was what the scene was like then," says Brodie. "Our image was four young pretty boys who could rave it up and all the tarts liked us. I think we were also pioneers of progressive heavy music, Hendrix-style stuff." In April 1968 the band won a talent contest at the Top Rank Suite in front of 2,000 people. It was recorded by Radio Luxembourg and introduced by Jimmy Savile who declared: "I've not seen anything like that since the Small Faces." Record companies became interested, including Saga. Brodie: "Saga wanted to sign us up to make cover versions of other bands' hits. We went with Immediate who wanted to change our name to Cicero and have us wearing pink outfits and Orange Music were going to make us some amplifiers also in pink. They wanted to completely change our image and aim us towards the female market." It came to nothing when Immediate, owned by former Rolling Stone manager Andrew Loog Oldham and home of the Small Faces and Fleetwood Mac, went bust. In October 1968 they received their Top Stars Award as top local group. Ten months later they lost keyboard player John Smith: "He wasn't happy being professional so he left and we used a foreign guy." The remaining threesome - Brodie, bass player Steve Pinder and drummer Mel Askham - remained just as popular with a flourishing fan club. "We continued touring but

Teen ravers Love or Confusion and, below, advert for their gig for Radio Luxembourg at the Top Rank

we weren't getting anywhere and it just didn't seem to mean anything anymore," says Brodie. He left to join Dave Berry, signalling the demise of Love Or Confusion, and went on to become a mainstay, from 1974, with another of Sheffield's most popular bands of the time, Bitter Suite. Another 'rave' group was the Da Da Strain who took old numbers and jazzed them up in rave style while Origators Creed was described as 'Sheffield's own auto-demolition group'. Mixing elements of pop with new contemporary sounds, the group became popular locally with a healthy fan club of mainly young girls.

Getting back to more basic music was the Blues Scene Club at the White Lion Hotel on London Road. With around 100 members the venue catered for blues fans even though another of the club's features was Pud's Psychedelic Light Show, named after its inventor. Probably it's most memorable night was when the legendary Champion Jack Dupree appeared. Organiser Percy Pringle remembers it as a bit of a disaster. "Champion Jack was living in Halifax at the time and came down on the train. Lots of people turned up but because I knew everybody they just said they'd pay later. Of course they never did and at the end of the night I didn't have enough money to pay Champion Jack. He left out of pocket instead." However, it was the more progressive blues, in the English and Chicago style, that seemed to be the most popular, reflecting the ever-discerning tastes of Sheffield's music followers.

24. SO NEAR YET SO FAR

Probably the most unheralded and unlikely Sheffield recording stars of the late Sixties were John and Anne Ryder, already veterans of the local pub, WMC and cabaret scene with the Whirlwinds when chart success came in 1969. Although they never achieved any success in Britain, they had two top 50 hits in the States. The first, I Still Believe In Tomorrow, written by Marty Wilde and Ronnie Scott, was also number one in, of all places, Memphis, Tennessee. It hit number one in Canada, the top ten in Germany, Holland, Spain, Australia, New Zealand (where they were amazed to find they also had a fan club) and Japan. The follow-up Signed For Love was another big hit.

Pitsmoor-born John Ryder - real name Holland - started out in the late Fifties with Ricky Knight and the Stormers. One of their biggest gigs was at the Carroll Levis Search For A Star show at the Empire. They came second - to Barnsley ventriloquist Tony Adams and Grandad. He then joined Johnny and the Nightriders (along with Frank White) and then the Whirlwinds. He first met Anne when the Whirlwinds played Barnsley Central WMC where she was appearing as a solo singer. They were married in June 1962, and six months later John left the Whirlwinds and they went out as duo, John and Anne Ryder. They played clubs at night while John carried on his daytime job as an engineering pattern maker for steel castings: "He'd come home at lunchtime, doze off, and be late back for work," says Anne. It wasn't until they were signed up by one of the first agencies, Stan Farrell, that the work spread further afield, particularly Sunderland and the North East. They went professional in 1965. They continued to play clubs, mostly in the north and mostly somewhere down the bill, until being spotted by John Simpson and a colleague of London management company, B&J, in early 1969. They were in Doncaster looking for new talent and legend has it that they were about to get the train back to London when it was suggested they stay to hear the Ryders at a charity event. "They came into the dressing room and they wanted to sign us." Recalls John, "We thought, 'Oh yeah, sure'. But they invited us down to their offices in Oxford Street and they already had a contract made up." Anne told Top Stars at the time: "It was lucky they came along when they did for about then we were beginning to get really fed up with doing the same places over and over again and feeling we were getting nowhere." John added: "I think we would have opened a shop or something."

Under the new management they got work on the cabaret circuit all over the country and abroad and also landed a recording contract

Johnny Ryder with singers Lyn and Jean

with MCA Records. Their first record, I Still Believe In Tomorrow, was released in March, 1969. The headline in Top Stars ran, "Promising first disc from Sheffield duo." It was described as, "a mixture of country and western and hard beat." It was also Record of the Week in Record Mirror: "It could so easily be a hit and this Sheffield-based couple treat it well, without getting that cloying feeling so often apparent in this kind of thing. I like this a lot - watch it." Nothing else was heard about the record until their management company phoned them up eight months later, just as they were about to go on stage at the Penguin club in Birmingham. "They told us to get a copy of Billboard magazine. We said, 'Why?' 'Because I Believe In Tomorrow is in the American charts.' We said, 'Pull the other one.' We'd all but forgotten about the record," says John. "We were then introduced on stage that night as being pop stars with a big hit in the States." They went on to make a video for the single, showing them sailing down the Thames with Windsor Castle in the background. The record sold steadily in the States, reaching number 42, and an American management company tried to persuade them to record in Nashville. There was also pressure on them to move to London. The Ryders were sceptical having seen enough of the fickle ways of show business to not let the success go to their heads. "We are basically northerners and will stay that way," John told Top Stars. "We don't really like London all that much - too many people and too much traffic everywhere."

The next single, Signed For Love, was also a minor hit in the States, reaching number 44. "We were the only English people in the top 100 apart from the Rolling Stones and Tom Jones," recalls John who was known as 'Rigor' by fellow musicians because he never moved on stage.

I STILL BELIEVE IN TOMORROW — John & Anne Ryder — Decca DL 75167
  This well-orchestrated LP features the pleasant voices of the young British singers who had a minor single success with the title song. The package is well put together to include currently popular tunes like "Everybody's Talkin'" and "Let It Be Me," plus some other pretty material from various composers. John & Anne are fully enjoyable, richly melodic and harmonic. The album has done them justice. Will be right for most MOR and some pop stations. Could see chart action.

US Billboard magazine review of John and Anne's album

Until, that is, the day he started tapping his foot. Anne: "The whole band stopped playing and I said, 'Look, Rigor has moved'." They went on to release five singles, including Hold On which not only had a gospel feel to it but featured a full gospel choir. They became the John and Anne Ryder Congregation for that one record. They also recorded a version of Paul Simon's Cecilia. They appeared on various television shows including the Leslie Crowther show, the Golden Shot and five times - for each of their singles - on Lift Off With Aysha. They recorded an album, I Still Believe In Tomorrow, which was reviewed in American magazine Cash Box on January 24, 1970: "John and Anne are fully enjoyable, richly melodic and harmonic. Will be right for most MOR and some pop stations. Could see chart action." It sold well. It was

recorded in three different studios in London, with a 60-piece orchestra and arranger Cy Payne, but it proved to be the beginning of the end. "We were staying in our caravan at the Crystal Palace caravan park and we had to be in the studio all the time, from ten in the morning until three or four the following morning. It had been like that for us for two years. We were once playing in Edinburgh and the management company phoned to tell us we were to appear on Top of the Pops in Holland. We drove down over night, flew to Holland, recorded the show, flew back, no sleep, and drove up to Edinburgh to complete that night's engagement," says Anne. "MCA wanted to put a lot of money into promoting the album. A member of the board flew over from the States and told us he wanted us to come over to the States for six months - he'd already booked us into the Playboy Club. But we were simply too exhausted and turned him down. Our management company phoned us up the next day and said that it was the end of our career. The money went instead to a brother and sister act called the Carpenters. Six months later they were at number one in the States. We were just so naive." Their career with MCA didn't end there and then, and the record company sent them a crate of Moet Chandon champagne when Anne suffered whiplash injuries in a car crash on ice on the Woodhead pass as they drove back from a show in Manchester just before Christmas Day in 1969.

The final straw came once Anne had recovered. A tour of American army camps in Germany in February, 1970, saw them teamed up with "third rate" musicians and a driver who was an alcoholic. They were then scheduled to play the Hilton hotels in Tokyo and Istanbul. Instead they headed back home to Kimberworth in Rotherham. "We phoned the management and said we were finished. Our contract was cancelled and we took a long break," says Anne.

Cabaret stars: John and Anne Ryder

They eventually went back on the clubs, with John also resuming his pattern-making job. They were voted South Yorkshire top club duo three years running. "That meant more to us than anything else," says Anne who, after John packed it in in 1988, went solo and won the award for top female singer. But other than on clubland they are still virtually unknown in their home city. "It's funny," says John. "When people recognise me they always remember me from the Whirlwinds, and that was just for two years in the early Sixties." The couple now live modestly in Greenhill village in south Sheffield with little more than memories from their heady days. Their two hits each sold more than 250,000 copies in the States alone and their album also sold well. "All we ever got was £350, which

Barry Marshall, formerly Dean Marshall

seemed a lot of money at the time, but nothing like the amount we should have had," says John. "We also wrote the B-sides for our records but we've never seen any royalties for that either."

One of the biggest and most popular groups in Sheffield in the late Sixties and Seventies were Bitter Suite who achieved a national profile without getting the success many felt they deserved. They were a versatile outfit who changed their music according to the trends, from soul and psychedelia to mod and rock. They were about the only band in that barren period of the early Seventies who looked like

making the big time. They were regulars on Radio 1 and on the same tour circuit as Mud, Sweet and Paper Lace. And perhaps it was their versatility which eventually cost them their chance of joining their contemporaries in the charts. They instead ended up making a good living on the workingmen's club and cabaret circuits.

Singer Barry Marshall can trace the roots of the band right back to skiffle: "I used to go to the working men's clubs, especially Stanley Street, with my parents and I saw quite a few bands there - the Greycats, Whirlwinds, Blue Harmony Boys - with the old tea chests and brushed nail things. But my first introduction to it and my first influence was probably Lonnie Donegan whom I saw at the Empire when I was about 13 or 14."

Barry was at the same school as Pete and Roger Jackson and Dickie Elroyd in the late Fifties. "They used to bring their guitars to school sometimes and they practised in the shed down at the bottom of Pete's garden and I used to go and listen," says Barry. "Initially I got them their first gigs at youth clubs and things like that. At that time it was all instrumentals. We turned up at one youth club and they said, 'You haven't got a singer?' They had a microphone and we had sort of semi-rehearsed in the hut, just playing around, me just joining in. And it started off like that really, I just got pushed into it. I was a mate, admired them, they were great musicians and it was ironic that I should join the band." Pete Jackson: "We wanted a frontman and Barry was the nearest thing we could see to Cliff Richard. We played just round the corner from my mother's at a place that was known as the 'tanner hop', it was just a community centre. Tuesday night and Sunday afternoon they used to come from Barnsley, Rotherham, everywhere. There would be about 700 people." The band became Dean Marshall and the Deputies. Barry: "We got quite a few gigs and the band improved, but we had to change material. The Beatle thing was breaking so we became a Beatles-type band. I wasn't the only singer in the band. Rog, Pete and Dickie were all good singers, so they would do nearly all the Beatles' stuff. I was sidelined, although I loved it. I was doing all the Johnny Kidd stuff. But Johnny Kidd wasn't as popular as the Beatles so I wasn't going down that well.

"We played everywhere. And one night in 1964 we were playing the Arbourthorne Hotel and Pete Stringfellow walked in. I didn't know him from Adam but he was a very forceful guy, 'Hi lads, I'm Pete Stringfellow. What are they

The Lizards, Barry Marshall, Gerry Scanlon, and brothers Pete and Roger Jackson

paying you here?' '£4.50.' 'I'll give you seven quid to come and play at my place.' That was at the Black Cat. Stringfellow started to manage us." Pete Jackson: "Stringfellow had got it all planned. He said, 'You're changing your name and I've got a great idea - go to the Toggery at Stockport and get four kinky green leather outfits and them Beatle boots.' We became the Lizards and were a Hollies-type band. Our tag was, 'Sheffield's most popular non-recording group,' and that stuck with us."

A tour of Scotland and Ireland was set up for the band but had to be cancelled because of a typhoid epidemic. They finally got their chance when they reached the final of the Mackeson contest at the Parson Cross Hotel. They went to London to record but sadly missed out, as Pete Jackson recalls: "We went down without an original song and that's what let us down so we didn't get anything down on record." Barry: "Dickie Elroyd had left by then due to girlfriend pressure. with Gerry Scanlon replacing him. Then Rog and Pete left to join the Hillbilly Cats. I think they were getting fed up of it. It wasn't a living, we were just playing for fun so while you are playing for fun surely you have got to enjoy it. If it's a job of work it's a different kettle of fish."

With new recruits Bob Grundy and Fred Guite, The Lizards continued and did make it on disc via a Rag Record, issued by Sheffield University Students Union. My Love Goes On was written by Chris Stainton and Malc Towndrow of the Knives And Forks and made up one side while the New Foresters folk group featured on the other side. The band continued but finally dis-

banded when Barry and Gerry joined the Square Circles for a short while. Barry: "It was enjoyable. The music moved on again, it all happened so quickly in those days. It became the mod era and we were playing Small Faces' stuff which suited us. We had a good following." They then joined forces in 1967 with Adrian Askew and Will Williamson and became Jigsaw. The band expanded, with guitarist Ray Ashton, plus Mick Bell on sax, Vic Middleton, tenor, and Ian Brooks on trumpet, the latter being poached from Stu Moseley's band, the Reflections. Moseley wasn't too pleased: "Saxophone players were like gods, there were so few of them. And trumpet players were even rarer. We used to have two brass players who were members of the Territorial Army and I once had to drive all the way to Leek to pick them up for a gig in Sheffield and then drive them all the way back afterwards. They got well paid for the job while the rest of us ended up with about a shilling to share between us. The sax players were always better paid than anybody else in the band." Barry: "We were doing all the Wilson Pickett, Otis Redding, etc. The mod scene had gone. We were all into the fashion thing, we'd go to London to buy our clob-

Bitter Suite brass section

ber. We'd spend all our wages on clothes - the Beatles boots, fasten-down collars, all the fashion. That's the way it was, music and fashion. But there was another band called Jigsaw coming out of Birmingham and they had the hit record with Sky High. We got a little bit of a nasty letter saying if we didn't change the name they were going to sue us, so we had to look for a new one. For about a month we were Seesaw but none of us liked it until Will Williamson came up with Bitter Suite."

The pop-soul band turned professional on January 1, 1970, not bad considering they were an eight-piece at the time. They were managed by John O'Hara's former manager Brian Hart and were already regulars on Radio One and Radio Luxembourg. They had linked up with top

Bitter Suite, soul band

songwriters Tony Macauley and Barry Mason and recorded a couple of their songs. "I'll eat my maxi coat in front of the Town Hall if one or the other is not a hit," Marshall boldly told Top Stars. Unfortunately the maxi coat had to go, as the release of Time To Put Your Tears Away and Bye Bye Lorelei, was scrapped at the last minute, as was Gasoline Alley Bred which the Hollies went on to turn into a hit. Not that the band were short of work with regular cabaret appearances and tours of Turkey, Greece and Germany. They had a stint in Hamburg, following in the footsteps of O'Hara's Playboys, doing the whole eight spots a night thing. Bitter Suite became one of the first commercial bands to play the working men's club circuit.

They did eventually release a single, Goodbye America, on the Bus Stop label in 1974, the now five-piece donning Uncle Sam costumes to promote it. It was written by Peter Callender, who initially offered them Billy Don't Be A Hero. "We didn't want that," says Barry of the song which took Paper Lace to number one in February, 1974. Goodbye America got a lot of promotion and looked like becoming a hit. Then there was

Bitter Suite with manager Major Brian Hart

a strike by BBC technicians which took Top Of The Pops off the air and scuppered Bitter Suite's all-important appearance on the show as a tip for the top. The record did well outside the UK as bass player Gerry Scanlon recalls: "We did a small film of Goodbye America [this was before video days] for television abroad. It appeared on the Dutch version of Top Of The Pops and that took the record in the charts over there. It also got to number two in Portugal and we were due to go there." Unfortunately a military coup prevented the band from making the trip, continuing their run of bad luck. "We never made any money out of the record," says Gerry, "A bit of glory, but that was it." There were also appearances on Lift Off With Ayshea on Granada and a showing for the 'video' on children's programme Magpie. They recorded at least one more single for Bus Stop, How Married Are You Marianne?

The band's versatility was perhaps their downfall. Barry: "We also did the flower power thing, playing the university etc. Whatever came in we did it. The whole thing. I can't recall any band who has changed as much we did, we were like chameleons." Typical of the band's versatility was their arrangement of The Bee Gees' New York Mining Disaster which mixed the cheesiness of the pop song with the full-blown jazz-rock of the horn section. There were also several near misses. Barry: "We were almost Edison Lighthouse. Tony McAuley had this song but no band. He had singer Tony Burrows so the band, minus myself, were going to go on Top of the Pops and mime to it while Burrows sang it. But Tony thought the band was too strong and he'd got other material so he got another band from a local pub and put them behind Burrows. They toured for years afterwards as Edison Lighthouse. We did a lot of Radio 1 work. We were always on somebody or other's show and also did Radio 1 Live from a disco or whatever. We drove down from Doncaster one night to a live show at Tenby, no sleep. The BBC lads said, 'Oh Bitter Suite, you know how this lot goes, set it up, we're going for a drink'. So we set it all up and we were on air at 12 o'clock. Radio was only allowed to play so many records - it was called needle time - so they had to play so many live bands. The money from that helped keep the band afloat. We were working seven nights, we'd do double spots and sometimes trebles, especially in Manchester. We'd go from one place to another. It was a slick operation. We were that sort of band, we were well managed. Our manager Major Brian Hart who also managed Little and Large, who were Sid and Eddie then, Paper

BITTER SUITE
"Good-bye America"
on
Bus Stop Records

Midland Management
Tel. Nottingham 53277

"How Married Are You Marianne"

Bitter Suite

BUS
1028

RELEASED
12th September

Bitter Suite on record

Lace, the Cresters and the Wolves, he opened a few doors for us, cabaret and the like. We had to be multi-faceted. We'd do a university one night and be sort of really avant garde and then we'd support somebody like Bob Monkhouse at the Cavendish or somewhere. We learned to be all things to all people. We went from Cliff Richard and the Shadows to the Beatles, Blood Sweat and Tears to Chicago, we did everything, and we did it well. We had silk shirts with ruffles from Carnaby Street, fashion was part and parcel of the music business. Clubs were initially to get the ball rolling but nobody in the band was a proficient songwriter. We wanted to make it. But

we were working seven nights a week so when could we get together to write material?"

Bitter Suite never quite found the niche they were looking for and eventually ended up specialising in rock cover versions and working the club circuit. "We were so good at copying everybody else we were able to make a good living doing what we enjoyed," says guitarist Phil Brodie who first teamed up with Marshall when he was recruited from Love Or Confusion to join Jigsaw. "We were driven into the clubs because there were not enough live gigs that would pay enough money. But for us it was also a trap. We couldn't break free and play our own stuff." There were several changes in the line-up over the years with one notable addition being John Parr in the early Seventies on guitar and vocals who went on to have a worldwide smash with St Elmo's Fire. An attempt was made to perform original material when the band became hard rock outfit Prisoner but there still wasn't sufficient money to survive and it was back to Bitter Suite. There have been various comebacks since, the most recent in 1997, albeit very brief. However the name of Bitter Suite will always be well remembered by Sheffielders.

John Parr on stage with Bitter Suite

Sob, featuring future Saxon members Steve Dawson and Graham Oliver, top

25. THE OUTSIDERS: SOB TO SAXON

One of the busiest bands of the early Seventies in Sheffield were Sob, featuring two musicians who were to go on to become founder members of rock giants Saxon. Bass player Steve Dawson and guitarist Graham Oliver, from Swinton and Mexborough respectively, started out with Blue Condition in 1969. They went on to become Sob, named after the Free album Tons Of Sob, then Son Of A Bitch and ended up as Saxon. Graham: "We did loads of pubs around Sheffield at first but then Steve took me and our singer Steve Firth to Sheffield to the Mustard Seed coffee bar on Norfolk Street where the greasers and biker-types would go.

There was this guy playing this big Gibson 335 blues guitar and we thought, 'Cor, this is it, Sheffield is the place to be.' I was 16 at the time and the only thing we had done before in Sheffield was get the bus down to Johnson Electrics music shop on London Road. We'd never gone for a night out or anything because we were too young."

Blue Condition's first gig in Sheffield was at the Cannon Hall Hotel on September 6, 1970, but it proved hard for them to make their mark, partly through their own ineptness. Steve Dawson: "It soon became apparent that what we thought was great nobody else did. There was a lot of booing and being paid up in the early days with Blue Condition. We've always written our own songs but that wasn't because we were clever it was just that we weren't very good at learning anyone else's. To sit down and learn say a Beatle or Chuck Berry song, it takes some doing. So it was easier for us to learn our own simple, not so good tunes, but out of that inadequecy we developed how to write better tunes. We did learn a few basic tunes that were popular at the time that we put in between our songs. If we did 20 songs in a night, eight of them would be other people's. If the audience was getting bored with our songs we'd throw in something they knew, like Bad Moon Rising. Obviously in Sheffield and around there were different areas that liked different things. We used to play at the Barrow Hill Hotel at Staveley and they loved all our stuff." Initially their set included numbers by Cream, Fleetwood Mac and Hendrix as well as Little Richard, Chuck Berry and Motown.

Their first booking agent was Robin Eldridge in Doncaster, but there was always a problem with communication because Steve and Graham were not on the phone. Graham: "The agent would send us postcards with our gigs on, saying you're playing at so and so next week." Steve: "And if it was short notice he'd send a telegram. One of those little red BSA Bantams would turn up at our house and my mother would almost collapse, 'Who's died in the family?' And the telegram would say, 'You're playing at the Birley Hotel tomorrow.' Three times a week me mother was having a heart attack because of these telegrams." Graham: "We'd never take any money from our gigs, it would all go into a band kitty. A good paying gig for us was about £15 and an average gig was between £9 and 10. We weren't a big name and we weren't playing music that was particularly popular. We tended to get gigs because the agent wanted some commission rather than the pub wanting

to book us."

They started out rehearsing at the Thurnscoe Hotel before moving to a now demolished pub in Rotherham. They ended up sharing a room with McCloskey's Apocalypse - Blue Condition's then drummer was Lawrence Higgins, brother of McCloskey's Ray - above the old Albert Inn (now demolished) opposite Sheffield City Hall. The Albert had its advantages, as Graham explains: "While you were rehearsing, if a big band was playing at the City Hall, you would keep one eye on the window. As soon as the first person came out you knew the band had finished their set. We'd be ready to leg it straight across the road because you could get in for nowt then. All the bouncers were at the front, nobody on the door, nobody cared by then, so me and Steve saw everybody - Deep Purple, Ten Years After... everybody for nowt. There was always another half an hour to go, encores and everything." Steve: "The rehearsal became a minor annoyance."

They did occasionally pay: "We went to see Delaney and Bonnie and Friends [which subsequently became the basis for the Mad Dogs and Englishmen tour band] when they were with Eric Clapton, George Harrison and loads of other people," says Steve. "Afterwards the shout went up that they'd be coming out of door B or whatever outside. We go heads down running and, whack. We looks up and it's chuffin' George Harrison, we'd run head first into George Harrison. And with him is Eric Clapton, both stood there in big maxi fur coats. We were that gob-smacked we couldn't even get any words out to ask them for their autographs. They just walked off and disappeared through the automatic doors into the Grand Hotel."

It was in the Albert that Blue Condition, or Sob as they soon became, did their first recordings, thanks to a friend. Steve: "We knew this lad Neil Hawthorne who was related to racing driver Mike Hawthorne and got left some money when he died. All bands had somebody who hung around with them, a bit of a boffin, and he was ours. When he got the money he said, 'I'm going to London.' We said 'We're coming with you Neil.' So we all got into our J4 van - going to London then was like going to New York now. We went to Shaftesbury Avenue, and he spent all this money on a Telecaster, new Fender amps and cabinets, a keyboard, tons of albums and bootlegs at Branson's first Virgin Records shop. He also bought a Tascam TEAC stereo tape recorder and when we rehearsed at the Albert he'd record us." One of the songs they recorded was the split tempo number Albert, inspired by

Son of a Bitch with the line-up that became Saxon

the name of the pub. Graham: "Neil would come to all our gigs and we'd finish with Summertime Blues which ended with a big freak out. He'd sometimes get carried away and come on stage and take the guitar off me and throw it about the room. A kid once came and said, 'Shall I get him for you?'. I said, 'No, it's his guitar'."

They signed with a new agency, Trend, based on Waller Road, Walkley. Graham: "They got us Friday night gigs at Monk Bretton Social Club [which later became Bailey's], we did it a few times, once with Dave Berry with Phil Brodie with his white SG. We were like the lowlife, they were in a dressing room and we were like stuck in a corner." Phil Brodie: "They asked me to join them but at the time I was earning 50 to £60 a week with Berry and that was good money then. They were only earning around £20 so I had to decline their offer." Graham: "Frank White turned up with the whole of the Grease Band, Tommy Eyre etc, and we all sat round the tables watching Dave Berry and for us it was like we'd made it. They treated us like equals." Other big gigs for Sob included the Bird Cage at Hoyland and Clifton Hall in Rotherham.

However, it wasn't always about how good a band was. Graham: "There was a pecking order among musicians. We used to judge bands on what guitars they played. George Gill [of George Gill's Farm] had always got a Telecaster and we'd think, 'Wow'. Most people had a Watkins Rapier, whereas Frank White had the double-neck Gibson. We'd got fuck all, but if you'd got

some money and you were going in to buy a Marshall amp everybody from Swinton to Johnson's knew that you were going to buy a Marshall. You'd walk into the shop, knock everybody out of the way, stride up to the salesman - we knew him as 'mate' - and say, we've come to buy the Marshall. But if somebody was buying a Les Paul you were behind them. That was the shop to buy everything, me and Steve bought all our gear from there. I've still got the HP agreements at home, £2 a week and it would take ten years to pay it off. I used to get £12 a week and pay six to the hire purchase." Steve: "Johnson's was a bit of a strange place. You'd go in and there would be five guitarists all trying to outplay each other and the salesman shouting, 'shuddup'. There'd be guitarists copying whichever guitarist was big at the time, Jimmy Page or whoever, and they'd obviously spent seven nights a week for weeks, getting these licks off. They'd be in Johnsons from nine o'clock in the morning to five o'clock playing this new riff on a guitar off the wall until the salesman gave them a clip and kicked them out." Graham: "It was a big meeting point, bands would always be exchanging ideas."

Steve: "Another meeting place like that was Woodall services on the M1. After every gig you'd go to Woodall services because there was nowhere else open at one in the morning. You'd do a gig in Barnsley, anywhere within 20 miles driving distance, and go to Woodall. At about one all the band vans would start rolling up.

Son of a Bitch on stage at Sheffield Top Rank Suite in the 'US' deodorant competition

Then you'd all be in there having cups of tea and meals and they'd all be talking, 'We've got this and we've just played there and we've got the best van in the car park.' The van business was another way you could show off. You were top dog if you had a long wheel-base Transit mini bus - not a van - with windows. And to take it one step farther it had to be hired from Smith's self-drive at Thrybergh, I don't know why. And another thing was having a big steel bar across the doors - the bigger the better. Then there was us with an ex-Post Office J4, we'd park ours round the back so nobody could see it." It can't have been as embarrassing as their first van, a Bedford, which they acquired in October 1969 - it had 'Tripe and Neat's-foot Oil' emblazoned down the side. But embarrassment never stopped Sob: "We'd even pretend that we'd done a gig and turn up at Woodall at one o'clock in the morning. That's how barmy we were," says Steve. "We'd even drive to London, set off at 10 o'clock at night, park up at Kings Cross Station and go down to West End and look at the guitars through the window. We did that on more than one occasion."

Graham: "One day in 1970 Ginger Baker came in to the services with all these people from his band Air Force - Stevie Winwood, Rick Grech, Graham Bond in a huge fur coat... - and there's all South Yorkshire's bands and club land there. All the drummers went to their vans and got their snare drums. Ginger Baker's trying to eat his dinner and he's getting all these snare drums shoved under his nose to be signed. When Ginger went outside to get into his Jensen with the Air Force circles on the doors, this lorry driver says, 'Oi, who the fuck's that?' And this other guy says, 'Ginger Baker, he's a living legend, that's all.' 'Ginger Baker my arse,' came the reply and it ended up in a great scrap. They squared up and knocked the shit out of each other, knocking bits out of each other."

Things began to look up for Sob. They even got a proper van. Steve: "We eventually got to know the bands, and ended up getting a nice Transit with bus seats and Steve used to drive Frank White and McCloskey's to gigs. If the van was doing nothing they'd phone up - by this time we'd had a phone put in."

Steve Dawson: "The Star was like the musician's bible. All musicians bought it. They didn't really read it. The reasons we bought it was because there were three or four advertising columns in the back - I used to know the numbers off by heart - Instruments For Sale, Musicians Wanted and Bands. We'd all look at those columns. I still buy it today and still look at them just out of habit. I bet a lot of musicians are still the same."

There was also inevitable rivalry between bands. Graham Oliver recalls run-ins with Greensleeper whose magnum opus was a song called Get You Rat Bag: "They were one of the first bands I ever came across that had an attitude problem, and they were fuck all. They were your typical 'If you are not from Sheffield you're rubbish'." Steve: "We'd play the day before or after them in pubs all the time and dressing room walls would inevitably be full of messages - 'Greensleeper go fuck off, from Blue Condition,' - there was a message from every band." Sob eventually got their revenge when they signed to another agency, Jetrock, run by former Greensleeper/ McCloskey's Apocalypse driver/ helper Dave Beaumont. Graham: "We ended up taking most of Greensleeper's gigs. Their singer Albert didn't like that, he hated us with a vengeance."

From 1973 onwards Sob stopped playing in Sheffield, partly because of the overwhelming

Son of a Bitch back stage with 'rock chick'

onslaught of discos and partly to find a friendlier outlet for their rock music. They became regulars on the lucrative circuits in the North-East and Wales. In 1975 they became Son Of A Bitch, a name suggested by Alan Bown of the Alan Bown Set. It was shortly after that that singer/ bass player Biff and guitarist Paul Quinn of Barnsley band Coast joined in 1975 after a chance meeting at an M1 service station at one in the morning, this time Woolley Edge. Graham: "Our singer Steve Firth quit just before a tour of Newcastle and ended up doing it as a three-piece. I did the singing, it must have been horrendous. On the way back home we bumped into Biff at Woolley Edge. We were already friendly rivals. We told Biff what had happened and he said he'd give it a go as long as Paul could come along as well. We did the first gig at the Dickens in Rotherham on Saturday dinner time and played Crewe at night. Half a set with me singing and then the other half of the set Quinny and Biff would come on and take over. The first half slowly diminished after that."

The final piece in what was to be Saxon came in 1976 when Sheffield drummer Pete Gill was recruited. He had started out with short-lived band the Epics and Manic Depression at the age of 16. But his first break came with soul band Lubi Souls who landed a spot on Yorkshire TV's Calendar. He then moved on to another soul band Travellers Express. From there he became a member of the Glitter Band and played on all of Gary Glitter's big hits, starting with Rock And Roll (Parts 1 & 2) and I Didn't Know I Loved You (Until I Saw You Rock'n'Roll) through to I'm The Leader of the Gang (I Am) and I Love How You Love Me between 1972 and '75. "After the Glitter Band I played sessions and with a number of bands in Germany but the sort of band I wanted was playing heavy rock," said Pete. "It was hard to shake off the Glitter Band tag and so I had to start from scratch again." He joined Son Of A Bitch following a determined search by Graham and Steve. "After our then drummer John Walker left, somebody had told us about Pete. Word got back to him and he left a message with my mother but she lost it," says Steve. "But we knew he lived in some flats in Sheffield with his mother, so we went round all the flats in Sheffield knocking on doors, asking people if they knew where Pete Gill lived and we eventually found him."

One rare foray back to Sheffield was when Son Of A Bitch won the area heat of a competition run by US Deodorant at the Top Rank Suite. That took them into the final at the Manchester Apollo where they came second. It wasn't long

afterwards that they became Saxon and for a short period in the early Eighties were one of the biggest rock bands in the world. Graham: "The greatest feeling for us was when we came back and did two sell-out dates at Sheffield City Hall in 1981. We thought of all the twats that that laughed at us - we did take a lot of stick. We didn't feel smug about it but we'd done it on our own. We never dreamed that we'd get there."

Being outsiders, Graham and Steve are perhaps able to form a better overview of the Sheffield scene than most of the musicians from the city. Steve: "Sheffield is very insular. There are fantastic musicians but they don't seem to able to get past bloody Walkley, never mind Penistone. Get more than 20 miles from Sheffield and it's like they have elastic on them that drags them back. Their biggest downfall is that they had an attitude that they are too good. We'd do any gig anywhere, it didn't matter if it was a WMC or a pub. As long as we could get there and back on what we were being paid, we went. If you've got that attitude, 'I am too good for that gig' you never get anywhere." Graham: "I sometimes wonder about people like Def Leppard and Jarvis Cocker, even Joe Cocker, whether they were appreciated as much in Sheffield as some of the other bands like McCloskey's and Frank White who had the same crowd week after week. It must have been like a security blanket for them. Maybe the ones who did make it were the ones willing to work that bit harder at it than some of the others." And the subsequent success of Saxon stands as testament to the hard work of Dawson and Oliver despite the reaction they initially had to suffer in Sheffield.

26. MUSIC IN THE PARK

One of the most popular venues became Weston Park where concerts were regularly held in the early Seventies. Sheffield's first open-air jazz concert, Jazz on a Summer Evening, had been held in July, 1968, 2,000 people turning up to see Humphrey Lyttelton's sextet, the Ian Carr/ Don Rendell Quintet and the Barry Whitworth Quintet. The success of that naturally led on to more pop-orientated sessions. The audiences may have been a little less restrained than that for the jazz concert, and the drug consumption somewhat more prevalent now that LSD and cannabis were freely available, but even the most addled of drug survivors has happy memories of Sunday afternoons in Weston Park. The concerts, organised by bookie Glyn Senior, attracted audiences of all ages. For instance, on Sunday, July 26, 1970, one pensioner, Horace Rogers, a retired builder, was quoted in the Sheffield Morning Telegraph. "All the old people should come. Get away from the telly, come here, get livened up," he said. The report went on: "What looked like a girl wearing a sleeping bag strode by and two elderly men smiled secret smiles under rain-glistening beech trees. To the sound of McCloskey's Apocalypse 1,000 teenagers and youths nodded their heads, snapped their fingers and smiled their smiles. Toddlers with ice creams pranced about between long legs in tail coats; and couples held hands and spoke through the music." Most of the bands were virtually unknown, including the jazz-rocky Superslug and the more theatrical Le Trombone Noir. There was also the famous occasion when Brighton band Redhead Yorke were joined on stage by Peter Green, the reclusive Fleetwood Mac guitarist, who left the band under mysterious circumstances and virtually disappeared. Green had been persuaded to do

Jazz on a summer evening in Weston Park

Shape of the Rain playing in the bandstand at Weston Park

the gig by a friend who shared a flat in Brighton with former Pharmaseutrical Earth Mover guitarist Pete Warren. It was a gig that Redhead Yorke - with McCloskey's Apocalypse drummer Dave Seville sitting in - and the audience would never forget. Stewart Tomlinson was in the audience that day: "The only trouble was that Redhead Yorke were crap. I saw them later supporting the Edgar Broughton Band at the City Hall. They were rubbish then as well." Graham Oliver: "One of our first gigs was at Weston Park in 1970. We'd been to see McCloskey's a couple of weeks before and they were doing Summertime Blues that the Who did on Live At Leeds. We decided to do it but we did McCloskey's version which was The Who's version but taken one step further, a bit punkified, really fast. Of course Ray would nut his fuzz box and eat things. And when we started it they were sort of fumbling about on stage getting their gear ready and they were grumbling. We had to apologise to them but they'd inspired us to do it." Steve Dawson: "They started to have like an alternative to Weston Park in Crookes Valley Park, at least twice. Headline act was Vinegar Joe, who had been on at the Black Swan the night before. Another band playing was Le Trombone Noir, can't remember much about the music. They were like one of these Global Village Trucking Company-type hippie bands. They came on and did their set and because we didn't like them it seemed to last longer than anybody else. When they go off we're waiting for Panic or George Gill's Farm or whoever to go on, but one of the Le Trombone Noir had this big drum and he walked round on to the top of this hill bashing this drum all the way through everybody's performance for about four hours. It was murder." Another concert was in Graves Park where the headliners were the then virtually unknown Supertramp. "It was like a rubbish tip," recalls Keith Riley from support act Shape of the Rain. And over in Rotherham, to celebrate the borough's 100th anniversary in 1970, the council held a weekend of concerts in Clifton Park. The first featured T Rex, Marmalade, The Crazy World Of Arthur Brown and Terry Reid. The latter didn't turn up, Arthur Brown wouldn't go on until it was dark because setting his head on fire would be a pretty futile gesture otherwise, and Marmalade refused to go on before Arthur.

27. DISCO AND THE EGG BOX

A contributory factor towards to the demise of live music in the late Sixties were discos. Early instigators included Ian Ramsay who began by playing records at parties and functions with his 'unique invention - a portable discotheque'. Another exponent was Alan Dale, former singer with the Square Circles and Lizards, who would also feature 'go-go girl dancer' Diane Pearson as an added attraction. Art Stereo Disco in Rotherham was also one of the very first and is still going 30-odd years later. Steve Dawson: "Art had a massive PA that they had built themselves. They'd rent a room in a club or whatever and put us on with the disco and take the money on the door."

The Blue Bell at Hackenthorpe was reported to be the first pub to combine discotheque with live groups. The Searchers, Wayne Fontana and the Fourmost appeared there in 1967. But the writing was on the wall, audiences were beginning to get complacent about live music, rarely showing any response while being entranced by flashing lights to the sound of top 20 records. To pub landlords discotheques also offered a more economical proposition with a full night's music presented by just one man, plus there were no problems with temperamental musicians either. Soon others such as Ray Stuart, Gaspin Gus and Lance Edwards followed to sound the death-knell for many local bands. Mal Hooley: "The discos cost us a lot of pub gigs. All the pubs were taking live music off and putting in discos." Steve Dawson: "People wanted to go and see a disco and hear their favourite records played because it was novelty, rather than see a band. A lot of the venues we played didn't really want a live band but because they had to get a music licence through PRS or whatever for discos, they also had to have a live band at least once a week so you got venues that didn't really want you and audiences that didn't really want you so you had to put up with it. They all went that way, apart from workingmen's clubs where live music was five or six nights a week."

Elsewhere not much was going on. David McPhie: "I don't think anything really original has come from Sheffield since Joe Cocker. I think that the environment is partly to do with it, particularly as there is nowhere for anyone original to play. There are very few places that want to book bands who play their own material. Most of them just want to hear the top 20 stuff. Before they would take the plunge, but now they won't. Also the people who come to listen have

Singer turned DJ Alan Dale and, below, go-go dancer Diane Pearson

got a bit too cool about the music. Many have got the attitude that they have seen it all before."

Even Top Stars Special gave up the ghost in November, 1970, after a decade of chronicling the Sheffield music scene. Roy Shepherd, who edited the monthly magazine for seven years, lamented the changing scene: "Today a lot of the gloss and glamour has gone from the pop business. The general public, saturated with entertainment by that little box in the corner, look for more value when they spend money outside. They demand more gimmicks. And who can blame them? Many so-called stars charge outrageous prices to be seen and give very little in return. One night stands, touring ballrooms and village halls, are no longer necessary. Usually the record is made first and the group and act come later. It's a great pity, I think, for

a lot of the excitement of the early days has gone from the business."

Graham Oliver: "'73 was a really bad year for bands, hardly no gigs. Discos took over completely. Steve [Dawson] did all the bookings and we ended up going to the North East, places like Ashington which had 21 working men's clubs and one pub. Same in South Wales. The club thing from the Sixties was on the wane so they started putting on rock nights. We'd go for a couple of weeks to play in Newcastle. We'd sleep in the van, put mattresses on the gear. All the clubs had rock nights with bands such as Man, Sassafrass, Orphean, even the Scorpions were on the circuit."

The folk scene proved to be an outlet for some of the new breed of singer-songwriter musicians. The main venue was the Highcliffe on Greystones Road where the Highcliffe Folk, Blues and Contemporary Music Club was held every Thursday before switching to Saturdays. It was started by Win White, then a student at Sheffield Training College, in the mid-Sixties. After he qualified he left Sheffield, returning in 1967, and reopened the club in October, 1967. The opening night featured Michael Chapman whose debut album Rainmaker had just been released on progressive rock label Harvest to rave reviews; Ralph McTell who had already had three albums out on Transatlantic; and one of the heroes of the folk scene Wizz Jones. Other regular visitors included Alex Campbell, John Martyn, Magna Carta and Scottish duo the Humblebums, with one Billy Connolly on vocals and guitar. Tony Capstick was resident singer.

While much of the Sheffield scene struggled on, one group of musicians were busy making their own music. The combined talents of ex-Cruiser Frank Miles and ex-Cadillacs Tom

Rattigan and Chris Stainton, formed a songwriting/recording partnership and wrote and recorded a number of their own songs basically as demos for other artists. Their studio started out in the converted outhouse at Frank Miles' house in Beighton and was probably the first home-made recording studio in Sheffield, put together solely by musicians. From the mid-Sixties and on through the next decade the 'Egg-Box' studio (so-called because the walls and ceiling were lined with egg-boxes) was a hive of activity. It was a case of everybody pitching in and among the many songs the threesome wrote together was a piece that eventually became Marjorine, Joe Cocker's first chart hit. Linda Harvey often helped out on the sessions and remembers some of the problems: "It was freezing cold in the Egg-Box, we just wanted to get in the kitchen to warm up but you couldn't as there was always another speaker to swing about. The reel-to-reel tape used to keep snapping and Chris used to go frantic every time it snapped. They used to have to stick it back together. That's why there's little gaps in those tunes." Now with a stockpile of demos of impressive well constructed songs like Right Satisfied, Time and Isabelle Blue, Frank, Chris and Tom secured a recording deal of their own with Fontana. Under the name of Made In Sheffield, they had a single released, Right Satisfied/ Amelia Jane. Frank Miles recalls how they got on record: "Tom went down and got the deal actually. He went round and tried to

Twisting by the pool: The Steelers

The former Micky and Johnny, now Gemini Duo

play them to Apple but nothing happened there." When Chris left to go with Joe Cocker's Grease Band, Frank Miles and Tom Rattigan joined forces with other local musicians such as Barry Brumpton, Ray Woodcraft, John Loftus, Roger Harrison, John Firminger. Roy Barber was another musician involved and with the help of Frank and Tom recorded his own song Poor Little Rich Boy. In 1970, Sheffield club band Popcorn made a one-off single, Don't Let It Start/ You Took Me By Surprise, two more songs written by the

Miles and Rattigan team. The group's two vocalists were Trevor Woodcock and Dave Bye who had been performing together for a number of years on the local scene, first as Mickey and Johnnie, then with the Cadillacs and offshoot band the Originals. When the disc was issued by RCA the band were billed as the Gemini. Although their efforts didn't produce any more major successes, the Egg Box Studio had an impressive catalogue of songs, some of which were recorded by fellow Sheffielders Jimmy Crawford, Frank White and Dave Berry. Moving from Frank's house, the studio was set up briefly in Woodseats before returning to Frank's upstairs room where he is still involved in recording and songwriting today.

There were occasional threats of other things happening. For instance, Larry Page of Penny Farthing Records signed the Tumblers after they won a Looking For A Star contest run by Top Stars in 1969. They played "top pops, slipping in ballads for clubs," and Page renamed them Barby Thatch, probably in homage to their ridiculous hair which looked like it was glued on. They were Alan Roberts, Terry Adair, Roger Rutland and Robert Jenkins. Nothing more was to be heard of them. More hopeful, and certainly more eye-catching, were the Steelers, a two brothers and two sisters act who also appeared in the competition, Page signing them to a five-year contract and managing them. They were Alan, Michael, Christine and Anne Greaves and they certainly made a splash in Top Stars when the girls were photographed in bikinis splashing about in an outdoor swimming pool. Their father, a director of a wrought-iron firm in Sheffield, was quoted in Top Stars as saying: "I think they have an excellent chance of succeeding. They have made my wife and myself into 'with-it' parents." Unfortunately we are still waiting for their first record.

Sheffield-based singer Steve Mongomery was signed up in 1969 by Gordon Mills, the man who guided the careers of Tom Jones, Engelbert Humperdinck and, later, Gilbert O'Sullivan. The former door-to-door vacuum cleaner salesman, a golfing companion of Engelbert, released a single, You've Still Got A Place In My Heart. Another Sheffielder Dianne Littlehales was the 'Lee' in Peters and Lee, joining up with blind singer Lennie Peters at a Rolf Harris show in Bournemouth in 1970. Three years later they won Opportunity Knocks and went on to have a number one single, Welcome Home, in May of 1973. The Crying Game was the follow-up but failed to chart although By Your Side, Don't Stay Away Too Long, Rainbow and Hey Mr Music Man were hits over the next three years.

28. RHYTHM & BOOZE: THE BLACK SWAN

The only pub venue which was to thrive following the implementation of the new entertainment act was the Black Swan on the corner of Snig Hill and Bank Street. Rebuilt in 1965, it had a large concert room and subsequently became a major stopover on the British pub-rock scene of the late Sixties/ early Seventies. Manager Terry Steeples, a larger than life 17-stone 6ft-plus character, could match Peter Stringfellow for charisma, ebullience and the ability to pick the right bands at the right time. Terry began his career managing what was the Empire Cinema (later the Essoldo) in Rotherham that had been built by his grandfather. It was there that he showed he knew a thing or two about enticing in the customer with something different or 'wild publicity stunts' as he called them, whether it be a live show by the Shadows or Denis Lotis or the woman lying in a coffin in the cinema foyer to advertise the opening of the film Bride Of Frankenstein. That led to him being asked to take over the Black Swan after the first manager left in 1965. The musical fare was sim-

ply organ and drums: "It was all very nice but it was a bit outdated. So I introduced groups, much to the horror of the organist and drummer, although we kept those on until it was all groups."

It was soon a success and a showcase for such bands as Bitter Suite, Chuck Fowler, Frank White, Shape Of The Rain, the Wolves, New Jersey Turnpike and Sheffield-based Scottish band, John O'Hara and the Playboys. Terry, still remembered fondly by bands and fans alike, knew what his customers wanted and went on to book a regular and varied selection of top up and coming national bands. Gracing the stage were names such as Mud, Timebox, Sweet, Brinsley Schwarz, Argent, the Cresters, Wishbone Ash, Average White Band, Kilburn and the High Roads, Genesis, Patto, Vinegar Joe, If, Christie and horror-rock band Light Fantastic. The early Seventies was the heyday of the whole pub rock movement and the Black Swan was right at the heart of it. Patto, one of the most popular bands on the circuit, played their farewell concert there. Terry recalls the many acts with great fondness: "Vinegar Joe were marvellous, Elkie Brooks and Robert Palmer together. Can you imagine that? Elkie Brooks had been up several times before that. Vinegar Joe came for about two hundred quid. Patto were so popular that we used to get crowds of 300 in the concert room that only sat 230. Their finale number was So You Want To Be A Rock'n'roll Star and the guy on the organ used to push it and it fell more than once on to the front row. One of the great favourites was mime act the Discos, their timing was superb. They used to get me up doing the mime with them as well. We had the Sweet on a Monday lunchtime and I thought they were bloody awful and a week later they were big stars. I booked a group for thirty quid, I can't remember their name, it was an organ set-up. They were so bad I had to switch the power off. I told them to get off and they wouldn't so I pulled the plug out. That was the only time I had to do that." One of the most popular local acts were Bitter Suite. Barry Marshall: "We were almost resident at the Black Swan. If we had a cancellation Terry Steeples would put us on. He worked hard for Sheffield and brought some right stars down there. When it was full it was as good a gig as anywhere, it was red hot, you'd sweat cobs and that was what a gig's all about. Come off stage wet through and you knew you have had a good gig." Graham Oliver: "We could never get on at the Black Swan, he (Terry) wouldn't have us. We got on once for a cancellation but we'd always go in

The entrepreneurial Terry Steeples

the afternoon so we knew all the scene and all the bands. One afternoon Limelight from Mansfield were on. We were sat in the middle and there were kids over here, kids over there, and they were shouting 'I've just been to Johnsons and I've got an Orange Graphic,' and there were these discussions going across the band while they were playing. They were all trying to outdo each other by bragging off about their equipment."

Terry Steeples: "The highlight for me, when things really got going, was the World Cup in 1966. I went to a magistrate to apply for a licence on the grounds that these people from Germany or wherever, wouldn't understand an Englishman who couldn't speak German trying to turn them out at half-past ten! And the magistrate said yes, and gave me the licence. It was an incredible experience in as much as when we were supposed to close at three o'clock all these Germans and heaven knows what came in and asked for beer. Rather than try to explain to them we're closed, I used to serve them as long as they wanted." Rising to the occasion for the

two weeks of the World Cup, Terry booked some big names including the Ronettes. However, this presented a problem: "When I arrived at the pub there were two dressing rooms - a female and a male. My office was in the depths of the building, three floors down, and I thought this was no way to carry on. So I took the ladies dressing room and the bands had to use one dressing room that was about three foot by five foot. So when you got groups of six or eight in of mixed variety, they all had to change in the one dressing room. But the Ronettes said, 'Not likely, we're not changing in that dump.' So I let them change in the flat at the side of the dressing room. And Auntie Dot, who used to take the money on the door said, 'They're not coming in here' but eventually they did." Also booked for the fortnight was singer/ comedian/ vagrant Harry Bendon whom Terry often put on to open up for bands at the lunchtime shows. Although a fine singer, his humour was often less than savoury: "Harry was a wonderful comedian and had a nice voice but he was an alcoholic unfortunately. But at lunchtime the fact that he was a bit drunk made him all the more appealing. He did so well at those sessions I bought him a gold-watch and presented it to him on stage. He was a great character."

The Black Swan became one of the first pub venues to charge on the door: "It was a necessary evil. I'm talking about charging about ten pence, 20 pence, albeit many years ago. In those days you were getting crowds of about 300 in so you've got sixty pound on the door. Some nights it was a disaster. People wouldn't pay, y'know, the lads who were looking for a 'bit of spare', but the people who wanted to watch the bands would pay. On one occasion it was fifty pence. That was for Joe Cocker." And in 1970 Terry found himself up before magistrates for breaking the Sunday Observance Act which dated back to 1790 and forbade payment for entertainment on Sundays. Asked by the chairman, Miss Mary Berry, if better class groups made more noise, Steeples replied: "Not necessarily. It's just the way they use their instruments." Brian Watson, drummer with the Works, recalls that Terry was always fair with bands: "He booked us for sixty quid and then he gave

us a percentage of the door money, making about a hundred quid. He could've just given us the sixty notes but he was happy with his bar takings and he loved us there. Apart from Joe Cocker and Argent, we got the biggest crowd." Singer/songwriter Nick Lowe, then in Brinsley Schwarz, also recalls Terry's generosity: "Not only did he pay very well but he would give us a crate of Sam Smiths to stick in the van for the ride home." Bobby Knutt: "If I was skint and wanted a £2 sub I could go and see Terry and he'd give it me, and then knock it off on Saturday. He knew it was safe." Barry Marshall: "Terry asked us to play at the Black Swan but we said we couldn't because the van had broken down. So he gave us our fee two weeks early so we could get the van mended and we could do the gig, a great guy."

For many Sheffielders the most memorable night at the Black Swan was Joe Cocker's triumphant return to the city as he was heading towards number one with A Little Help From My Friends. Terry Steeples: "There were 500 people on the hill and we couldn't control them and the police came and said, 'If you don't move this

Flying high: Jimmy Crawford at the Black Swan

crowd in two minutes we're going to do you for obstruction.' I didn't like to tell them I couldn't get 500 in the concert room legally. But I thought, 'If you say so, sir,' and the whole 520 went in and paid fifty pence to get in. At the end of the night, because I'd never agreed a fee with Joe, I said, 'How much do I owe you?' He asked how much we'd taken. I said '£260.' So he said, 'Give me £200 and share the 60 out between you and the staff.' A gentleman. He sent me a telegram thanking me for all I'd done for him."

And what if a band failed to turn up? "Occasionally they used to break down. I always had a poor selection of records so I used to get up for about an hour and a half and talk to the people. There would be jokes and various stunts and gimmicks like beer drinking contests with a girl climbing on her boyfriend's shoulders while still drinking her beer." Finally, when it became apparent the band was not going to make it, he'd offer the crowd their money back, by which time they'd drank enough beer to not care anymore. "The highlight of the whole week was hen party night on Thursday. Dave Newman, the Roy Orbison lookalike, was the most popular of the hen party night entertainers. There were no blokes allowed and we used to play daft games. The girls used to get on stage and have a Merry Terry which was a mixture of brandy, lots of crushed ice, pernod, vodka and a measure of blackcurrant topped up with lemonade. It's firewater, not many of 'em went home sober. And there was confetti - by the end of the night we'd have to shovel the stuff away." There was also talent night - "There was one bloke who thought he was a star. He would come every week and do farmyard impressions. They would always sound the same. He became very popular but we fell out when he started demanding an artiste's wage." And then there were the topless go go dancers, but that's another story.

Indeed, Terry Steeples ended up becoming just as popular as many of the artists he put on at the Swan. "The secret with pubs is communication. You must be there, you must be seen. I dressed up in an evening suit every night so they knew who was the boss. There were other music venues around, including the Marples and the Top Rank, but times were changing. The talent night and even the hen night had disappeared by the mid-Seventies and nightclubs such as Baileys and the Fiesta were taking business. In the early Seventies I got a 2am licence for a disco. It went well until one night someone was hit in the face with a beer glass. That was it for me. I think I got out at the right time."

Six months after he left, the Black Swan was closed, to be converted into the Compleat Angler. But there was a last chance for the pub to make history. On Sunday, July 4, 1976, the Black Swan hosted punk legends the Sex Pistols, with support from The Clash, since immortalised in a documentary on the London band who were performing their very first public gig. That first line-up was Joe Strummer, Mick Jones, Paul Simonon, Keith Levene and Terry Chimes. "I wouldn't have had anything like that. Even now I still find them revolting," said Terry. No one had the commitment and flair of its former landlord and after its change of name to the Compleat Angler, it became just another city centre pub. That lasted for more than two decades, under various names, including the Mucky Duck in homage to its illustrious predecessor, before re-opening as a live venue in 1997 as the Boardwalk.

29. ROCKABILLY REBELS

From mid-1965 to late 1968 there was a group of Sheffield bands who detached themselves from whatever the current musical trends were to play the kind of music they liked best - early rock'n'roll and country music. These included the Hillbilly Cats, Dave Hawley Combo, Steve Denton Band and the Chuck Fowler Four and they soon found a lot of people liked what they were doing too. The Hillbilly Cats comprised of members of The Lizards and the Dave Graham Four, bass player Pete Jackson: "We used to get as much work with the Hillbilly Cats as we did with the Lizards. It was so much of a change yet people seemed to want it. It wasn't a gimmick because we'd got it together with the stand-up bass and then Brian Terry joined on steel. It went brilliant because we used to throw in a lot of stuff that we liked to play but when Brian joined we used to do corny stuff like Old Shep that went down great. We tried not to make it gimmicky, but do it in a proper way." The

The Hillbilly Cats

NOT LIKE A PROPER JOB ▲ 115

bands were all very supportive of each other. Pete Jackson: "We seemed to follow each other on the pubs. We were on one night and one of the other rock'n'roll bands were on another night, like a procession. It was camaraderie. If we thought that someone might be struggling at a venue, we'd take a gang down to watch them." With ex-Cruiser John Riley taking over on drums from Roger Jackson and later Johnny Pearson, the Hillbillys went from strength to strength, becoming something of a cult band among Sheffield fans.

Frank White, following his departure from Dave Berry's Cruisers, also for a time became part of the rockabilly scene with his own band Frank White's Katters. Then there was Frank's brother-in-law, Dave Hawley, who had a good track record as guitarist, beginning with the Del Vikings: "We started out at the Parson Cross Hotel, and I think we were one of the first under-age bands to play the workingmen's clubs." He went on to play with bands like the Whirlwinds, the Scott William Combo and Hillbilly Cats. He also joined a band who became one of the most popular club bands of the early Sixties: "Johnny and the Nightriders were playing and their guitarist Frank White hadn't turned up and I ended up joining them there and then. We rehearsed

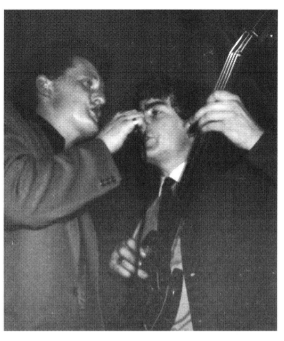

Steve Denton and Nick Farrelly

and that became the Whirlwinds. Lynne (Dave's wife) and Jean (Frank's wife to be) were already there, doing rock'n'roll and stuff before the commercial stuff started to creep in. I left because I wanted to play rock'n'roll, they were playing all Shadows stuff. I formed the Dave Hawley Combo for a while after the Whirlwinds but that didn't last long. I couldn't do what I wanted to do but I could with Scott William." After a stint with Scott, Dave formed his own band again giving him the opportunity to perform his own kind of music. "I stuck rigidly to what I wanted to do. Sheffield has never been known as a country orientated audience. Never got big audiences, but what we got we gelled with them." Alan Wood played rhythm/second guitar in the Dave Hawley Combo: "He was an outstanding guitar player and great vocalist with plenty of charisma. Everything Dave Hawley did - rockabilly and all his instrumentals - he had it all. It was a very good band." In 1968 Dave left Sheffield to go with British country singer Lorne Gibson. "Frank (White) saw an advertisement in the NME and I phoned, got on the milk train to London, on at 9pm, it delivered about four million bottles of milk and got in London about five o'clock in the morning. Went to Putney and the same night we were off to play an American base at Ruislip. It was good money - £12 a night. Two or three months later I joined the band, jumped at the chance, and went on tour to Germany, Malta and the Middle East, it lasted about a year."

Steve Denton was probably one of the best Elvis soundalikes in the UK, specialising in

Dave Hawley

Gaspin' Gus at the Sun Sound seen here with regulars at the Staniforth Arms

Presley's early and best work. He began singing in public as a teenager around 1956 when he would take sheet music for the latest hits round some of the city's pubs, getting up to sing with the resident pianist. Later, as the group scene developed, he would appear with his own bands who through the years were the Wailers, the Dentonaires, the Steve Denton Four as well as teaming up with Chuck Fowler both on stage and on record.

One musical sanctuary for both fans and musicians was the Sun Sound Club devoted to rock'n'roll and country and western. The Hillbilly Cats, Steve Denton and the Dentonaires, Chuck Fowler Four, Dave Hawley Combo and Frank White's Katters featured regularly and found an appreciative audience. The Sun Sound Club was

Chuck Fowler Four: Dave Hopper, Dave Green, Chuck Fowler and John Firminger

led by DJ extraordinaire Gaspin' Gus (Maurice Chapman) along with his co-organisers and operated between February 1966 and May 1969. It was self-financed by charging an admission price of around 3/6 (17.5p). This was possibly the first time a door-charge was put into operation and was met with disapproving scowls when the club first opened its doors in the upstairs room of the Ball Inn at Crookes, later moving to the Old Blue Ball on Broad Street and the Staniforth Arms at Darnall. However audiences seemed willing to pay to enjoy the music in the company of others with the same musical tastes. Sometimes a few more paying customers were needed but the bands would often drop their fees a little in order to help with running costs and play for audiences that appreciated their efforts. In a Top Stars Special feature on the Sun Sound Chuck Fowler said: "I think everyone enjoys it here, the club has a very good atmosphere." He was seconded by bass player Dave Green: "The people who come along are those who are really interested in the music. That's why there is no rowdyism." Special Sun Sound memories remain: the rockabilly powerhouse of the Dave Hawley/Chuck Fowler Combo at the Ball Inn; Doncaster's Jack Parkes and the Winchesters bringing some great country music to the Old Blue Ball; the opening night at the Staniforth Arms with the 'Green Goddess' herself, record shop owner Violet May, toasting the venture with champagne; and a great note-for-note version one night of Vince Taylor's rockin' Brand New Cadillac performed by the late

Rock around the spire: Bill Haley in Chesterfield, April 1968

Johnny White and his brother Frank on guitar. The club also had its own magazine, the Sun Sound Special, that featured all matters rock'n'country both locally and nationally. The club also organised trips to various concerts including Johnny Cash, Carl Perkins, Jerry Lee Lewis and Bill Haley.

In April, 1968, Bill Haley and the Comets appeared at the Victoria Ballroom in Chesterfield, headlining a bill including Frank White, Steve Denton and Chuck Fowler with one of their great rock'n'roll heroes. The Sheffield performers all played for free that night, at the request of the Vic's management and, of course, for the prestige of playing on the same bill as the 'father of rock'n'roll'. With maximum publicity in Top Stars, the place was packed with 700 people and the atmosphere electric. Bill and the Comets were magnificent, blasting away with a great set consisting of all their rock'n'roll classics. Unfortunately, in Top Stars' double page spread on the night the paper failed to mention any of the the local bands, who had all played well, particularly Chuck Fowler, focusing on the reaction to Haley. The night ended on a sour note. The only piece of equipment the Comets' drummer had brought with him was a brand-new Gretsch foot-pedal, which cost a then massive £50. He used a drumkit belonging to one of the Sheffield bands and at the end of the night the foot-pedal was missing. Every musician on the show was searched but it was never found. Alan Wood also recalls someone trying to get in to the show: "The bouncer came up and said, 'There's some geezer here who says he's Joe Cocker, he's in the charts and he wants to see Bill Haley and he can't get in.' So I said to the bouncer, 'It is Joe, go on let him in,' and they let him in." The night finished off with an after-hours party for all the Sheffield musicians at the Barrow Hill Hotel.

As the Sixties drew to a close the local rockabilly scene turned more towards country

Pete Carson rolls out the red carpet at Sheffield Country Music Club for special guest George Hamilton IV

music. The Sun Sound Club metamorphosised into the World Of Country Music, holding weekly country sessions at the Burgoyne Arms on Langsett Road and featuring resident band Hickory Wind. In November the Black Swan on Snig Hill played host to the first Northern Country Music Convention, featuring bands from Sheffield, Wakefield and Doncaster. The event was repeated in March 1970. Country music was starting to become more popular locally, backed up by a regular page in Top Stars. In one issue, London fan and regular visitor Hank Taylor wrote a half-page feature in February Top Stars Special praising the local country/ rockabilly scene. Country music clubs continued to run in the city throughout the Seventies. Over in Whittington Moor, Chesterfield, a weekly session was held at the small Social Club. In the summer of 1972 country music enjoyed a brief run when fans Don and Audrey Darrington staged shows at the Penguin Hotel, Shiregreen, kicking off with ageing US star Patsy Montana, the first female artist to have a million-seller with I Want To Be A Cowboy's Sweetheart. Country music then resurfaced in the city around September, '74, when the Sheffield Country Music Club began operating every week in the concert room of the now demolished Old Blueball on Broad Street. Featuring mainly bands and artists from out of town, the club enjoyed a memorable visit in the summer of '76 when Nashville artiste George Hamilton IV, who was appearing at the Fiesta, dropped in. Co-organised by Pete Carson, Reg Heath and John Firminger, during its nine year existence the club continued to survive, albeit with mixed fortunes, thanks to a loyal membership.

30. MY KINDA TOWN

With a lot of musical activity in and around Sheffield many musicians from further afield gravitated to South Yorkshire. They would use the city as a launch pad to greater things or just to make a living.

Prime examples were Scottish band O'Hara's Playboys who came to Sheffield in 1966 - and became extremely popular. They were fronted by Glaswegian John O'Hara, a former Salvation Army brass player, who formed the band in his home city in 1963. They went out on the road and were spotted by a German agent at the 2I's coffee bar in Soho. John O'Hara: "We went to Germany for a month and stayed four years. After virtually starving in London and sleeping on top of each other in the van, we got to Hanover, the van had bald tyres - and then the engine seized up. I said to the boys, 'This is it, if we don't put on a good show and we get paid off there's no way we can get back.' The guys went on stage and did somersaults, the lot, absolutely fantastic. The Germans loved it." They went to Hamburg and met the Beatles - drummer Davy McHarg still has their autographs - and went on to have hit records with their own energetic soul and beat music, as well as recording German beer songs. They were also struck twice by tragedy. The original line-up was decimated by a road crash which left three of them unable to play their instruments. Then their manager and his wife were killed in another crash. John O'Hara: "The Fortunes were number one in England and we were number two in Germany and we were going to do a swap - we'd

O'Hara's Playboys seen here at the Playboy Club, London

Caped crusaders: O'Hara's Playboys

tour in England and they'd crack Germany. Then a week before we were due to go, our manager and his wife were killed. The wheels came off everything. We were heartbroken. We had been rollercoasting - England next. We just bummed around for a bit afterwards, everyone wanted to manage us, even Brian Epstein."

They eventually hooked up with a new manager, Captain Brian Hart of the York and Lancaster Regiment who had been a recruitment officer in Sheffield, and moved there in 1966. "We just loved it," says John. "Loved the people, everything. Not just me but the whole band. We are all still here, apart from one. I call it the big village - everybody knows everybody else and what they are doing." Their first gig in Sheffield was at the Mojo and they became hugely popular around the clubs and pubs, particularly at the Black Swan, with a spectacular soul music show. O'Hara on lead vocals and tenor sax was ably assisted by the equally adept vocals of keyboard player Bobby Campbell. The band was complemented by a tremendous brass and rhythm section and could play all the top soul and chart hits of the day with expertise and flair. Barry Marshall of Bitter Suite: "When they first came to Sheffield they made a lot of jaws drop. We were only young kids at the time and they inspired us. When you see something that good you want to get on a par. They were an excellent band." They also wore flamboyant stage costumes, including ruffled shirts, flared trousers and velvet capes. The costumes weren't their only gimmick. Sax player Peter Green, who also played bagpipes, had his own bizarre party piece. John: "He thought he'd do something spectacular - he would fall over on stage. He did it on TV. And people would come up to me and ask, 'What happened?'." Davy McHarg: "I thought it was as funny as toothache." A funky driving version of Little

Richard's Lucille often provided the finale to the set. Davy: "We would work up into a frenzy and John would start smashing up the chairs and that, and the rest of them would lie on their backs waving their legs in the air. O'Hara would get hurt sometimes when a chair wouldn't break. He'd just end up chucking it away. He'd swing on the curtains instead. Venues would start putting a rope up to save the curtains. Terry Steeples at the Black Swan got fed up and started leaving the broken chairs out, 'Here break these not the new ones,' he'd say. I used to get a bit worried. There were bits flying all over the place." By the end of the night most of the audience was usually on the stage as well. Reflecting both their humour and musicianship is the band's live recording of one of their own songs simply titled Harry.

The Playboys also made regular appearances on television - Wogan, Opportunity Knocks, the Golden Shot etc - but not always with great success. Opportunity Knocks saw them finish joint third with the Sidcup Ladies Chorale. A week later they were on the Golden Shot. Davy McHarg: "We played with an orchestra in another studio doing the backing but in those days you never had cans or anything like that so we weren't in time with the orchestra. We could hear them but it was all echoey." More successful was a live recording for TV pop pro-

O'HARA'S PLAYBOYS are a group to be reckoned with as anyone who has seen them live can tell you. "In The Shelter Of Your Heart" has a good opening and clear-cut voices. I could have done with more strings earlier on but a good record (Fontana).

Record Mirror review

gramme Colour Me Pop, half of which was recorded in the Black Swan and the rest in the studio. One of the highlights of their career was a residency at the newly-opened Playboy Club in London in 1966. On the night of England's World Cup final victory over Germany they were joined on stage by England's captain Bobby Moore on a version of Len Barry's 1-2-3. "He just got up and grabbed the microphone off me and started singing," recalls John.

Yet, despite their popularity and professionalism as a live act and regular exposure on Radio One and television, they were never able to translate it into the charts, although they did reach number two in Beirut with the self-written Ballad Of The Soon Departed which resulted in a trip to the Lebanon. "We'd no idea where Beirut was," admits John. They recorded at least seven singles and a couple of albums for the Fontana label, including a version of the Bee Gees' Spicks And Specks and an O'Hara solo recording of I Started A Joke. They also recorded In The Shelter Of My Heart, written for them by top songsmith Les Reed. Top Stars Special gave a full page to the recording session in the March '68 issue. Plans to record a live album almost came to nothing when the chosen venue - the Mojo - closed in October, 1967, which also thwarted Amen Corner's plans to record a 'live' EP there. Instead O'Hara's moved it to the Nite Owl in Leicester taking two coachloads of fans with them, plus compere DJ Johnny Moran. Davy McHarg recalls the crowd's enthusiasm: "One fan was on stage singing along with John, he was singing so loud I couldn't hear what I was doing. I ended up shouting, 'For fuck's sake shut up, we're trying to make a record here.'" Davy: "We used to do doubles with Joe Cocker at the Black Swan and then the Penny Farthing. He'd be on first and then go to the Penny

TOP OF THE POLL

The Staggerlees

Farthing and we would follow him up. We were on equal standing at that time but Joe had something original about him, Joe was something else. We were a good showband, we did get people queueing down the street at six o'clock at the Black Swan and at the working men's clubs." They eventually ended up on the working men's club circuit. John O'Hara: "Peter Stringfellow told us, 'There's two ways you can go - you can either do the club scene, the night scene, like, say, Edwin Starr, where you will earn no money and try to get a record out, starve, go round the clubs and promote the record. If you want to earn money, go round the working men's club scene.' We needed the money so that's where we went." They went on to become one of the circuit's biggest draws, splitting up in 1970.

Another band that moved to Sheffield were club band the Staggerlees who took The Top Stars' top group award for 1964, presented to them by Jimmy Savile on stage at the City Hall. One member was Lance Fortune, an ex-college student from Liverpool who had had a British top five hit of his own in 1960 with Be Mine, followed by This Love I Have For You which got to number 25 in the same year. The other three members - rhythm guitarist Clive Gunn, drummer Tony Lee and lead guitarist Tony Grigg - were from Cornwall. They moved to Sheffield in 1963 at the suggestion of their manager Tony Cooper. They were regulars at the Top Ten Club in Hamburg and released singles Dance, Dance, Dance and Sweet And Lovely on the Oriole label. "Things have just mushroomed while we've been here," Fortune told Top Stars in October 1964. The band mixed comedy and music and were popular on the clubs and abroad. They became a trio at the end of 1965 when Clive Gunn quit the band for 'domestic reasons' and Tony Lee was replaced by Bill Covington. In 1967 they landed a five-month season at the Prince of Wales theatre in London, supporting the Frankie Howerd Show. The Staggerlees continued into the Seventies until Fortune and Grigg became a clubland duo working as Stagger and Lee.

The Fortunes, from Coventry, were that pleased with the response in Sheffield that they made it their home for two years before going on to major chart success. Rod Allen (bass), Glen Dale (guitar), Barry Pritchard (lead guitar), Andy Brown (drums) and Dave Carr (keyboards) became a popular draw around Sheffield pubs and clubs with their tight vocal harmonies. Their knack of re-creating the Beatles hits - they'd buy the record in the morning and perform it note-for-note that night - was impressive. Following

The Fortunes: Barry Pritchard, Glen Dale and Rod Allen

their first single Caroline, they went on to have big hits with You've Got Your Troubles, Here It Comes Again and Storm In A Teacup. At the height of their success rhythm guitarist and singer Glen Dale suddenly left to carve out a solo career, staying in Sheffield. He put together his own band Glen Dale and the Kandies who included guitarists Tommy Eyre and Ron Blythe and had a brief recording career with labels Page One and CBS, but it was clubland where he became popular. As they became successful The Fortunes left Sheffield and eventually returned to Coventry. Today with Rod Allen still fronting the band The Fortunes continue as a popular name on the 60's circuit.

As well as those who lived and worked in and around Sheffield, the area also has some other interesting and surprising musical connections.

Mick Jagger's grandparents on his father's side are from Eckington. His father Joe went to Greenfield School in Eckington and Mick, brother Chris and dad Joe were regular visitors to the Derbyshire village while their grandparents were alive. His grandmother is buried at Eckington and Mick went to pay his respects with flowers when the Rolling Stones played at the Don Valley Stadium in 1995.

David Bowie's father Haywood Stenton 'John' Jones was from Doncaster and his Uncle Jim worked at a steelworks in Sheffield - "He was an absolutely extraordinary bloke," Bowie told Q magazine in October 1999. "He learned every single word in the Oxford Dictionary." A most useful skill to have in a Sheffield steelworks!

The mother of Beatles' manager Brian Epstein was from Sheffield. Queenie Hyman, aged 18, married 29-year-old Liverpudlian Harry Epstein at the synagogue on Wilson Road, Hunters Bar, on September 6, 1933. They met on holiday at St Ann's On Sea. They were both involved in the furniture industry. Queenie owned the Sheffield Cabinet Company which made the Clarendon bedroom suite, a popular range in Sheffield at the time, while Harry worked with his father's business at Walton

Road, Liverpool. The couple moved to 197 Queens Drive, Liverpool, where son Brian Epstein was brought up. John Lennon and Paul McCartney were regularly entertained at the house in the early Sixties and it was there that John celebrated his 21st birthday.

Gerry Dorsey, later to become Engelbert Humperdinck, was a regular on Sheffield clubland in the late Fifties, making his first appearance in the city at Queens Social Club, Queens Road, on August 30, 1958. It was at the invitation of Charlie Wainwright, secretary of Sheffield Lane Top WMC, who had heard him in Leicester. "After his first performance the phone never stopped ringing," said Charlie. "And he got bookings at local clubs for the next 18 months." He stayed at Charlie and his wife Nance's home at North Quadrant, Firth Park, whenever he appeared in Sheffield. "He preferred working in this area than in his home town Leicester," said Charlie. "Probably because there were more clubs."

Wilko Johnson, guitarist with Dr Feelgood and Ian Dury and the Blockheads, was born and bred on Canvey Island in the Thames estuary but Sheffield can claim half of him. His mother Betty Morton was from Sheffield and her parents lived on Everingham Road, Southey Green. Wilko, or John Wilkinson to give him his proper name, was a regular visitor to their house in the Fifties and was evacuated there in 1953 at the age of six when Canvey Island was hit by flooding. "Me and my brother even got sent to school in Sheffield for a couple of weeks. I think we were a bit of fun for the other kids," said Wilko. "When my mum left Sheffield for Canvey Island she always claimed she had come down a step or two." The Black Swan in Sheffield was also one of the first venues Dr Feelgood ever played at in the early Seventies. Wilko remains a regular visitor with his own band and looks back on his Sheffield connection with fond affection.

The late official leader of the Raving Monster Loony Party and the original British horror-rock act, Screaming Lord Sutch had strong connections with Sheffield. His mother was from Woodhouse and after moving to Middlesex David Sutch was born. He lived with his grandparents, who lived at number 10 Coisley Road, Woodhouse, until he was four. "That was the nearest I got to Number 10," said Sutch shortly before his death in 1999. One of Sutch's last shows was at the Boardwalk in Sheffield in '98, invited by his former guitarist, Herbie Armstrong. Unfortunately by this time he had become better known for wacky political endeavours.

Sheffield had a profound effect on the Move

when Carl Wayne quit the band after an incident at the Fiesta in early 1970. A member of the audience took one look at Roy Wood with his hair to his shoulders and sporting a huge drooping moustache and shouted, "Hey, get off, you fucking poofta." Wood threw his glass of vodka and lime at the man. It shattered on his head, splitting it open. The man replied by lobbing his full pint of lager at Wood. The glass exploded on the middle of the stage only for the bouncers to intervene and drag the man out of the club. The audience was stunned, the band carried on to restrained applause and at the end of the show Wayne declared he had enough and quit the band. He was to be replaced by Jeff Lynne which led to the forming of the Electric Light Orchestra and the end of the Move.

Sheffield almost put paid to the career of future Led Zeppelin guitarist Jimmy Page in 1962. The 18-year-old was playing with Neil Christian and the Crusaders and collapsed outside a club in Sheffield, most likely the Black Cat. He woke up on the floor of the dressing room where a doctor diagnosed glandular fever complicated by exhaustion and fatigue. He was undernourished and emaciated, and had a bronchial cough. The continuous touring and the on-stage acrobatics he had to do, arching over backwards until his head touched the stage, had taken their toll. He left the band and enrolled in art school in Sutton to study painting. He went on to become one of Britain's top session guitarists but it wasn't until 1966, when he joined the Yardbirds (which slowly evolved, via the New Yardbirds, into Led Zeppelin), that he was to be in another band.

One of Britain's greatest jazz guitarists, John McLaughlin, who played with Miles Davis' in the late Sixties and was also responsible for one of the era's most acclaimed albums, Extrapolation, as well as being driving force behind fusion band, the Mahavishnu Orchestra, was born in Kirk Sandall, near Doncaster, in 1942. He played at the Mojo and Esquire with George Fame and the Graham Bond Organisation.

Kurt Wagner, singer/ songwriter with Nashville band Lambchop, went to Silverdale School in Sheffield in 1972 when his father took a sabbatical from the university he taught at in the States to research at Sheffield University for a year. Kurt gained his first musical experience in the city, playing cello with a youth orchestra. "Everyone seemed to play better, but I enjoyed trying to blend in. It was nice to be part of a large group of musicians, you feel better than you are, I guess." Perhaps that experience was what inspired him to form Lambchop which has

been known to use anything up to 20 musicians on record and stage. Wagner still has fond memories of the city and is a Sheffield Wednesday supporter to this day. He returned to the school in December 2000 to play a solo concert in the school hall. He admitted to being 'terrified', wore his old school tie and was spooked by the piano, the same one on which he had written his first piece of music 28 years earlier.

The steel mills in Sheffield were cited as the inspiration for the B-side of Birth, a hit for the Peddlers in August, 1969. Vocalist/ organist Roy Phillips said: "We have worked a lot in this area and we thought it would be a challenge if we tried to produce 'boom clang boom' sounds of Sheffield." They were joined by four percussionists - three from the Royal Academy of Music plus Errol Garner's drummer, on the instrumental track Steel Mills which also featured a hooter to represent meal breaks. It remains a tribute to the city from this once highly acclaimed group.

31. BEST OF ORDER

One source of revenue that has always been available to bands in Sheffield has been the working men's club circuit. Nearly all Sheffield's musicians played WMCs at some time or another, some settling into it for a living, others finding that the audiences were so unresponsive to original material or even slightly obscure cover versions that any ambitions to be pop stars had to be put on hold for the night. It was a case of supporting the meat pies and fitting in around the bingo, but it did have its moments.

Pete Wardlow, of the Twin Cities, remembers when rock'n'roll bands first started doing the clubs: "We used to work five nights a week in pubs and then work clubs at weekends. The first one was the old Philadelphia WMC at Upperthorpe. We were on good money. For a noon and night show we were getting £8 and then it went up to £10, with four spots at dinner time and perhaps five spots at night. We started going away from the pub scene and concentrating on the clubs. There was a bit more money on the clubs." Pete also recalls another form of entertainment just starting out on the clubs: "Rock'n'roll came out just as the first stripper started on the clubs, that was a woman called Lena Marlene. She'd pack a club out at dinner time. I can remember her causing a riot at Walkley Club, it got smashed up. The drummer's wife wouldn't let him play while she was on so I went up there and there's me, a 14-year-

THE
"WHIRLWINDS"

FEATURING.

Johnny Ryder. & Georgia.

Contact :- Mr H Bridges.
75 Horndean Rd
SHEFFIELD 5.

old on stage, I didn't know owt about this stripper and I'm wondering what was happening. She was a bonny lass! And she turned her back on the audience and she's chucking all sorts on me drums. Then she chucked her bra in the audience and this guy called Scotty caught it and wouldn't give it her back. She had these two bouncers and in those days Walkley was like a village. These two blokes started on Scotty and the lot went up and there's me still up on stage playing away and saying, 'Do you want your clothes back missus?'."

To get on the clubs most artists had to go to the Wednesday night auditions at the Stanley Street Trades & Labour Club (now Ceasars Massage Parlour), just off the Wicker. Jim Greaves explains the procedure: "You went downstairs for nowt and if you were good enough you got upstairs where all the concert secretaries were. In those days they didn't use agents, they'd have a notebook and they were gods. If you were still good enough you'd get a few quids worth of bookings, and we always got a fair amount." Trevor Woodcock: "That was the place to go in those early days. I can remember going home on the bus with the guitar and amplifier. We were on cloud nine as we'd got about £150s worth of work, at £12 to £15 per booking."

Although many musicians found it soul-destroying playing clubs, if you were versatile, you could make a steady living. There were many bands who became hugely popular. Perhaps one of the first Sheffield groups to emerge as clubland favourites were the Whirlwinds, led by Johnny Ryder, along with girl singers Jeannie and Lynne, drummer Tony Wallace, piano and bass man Keith Oldfield, and guitarist Neil Bridges: "We used to get to clubs and there'd be a queue down the drive and the club was full. I used to go to Cleethorpes and people who'd seen us in Sheffield used to come and ask me for my autograph. It was embarrassing." Alan Wood: "The club circuit was fantastic then. To join a club band and go to well known working men's clubs like Smithywood and Woodseats and know they were queuing at six o'clock to see your band, that was great." Johnny Ryder: "We would play Sunday lunchtime and people would stay through the afternoon so they could keep their seats for the night show." The Whirlwinds were also a breeding ground for talent in Sheffield, with Johnny Ryder and his wife Anne going on to become one of clubland's

The Kenny Pete Four: in Mexican mood

best known duos as well as having two minor hits in the USA. Comedian Bobby Knutt learned his trade with the band and there was also the larger than life voice of Georgia who, under her real name of Jean Rogers, got a one-off record deal with Columbia, as Roger Harrison recalls: "That was a result of that Mackeson contest at the Parson Cross Hotel. She went down to Abbey Road with Norrie Paramor and got a record released." The original demo version was recorded in Sheffield and was a song written by local singer guitarist Pete Jowell, once of the Cherokees and now known as Peterson, called Baby What Are You Gonna Do. Neil Bridges: "Georgia was the best singer I've ever heard."

Another popular act was the Kenny Pete Five, fronted by the late Ken Drennan. Roger Harrison was dropped in at the deep end when he replaced their drummer: "My first job with them was doing Opportunity Knocks. They'd won it twice and drummer Mick 'Flapper' Beaumont left in the middle of them doing it. It was a last minute thing and they were trying to teach me the song travelling over in the van and then in the toilets before the show." The band - Pete on bass, John Grace, rhythm guitar, organist Paul Black and new drummer Roger went on to win again. "They then did the all-winners show. They

Patt Leslie and the Greycats

got a lot of work out of that, a lot of travelling all over the country. We used to do a lot of cabaret and do comedy as well as the music. He was a nice guy Ken." Another member was Roy Barber who, after the group split, went on to form a duo with Kenny Pete: "We were Kenny Pete and Roy and we used to get more money 'cos they thought we were a trio."

The Greycats, with a long history on the Sheffield scene, were another popular act on the clubs. Their singer was Pat Leslie: "We could do no wrong on the clubs. People wanted entertaining and so long as you did your job you were OK." She was known for her powerful vocals and one reporter described her singing as, "Sock! Bang! Whoosh! Kapow! Then the room burst apart at the seams." Pat simplifies: "It was just posh phrasing for, 'She's got a big gob'. Another time while I was singing a fight started outside the club, one bloke was laid on the ground and said, 'Hit me again, I can still hear her'." Pat's impressive performance on the September '62 Top Stars Show at the City Hall led to the group being asked to make a test recording for Pye Records singing A Fool In Love. "We went down to London through the Noel Gaye Agency and recorded in the same studio as the Rolling Stones," recalls Pat. "But they wanted to take us over completely, telling us what to sing, what to wear, and me to lose weight even then. We didn't want to be dictated to so we told them we weren't bothered." Pat was also approached by a scout from the Jack Parnell Orchestra. "They offered me a job as the band's singer but I turned it down as I was very happy singing with the Greycats."

Comedian and actor-to-be Bobby Knutt first started playing the clubs when he joined the Whirlwinds. "They came to see me. They were top of the tree in the clubs. They asked me if I wanted to join them purely as a comedy vocalist. First job was at Darnall Green on £35 noon and night in about 1964, a lot of dough then." Neil Bridges recalls Bob's speciality: "He joined the group because he sang Donald Where's Your Troosers and he got dressed up in a kilt and used a whitewash brush as a sporran. And he could sing and play the guitar." Bobby admits he had taken his act from the group's drummer Norman Aistropp: "He used to do a comedy spot. Sometimes we'd do three or even four spots and in the second one we'd do one song and then Norman would come out to the front and say 'C'mon, I want to sing.' I'd say, 'Tha can't sing, go and sit on the drums.' He used to sing Granada all out of tune so we would put the guitars down and leave the stage and he used to do this 20-minute patter. He would do the same word for word every night. Anyway, we were working at Wincobank and Blackburn club on Saturday night and we were due at St Philips Sunday noon and night and as Norman is packing his drums away he says, 'By the way I'm leaving tonight'. No notice or anything, dropped us right in it. So Sunday noon not only did we not have a drummer but we didn't have a comedy spot. We managed to get a drummer from somewhere and I said I'd do Norman's spot. I did his act word for word, I knew it parrot fashion. Most of jokes were horrible, like the one about him meeting a big negress - that was the way it was told - walking down the road and she says to him, 'Do you want to come home with me?' 'What? Africa?' That was the standard. I got a few laughs and that was it, I'd got the bug reight then. I went home that afternoon and told my father what I had done and he said why don't you do that one or this joke. When I went back to the club that night I had half a different act. I wrote them all down on a piece of paper and put it on stage in front of the spot lamps. From then on I was the comedy man in the Whirlwinds. I'd replaced all of Norman's stuff inside a week."

Probably the zaniest band around on clubs was the Daizies with Paul Jarvis on bass, Spud West on guitar, Phil Galley on drums and Dave Robinson on lead guitar. They had formerly been Frankenstein's Monsters and it was Top Stars readers who renamed them, first as the

The ever zany Daizies

Psychedelic Daizies. Dave Robinson recalls how they transformed from horror to comedy: "We were doing that thing with Count Lindsay and we started doing this spot. Spud used to put wigs on and balloons up front for tits and acting about. We started doing a bit of George Formby and just pissing about." The offbeat humour was influenced by another wacky outfit. Dave Robinson: "We got to know the Bonzo Dog Doo

<table>
<tr><td align="center">WEDNESDAY, MAY 31st
GRAND DANCE
M.C.—CHARLIE SIMPSON.</td></tr>
<tr><td align="center">THURSDAY, JUNE 1st
The Two Tommies
Maureen Mappin   Dave Newman
TOMBOLA — Five Houses.</td></tr>
<tr><td align="center">FRIDAY, JUNE 2nd
TOMBOLA — 10 £2 Houses</td></tr>
<tr><td align="center">SATURDAY, JUNE 3rd
Gordon Jones & Partner
Paul Ashwood
TOMBOLA — Five £4 Houses.</td></tr>
<tr><td align="center">SUNDAY, JUNE 4th
Dave Harman's Collumbians
Con Martin
TOMBOLA — 5 £4 Houses</td></tr>
<tr><td align="center">THURSDAY, JUNE 8th
Grand Concert</td></tr>
<tr><td align="center">"Jock" Lee at the Organ</td></tr>
</table>

Bill of fare at Attercliffe Radical Club

Dah Band and got chatting and Spud had all their ideas in his head, and that's how the Daizies got their act." Roger Harrison: "It was very different at the time. Lots of props. Not just telling gags but doing sketches. There were certain things that we were all involved in, although Spud was the main man for the comedy. They were doing that before I joined when Phil Galley was still on drums. The first time I played with them was Sunday lunchtime at the Spa Club at Frecheville. The used to use electrical bombs in the comedy. They'd set the bomb up under my drum stool. I didn't know it was there. When the bomb went off, God it really made me jump! But not only that, it paralysed my legs, they went totally numb. I just sat there shaking with shock. I couldn't play. That's the sort of thing they used to do. They were very offbeat." The Daizies were another club band who progressed to cabaret, doing the Bailey circuit and the Fiesta. Dave Robinson: "We hit Leicester, you'd get to the club at half-past-six and the place would be packed. It was a great feeling." Like a lot of other club bands, The Daizies seemed to miss out on real success due to the confines of club work as Dave Robinson explains: "Those years were very good, but in another way they were a disaster. It put us off our guard. A lot of bands would get some original ideas and do things we

O'Hara's Playboys: 6d door charge

should've been doing. We'd got this great act on the Bailey circuit, plain sailing y'know. But it isolated us from what was happening musically." One of the few songs that the Daizies put on record was their version of Time, a song written by Frank Miles, Tom Rattigan and Chris Stainton.

Just about all of Sheffield's musicians have played working men's clubs at some stage. They were the bread and butter for most, a necessary evil for many. Mal Hooley: "You could never really get into the music. You'd go on and do perhaps six numbers. You were just warming up. Then they'd kill it all by having a break and playing bingo. You could earn more money playing clubs, more than pubs, but you were never appreciated." Dave Berry also recalls the lack of appreciation at one of his early club gigs: "I asked this chap why he hadn't clapped us and he said, 'Tha' dun't clap me when I cum ah'ter cage after an eight-hour shift dan't pit!'"

Karen Young, who sang with the Counterbeats at WMCs in the Sixties, also has bad memories of clubland. "They used to fill me with dread. The worst was having to do Sunday lunchtimes. They were just awful, filled with blokes swilling down a few pints. And when I went out on my own I had to rely on the resident musicians in the clubs to back me. More often than not they

destroyed the songs. Some of them were really dreadful. But I was never out of work for ten years. I had to beg my agent for a weekend out." Then there was the somewhat unprofessional or unknowledgable attitude of many club committees. Glyn Owen: "This chairman was rushing the show along and he said to the band in the dressing room, 'Come on lads, can we get you on. We're running late.' The guitarist said, 'I'll not be a minute, I'm just tuning my guitar,' to which the chairman said, 'For christ sake, tha's had t'booking for two months.'" Trevor Woodcock sang with club bands Popcorn and Time Showgroup and recalls how they had to close the night: "The chairman was the same old guy who was there every time. He'd been there throughout the night, introducing us and signing us off and closing the curtains. And he'd say, 'Now I want you to do up to half-ten and when you've done that I want you to do one more and then when you've done that they'll be shouting for more, because they always do! Then I want one of you to press this button on t'side here to draw t'curtains and give 'em a false tab, then you can come and do 'em one more after that, then close the curtains again. I've got me last bus to catch and it leaves at half-past ten." John O'Hara of O'Hara's Playboys: "Burngreave Liberal Club said 'John, you're asking good money now, we've got to put a cover charge on.' I said, 'That's up to you.' I get to the door and there's this piece of paper the size of a postcard, that says, 'O'Hara's Playboys 6d'. That's two and a half pence to you. I couldn't catch my breath, I thought it was going to be a quid or something." The Playboys also found themselves barred from Manor Social Club - "It was because there were too many people in. The committee couldn't get to the bar, that was the reason they barred us," says John. "At another place we were barred because we were on too long. People kept shouting for more so we did five or whatever encores. We were barred because the concert secretary missed his bus. In many places the concert secretary would say, 'When you've finished could you switch the lights off because I'll have gone.'" Glyn Owen: "This chairman was sat in the box one Sunday lunchtime at Attercliffe Non-Pots and brought the proceedings to a halt. He said, 'Right, there's been a lot of ill-feeling in this club with allegations flying about right, left and centre. I'm going to put an end to it now so will the alligator please stand up!" Another funny incident involved Frank White, who at one time used to call everybody 'Captain'. One night he's knocking on the back door of a club, trying to get in, and voice inside shouts, 'Who is it?' Frank shouts back, "It's the group, Captain," to which the voice replied, 'Group Captain who?'

Another side of clubland was the way they'd often get the names of bands mixed up. Literacy was never a strong point and the more tricky the name, the more it would get spelt wrong or changed completely. As a result, posters and noticeboards would advertise some quite strange names. Things were much the same coming from the chairman's box too as groups were announced wrongly. Graham 'Satch' Sargeant of the Hillbilly Cats: "This one chairman had had a few too many and he just kept getting our name wrong every time he announced us, the Killbilly Hats, that sort of thing. And at the end he announced us as the Wild Billy Smoke Men." Frank White also remembers when Frank White's Katters were transformed: "I walked in and there was a poster as big as the wall saying, Sank Wide Sk'taters. Do me a favour!" Alan Wood: "Frank White's Kommotion became Frank White's Komode a few times." Roy Ledger: "When we were with Johnny Tempest and the Cruisers we used to get called Johnny Tempest and the Crestas a lot. I mean, how long does it take to write it down so they know it?" Phil Brodie's first band, Fleur De Lys, changed their name to Xaviers after a WMC club thought they had booked a stripper called 'Flirty Liz'. Mick Wilson of McCloskey's Apocalypse: "We tried playing a couple of working men's clubs. One couldn't get the hang of the name so they chalked us up on the board as the Three Macs. We got paid off at the end of the first set anyway."

Many performers were paid-up before they had finished. Chuck Fowler was doing his act that included playing the piano with his foot when he was promptly stopped by the chairman. Chuck: "This silly concert secretary said, 'What tha doin' wi' that piano then? Nobody does that to our piano. Get your gear off the stage and get your money, you've done!' Another time at Arbourthorne I stood on this chair and I'm chucking bits of piano all over the stage. I'd got my back to the chairman and he's shaking his fist at me." But, as Pete Jackson explains, being paid up could often be a case of simply being in the wrong place: "It is nowt to do with whether you're crap or owt, it's if you're a fish out of water. I was paid up with Chuck Fowler at the Mona Club in Conisborough. The club had all pop acts and we did rock'n'roll. They said, 'Rock'n'roll? They don't like rock'n'roll here.'" Alan Wood: "Only once have I been paid up - with Jumbo at Dodworth Central Club. We went to a

noon show and we had long hair and everything. But we also had black suits, orange shirts and black dickie-bows. We thought by wearing suits and dickie-bows people would think we were a cabaret band when in fact we were doing Purple Haze and Hey Joe. And as we walked into the venue on a Sunday dinnertime, we heard military marches being played and we knew it wasn't going to be easy. So we thought we must try our best not to offend anyone. We reverted back to some of the stuff I'd done with the Wolves and Billy Simpson did the stuff he'd done with O'Hara's Playboys. We played all right and sang all right, but it was disastrous. I think they would have preferred somebody with spoons. They came in the dressing room and said, 'Don't bother coming back tonight lads, we don't want you.' We'd given it our best shot and we just weren't suitable." Glyn Owen: "We were at Heeley Bottom Club and I commented to someone that I didn't think we were going down that well. We were doing songs that we had an interest in rather than for the audience, I Think I'm Going Out Of My Head springs to mind, and I said to this committee man, 'I don't think we're going down well, I think it's going over their heads,' and he said, 'Well I'd drop the speakers down if I were you!'" Dave Berry recalls the time he got paid up: "It was at Darnall Liberal Club and was the only time I did a noon and night. Some guy came along to see us play at Darnall Public Hall and booked us even though we weren't a club act. We did the Sunday lunchtime and they hated it, and said, 'Would you mind not coming tonight?' and we said, 'Well thank you'." Cruiser Frank Miles: "It was the kids who wanted us but we didn't go down well with the older people." Dave Berry: "That's one of the things about my career that I'm really proud of. I never started on the working men's clubs, I've never done them regularly. I do them now but it's a special night and they charge to come in. But I've no intentions of doing them regularly." Roy Barber: "The kiss of death really, clubs. It's always annoyed me a bit, the generation of people that thinks that clubs are the bees-knees and if you can please them on clubs you can work anywhere. That argument just doesn't work. If you think of the thousands of groups that've gone on the clubs, you struggle to name four that've made it. There's people that have done the clubs on the way back down, but there's no legendary bands that've served their time on the clubs." Roy Ledger: "It's just South Yorkshire, they're hard work. The mentality is, like, you're getting paid to entertain, now entertain me."

Whirlwind members: Neil Bridges, Geoff Morton, Jean 'Georgia' Rodgers and Bobby Knutt

One entertainer who did go on to better things was Bobby Knutt: "I got fed up of the arguing and bickering with the Whirlwinds. By the end I was driving the van, doing all the comedy and playing lead guitar and singing. I thought I'm a mug here I'm only getting a fifth money. One night we worked at Woodfield Club at Doncaster and we were on with Johnny Ball, Zoe's father, he was a comic then. And in those days when you used to go and sign for your money in the clubs you'd know what they were on because they were the name above yours. We were on £30 noon and night and he was on £25 on his own. I thought, 'What?' A few concert secretaries had said, 'You owt to be on yer own, thee.' I didn't have the bollocks then so I went with Geoff Morton from the Twin Cities. Sid Brightmore, concert secretary at the Spa Club, gave us a booking. He said, 'What do they call yer?' 'I don't know.' 'Well call y'sens Pee and Nut.' And that's what we became. But Geoff wouldn't go professional, I was working as a roofer, bitumen under me nails, I knew I wouldn't last long, working and going off to bookings at night." Knutty ended up hooking up with his mentor Eddie Grant, a veteran comic who showed him the ropes and got him bookings. The rest is history.

There was also the problem of the committee men's sense of humour, or lack of it. John Firminger can recall one committee man coming up while he was setting up his drum kit, and asking if he was the drummer: "So I jokingly replied, 'No, I'm the trombonist,' to which he retorted, 'Don't get funny with me pal!'" Another wisecrack at a North East club brought about a hasty finish to Trevor Woodcock's band's performance: "We'd set up and we'd done four spots. We thought we'd done a fair amount, but we were going down so well we didn't mind. Anyway, we're in the dressing room and the

chairman comes in and says, 'C'mon lads, let's get you on another once before you go.' And Barry [Brumpton] turns to him, with a straight face, and says, 'What was tha' job before y'come here, slave driver?' And he didn't mess about at all this bloke, he said, 'That's it, put y'coats on.' And we just laughed at him and Barry said, 'We're only pulling your leg mate,' but he said, 'Get your coats on.' But what he didn't know was that we'd been paid after the second spot. So we said, 'We ought to tell you that we've been paid. Surely you want us to go on now?' He said, 'I'll get that back, you'll not be able to take that away. Get your coats on.' We did our best but he wouldn't have it, so we packed up and kept the money, and they didn't have anybody for the night time either." Barry Marshall of Bitter Suite recalls another incident: "We were playing St Philips one night, it was absolutely chock a block. We would start off by hitting them with three songs, bam, bam, bam, and then say 'Good evening'. We were just getting into the second song and this guy comes running down the club and shouted, 'Are you on VAT?' He stopped the show to see if we were on VAT. We thought there was a fire in the place or somebody had died. This was a professional band trying to do a show." Steve Dawson of Sob: "The biggest bone of contention for us in WMCs was the decibel meter, it must have been some smart rep going round, but all of a sudden around 1969/70 decibel meters started appearing. You only needed a slight tap on a snare drum and this meter went to the top and cut the supply to the equipment. You'd have this daft situation where you'd hit the first chord and it'd go dead and some power-crazed concert sec come from the back and say, 'tone it down a bit lads,' so you'd make this massive gesture of turning round and acting as though the knobs on the amp were four foot round and turn them right down and say 'all reight?' and he'd be suddenly like your best mate, thumbs up. You'd start again, whack, it would go off again. 'Tone it down a bit more lads.' You'd go ridiculous then, turn your amp down to nothing, so there was this little squeaking noise coming out of the speaker. We hated it, the audience hated it but because this concert sec's little meter was going up to the pre-set level, he loved it."

Roger Harrison: "They were ordinary working men who didn't know anything about showbusiness and who were put into a position of power one night a week, or at the weekend, and they just used to abuse it and show off." Alan Wood explains the lack of understanding between club officials and entertainers: "I have to be very careful because I still make my living out of clubs. I have to speak to these people called concert secretaries, etc. I think it's the inability of the working man who suddenly becomes powerful as a committee member with a badge, to say, 'I know you've been here since six o'clock and I didn't arrived until seven-thirty although I should've been here at six-thirty and I know you've taken all your time to meticulously set up all that equipment but it's in the way of the bingo machine. Is there any way that you may consider moving it a few feet please?' What you're usually met with is, 'Tha'can't put that theer, shift it.'" An apt description of some club committees comes from Jim Greaves of the Barton Brothers: "The unsuitable, chosen from the unwilling, to do the unnecessary. They hadn't a clue, they didn't know what they were doing, they wanted the best entertainment in the world for the least money."

One of the few bands with enough clout to challenge the rules and regulations of clubland were Bitter Suite. Barry Marshall: "No two ways about it, we were one of the pioneers in that department. The nickname of the band among the club fraternity was the Rolling Stones of clubland. We were the first band to go on there and not wear suits. All the other bands wore suits. They were called showbands and we rebelled against that too. And against the noon and night situation. We said, 'If you want the band you can have us at night.' Nobody was interested at noon. It was predominantly a male audience, they'd have the Green Un, looking at the results, and we'd be on stage working half asleep, so we said we wouldn't play them anymore. So the club said we weren't going to play their club anymore. It didn't last long. It turned round and other groups followed us. We also refused to do three or four spots. We made a stand. And that was it, it became two 45-minute sets and so it did for other bands. We made change by refusing to do what was expected. We thought a lot of the rules and regulations were

silly. It didn't apply to the day and age. We said you either book us or you don't. That attitude still prevails and that was what has brought a lot of them to their knees. There are still con secs who think they can shout and bawl and they are probably sweeping the shop floor by day. And they are in charge of running a business at night and they wonder why they are in the state they are in. And they are blaming the acts. It's not the acts. There was a club in Doncaster and it was charging £5 to see Bitter Suite. That was ridiculous with the money we were on, so we had words and said we weren't going to play and that was it. It made the national papers. Rebels again. We turned up the week after at Rawmarsh Progressive, with John Parr in the band, and they were all shouting, 'Rebels,' taking the mickey."

One group which got its own back on club committees was the Daizies as drummer Roger Harrison gleefully remembers: "A favourite trick of ours was to carry a set of bingo balls about with us. If we had any bother from the committee we just used to put another ball in the machine. So they'd got two number 31's or whatever it was and eventually, as they're playing the games of bingo, they'd get two of the same numbers out on the same game. And that would cause all sorts of trouble. Because not only did they, basically, have a committee meeting but invariably they used to decide that all the other games they'd played up to then were null and void because they'd got too many balls in their machine! So they then had to start playing right from the beginning again. The end result was, instead of doing three spots, we used to just do two! They never knew it was us." Pete Wardlow recalls another funny incident on stage: "The Twin Cities were playing at Intake Sports and Social and they used to have two palm trees on either side of the stage. Dave Fish tripped over the palm trees, fell backwards into the bass drum and got it stuck on his arse! He carried on playing like that until we prised him out."

Whirlwinds: Neil Bridges, Arthur Hutchinson, Georgia, Eddie Falcon, Tony Walsh and Dave Friskney

Neil Bridges recalls one wild night at the old Attercliffe Victory Club: "The audience was full of beer. This woman stood up with a pint pot and she threw it right across the club and it hit this other woman on the head. The pot exploded, the place was in uproar. We just stopped singing and went into the dressing room. A woman had a baby - she was due - and she blamed us!" Bobby Knutt: "I was with the Whirlwinds at Park and Arbourthorne and Georgia was singing with them. What a voice but she used to swear. She used to get dead upset if they weren't listening to her. She saved her two best numbers for last, Tall Dark Stranger and Somewhere Over the Rainbow. Normally when she did those you could hear a pin drop, but they were all talking and she walked off. But once she was behind the curtain she said, 'They're all a shower of fuckin' bastards,' without realising the microphone was still on. We had to wait until the club cleared before we could get her out. All the women were trying to kill her." Barry Marshall: "Bitter Suite played at Rawmarsh Cricket Club and our publishing company Chapel brought along Jim Capaldi, the Traffic drummer. He'd never been to a working men's club before. It was midweek, it was full and, as happens from time to time at these places, there was an almighty scrap." Gerry Scanlon: "It all started when a lighting gantry toppled over. The next thing we know the tables are going, glasses flying, the toilets smashed up, all the windows down one side smashed in. We legged it to the dressing room and locked ourselves in. Then there's this loud knock on the door and it's Jim Capaldi looking for somewhere to hide." Barry: "Eventually Jim Capaldi says, 'Wow, what a gig.' He couldn't believe it."

Another popular Sheffield club group of the late Sixties was Kalender, which began as a rock'n'roll band with Elvis Presley soundalike Steve Denton. Dave Hopper recalls the transition: "We'd had a fall out with Steve and decided to carry on using the name Kalender." Alan Wood took over on vocals temporarily and also played keyboards and he was joined by Dave 'Cannon' Smith on drums and Graham Davis on bass but the group is probably best remembered for its extraordinary young singer, Johnny Kalender. He was discovered after the band had auditioned several other hopefuls. Dave Hopper: "Cannon says, 'I've just found him hiding at the end of the bar. He says he's a singer but he's scared.' Anyway he had a go and sang My Prayer and he knocked us out." Dave Hopper: "That was a good band because it was in a really good musical period where everything was being

stirred up in like a big melting pot. We did a bit of everything: My Prayer, Born To Be Wild, Ragamuffin Man... from the sublime to the ridiculous." Kalender also recorded a couple of demos for EMI. Alan Wood recalls the experience: "Ray Stuart had seen the band and rang Bob Barrett at EMI and said, 'I've found the best band since sliced bread,' and arranged for an audition down at EMI. As we were carrying the equipment in we were told we didn't need amplifiers. I started to set up my Vox Continental organ and Bob Barrett said, 'You don't need that. Use that one over there.' 'That one over there' being a Hammond which the Beatles and Billy Preston used. I'd only just started to play keyboards and I had cunningly stuck on my little black and white organ little white circles with key symbols E F and G written on them. So I went to take these stickers off and stick them on Billy Preston's organ, and Bob Barrett's saying, 'What's he doing?' and I had to explain to him that I'd only just started playing keyboards. We went on to record a song that was going down a storm in the clubs at that time, an old Tom Jones' track called Two Brothers and because we didn't really know what to do for the other side, we did the Billy Preston song That's The Way God Planned It. So it was quite something to play Billy Preston's organ on a Billy Preston song and the main thing that sticks out on the demo, for some strange reason, is the organ. It's phenomenal!"

After the demise of Kalender Alan Wood went on to join another club band: "The Wolves were a very popular five-piece harmony band, recording with Pye Records and doing summer seasons. I auditioned on bass and also sang falsetto. When I joined, by their own admission, they were stale and a bit old fashioned and because they worked seven nights a week up and down the country, they didn't see a lot of other acts. Now I'd seen loads of acts in Sheffield like New

Clubs to cabaret: The Wolves

Sheet music for Quinceharmon's recording of
On The Buses

Formula, Second City Sound, the Fortunes, all these harmony bands making it. I came up with certain songs like Up, Up And Away done in a certain style and Touch Of Velvet, Sting Of Brass was a vocal harmony acapella thing and I did a song from Hair, Good Morning Starshine, and Mama Cass's It's Getting Better. We then looked into what the Beatles were doing. They'd dropped stuff like Penny Lane so I got us doing things like Dear Prudence and She Came In Through The Bathroom Window. With the five-piece harmonies it was fantastic." With this new

impetus the Wolves set a new standard for harmony bands on the club and cabaret circuit.

After the Wolves Alan was involved with Hollywood: "We'd been billed as 'Hollywood - ex-O'Hara's Playboys, ex-Wolves,' and people came expecting nice harmonies and suits, orange shirts and the black dickie-bows. Instead they were treated to beads, flared trousers, head-bands, wah-wah pedals and large bass cabinets. We were too loud, tried to educate them and they didn't want it." Hollywood had Every Little Touch released as a single On Beacon Records. They became Jumbo: "We were good musically, but we were too self-indulgent, head-bands and beads, a bit hippy-ish." They then received a solicitor's letter from the Tremeloes saying that they'd just signed a band called Jumbo who'd got a record out and had to drop the name.

One band who did find success following in the footsteps of the Wolves was Quinceharmon. The band's main claim to fame was recording the theme for the film version of popular TV show On The Buses. Drummer Pete Wardlow: "They had the premier at the ABC on Angel Street and we went there as honoured guests." Although the film was a big success, the record, released on EMI, wasn't. "EMI should have had everything done for the release of the film, they should have been in the foyer. They were supposed to have been there with all the publicity and EMI went and loused it up and things weren't ready so it didn't do anything. The film made something like eight million pounds in America, which was a lot of money then. We didn't get a penny, but we still get included in the titles 'Recorded by Quinceharmon'." Roger

Quinceharmon with the stars of On The Buses, Bob Grant and Reg Varney

Harrison was drummer with the five-man vocal/instrumental band: "It was a good harmony sound and there were some good singers in the band. There was Pete Jowell, he was in the Cherokees with me. Bob Holt was the main singer and had a great voice, and the one with the high voice was Ross Grant. So the three good voices together did sound great. There was Ivor Drawmer, he used to work all the harmonies out. He was very good at that and me and him sang as well. Before I joined there was Pete Wardlow singing, so it made a big sound."

With the departure of Jowell and Holt to form the duo Rockafella, Quinceharmon's Ross Grant, Ivor Drawmer and Roger Harrison regrouped as New Jersey Turnpike: "We got Bob Campbell who'd been with O'Hara's Playboys and Hollywood. He's a very talented guy, and we got another lad in from Liverpool called Paul Warren." However, the Liverpudlian was not all that he said he was: "He said he could sing and when we auditioned him he said he'd got a bad throat, so he never actually sang. It soon became apparent once he'd started working with us that he couldn't sing. So I had the unfortunate job of telling him he wasn't required any longer which is never a nice job." Carrying on as a four-piece the super-talented New Jersey Turnpike went on to become one of clubland's top bands for around three years. "We tended to do unusual stuff, stuff that was difficult to do. We used to do things like McArthur Park, Supertramp's Dreamer and John Miles' Music. We did Queen's Bohemian Rhapsody, which caused as stir at the time on the clubs. It was all smalltime really, but at the time we were the first band to do that song live. We did it for the first time up at Dial House and it got a standing ovation. It was a difficult song, I didn't think we'd get it off. It was Bob Campbell who wanted to do it. He brought the record and he said, 'We ought to be doing this.' I listened to it and thought, 'God, that's about six songs all in one, so complicated.' But we did it and we got a bit of a name for tackling stuff that was difficult to do. Ross Grant and Bob Campbell had both got exceptional voices."

Although the acts progressed many of the clubs didn't. Mal Hooley: "They never changed. It was still the flat-cap and meat pie image. That's why they've gone, they didn't change with the times." In November 1968 disc jockey Peter Brookes made a brave attempt to change the clubs' image with Tuesday afternoon dance session at Rotherham Trades. He told Top Stars: "We intend to make these dances as big a success and as removed from the traditional image of a workingmen's club as possible," - a rather impossible task. Agent Alan Wood: "Workingmen's clubs are a dying institution because they haven't encouraged youth. They haven't encouraged young people to come in working men's clubs, they've made them be members, they've made them be quiet while the bingo was on. And as young people don't want to play bingo they've gone into another room away from the bingo and it's on in the lounge. They can't get away from it. So subsequently young people don't go into clubs and they're now beginning to struggle."

32. THE NEXT GENERATION

For much of the early Seventies the charts were dominated by glam rock in some shape or form, whether it be brickies in make-up and tight satin trousers - Sweet, Slade, Mott The Hoople or Rod Stewart and the Faces - the more futuristic Roxy Music or pantomime dames David Bowie, Marc Bolan and Gary Glitter. Sheffield was no different. There were regular Tuesday and Thursday glam nights at the subterranean Crazy Daisy on High Street, just a few cellars up from where Stringfellow had his Down Broadway venue. Sure enough it was full of blokes wearing painfully tight flared pants and their girlfriends' make up. Other popular hang-outs included the Buccaneer bar, in the cellars beneath the Grand Hotel, which is where George Webster, later to open the Limit Club on West Street in the late Seventies, learned his trade as a DJ. There were also pubs such as rock refuge the Wapentake and the Penguin at Shiregreen. But live music was off the agenda for most teenagers.

As the decade wore on, with the miners' strike and Ted Heath's three-day week, the rise of the National Front, the Labour government's struggle against inflation and the International Monetary Fund and, in February 1975, the election of Margaret Thatcher to the leadership of the Tory party, things didn't look quite as glamorous as glam may have had us believe. In Sheffield the steelworks started to close down. And in surrounding areas such as Barnsley and Rotherham it was the pits that were being hit. A job for life? Forget it. Punk rock was to become the antidote for Britain's youth, and quite a few oldies, truth be told. But in Sheffield something else was bubbling under. Roxy Music and David Bowie are quoted by many Sheffield musicians as their main influences during that pre-punk era but there was also a penchant for German bands such as Kraftwerk, Can, Neu, Faust, even Tangerine Dream etc, almost all of whom eschewed using drummers and utilised electronic instruments. One of the main meeting grounds for many future musicians was a youth drama/ arts workshop project called Meatwhistle where names that would become familiar, including Martyn Ware, Ian Craig Marsh, Glenn Gregory and Adi Newton, met up. Ware: "It was a sort of intellectual youth club where we were encouraged to create imaginary bands with names like Musical Vomit and VD K and The Studs." Meanwhile Ware's old school chum at Myers Grove, Philip Oakey, sported a lop-sided haircut, a penchant for motor-bikes and was working as a hospital porter.

Youthful rockers Joe Elliott, Richard Savage and Pete Willis were already showing signs of musical rebellion while still at school and the Broadfield was the first venue to witness the vocal power of Bruce Dickinson, the future Samson and Iron Maiden singer, who was born in Worksop but raised in Sheffield. He joined up with some school mates from King Edwards School (which also spawned Graham Fellows, better known first as Jilted John and then John Shuttleworth, and Housemartins/ Beautiful South singer Paul Heaton) to sing with their band Paradox. Dickinson insisted they rename themselves "something big and mythical like Styx," unaware there was already a big American rock band of that name. He had previously got himself into trouble laying waste to chairs at one of the Weston Park Sunday afternoon concerts. In Rotherham, guitarist Steve Fellows and drummer Mik Glaisher were in the process of putting down the roots of what was to become the Comsat Angels while in Chesterfield teacher Tom Bailey was looking for an outlet for his musical ambitions that would eventually come to fruition in the Thompson Twins. Various other characters were in the process of applying for places at Sheffield University which was also about to become a fertile spawning ground for the new wave of musicians.

But it was another youthful outfit who were about to launch Sheffield into a new musical era. Schoolboys Stephen Mallinder, Richard Kirk and Chris Watson had been busy making experimental electronic music in the attic of Watson's parents' house in Totley since 1973. Named after Hugo Ball's 1916 Dadaist venture Cabaret Voltaire, they became the first of the next generation of Sheffield bands to play a gig. It was at the Upper Refectory at Sheffield University on May 11, 1975, and ended in a full scale fight. Which seems to be the perfect point to end this history of music in Sheffield - to be continued in a second book.

PART TWO: THE MUSIC MAKERS

1. I LOVE HOW YOU LOVE ME: JIMMY CRAWFORD

In 1962 the Sheffield scene was flourishing but of all the groups and singers only one, Jimmy Crawford, had achieved anything approaching a national profile. He was also the first Sheffield performer to have a hit record, Love Or Money - one week at number 49 in June 1961 - followed by his recording of I Love How You Love Me which reached number 18 on November 16, 1961. That was the height of his chart success but if anybody can claim to be Sheffield's first pop star it is former draughtsman Ronald James William Crawford Lindsay. Chart success may have been short-lived but he was a survivor who turned to the club, cabaret and WMC circuit to earn a living.

He first took to the stage as Ron Lindsay, with his backing band the Coasters, in the late Fifties. As well as being a junior swimming champion he had a promising career in motorcycle racing and used to turn up to work at Davy United - where he shared an office with one Terry Thornton, of future Club 60/ Esquire fame - on a massive Norton International. He competed at Silverstone, Brands Hatch and Crystal Palace. "Every penny counted," says Jimmy. "I had to eke out expenses during the three seasons I was riding. I waited-on in WMCs and even applied for a job as a grave-digger."

He started out watching local early rock'n'roll bands but his own musical start didn't come until 1958 at a party. He was encouraged by his sister Jeanette to get up and sing a number with local band the Harlequins. Jimmy: "Tony Cooper, who worked in the same drawing office at Davy United as me and Terry Thornton, was in the Harlequins out at Kiveton. I went to see his band because I wanted to be the singer. He auditioned me and said I had no chance, no hope." Cooper was later to become his manager. The setback didn't stop Jimmy as Terry Thornton recalled: "Although it was rather a disastrous performance, Jimmy and I immediately went home and got together to start a group of our own." Crawford: "I thought 'right I'll show him' and formed my own band with Terry on keyboard, Alan Smith on sax and guitar, Haydn Percival on guitar." They first got together in the canteen at Davy United and became Ron Lindsay and the Coasters. It wasn't long before the band started making a name for themselves and turned professional. Terry Thornton: "They were a wild bunch that I think the steel works were glad to get rid of. We had a sticky time at first, coming in at a time when the waltz and the quick step were the thing in the dance halls. We went for a booking at the City Hall but they wouldn't touch us." They found their audience on the Saturday Morning Teenage shows at the Gaumont where they became local stars with their own fan club which was started in February, 1960, by four teenage girl members of the Star's Teenage Club.

After a number of personnel changes the group became Jimmy Crawford and the Ravens. Lead guitarist Frank White explained the name change: "There was another Coasters and Ron Lindsay was not a rock'n'roll name. It was the management that decided that." Haydn Percival, on rhythm guitar, was retained from the previous line-up, and he was joined by fellow former Mainliner Mick Beaumont on drums, and Art Jacobs (Arthur Hutchinson) on bass. The new band's presentation became a lot more showy and some people have said that Jimmy Crawford was pushy. Trevor Woodcock: "To become successful you've got to have that attitude. You've got to make the break rather than hope someone will give it you." Frank White: "He was a very hard worker, I'll give him his due, bursting with ideas and energy."

Jimmy Crawford and the Ravens also became popular at dance halls in Chesterfield, Mansfield and Ripley. Crawford: "We had a fan club pretty quickly, and we ran two buses down to Mansfield Palais where we used to be very popular. We'd play every Friday night, and Sunday lunchtimes we'd do a teenage rock concert. People couldn't get in, it was so full."

Jim was the envy of the other bands. Dave Berry: "We were always very jealous of Jimmy Crawford because he'd got a rich grandma who used to buy him all the equipment. We always felt very peeved that he should have good suits, good van and first class equipment while the rest of us were struggling to pay for amps and things." Crawford: "I had got a red Transit van but before I started there was a band called the Blue Harmony Boys, who had a lovely Ford Transit with 'Blue Harmony Boys' painted on the side. I saw the standards they set with the van and the equipment, the suits, everything done pro and I thought, 'Nothing less than that, we have got to do it that way.' We got tailored gear, matching amps, real pro. My grandma helped, she spoiled me rotten.

Haydn Percival (Rhythm Guitar)

Mick Beaumont (Drummer)

Brian Smith (Tenor Sax, Clarinet)

THE COASTERS

Frank White (Lead Guitar)

Ron Lindsay (Vocalist)

She had a big heart and loved music, as did my dad, and she just wanted to see us get on. She signed guarantors for organs, drums, guitars, anything. It made a difference obviously. I got every help in the book." Linda Harvey: "He was very good with his grandma. He used to take her everywhere with him so she gave him everything he wanted." Image-conscious Crawford, who geared a lot of his act towards the opposite sex, sported a large blond quiff together with a flashing smile showing off a set of white capped-teeth. The latter were also paid for by his benevolent grandmother. Jimmy's hair was the subject of some curiosity when he was part of the Steel City Special trip to London in May, 1960: "Cliff Richard's agent, Hymie Zahl, turned up and I had got this silver stuff that I sprayed on my already blond hair. It looked outstandingly differ-

ent, I don't say good. The agent came up to me curious about my hair. He touched it and some of it came off on his hand. It was just the colour. He was going, 'Curious, curious.' I think I was the first one in Britain to do that, before Wee Willie Harris with his red hair, and Heinz in the Tornados. It got me noticed a bit." Alan Wood: "Everybody thought that Crawford used to put milk on his hair to make it look blond, so this singer of ours used to put milk on his hair. He didn't realise it was dyed!"

In July 1960 Jimmy and his band made another trip to London, this time to play at the birthplace of British rock'n'roll, the 2i's coffee bar in Soho, alongside Anglo-American rocker Vince Taylor. Crawford: "We decided to go down to London to try and get discovered, Dick Whittington and his cat and all that. So we took two coach loads from Mansfield and Sheffield down to the 2i's. In those days it was small. The guy on the door wondered what had happened, all those kids trying to get in to see somebody he'd never heard of so he got on the phone and called some agents, telling them there was something funny going on, 'There's some kid pulling a complete capacity, they are out on the pavements.'" Frank White: "When we went down to the 2i's, we all dyed our hair black and took two coach loads of fans. It seemed like a sure-fire thing. Crawford had got this Thames van and he'd got posters all over it and after we'd done the gig, we slept in the van and these louts came and urinated all over it." But for Crawford the trip was well worth it: "An agent turned up from EMI and signed me there and then and I went to EMI's headquarters at Berkeley Square that night and signed a contract with EMI and two managers." A demo

Disc reviews Jimmy's first release

recording of Jimmy and the group was made and sent to Columbia recording manager Norrie Paramor by the managers Roy Tuvey and Morris Sellars. Things weren't quite as straightforward as they seemed. Crawford: "We were signed to Top Rank and then EMI swallowed them up and I then went under Norrie Paramor and there was a chance I wouldn't get a record out after the change. But Norrie listened to the Top Rank artists and picked out the ones he wanted to record and luckily I was one of them and away we went." Jimmy also learned to make all the right moves in his quest to become a pop star. When he was signed up he kept quiet, at the behest of the publicity people, about the fact that he was married, to his childhood sweetheart Maureen (sister of former Sheffield Wednesday manager Howard Wilkinson) and they had a couple of children. "We rented a nine shillings a week house in Aberdeen Street in Walkley. It has been flattened since. I went out and bought an American Oldsmobile car. It was bigger than the house, but it was all part of the image of being a pop star." He also found he couldn't pursue his favourite pastime, motorcycle racing. He told Top Stars: "My record company Columbia feel that it is too dangerous and there is a clause in my contract that bans me from motorcycle racing." Not that Jimmy's driving could be trusted at the best of times: "I once turned the van over, I went through the window and the farmer threatened to sue me for smashing five plant pots. And we'd nearly been killed."

Crawford's first record, as part of a seven-year deal with Columbia, was a latin-american moody ballad, It's Unkind, backed with a typical British rock'n'roll number, Long Stringy Baby.

The punters weren't very kind and it failed to chart. But Unkind did bring work further afield in places like Liverpool, Sunderland and Coventry. Frank Miles: "He was a good looking kid and, let's face it, having a record out in those days was a big thing." And Long Stringy Baby can still be heard in a Dirk Bogarde film, playing on a jukebox in a cafe in Soho.

For the big dances the Ravens expanded to a six-piece with two sax players Norman 'Jock' Horan and Jerry Gilmore from the Twin Cities Beat Group. Twin Cities drummer Pete Wardlow: "He'd got more money than anybody else so he got what he wanted. He came to see us and he'd seen Emile Ford and the Checkmates at the Gaumont so he must have saxes in his band. We turned up one night waiting for our sax players and we got a phone call saying, 'We've joined Jimmy Crawford.'" With the larger line-up the band recorded a record of their own as the Ravens Rock Group for Pye International, two instrumental tracks - The Ghoul Friend, written by the sax player with Lord Rockingham's XI - and Career Girl. With all this impetus as 'recording stars' Jimmy and co were also signed up for a series of package shows around Yorkshire. "It was a big band - two drummers, two sax players and three guitarists. We did a big tour with Clarence Frogman Henry, Tony Orlando, Bobby Vee, Springfields and comic Billy Burden. And the band backed the lot, with difficulty. We didn't know they were going to back the whole

show. It worked out all right but it was a bit of a nightmare at first." Jimmy remembers Tony Orlando as being something of a consummate performer: "He showed a lot of knowledge in the way he worked an audience, he was a very astute person - sort of a 'musical conman'. I learned a lot from him. He'd win his audience over not by his singing or his songs but the gift of the gab."

By spring 1961 Jimmy Crawford was Sheffield's brightest star and released a second single Love Or Money. Producer Norrie Paramor tipped him as, "the voice of 1961, successor to Britain's king of rock Cliff Richard." On June 10, Jimmy performed his new disc on ITV's Thank Your Lucky Stars. However success wasn't long in coming: "Unkind just caused a bit of a stir, with the managers promoting it a bit. It got airplay. But the second one Love or Money didn't need any help." Third single I Love How You Love Me became Jim's biggest hit but it should have been bigger, as he explains: "It had done over 100,000 but the worst piece of luck happened to it. It was selling 10,000 a day just prior to Christmas and it was on Two Way Family Favourites three successive weeks, record of the week, all that sort of stuff, but then EMI, with the record in full flight, went on two weeks holiday, closed the factory and killed the record dead. I've still got a letter from Norrie Paramor apologising. It had sold out but there were no more."

In May 1962 Jimmy appeared in the pop film Play It Cool starring Billy Fury, Shane Fenton and Helen Shapiro. Crawford: "The director was Michael Winner, I think he was experimenting on that Billy Fury film to see how bad he could get before he got good. I got the part after Norrie

Paramor phoned me and told me I Love How You Love Me was doing 10,000 a day and he asked me if I would be interested in doing a film and I said, 'Would I?' I met the director, and that was it." Jim is seen performing Take It Easy backed by a trad-jazz band dressed in chain-gang costumes. "Norrie Paramor wrote the songs for the film but the one he wrote for me must have been written between lunch and sweet because I could write one better in a thick fog with a blindfold on now." On television he was seen as rock singer Ricky Rampant in the BBC play The Big Eat.

Jim was now in demand and was asked to open Dobson's new record bar and teenage showroom in Staniforth Road, Darnall. The Ravens' line-up had changed to include two drummers, Mick Beaumont and Paul Allen, along with Arthur Hutchinson, Frank White and rhythm guitarist Chick Wilson. But, despite the success of I Love How You Love Me, Jimmy's career was about to hit its biggest glitch. Norrie Paramor suggested he should do a Eurovision Song Contest song. "I represented EMI in the Song for Europe, sang the song they told me to, but it didn't get into the top three to get into the Eurovision. And I didn't do another record for nine months and I really was dead after that. In those days you had to be around every two or three months with another record." Crawford continued to record but without success: "I did Don't Worry About Bobby, I Should Have Listened To Mama, Does My Heartache Show and they didn't move so EMI dropped me and I signed to Oriole. I had a couple of releases with them, then a couple with Pye, and even CBS. I got a few airplays but my bubble had burst. But I was also moving in a different direction myself.

Jimmy sings Take It Easy in the film Play Cool

I was moving from rock, which I should have stayed with, to more cabaret style stuff, entertainment and that I think was my big mistake."

As Merseybeat and R&B took over from the earlier sounds of the Sixties Crawford's music began to sound dated, as Dave Berry recalls: "We were all playing at that same time but Jimmy was still from the old school. He was like Cliff Richard and Marty Wilde. But we were aware that Jimmy Crawford was a very popular performer around Sheffield. But sadly he recorded before the Beatles and that was absolute taboo by 1963. Although he was probably the same age as everyone else, he belonged to a different era." In an attempt to keep up with the musical changes, after disbanding the Ravens, Jim re-emerged with a new outfit, Jimmy Crawford and the Messengers, in early 1963. He recorded another single, Another Of Your Toys, with Paramor, but once again it didn't chart. The new four-piece band featured two star players in London-born pianist/singer/harmoni-

Jimmy Crawford and the Messengers

ca player Johnny Alexander and drummer extraordinaire Kenny Slade, freshly poached from the Cruisers. The line-up was completed by ex-Ravens' guitarist Chick Wilson and Gran Lawson on bass. Crawford: "Johnny Alexander came up from Wayfleet. We got snowed in at Buxton and he came up by train to play with us and we couldn't get back to Sheffield. We slept in a hotel foyer. We were together from then on. He eventually left to form the Sheffields and was well in with Stringfellow but he came back years later to join the Jimmy Crawford Blend." As always with Crawford, the act looked and sounded very professional but it was a more rhythm and blues-influenced show and quickly put Crawford's name back on the local scene. Kenny Slade: "It was a good band, they rocked a bit and he put it over good. We used to do Tonight [from West Side Story] latin-styled.

London's GREATEST Ever
OPEN AIR POP FESTIVAL
WHIT MONDAY, 3rd JUNE, 11 a.m. to 6 p.m.
DEL SHANNON • GERRY & The Pacemakers
VINCE TAYLOR • EDEN KANE • KENNY LYNCH
BILLY J. KRAMER & The Dakotas • BRIAN POOLE & The Tremeloes
FREDDIE & The Dreamers

Jimmy Crawford & The Messengers	Rey Anton & M Squad
Screaming Lord Sutch	Mickie Most
Cherry Roland	Robb Storme & The Whispers
Cliff Bennett & The Rebel Rousers	Jackie Lynton & Teenbeats
Tony Holland & The Pack-a-Beats	Johnny, Mike & The Shades
The Cresters	The Golli-Golli Boys
	The Blue Diamonds

· FUN FAIR — REFRESHMENTS ·
BOTWELL—Centre of Hayes, Middx.
by road—near London Airport   by train—25 mins. Paddington
Admission 7/6.   Seat near stage 2/6 extra
Tickets (s.a.e.) from Botwell House, Hayes, Middx.

Nobody had ever heard it done like that."

Like many others, Jimmy and the band made the trip to Germany where their R&B-styled cabaret show was well received. "We did American bases and the clubs. We were playing the music they wanted but there were a lot of entertainment acts around. We followed the Beatles to the Star Club in Hamburg. We had a right eight weeks in Hanover and Hamburg, couldn't believe it. But it was hard work. We ended up going on stage in pyjamas on Sunday. You'd kick off at four on Sunday afternoon, an hour on, an hour off, an hour on... and at seven on Monday morning you'd still be at it. The owner and his 23-stone right-hand man bouncer would sit there in an empty room and watch us on stage at seven o'clock and we'd be in pyjamas to see if they would take a hint. That was what all the bands would do. The lads would get taken over by prostitutes who would adopt them. The lads couldn't find a way to the clinic quick enough. They'd buy them leather coats, booze

Jimmy Crawford with the Chantelles

etc. The lads would get pilled up, poxed up, boozed up and fucked up. I flew my wife over there. We used to live in this 36-seater coach which belonged to a Nottingham band, the Beatmen. Maureen cooked every Sunday for them - roast beef and Yorkshire puddings - and every Englishman in Hamburg would turn up for it."

The Messengers was short-lived. By September '63 Crawford had disbanded them and teamed up with a new band the Shantells, led by guitarist Jim Ryder. Jimmy spotted the band, who were from Scunthorpe, at the Birley Moor Hotel. He also began to introduce comedy into the act. "Everything interests me, nosy I suppose, so I started to play around with it a little bit." Jimmy's act went down well with the American airmen at USAF bases in England. This led to him playing more successful gigs in Germany and, subsequently, Paris for an eight-day stint in October '63. Back in the UK Jimmy and the band recorded a new single Don't Worry About Bobby on which they attempted to get the Phil Spector sound. Jimmy's friend and manager Tony Cooper forecast in Top Stars: "It will be in the charts before Christmas." Sadly it continued Jimmy's run of flops.

As well as performing, Crawford also became an agent with ex-Harlequin Tony Cooper. They set up Mini Entertainments in an office on Eyre Street. "We used to book bands from the Plymouth area and one of them was Rocking Henry and the Hayseeds. The same band used to dress up and become Danny Collins and the somethings and the third trick would be to wrap up in the monster gear so you would get three bands on the same show - and they were all the same band. We ran the agency for three or four years, booked people like the Small Faces and Rod Stewart who actually came to the office. We'd book the bands for a bit of a commission. Then the landlord at the Queens at Maltby rang

up and said he didn't mind the bands but one was complaining about the commission he had to pay out of his £14. It was Ray Stuart. I caught up with him at a show. The bastard! He was a big lad but I was that annoyed with him it wouldn't have made no difference."

A previous attempt at promoting bands was less successful: "One of the biggest troubles I got into was when a guy tapped on the door at Aberdeen Street before I was married. He said he came from Whittington Moor at Chesterfield and he owned a big ballroom, the Carlton. 'I understand you and Dave Berry are the leading lights for rock music round here. I'd like to book you and Dave Berry for four weeks each.' I said, 'Can you organise it?'. He said, 'Yes' and and I said he needed Shane Fenton and the Fentones as well. I said I'd get it set up. Got hold of Berry and Fenton. We booked it up for four months. Shane Fenton was first. Come the opening night, Shane goes along with his dad and the van and band and the gear and the place is boarded up and locked up. So Shane Fenton's dad sues me and it makes headline news in the local Mansfield newspaper. I defended myself with Tony and I called myself Spencer Churchill and he was something like Dick Wray. They made mincemeat of us in the dock. The magistrate said, 'Have you got no idea how to conduct yourselves in a court of law regarding showbusiness?' And we said, 'We can only tell you the truth, sir.' He murdered us did Shane Fenton. I was on with Shane Fenton later at the Finsbury Park Empire. His manager was there. I said to the manager, 'Where's Fenton.' 'He's not arrived yet. Why?' 'Well I hope he sings well with broken teeth.' 'What you are talking about?' 'He's going through that window as soon as he walks in.' Nothing happened of course but he had got us into hot water."

By 1967 Jim had moved firmly into WMC and cabaret work, with comedy an essential part of the show. The Jimmy Crawford Four wore tartan jackets and the line-up often swapped instruments, Jim Ryder playing guitar, bass and drums, Dennis Mathews bass, sax and banjo and Nick Cowling drums and trumpet. He twice won ABC TV's Opportunity Knocks, appeared on the All Winners show and had a 12-week summer season with Solomon King and Don Partridge at Blackpool's Central Pier in 1968. Jimmy's costumes and appearance became more and more outrageous. He started wearing tight fitting satin suits, had his hair permed and grew a luxuriant moustache. He bore more than just a passing resemblance to actor Peter Wyngarde's Jason King character. The show

Jimmy Crawford Four on Opportunity Knocks

Showtime! Jimmy and Big Jim Ryder

resembled more of a variety act with comedy routines centred round Cowling. A trip to South Africa, in March, 1969, was inevitably controversial with the anti-apartheid movement at its most vociferous. Crawford, by now sporting huge sideburns, toured the country with Vera Lynn and Tommy Trinder and had Top Stars on his trail for a picture spread. In Cape Town he was asked by a local newspaper to model clothes. He ended up in an evening suit in midnight blue with waistcoat and matching lapels "in lush gold and blue brocade".

Crawford: "The Jimmy Crawford Four became the Blend, doing impersonations such as PJ Proby, Mick Jagger and crap like that. It was the death of a solo singing career. Dave Berry came to see me at Leeds and hadn't seen me work for a while, and we finished the act with There's No Business Like Showbusiness. And Dave Berry couldn't stop laughing, he couldn't believe it. I should have known better. I said to him, 'That's showbusiness,' thinking he's in a different branch of it to me. Yet we could fill clubs like the

> **JIMMY CRAWFORD: "I Can Make It With You" (CBS).** Jimmy Crawford, says the handout, is one of the most popular club and cabaret entertainers in the country. He was also a swimming champion and motor cycle racer. The Chip Taylor song is quite a strong one and the versatile Mr Crawford does no harm to the ears. They should be proud of him in Sheffield

Record Miror review, March 1970

Showtime at Derby which had acts like Tony Bennett, Billy Eckstine, Sarah Vaughan, but there was only us that could fill it for a fortnight every three months. We played Australia, Rhodesia, South Africa, Gambia, American bases throughout Europe and Vegas with Kenny Rogers. The Americans like a bit of confidence and I moved a lot." From this period is a live recording of Jim and his group at the Embassy II Club in Plymouth, performing with his typical confidence and exuberance Leave Me Alone.

He released a new single, the gentle singa-long ballad Love Wonderful Love in July, 1969, followed by another pleasant ballad I Can Make It With You in April, 1970. In the summer of 1970 Jim made another appearance on Opportunity Knocks. This time he appeared solo. He was a last minute choice for the show's special for the remaining place in the Knokke

Jimmy and Jan Lesley

Song Festival in Belgium. After leaving Sheffield in 1976 to take a pub in Bristol, Jim was still performing and, as the Jimmy Crawford Blend, came second on another TV talent show New Faces. This landed him a spot at the London Palladium behind headliners the Supremes. He also looked to revive his recording career with an updated version of I Love How You Love Me. He has since travelled the world, playing everywhere from Butlins to Las Vegas. In the early Eighties Jim teamed up with another Sheffield singer Jan Lesley. Alan Wood produced an album: "Jimmy has a very fast vibrato and I managed to slow it down. He did a song, With You I'm Born Again, with Jan Lesley and you wouldn't know it was Jimmy Crawford. He said, 'God, that's the best I've ever done.' It was a great version of it, excellent, so much soul and feeling." By 1986 Jim and wife Maureen were running a family hotel in Malta. Two years later they moved back to England and Derby where he still lives and does the occasional cabaret gig. He is also an accomplished artist, and in March,

2000, teamed up with Dave Berry to put on an exhibition of Jimmy's paintings at the antique emporium on Dover Street where Dave and Marthy have a space.

Looking back, Jim reckons he never made more than £1,000 from his hit records - "I was green in those days, and they knew it. The story of my career is out of time, out of place. Every time I have done something good it has been at a time when it didn't count." But Jimmy, now in his early sixties and the first to admit he is not a great singer, has one accolade nobody can take away from him - Sheffield's first pop star.

2. LONG DISTANCE INFORMATION: DAVE BERRY AND THE CRUISERS

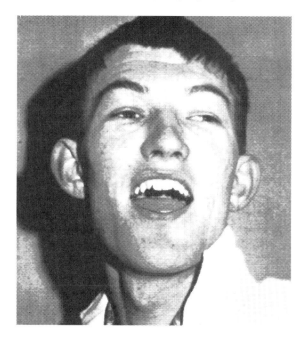

Dave's letter for the Singing In Harmony competition

With eight UK hits and numerous big sellers in countries such as Holland, Woodhouse-born Dave Berry remains the first Sheffield artist to achieve international fame. His most successful period was the Sixties but he has managed to sustain an active and successful career in the music business ever since.

Dave Holgate Grundy's first musical influence was his father Arthur, a Coal Board property repairer who played drums in The New Mayfair dance band. He would interrupt the youngster's sleep by bringing home his fellow musicians to listen to jazz records. At 15 Dave started work at Beighton coke ovens and attended Sheffield Polytechnic to learn welding. Dave was also a promising goalkeeper and played regularly for

Beighton Youth Club in the East Derbyshire League. Music also came quite naturally and in 1958, at the age of 18, he won a rock'n'roll dance contest at Butlins Holiday Camp at Filey, hitting local headlines as "Rock'n'Roll Champion For Beighton?". He also worked as a brickie at Tommy Ward's and he would entertain his mates by singing on the bus home from Sheffield on Saturday nights. Dave teamed up with another pal, Malcolm Green, and called themselves the Dominoes. "It started in 1958. Malcolm decided to buy a guitar and I'd got my dad's drums, just the two of us singing in harmony doing Everly Brothers and Buddy Holly songs. It sounds ridiculous now just guitar and drums but that was the beginning of music here so it wasn't so unusual at the time to have these silly line-ups. We got 15 shillings a night for performing in pubs and we were pretty crude then." The duo were together for around ten months, and in August 1958 they were joint winners, along with singing duo Mickey and Johnnie, in the Sheffield heat of the national Singing In Harmony contest at the Locarno on London Road. In the finals at Manchester Dave and Malcolm sang the Everly Brothers' Wake Up Little Susie backed by the Basil Kirchin Band and came second. This allowed them to get better bookings at dance halls, private functions and clubs, only for Green to receive his call-up papers which ended the Dominoes.

Dave, by now living in Beighton and working

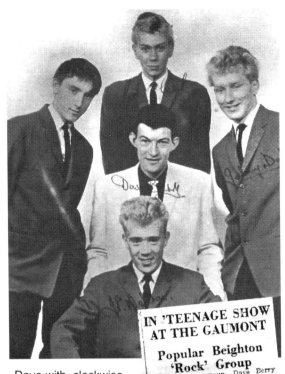

Dave with, clockwise, John Fleet, John Hall, Frank Miles and Alan Taylor

IN 'TEENAGE SHOW AT THE GAUMONT

Popular Beighton 'Rock' Group

A Beighton group, Dave Berry and the Cruisers, are to appear in the 'Teenage Show' at Sheffield Gaumont next Saturday, following a successful audition after which they were booked immediately.

Members of the group are David Grundy (vocal), Alan Taylor (rhythm guitarist), Frank Miles (lead guitarist), John Fleet (piano), Ray Cuffling (drums).

The boys are well known in the area through playing regularly for 'rock' sessions at the Leeds Arms, Wales, and Swallownest Miners' Welfare.

The group have been together about five months and the vocalist and guitarists were in the very successful 'Frantic Four' rock group which is now disbanded.

as an electric welder, would go along and watch another outfit from the village, the Frantic Four, led by singer Brian 'Chuck' Fowler. "Chuck would invite me up and I'd sing about half a dozen Chuck Berry songs, just as a jam really." Chuck Fowler: "He was all right, pretty much the same as he is now, a distinctive sort of voice and he'd obviously got some appeal." Eventually Dave joined the Frantic Four as drummer: "Then Chuck did an Elvis on us and did two years national service. So the band split." He then teamed up with lead guitarist Frank Miles to form a new outfit in 1960: "I approached Dave to do the singing as he was also into Chuck Berry." They were joined by John Fleet from nearby Killamarsh, first on piano then bass, and Alan Taylor, a neighbour of Dave's, on rhythm guitar to form the first line-up of the Cruisers. They played at venues such as Swallownest Miners Welfare with Dave still on the drums before Ray Cuffling took over. Following in the footsteps of Chuck Fowler who named himself after Chuck Berry, Dave decided to use the other half of his hero's name and became Dave Berry. "It sounds strange now but Chuck Berry really was unknown in Britain at the time. Those

sort of rock'n'roll people, especially the black artists, were not really known apart from by musicians who used to listen to their music." The Cruisers, as with with a lot of local combos, also had stage-names with Frank Miles calling himself JP Nelson, Alan Taylor was Wilson Shane and John Fleet was known as Red Fleet.

Dave Berry: "People liked us because we were doing something different. We still played a mixture of stuff, not just r'n'b but chart stuff of the time and rock'n'roll. Joe Cocker was the same. But it was not just me it was the whole band. John Fleet had a jazzy feel, Frank Miles was stationary and intense, playing his Chuck Berry riffs, while Alan Taylor had been to Chelsea Art College and was more arty. It was that combination, not that we were aware of it at the time. And people came along to hear songs they hadn't heard before." Berry may not have had a great voice but he had charisma and he picked some great material, predominately Chuck Berry. He had a way of putting a song over and he was probably the first one local followers remember doing Bo Diddley. He also had a great act with all the mystique. He started off with the Gene Vincent hunch over the microphone and the Elvis leg wiggle before developing his own act. He also had a knockout band.

Initially, Dave and the boys did a lot of their own promotion by going round and getting bookings themselves: "I don't believe in the word 'luck', we worked for what achieved in those early days. We'd built up four residencies which gave us the opportunity to turn professional. We were doing four regular gigs a week and they were small venues - the Leeds Arms at Kiveton Park, Monarco Ballroom, Worksop, Co-op Hall at Frecheville and Darnall Public Hall." Dave's family also helped out: "My mum was on the cloakroom, dad was helping taking the money and somebody's friend putting the records on with Martin my cousin. It was very family-based."

Five months after getting together Dave and the Cruisers had a steady following and suc-

Dave and the band on stage at Farm Grounds

cessfully auditioned for the Saturday Morning Teenage Show at the Gaumont Cinema. They soon became one of the show's leading names. "To get on the Teenage Show was very good. What people forget is that it was great preparation for doing the big theatres." They also performed at the city fair on Farm Grounds as one of the attractions in the Telegraph and Star talent contest. In September 1960 Berry hit the national newspapers with a piece in the Daily Mirror about his size 12 feet. With the headline 'A rocker - on his uppers', Dave jokingly bemoaned his outsize shoe repair bills. However, it was a useful bit of publicity for a young rock'n'roller about to turn fully pro.

At the beginning of '61 Dave and the group consolidated their following with more regular gigs at places like the Queens Hotel at Maltby, Swallownest Miners Welfare and the upstairs dance hall at Frecheville Co-op which was a favourite Wednesday night haunt for the group's followers. Often there were other up and coming musicians in the audience such as Dave Hopper: "We all stood in a row in front of the band. We weren't bothered about birds or dancing at that time, we were just mesmerised watching the band." Mal Hooley: "I thought John Fleet's bass playing was fantastic." In April Dave and the band, made the then long, arduous trip down to London, to appear at what was then the home of

British rock'n'roll, the 2i's coffee bar in Soho. Frank Miles remembers the gig: "Berry must have been very nervous. Somebody came up and said he sounded like a male Eartha Kitt. I thought, 'Well he's not supposed to,' although I did notice his voice was trembling. It'd got to be nerves. I don't blame him, we were all nervous. That was the first night and once we'd been accepted they wanted us to come back. I think we'd gone down for the week and we played there two or three times. They were that used to folks going down into the 2i's and playing Shadows-type stuff, they thought nobody could play anything else. So of course when we started up we were playing all Chuck Berry and they're thinking, 'God, what's going off here?'"

A look through the band's 1961 diary reveals just how busy they were, playing four to six nights a week in and out of town with fees ranging from £10 to £20 per gig which was good money when an average week's wage was around £8-£10. Frank Miles: "I was working for a fiver a week and if I went out and played three nights I'd get something like £7.50. So I thought, 'What am I working for? I might as well do something I like doing, 'cos we all loved it.'" By late '61 the band were playing regularly at rock'n'roll dance venues in surrounding areas like Doncaster, Worksop, Barnsley, Scunthorpe and Lincoln, travelling around in their eye-catching Bedford Dormobile van emblazoned with 'Dave Berry and the Cruisers' down each side. Another residency was every Monday night in an upstairs room of the Albert pub, Barkers Pool. The session was called Bluesville

DARNALL PUBLIC HALL

BARNARDISTON ROAD

EVERY THURSDAY
COMMENCING 2nd FEBRUARY

BIG BEAT NITE

WITH

DAVE BERRY AND
THE CRUISERS

YOUR RESIDENT DISC JOCKEY MIKE

NON STOP ROCK 'N' ROLL 8 p.m. to 11 p.m.

ADMISSION – TWO SHILLINGS & SIXPENCE

Sissons & Son, Ltd., 31—33 Bridge Street, Worksop.

Local gigs. Card below shows wrong address; it should have read Barkers Pool

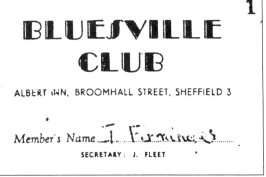

BLUESVILLE CLUB

ALBERT INN, BROOMHALL STREET, SHEFFIELD 3

Member's Name J. Firminns

SECRETARY : J. FLEET

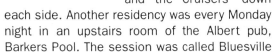

and was organised by Berry, with 'J. Fleet' as secretary.

When Alan Taylor left to go to university, the lead guitarist with Johnny Tempest's Mariners Roy Barber became the Cruisers' new rhythm guitarist. "I was a bit mystified as I'd only just started playing really. I'd only been with Tempest about 18 months. Somebody must've told them about me and Berry and Fleet came down to the Dog and Partridge in Attercliffe. I don't remember them coming down there before, they were big time. I was into the Shadows and it was years before I was into what Berry was into and I remember thinking, 'How am I going to play Georgia On My Mind?' 'cos I knew they did that and the thought of that was intimidating, lots of chords." After Ray Cuffling and then Brian Gee, the Cruisers' third drummer was the solid and precise, yet quiet and unassuming John Hall ('Johnny Dale') from Frecheville but when he fell ill with jaundice a stand-in was sought. Kenny Slade was asked to help out: "Berry came into the betting office at Swallownest and asked me if I was Ken Bates [Kenny's real name] and I said, 'Who wants to know?' He asked me if I could play with the band but I said I didn't know anything about Bill Haley, Elvis Presley and all that rock'n'roll stuff. I was into Count Basie, Dizzy Gillespie, Duke Ellington, etc." Roy Barber: "We knew nothing about him except that he was supposed to be an amazing drummer that could play with big bands." Kenny Slade: "I'd never heard of Chuck Berry, it was all foreign to me." Some guidance came from fellow drummer John Riley: "I had to show Ken how to play a back-beat. I think he was unfamiliar with it, being a jazz drummer. He couldn't catch the beat on stuff like Johnny B Goode and Beautiful Delilah, I kept just telling him to just play, bang... bang... bang!" Kenny became a powerful rock drummer and gave a new impetus to the Cruisers' sound. Unfortunately for John Hall, Kenny's power-

house drumming made such an impression on Berry he decided to keep him in the band. Roy Barber: "Berry knew a bit about drumming from his father and decided that Kenny was altogether so much better." Kenny Slade: "Three weeks later I'm off to Manchester to buy a kit - a Trixon, green sparkle." He became a popular figure with the group's followers, but Kenny was constantly at odds with the rest of the band, probably due to his more mature musical outlook. Roy Barber: "He'd got no respect for what we were doing. It was all a bit beneath him the rock'n'roll stuff. But at the same time we were intimidated by him because he was older, wiser and a better drummer technically and a better musician than for the purpose we needed. There was a certain crudity to what we needed. We were doing basic rhythm and blues stuff, you didn't want sophistication. Kenny was trying to do that and, to be fair, he didn't really mix with the rest of the band." This led to heated arguments and, on occasion, fighting with the other Cruisers. Subsequently, Kenny had to go and the band were on the lookout for another drummer. Ironically, Kenny beat them to it when he announced he was leaving to join Jimmy Crawford's new band the Messengers. "Crawford and Tony Cooper came round to my house in their matching pair of pink Vauxhall Crestas and offered me three quid a week more!" Roy Barber: "It was all really underhand, although when Kenny announced that he was going with Crawford it was the best news that Berry had heard in years!" Stroller's drummer Graham Swift helped out briefly until a replacement was found in Pete Thornton who had impressed with his tight, solid playing with Doncaster band Lee Walker and the Travellers. Unlike Slade, Thornton was quite a suave character, although both men had a penchant for gambling. Roy Barber: "We still drifted away from that raw rhythm & blues thing. He was a tidy drummer but he was 'twee'. It was probably Berry again recognising his drumming ability, but not recognising what was necessary."

By now Berry's stage-act had become highly visual, developed from influences like Gene Vincent, Elvis and Chuck Berry. Pete Stringfellow: "Dave Berry was the sexiest thing I had ever seen on a stage. I thought he was brilliant." Hunching and creeping around the stage, he'd use anything that caught his eye. He would look into the ear of one of the band or simply pick up a cigarette-end. He got everybody's attention with his antics. Berry: "I used to read a lot about American singers who did somersaults in the aisles, while British singers like

Kenny, Dave, Roy and Frank in Trafalgar Square

Go Johnny go: Frank, Dave and Roy

Adam Faith and Cliff would just come on and sing. I began developing my act at the Esquire, which had a central support in the middle of the stage. I did stupid things with this. People liked it. Now when I go on stage I look around to see what I can work with - curtains, all sorts of strange things. I just do it. I don't rehearse. That would just kill it." Terry Thornton summed up Berry's appeal: "He is an artist you have to see. He has a tremendous visual appeal. He seems to put over a mass hypnosis. Even those who profess not to like him can't help watching him. Even I find it hard to tear myself away when he's performing - and I've seen him hundreds of times."

A big part of Berry and the band's appeal were the songs, obscure, yet excellent material that they would introduce to audiences and soon make their own. Dave: "I always liked to do unusual songs. People used to come along to our shows because they knew we'd do numbers they'd never heard of before." These would include Sanford Clark's Go On Home, the Coasters' Shoppin' For Clothes, Johnny Cash's Five Feet High And Rising, Jesse Hill's Ooh-Poo-Pah-Do (the latter would attract much audience participation in its wailing intro). Gems like Diddley Daddy and Bring It To Jerome from Bo Diddley and, of course, lesser known Chuck Berry masterpieces such as Down Bound Train, Too Pooped To Pop and the great jungle tale Jo Jo Gunne. They also did some novelty things, with Berry and John Fleet duetting on the Stan Freberg novelty monologue John and Marsha, or the Highwaymen's sugary pop/folk song Gypsy Rover featuring the melodic whistling of Frank Miles - hardly rock'n'roll. Original instrumental numbers were also featured including Cruisin' and Tombsville along with covers which gave the Cruisers a chance to shine like the Ventures' Ram Bunk Shush, the Shadows' Nivram and Big Noise From Winnetka in which drummer Kenny Slade would go round the kit and end up playing the drum solo across the strings of Frank Miles' guitar. Dave Berry: "When Kenny left I used to do it. Obviously the sticks weren't controlling what was being played. I was just hitting the strings and the guitarist was doing the playing."

Evidence of just how good the band was exists on a tape recording live at the Plaza, Handsworth, from the summer of 1962. They perform Roll Over Beethoven, Hoochie Coochie Man, Memphis, Sweet Little 16, I'm Coming Home, Georgia On My Mind and No Money Down while the Cruisers play Blue Moon and Cruisin', the latter featuring Kenny Slade doing his round-the-kit solo. After Slade's departure, Berry would take over the drums on Chuck Berry's Guitar Boogie while drummer Pete Thornton came to the front to offer humorous asides and bits of distorted nursery rhymes in between Frank Miles' inventive guitar passages. This type of feature number always went down well wherever the band performed and it was the combination of both Berry and the Cruisers that made them such a popular and influential force on the local scene as Alan Wood testifies: "The Cruisers were by far the best live band around at that time, absolutely sensational."

In 1963 Berry and the Cruisers went to Germany to play for a month. Although it was reported in Top Stars that the group were having a good time, the band don't remember it that way. Berry: "It was absolutely disastrous. I hated everything about it. We arrived over there with a so-called contract and were told it was two 45 minutes per night which was our normal set. We finished up doing an hour on, an hour off from like eight o'clock at night till three in the morning. Saturdays we'd start at something like eight at night until six o'clock the following morning with an hour on and an hour off. To this day I could never understand how anybody could come back and say that it put the bands together. Someone did say that they heard us when we came back and thought the band was tighter. It could've been for the musicians, but for the guy out front, involved in the theatrical side of it, I found I couldn't sustain it for five or six hours. It lost it for me because we didn't have enough material. We'd be repeating stuff and half playing songs we didn't really know or probably like. It's very difficult to play six hours a night and do anything new." Roy Barber: "I found it horrific, we all did. It was just incredible hard work. The living accommodation was terrible, it was more like a dormitory than a bedroom. The owner of the club used to get roaring drunk and he'd come up with these Alsatians scaring you to death while you were asleep in bed. We ate badly and we didn't come back with as much money as we were supposed to do because when we got there they said, 'We forgot to mention tax and you were supposed to pay so much for your living accommodation.' I came back with perhaps 30 or 40 quid and the rest of the band spent their money flying back. Of course when we came back to Sheffield it was a bit of prestige. You'd been to Germany and the last people who'd been to Germany were your dads under different circumstances. Ours were tougher!"

Back on English soil they were topping the bill at rock and beat shows around the country at venues like Boston Gliderdrome, Manchester Oasis, Cleethorpes' Cafe Dansant, Hanley Place, the Picador Club in Blackpool and the Floral Hall, Morecambe (nicknamed Florrie Hall, Malcolm). It was at Morecambe that Berry and the boys headlined over an up and coming group from the south calling themselves the Rolling Stones! Roy Barber: "They were totally amazed by us and we outclassed them without a doubt. The Stones were discovering the music through us. We were copying Chuck Berry, but they were copying Dave Berry copying Chuck Berry, which was a compliment in a way, but the Cruisers, like the Stones, had earned a reputation as a top driving R&B outfit." At out of town gigs Berry and co started to come in contact with other bands who also had similar musical inclinations as their own. Roy Barber: "It was a revelation. Of the bands we respected in Sheffield, there wasn't any of them that could compare to say the Pete McClain & The Dakotas or the Big Three. They stopped you in your tracks."

In the wake of the Beatles, record companies were on the look out for northern combos playing this revitalised American music. Roy Barber: "The time was right, it was happening all over the place." Doncaster Baths was a regular gig for Dave and the lads and it was there, supporting Freddie and the Dreamers, that Decca Records A&R man Mike Smith, along with Mickie Most, went to check them out. Suitably impressed, a recording test was arranged for Berry and after delivering the goods with a song entitled Tongue Twistin', Decca signed the Beighton rocker. Initially Mike Smith suggested Dave change his name, probably to avoid confusion with the other two Berrys - Chuck and fellow Brit Mike. They suggested 'Dave Rand' which caused great amusement among Dave and the band. Thankfully, in the end, it was decided to keep his more familiar name and in August, 1963, Dave and the group recorded two tracks for their first single in the label's West Hampstead studio. Chuck Berry's Memphis Tennessee had been popular in their live shows and a slightly rearranged version was designated as the A-side, coupled with a cover of Tossin' And Turnin' which had been a million seller for Bobby Lewis in the States.

With impressive publicity from Decca, Memphis Tennessee sold well, despite being voted a miss on Juke Box Jury. Berry also made an appearance on Granada Television's Scene At 6:30 on September 17, 1963. Berry was accompanied by Frank Miles on guitar and they were both, for some reason, wearing flowered Hawaiian shirts. After the appearance Dave and Frank quickly returned to Sheffield where they joined the rest of the band for their gig at Frechville Church Hall. On October 12, Dave was seen in his more familiar leather gear, creeping on to a mock railway platform on the big Saturday TV pop show Thank Your Lucky Stars. As the record entered the UK charts at number 20 on October 20, the Sheffield Star proclaimed 'Sheffield Blues Singer Hits The Hit Parade With His First Record', along with a picture of the

group posing in Barker's Pool taxi rank. Dave's success also, in a roundabout way, helped namesake Chuck to his biggest hit to date when Pye Records decided to issue the original of Memphis Tennessee, coupled with Let It Rock, which subsequently climbed to number six in October. Dave's version had stalled at number 19 in September, staying in the charts for 13 weeks.

Berry, after three years working his rather large socks off in Sheffield to little avail despite pre-empting the rhythm and blues boom by almost four years, had finally arrived. "I must admit we are grateful to the Liverpool lads for giving our type of music such a boost, but we don't want anyone to think we are simply cashing in on the beat trend. Our style is pure rhythm and blues and we haven't changed one iota in four years," he said at the time. The band's local followers were delighted to see the record become a hit and in a personal thank you message in Top Stars, Dave and the Cruisers said: "We'll give you another one soon!" The group then undertook their first major nationwide tour in November '63. The package also featured Freddie and the Dreamers, Brian Poole and the Tremeloes, Susan Singer (cousin of Helen Shapiro), the Searchers and Dusty Springfield who was making her first solo tour. The Cruisers also found themselves backing Dusty which, as Roy Barber recalls, was quite demanding. "She'd done I Only Want To Be With You which was a big production with a big band and it was only on the night before the tour opened we

found out we were backing her. We got sent the record and some music. We had to collect some new suits from the Toggery in Manchester and then have a rehearsal in the afternoon. Of course it was hopeless. We couldn't do a song like that, we were a rhythm and blues group. Musically, it must have been awful. It made us look really stupid because we were billed in the programme as being 'outstanding musicians, not your normal run-of-the mill'. They really dropped us in it." But on the road Roy and co had a lot of fun with other members of the tour. "There were a lot of jokes being played with peashooters, especially on the last night."

Dave also found himself being taken to court after the success of Memphis Tennessee when his management company Martin Yale took him to the High Court after they had not received a percentage of his earnings as agreed in a five-year contract signed in November 1962. Dave told the Star: "This could mean complete ruin. Martin Yale has never done anything for me. Until I had my first record I hardly ever heard from him at all. If I lose I will be finished." Dave eventually settled the action out of court.

There were also the first signs of unrest in the band when for the next single the Cruisers found themselves relegated to the B-side, a moody version of the Muddy Waters' blues classic Hoochie Coochie Man, another song the band had been performing for about 18 months prior to the recording. Roy Barber explains: "The sad thing was, nobody at Decca wanted to know, we were too crude for them. They weren't getting our sound, it wasn't working for them or for us. They were trying to turn us into the Tremeloes or something. They didn't understand what a group should sound like. Most bands weren't capable of making a decent record but, in theory, the Cruisers were. The Stones obviously thought so." The original British cover of Buddy Holly's Not Fade Away was cut by Dave Berry with the Cruisers for Decca. Apparently Buddy's former manager and record producer Norman Petty was quite impressed upon hearing it, but the UK hit version was by the Rolling Stones who had become label-mates with Berry on Decca. Dave Berry: "We were all playing the music from the same source. We were all doing John Lee Hooker, Muddy Waters, Bo Diddley and Buddy Holly tracks. The Stones had been doing Not Fade Away live on stage and I had." Roy Barber also recalls how the Stones may have come to put their version out: "We did a half-an-hour set in the studio and Decca recorded it. We did Not Fade Away and some Bo Diddley stuff with maracas, including You Better Move On, which were totally obscure to Decca. The Stones were releasing records through Decca and they quite obviously listened to the tape and made a hit record out of it." Replacing The Cruisers on record were a group of elite session players who included guitarists Jim Sullivan and Jimmy Page, bass player John Paul Jones, pianist Reg Guest and John Bonham on drums.

this is it!!

Dave Berry   DECCA F11937   The Crying Game

Direction & Agency
DANNY BETESCH
Kennedy St. Artistes
Limited,
14, Piccadilly,
Manchester.

Music Publishers
SOUTHERN MUSIC
8, Denmark Street,
London, W.C.2

This line-up was used on Dave's next A-side, a rip-roaring version of Arthur Crudup's My Baby Left Me, featuring tremendous lead guitar from Jimmy Page. It only reached number 37 in January '64 but it helped to further establish Berry's name. For the next single he went for a more overtly commercial song, Baby It's You. Written by Bacharach, David and Williams, it had been a US hit for female group the Shirelles but had been popularised in the UK by the Beatles' live performance of the song. It proved to be a move in the right direction as in April '64 it made it to number 27. More major packages followed with Dave and co touring with the likes of Adam Faith, Roy Orbison and three young American girls, the Ronettes, who had all the band drooling. Roy Barber recalls one of the stars: "Adam Faith would turn up in his Roller and we'd never been that close to somebody who owned a Rolls Royce. He was a very decent bloke. He'd chat to you and not patronise you. There was no side to him, no 'big-time'. One of the better pop stars."

Berry's own credentials as a bona fide pop star were confirmed in September 1964 when he released the song that was to become his signature tune. The Crying Game was a complete departure from the rhythm and blues that had characterised his sound until then. Written especially for him by Geoff Stephens, The Crying Game was a slow, spooky piece of pop music featuring equally spooky guitar from Big Jim Sullivan. It became Berry's first big hit, reaching number five in August '64 and paving the way for a long-term, successful career. There was further recognition as Dave and the Cruisers laid down tracks at the Cavern Club in Liverpool for inclusion on a live album, along with other British beat groups.

Although success meant much more work for Dave and the Cruisers, unrest had begun to set in among the band. "It was never a personal thing with the original band," says Dave. "I was the owner of the vehicle - I was the only driver, no one else would take a driving lesson. I was the guy who sorted out the equipment in the afternoon. If it wasn't working I'd be dashing along to Woodhouse to have an amp repaired. There for an hour and a half and then dashing back, while the rest of the band were sat at home." Berry had become the focal point of the act causing the band to start to show lack of interest. "There were things like when we did our first radio show for the BBC. I remember being in hotels and saying, 'It's on at half-past five,' or whatever it was, and they couldn't even be bothered to come out of the hotel dining-room to listen to the programme we'd just

recorded. And there was the occasion we were doing four numbers for a live radio show at lunchtime. I got there and the band said, 'We went to pick Pete up and he wasn't

DAVE BERRY

Q. I heard that The Cruisers, Dave Berry's backing group were leaving him. Is this true? (Danny Martin, Crosby, Liverpool.).

A. "Fraid so Danny. The group (pictured right with Dave) were not satisfied with their wages, goes the story. Dave's new backing group will be another Sheffield group The Frank White Combo.

there.' So I actually put the drum track down, did the harmony and then the lead vocals as well. So somewhere in the BBC archives there are four tracks where I'm on drums, backing vocals and singing lead. Then you go round somewhere and somebody wouldn't be ready because they got back late after being out with the girlfriend all afternoon. So you can see why I got disillusioned by musicians at that time. They sound trivial now, but that's what happens."

Because he was doing most of the organising, Dave felt he deserved a bigger cut of the proceeds. "When success starts to come along, one starts to think, 'Well maybe I should be the one who should get a bit more out of it?'" Roy Barber: "There's always somebody in the band who does things, the running about, but Dave had got the van. We didn't have any transport at the time." Putting the rest of the group on wages hurt them bitterly, especially Frank Miles who had originally formed the band with Berry. Eventually the band decided that in order to get some recognition of their own, they would have to go their own way. Berry showed his displeasure by parting company with the band before the date they had set to leave, compounding the ill-feeling even more. When the split came, many of their followers thought that would be it. Dave Hopper: "When Berry split with that band he lost his sound really. It was like the end of an era

once they'd gone." Ernie Booth: "I thought that was the end of Berry." The split was aired in November, 1964, Top Stars with one promoter stating that, "Even if the Cruisers had had a change of vocalist in the early days, it would have been a setback but they were so good on their own account that it certainly wouldn't have been a disaster." Dave Berry: "In all their appearances the Cruisers did the first three numbers on their own before I came on the stage. It was up to them to make the most of it but they were slow in putting themselves across."

Following the split, the original Cruisers attempted to continue working as a band in their own right but were hampered by being teamed up, thanks to a Doncaster club agent, with singer Tony Lindell. His pretty-boy looks and Cliff Richard-esque presentation were far removed from the band's tough R&B approach and it wasn't long before they parted company too. Pete Thornton left soon after to be replaced by one John Firminger who made his drumming debut at the Esquire on December 13, 1964. But his stay was to be short-lived. The band found bookings hard to come by, and they soon realised that without Dave Berry they meant very little outside Sheffield and decided to call it a day. Roy Barber: "We had to try it because the alternative was to go back to work. Of course we'd got to face all the Sheffield public as one minute we were stars and the next minute we were not. What is sad is that whatever the Cruisers had they lost once they stepped out of Sheffield. They were never appreciated, apart from by other musicians." Berry simply recruited a readymade set of 'Cruisers' - the Frank White Combo. Frank White: "He just kept on at me until I had to put it to the rest of the band." John Riley: "Berry just wanted Frank really, he intended to keep Pete Thornton but when he went with

The Cruisers: Pete Thornton, Roy Barber, John Fleet and Frank Miles with new singer Tony Lindell

Dave with Frank White and John Riley

the old Cruisers I joined."

Berry also dabbled in acting. In 1964 Dave got the starring role as Bongo Herbert in the stage musical Expresso Bongo at Westcliff-On-Sea, apparently beating Adam Faith for the part. "I couldn't believe my ears when I was asked to take the part," Dave told the Sheffield Star. "I just burst out laughing. I've only been in school plays before but I'm sure I'll enjoy this, although I've never been more nervous." Was he trying to become an all-round entertainer? "My management thought it would be a good idea to try and branch out. I acted and did all the songs, Voice In The Wilderness, The Shrine On The Second Floor, etc." Three years later Dave enrolled on an acting course with Miss Helen Goss, one of London's top acting coaches, with a view to going into films. She told Top Stars: "It is difficult to say how long it will take for Dave to complete the course. It varies from person to person, but I am teaching him in his spare time until he attains the standard necessary for him to go into films." The only film he did appear in was The Ghost Goes Gear in 1966 a typical

Dave receives Top Stars Special Awards for top singer and top group from Star reporter Richard Redden

lightweight pop outing in which Berry is seen singing Mama up a tree. The film starred the Spencer Davis Group and Nicholas Parsons.

The Crying Game finally established Dave Berry as a major star, despite the relative failure of the follow-up, One Heart Between Two, which only made number 41. By 1965 he was house-hunting in Derbyshire, looking for a big old house with enough land to have a swimming pool built. He and the new Cruisers were in demand seven nights a week across the country as well as making more TV appearances on Top Of The Pops, Thank Your Lucky Stars, Ready Steady Go and Scene At 6.30.

It was also around this time that he met the man who had been such a big inspiration, Chuck Berry. How did Dave find him? "Awful. I went over to Manchester and met him there. We went

Dave meets Chuck

to the hotel and picked him up and took him to the theatre, but there was no communication. He's not a very nice person and I'm speaking just as many other people would. If you met the guy in the pub he'd be the guy people would be smacking in the mouth every few weeks!"

The new Cruisers also got a chance to share the limelight when they had their own single out, a cover of Bob Dylan's It Ain't Me Babe. At the session Dave had also put his vocal to the song but told Top Stars: "Their version was much better than mine." It Ain't Me Babe was released on the same day, March 12, 1965, as Berry's new single, a cover of Bobby Goldsboro song Little Things. With its distinctive arrangement featuring 12-string guitar, Little Things went on to emulate the success - and chart position - of The Crying Game. Berry and the band also played an increasingly rare home town date on the same bill as the Rolling Stones at the City Hall on March 11. Another package tour followed in May with Billy Fury, Brian Poole and the Tremeloes and Pretty Things, although it was Berry who got rave reviews, his set being described as "nothing short of brilliant, professional, stylish, attractive, dramatic." Guitarist Dave Hawley once filled in for Frank White with the Cruisers: "Dave Berry said, 'Can you play the Jim Sullivan guitar solo on The Crying Game?' 'No'. 'You've got three hours to learn it'. I'd got the De-Armond foot-pedal so I was half way there, it was just the tricky bit at the end. Instead I sang it, and I'm sure Berry thought I'd really played it."

In June Berry appeared at Brighton at the first British pop song festival, along with the Moody Blues, Marianne Faithful, Helen Shapiro and the Ivy League. He performed the Ray Davies' song This Strange Effect and made a big impact by appearing in a striking all-white stage outfit. The following month Dave represented Britain in another song festival in Knokke-le-Zoot in Belgium, performing Can I Get It From You? In November Dave and the Cruisers were added to another nationwide UK tour starring US singer Gene Pitney. The end of the year saw Dave receive silver discs for topping both the Dutch and Belgium charts with This Strange Effect, plus two awards from Top Stars. Back in Sheffield he made an appearance at the City Hall, performing this time in the Ballroom. "I was wondering what the reaction would be," Dave told Top Stars. "But it turned out to be one of the best receptions I have ever had." By the end of 1965 he had established himself in the Netherlands with, in December, no less than four records in the top 20 at the same time - This Strange Effect (still the biggest selling records of all time in the country), I'm Gonna Take You There, Can I Get It From You? and Little Things.

In August '66 Dave made another appearance in Sheffield at the Gaumont, on the same bill as the Small Faces. Dave made a great impression with local followers such as Jo and Sue who wrote in Top Stars: "At last Sheffield has a top

star that shines above all the rest. He was so professional and bewitching that he stole the show."

Following the departure of Frank White and John Riley, the Cruisers were joined by Hillbilly Cats drummer Roger Jackson and the guitarist with the Sheffields, Roy Ledger: "I'd known Berry since I was about 15. I used to go with him to Hathersage Baths swimming regularly. All the groups used to go out there." Roy and Roger were also in Dave Berry's Showbiz 11 football team. In a photo taken at Beighton, Berry's team included Cruisers Roger Jackson, Roy Ledger and Allie Taylor, guitarist Pete Jackson, Dave Hawley roadie Keith 'Sam' Simpson and Ron Barton, all looking frozen to death and far from pro-footballers. How did Roy find it working for Berry?: "Great. Bigger audiences, bigger theatres, we went on the continent... The band weren't much good though. I never enjoyed playing with that band. They weren't as good as the Sheffields."

In 1966 Berry enjoyed another big hit, albeit his final one, with a song from another US songwriter BJ Thomas. Mama, a soppy waltz-time ditty full of maternal gratitude, was a far cry from his R&B and rock'n'roll roots. There were more singles over the next three years, including the stomping If You Wait For Love, another Bobby Goldsboro song, which was a hit for him in Holland; Stranger, originally a hit for country star Lefty Frizzell; Just As Much As Ever which Dave later described as a "diabolical mistake"; Tuesday Afternoon, a song written by the Moody Blues which had been a big US hit for the group; and (Do I Figure) In Your Life written and recorded by British group Honeybus. The latter's B-side Letisha, a song co-written by Dave and guitarist Alan Taylor, was recorded in London and featured ex-Cruisers Frank White, Taylor, Roger Jackson and Pete Jackson providing the backing. He also recorded Change Our Minds, written by ex-Cruiser Frank Miles with Tom Rattigan and Chris Stainton (who played piano on the track). In May 1969, Dave cut Huma-Lama, on which he

Cruisin' in '66: Roy Ledger, Pete Cliffe, Dave, Roger Jackson and Alan Taylor

was backed by a band called Sponge made up of regular Cruisers and session musicians. That was followed in 1970 by Chaplin House written by two members of Hotlegs (later to become 10cc). But none of them registered in Britain. The third set of Cruisers worked with Berry for two years before he decided to make another change. Roy Ledger: "He didn't have any hits and the work started dropping off. It sort of faded out."

By the summer of love, in 1967, Dave had adopted the full hippie regalia, and was pictured on the September edition of Top Stars in tassled jacket and draped with the full "bangles, baubles, beads and bells," as the magazine put it. "It's fantastic," said Berry of the new craze. "I don't know whether it will last and I don't care. If people can just be nice to each other for six months it'll solve a few problems. It's better than shouting and fighting with each other for six months." He was also due to pay his first visit to the USA, and the home of flower power, San Francisco, in particular. The Stateside visit never materialised, something that Dave attributes to the lack of interest in him in America and it remains one of his biggest disappointments that he never played the States. He also noticed changes in his audience in the UK: "The kids are somehow more receptive and more willing to chat with you. They're not as inhibited."

Splitting with the Cruisers at the beginning of 1968, Dave moved more into cabaret and universities and needed a band with more scope. Birmingham-based seven-piece the Richard Kent Style, who had previously backed Del Shannon and Paul Jones, fitted the bill. "I saw them backing both these and I thought they were brilliant," Dave told Top Stars, "I need a bigger sound and that's what this group provides." This combination worked together well for a couple of years before Berry hired Sheffield club/cabaret band

the Daizies. Drummer Roger Harrison: "We played with Berry when he needed us and carried on working ourselves doing our own act as the Daizies. It opened up a whole new set of better venues and a lot more travelling abroad." As Dave Robinson also recalls, their link-up with Berry also gave the Daizies a much-needed kick up the arse: "We were stale, so it was great. We had to think. For me it was fabulous as the lead guitarist 'cos it was a challenge to try and learn Jimmy Page's and Jim Sullivan's solos. Roy Barber showed me quite a few of them." The Daizies were known for their comedy act but with Berry they were required to play it straight. "Before Berry came on we used to do a Beatles' medley, between five and ten minutes long. This was unusual because, prior to that, it would just start with Berry. It was his suggestion." Berry: "We had a really tight show. They were a great harmony band and they'd start off and then I'd come on stage for about 40 minutes."

Comedy did creep into the show, although most of it was aimed at Berry himself, thanks to guitarist Spud West. Roger Harrison explains: "On stage he wanted it, y'know, Dave Berry creeping about and us providing the music. And of course it didn't work like that. Not when you had someone like Spud in the band. Lots of things used to happen. Tell Spud not to do a thing and you could guarantee he would. Berry always used to come on stage with hardly any lighting, just a pencil spot on his face. That was the time when Spud used to often do something. Berry didn't like it a lot of the time, certainly not when he was on stage. Quite often the audience used to laugh. It was alien to what he was intending to give off as a show. It used to ruin it for him but he used to laugh about it when he got over it. It was good playing with Berry, I enjoyed that period. We used to do a lot of gigs with all the well known Sixties bands. Lots of people used to come and see Berry, people like

Vote for your top pop favourites inside

Free pin up in this issue The Pink Floyd

Adam Faith, and that was nice all that." Dave also remembers the time with fondness. "When the Daizies were backing me, those years were the best laughs I've ever had. Then it became a pain after a couple of years. The things that you found funny, you didn't find funny anymore. But in the early days we had some really, really good laughs. It was a very, very funny band."

Dave was still in demand abroad and in 1970 he flew to Yugoslavia for a song festival appearance - representing Malta! Eventually the Daizies parted company with Berry. Dave Robinson: "We got fed up of all the inconveniences like you're in Dover one night and Inverness the next, and the way we got used." Berry had no permanent backing group for the next eight months or so. He used an assortment of different bands, including the Bob Davis Band, John Verity Band, the Daizies again and another brief reunion with Frank White. Eventually he reverted back to using the Cruisers name with a line-up of John Reid on guitar, John Broxholme on bass, Phil Brodie lead guitar and Dick Emory on drums. The latter had just switched from bass as Dave Robinson recalls: "I says to him, 'How long have been playing drums?' He said, 'I don't know.' 'Does Berry know?' and he said, 'Don't tell him, don't tell him!'" With Brian Watson taking over on drums, most of the work was now mainly on the thriving cabaret circuit and Phil Brodie recalls how Dave would still keep up his mystique:

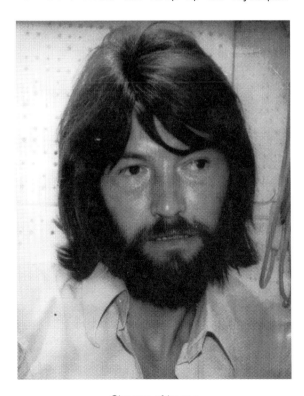

Change of image

"When we arrived at a club he'd always have his coat over his head when he came through the back door so no one could see him." Dave enjoyed the life: "It was great to work in one place for a week, with no travelling and just take it easy. People were just out for fun. A lot of the people hadn't come to see me in particular, they'd come because it was a night out at a night club. The audiences were in their mid to late twenties, they'd be aware of me or a particular artist who was on, but you weren't having to keep this Dave Berry image going all the time, so it could be fun."

Dave's main aim has always been to entertain the audience and isn't really bothered about whether every little note or solo is spot on. "My dad used to have an expression, 'Most people can't tell a crotchet from a carrot.' In other words, the audience don't know. It should be the overall thing they're looking at, nobody dissects it and thinks, 'I didn't like the third number when he came in after the solo or I didn't think he sang that bit very well.' Audiences don't do that."

Dave's stage movements have always been highly visual and people took notice of his stage act. In the 1965 documentary film Don't Look Back, then Animal Alan Price is caught trying to explain to Bob Dylan how Dave slithered around the stage. Dylan looks bewildered. In his 1969 book, Pop From The Beginning, pop chronicler Nick Cohn wrote: "Dave Berry was great fun - he moved like a snake, all arms and legs, very spooky in black, and he said he was going to be reincarnated as a snake." Berry: "The English audiences never saw any humour in it. They always thought I was very weird and strange, which is fine with me. The Dutch and the Belgians got the humour. On my first appearance on Dutch television the humour came across. Whether it was just a look into the camera or something that they knew was just tongue-in-cheek. That never came across here, but that was maybe my fault because on the TV shows I wanted to do something weird which would stick in their mind. I don't think it's neccessary always to be safe. I didn't go into this business to be safe. If I'd wanted to be safe, I would've been an accountant. But I do feel there should be a little bit of danger and y'know, if they don't like it, well... tough."

Throughout his career Dave has had his share of controversy. In 1965 Dave was part of a British team in the Knokke Song Festival. However, he was labelled 'immoral' and a danger to teenagers by German judges because he was the only one not to wear evening dress. He

was also dragged off stage by screaming teenagers and injured at Kirby, near Liverpool, with a startled Princess Margaret sitting just five yards away. Strangest of all, in 1971 he was dragged into court at Ossett - as the alleged 'villainous Mr X' - to face being accused of fathering a child by a 29-year-old hairdresser. She alleged he asked her to marry him and said that Dickie Valentine would be the best man and guests would include Cilla Black. The minute Dave walked into court she said he wasn't the man. The other Dave Berry had a mole in the middle of his forehead. He was also accused of running up a bill for £17,000 at a firm's expense on a chat line in 1989. Again it was an impersonator, a lonely nightwatchman in Redditch who even sent signed photographs of Berry to one woman he had chatted to.

In the mid-Seventies, with live work his main source of income, Dave was offered another recording deal with independent London producer Derek Lawrence. In preparation he recorded a demo session at the Look Studio in Huddersfield. Guitarist John 'Vinnie' Reid recalls the naivety of the drummer involved: "The engineer asked him if he wanted any cans. To which he replied, 'no thanks we had a couple of pints on the way over.'" At the London sessions Dave recorded Queen Of My Heart written by Billy Swan and I Am A Rocker written by Chas Hodges and Dave Peacock: "I thought they were good tracks but sadly nothing happened." But his career got an unexected boost when punk emerged. Most of the older acts didn't understand punk and felt threatened by it. Berry found himself an unlikely influence. "It was a bonus for me. When it all started I was doing a gig on the outskirts of London. There were lots of different age groups that I was pulling in at the time. But there were these 17 and 18 year olds coming along. At first I thought they were taking the piss, 'cos they were stood at the front of the stage. Then some of them came in the dressing room and told me that the Sex Pistols were doing Don't Gimme No Lip Child, which was the B-side of Crying Game, and they were also doing This Strange Effect. Siouxsie Sioux was also a fan and somebody else was also doing a couple of other things, so they liked me. Then in the late Seventies I was invited to do three or four shows with Adam and the Ants when they were really into their heavy punk thing. And I went to see the Monochrome Set at the Leadmill and they did Little Things."

Recently Dave has been getting back to his R&B roots. "It started at the Rockingham Arms at Wentworth. I wanted to do more of a blues set to suit the venue. That got me putting more blues things in, which I love. I've done the Rockingham every year as well as other blues type venues." He was also the surprise hit of the annual Alexis Korner Tribute at the Buxton Opera House in 1995. "I'd met Alexis Korner in the Sixties on two or three occasions and I knew other artists who'd been on the show so I phoned up the guy who runs it, Norman Beaker, and told him I'd like to do the concert. It was one of the highlights of my career. I didn't know whether the audience would go, 'Oh Jesus Christ, what's he doing here?' I should've given them more credit. If they're blues and R&B fans, they should know their history of British blues - and I was there at the beginning. It was a revelation for me. The audience were just up as soon as I was announced."

Another contributory factor towards Dave's longevity is his efficiency. "I've always liked to be organised. I think that the people I'm working with like to know that you're organised, that why musicians tend to stay with me for a while. As we all know, it's not the most secure job being a musician. The money's never all that brilliant, but the fact is that I've been able to pay reasonable money. If ten or 15 years ago I'd been paying completely over the top to musicians I might've had to pack it in because I wouldn't have been able to afford to sustain it."

His period in the limelight in Britain was relatively short-lived, starting in September 1963 with Memphis Tennessee and ending with Mama three years later. However, he packed a lot into that time and has never become one of those pop stars whom people asked, 'Whatever happened to...?' "I'm playing to bigger audiences now than I ever did in the Sixties," says Dave now 'around' his 60th birthday. And he continues to be as active as ever. April, '97, saw him start the longest tour of his career, along with fellow Sixties veterans Gerry Marsden, Wayne Fontana and Peter Noone. With tours abroad and playing before audiences of 8 to 11 thousand at UK festivals, people still want to see and hear the 'man of mystique'. "Being a rock star is like being a cowboy. You drive into town, have your fun, and then ride out a free man the next day," says Berry.

His recordings have been fairly few and far between after his initial success. Compilations of his Sixties' recordings continue to appear

while odd tracks from the Seventies see the light of day on various collections. In 1987 he released an album Hostage To The Beat, but only after the original master tape was recovered after being stolen from his dressing room at a Manchester rock club. His version of The Crying Game was also used on the successful 1992 film of the same title but, much to his chagrin, Boy George was employed to sing the title-track which was then released as a single which made the top 30. In 1997 he recorded a set of tracks that were decidedly more rootsy, including versions of JJ Cale's Cajun Moon and the Allman Brothers' Pony Boy but still awaiting an outlet. Dave's interpretation of Jacques Brel's Amsterdam was included on a 1998 tribute album to the French songwriter.

Berry has always been fairly relaxed about things, never taken himself too seriously and, if anything, almost relieved that he didn't become a huge star. He can still earn a good living, but hasn't got the pressure of being a headliner. How relaxed? When the Crying Game was big in the charts, Berry was nowhere to be found. "I was in Algeria, on my own in the casbah. I had met a girl in Spain and flew on my own to meet her in Algeria. When I got there she had gone back home - with her husband." That was before he married Marthy van Lopik in February 1967, sneaking off to Weston-Super-Mare to marry secretly. She was a Dutch TV personality whose achievements included being fired out of a cannon. In 1970 they bought a £7,000 house in Dronfield where they still live. Even in his sev-

Dave Berry: the Sheffield Flash

enth decade he is lean and lanky, a craggier version of the high cheek-boned youth who made girls scream and swoon. And he still puts those size 12 (or is it 13?) feet to good use, pounding the countryside as a devoted walker. And longevity? "From the beginning I wanted to sustain my career. After my initial success with the records I was looking at it and thinking that if I could handle things carefully those songs would be with me for the rest of my career. It's just a matter of having the right attitude and always playing with good musicians. My nightmare is to work with musicians of my own age, people who are thinking about the next round of golf." Throughout it all Berry has maintained his keen interest in the music. "If I listen to new music or the old stuff that I was brought up with I still get a great buzz from it." And even in the year 2000, he could still prove he had got it. When Van Morrison asked him to support him on two dates in England, Berry almost stole the show.

3. NICE TO BE ON YOUR SHOW: FRANK WHITE

Guitar hero Frank White, born Frankie William White, is something of a local legend, and has been playing around the city's pubs and clubs since the late Fifties. An outstanding musician by anyone's standards, he has also developed into a soulful singer and prolific songwriter and continues to be an inspiration to other musicians, young and old.

Frank, born and bred in Darnall, got his first guitar when his grandmother bought him a secondhand acoustic model for £2.50. At first he struggled to teach himself to play: "I found by accident a piece of paper with a chart showing how to tune the guitar and I just took it from there, completely self-taught." His earliest musical venture was getting together with some City Grammar school friends and forming the Zodiacs skiffle group. "That didn't amount to

Frank (left) with his first band, Johnny and the Nightriders

anything because we were only kids with loads of guitars and it fizzled out once we'd left school." For the next two years Frank held down a variety of clerical jobs, first in the Town Hall Housing Department, then at Bassetts and the Tinsley branch of English Steel. Work began to take second place: "Music always got in the way of everything, it just totally took over." Jim Greaves of the Checkers recalls how Frank had wanted to join them: "This young kid with glasses used to tell everybody that he was with the Checkers and he used to turn up to all our gigs and say, 'Can I play with you?' and we used to say, 'No, sod off, you're not good enough!'" Frank eventually got together with some other young musicians and formed a rock'n'roll band, Johnny and the Nightriders. At nights they would practise at a Darnall pub known locally as the Monkey because the landlord kept a pet monkey on the bar.

Inspired by rock'n'roll, Frank had developed into an impressive guitar player and in 1960 it got him noticed by one of the city's top bands. Jimmy Crawford: "Harry Murray at the Gaumont didn't provide backing bands, so if a solo singer wanted to do Teenager In Love Harry'd look around and see if anybody would help out and Frank White would invariably get up." Jean White sang with her sister Marilyn as Lynn and Jeanie and it was at the Gaumont shows that she met her future husband Frank. "When we went to sing Bye Bye Love the manager asked, 'Where's your music?' And we said, 'What music? We don't have any.' And then he said, 'Don't worry, I know just the man who can play for you.'" Jimmy Crawford: "He would know all the chords so he stood out. I thought, 'I'm going to get him in my band,' and I did. He was outstanding when there were no good ones about. In those days Frank White and Frank Miles [of Dave Berry's band] were the ones that were the leading guitarists. And a lad from Leeds called Richard Harding. They had got what it took. There were some good guitarists on set-pieces but Frank had the knowledge of chords and, completely from scratch, could help somebody out, just strum through it." Frank jumped at the chance: "I'd had enough of work and the band I was with. Jimmy had management and they wanted us to go to London for a gig at the 2i's coffee-bar." As a result of the trip to London Crawford was signed to Columbia Records and Frank played on his first single Unkind/Long Stringy Baby. In 1961 he became the owner of only the second Fender Stratocaster in Britain (after Hank Marvin). Frank's dexterous playing soon became a feature of Crawford's band the Ravens.

Roy Ledger recalls how Frank used to guard some of his know-how: "There'd be one solo that nobody could play so we'd go and see Frank 'cos he'd know how to play it. He'd get to the solo and he'd turn his back to play it." Dave Hopper: "Everybody knew him then as Frankie White. People used to go along to watch him, they didn't take a lot of notice of the rest of the band. On one occasion at the Foresters on Division Street we'd been watching him for a full set before we realised that Jimmy Crawford wasn't there. He'd turned the van over and was recovering. This was in 1960. Frank's there sat on a stool at the front with his back to the audience playing Three-Thirty Blues so nobody could see what his fingers were doing. That added to the intrigue." Lynn Tomlinson recalls how Dave Hopper followed Frank's example: "The kids used to go along to watch Hopper play lead gui-

BOBBY VEE CONCERT REVIEW

THE long-awaited Bobby Vee package show opened its tour at the Gaumont, Doncaster, to packed houses. And Bobby was wonderfully supported by Clarence " Frogman " Henry and Tony Orlando, who each had phenomenal successes.

Jimmy Crawford and the Ravens were the first off, working through several solid rock numbers like "Runaround Sue" and "September In the Rain"—with Jimmy really going to town on the latter. He also included his recent chart entry, "I Love How You Love Me".

Jimmy and the group were already firmly established in Doncaster through regular appearances in ballrooms. An extra feature for the Ravens was a dual drumming session on "Let There Be Drums"—and the boys backed, most efficiently, all the acts of the bill.

Part of Record Mirror show review, February '62

Jimmy sings and Frank plays

tar and he'd turn his back to the audience." The Ravens went on to secure a recording deal of their own with Pye Records. They recorded a one-off instrumental, the echoey Ghoul Fiend, backed with Career Girl. Frank: "That was through Jimmy Crawford, his management - Roy Tuvey and Maurice Sellars - who you may see on credits on various films. They just did a separate deal with a separate company." Pop weekly Disc reviewed Ghoul Friend in April, 1961, as a "sharp edgy noise with some gimmicky twanging effects behind saxes for the beat instrumental." Crawford and the band then went on a major

THE RAVENS (left to right): MICK MEREDITH, FRANK WHITE, PAUL DENTON. Kneeling: CHIC WILSON, and ART JACOBS.

nationwide tour with US stars Bobby Vee, Clarence Frogman Henry and Tony Orlando, plus British acts the Springfields and Danny 'Moon River' Williams. The Ravens found themselves with the task of backing all the artists. Frank White: "I was thrown in at the deep end. None of them had bands. Jimmy had got one and that was it. A few rehearsals, then two to three hours on stage every night for a three-week tour." The experience proved formative and earned Frank and the band some good press. "After that tour had finished we did a week of gigs with Tony Orlando. He was really good with us. He gave us a tip at the end of the week, he was really into the band." Frank stayed with Crawford for three busy years, although he didn't find the job musically fulfilling. "They were taking Crawford away from rock'n'roll and making him a pop star. He was a good frontman, but it was just entertainment. I needed to be playing the music I was listening to, like Howlin' Wolf, Muddy Waters, Little Richard, Little Walter, Elvis, Carl Perkins," said Frank. "We did some of that stuff with Jimmy Crawford. He was a good front man but he couldn't sing the blues."

Frank left Jimmy Crawford in 1962 and, at a loose end, joined Pete Fender and the Strollers. Mal Hooley: "We thought it was fantastic to have Frank in our band. It was like having Hank B Marvin playing with us!" Frank stayed with the Swallownest band for about five months before moving on to another local band, the Vampires. Rhythm guitarist Pete Cliffe: "Frank came to play with us for a while before I went with him to form his own band." In August '63 the Frank White Combo was formed, with Cliffe on bass, ex-

Debonaires drummer Johnny Riley and former Whirlwind Dave Hawley on rhythm and vocals. "Frank bought us all black mohair suits, borrowed the money off his grandparents," says Dave Hawley. Now able to play a more down-to-earth style of rock'n'roll than their previous bands had allowed them to. The group played their first gig on home-ground at Darnall Liberal club on Boxing Day, 1963, performing a gutsy blend of rock'n'roll, country and R&B with Frank taking lead vocals for the first time. "It was a bit scary, I remember one person in the audience made an adverse comment about my singing." Another memorable gig, by which time Hawley had left, was on May 30, 1964, at the Esquire Club when the Combo was booked to support one of their idols, rockabilly great Carl Perkins. Frank and company surprised Carl by including a selection of his songs in their opening set. John

Hero worship: Frank, John Riley and Pete Cliffe with Carl Perkins

The guitar's the star: Frank shows off his brand new twin-neck at Club 60

Riley; "We were just 20 year olds and it was fantastic to be playing on the same show. Carl was very impressed by the fact we were a bunch of young English musicians playing his songs. I remember, as we played the solo in Lend Me Your Comb, Carl stuck his head through the curtain at the back of the stage and just shouted, 'yeeeah'." In the press Perkins reckoned that Frank's band was, "One of the best rock'n'roll groups in the country," and suggested they back him on his next British tour. A return to the Esquire on October 3 saw the band supporting and backing legendary bluesman Little Walter. John Riley: "He was really stoned. We'd suggest he do so and so but even then every song he played virtually sounded the same as My Babe which was what he was known for." A few weeks later the Combo was recruited by Dave Berry to be his new Cruisers after the split with the original line-up. Dave Berry: "They were an excellent band." Frank White: "I always wanted to have my own band and I'd resisted Berry for ages. He must have asked me to join him for nearly three years."

Around this time Frank acquired his trademark white double-necked Gibson featuring a six-string and a 12-string neck. "I saw it in a Gibson catalogue. I just thought, 'I like that, it's really cool, I need one of those,' like you do when you are young." He ordered it from Wilson Peck's music shop at the then astronomical amount of £400, but the instrument took nearly a year to finally arrive from the States. When he eventually went to collect it, Frank and his friends just stood in the shop and looked at it in complete awe for about an hour. The guitar also added a bit more mystique to Berry's offbeat stage-act. However, because of its weight, the guitar did take some getting used to as Dave

Hopper discovered: "It was a knack. You'd just got to get it balanced right, if you hadn't it kept falling down to the left." The guitar became Frank's trademark for the next decade or so before he swopped it for a 'more manageable' single-neck Gibson. "The twin-neck was solid mahogany and like having two guitars around your neck. That was all right when I was young but I didn't want to get a hernia." In 1984 the instrument became the property of Frank's one-time manager and Chevrons' guitarist Dave 'Rusty' Rogers who in turn sold it on and today belongs to guitarist and collector Phil Brodie.

With Berry and the Cruisers, Frank's career was elevated to concert package tours with the likes of the Rolling Stones and Herman's Hermits, and TV appearances at home and abroad. The second set of Cruisers also landed a recording deal with Decca who obviously thought the 'new' Cruisers had more potential as a recording unit than the previous line-up. Frank: "Well, I don't think there were any singers in that band anyway. In this one there was John Riley and myself and we'd already been doing it as a band anyway." Dave Berry: "I'd been talking to producer Mike Smith about how good the band were on their own and we thought it would be a good idea to record them." The band, with Frank sharing vocals with Riley, recorded Bob Dylan's It Ain't Me Babe, backed by Jimmy Reed's Baby What Do You Want Me To Do. The Melody Maker review of the record gave it a somewhat back-handed compliment by saying it sounded "like another old recording made in 1958! A cross between folk and country and western." Unfortunately, Johnny Cash's cover of the Dylan song got more attention and Frank and co's efforts failed to make any impression, except with local fans.

Dave also recalls how Frank saved the day on

Decca publicity picture for the Cruisers one-off single

one of his European trips: "I did a week at this big theatre in Brussels. I was working with an orchestra and Frank was travelling with me on lead guitar. We got there and the roadie, Sam, had left the music parts back in England. And we were doing the show that night. So Frank wrote the parts out for the orchestra in a fashion so that we could do the show. Frank just sat and talked to them in broken English so they could understand. Also he came to Ireland with me once in about 1970, after we'd parted company. He came over as guitarist and we were on this show with an Irish showband, and you know how good they were, and Frank went and sat in with them after my gig. He was playing stuff like Dave Brubeck's Take Five, Twistin' The Night Away and then a soul number. They were absolutely amazed with Frank. They couldn't believe it. They were saying, 'This guy can play anything.'"

In October '65 Frank and John Riley decided to leave Berry, and resume working with their own band, recruiting Dave Hopper on second guitar and bass player Dave Green. Frank looks back on his stint with Berry with great fondness: "I enjoyed it, there were aspects of it that I didn't particularly like, 'cos I've never been a heavy showbiz-er. It was a brilliant experience touring with the Stones and the Hollies and bands like that. It was a great time." In Top Stars John Riley added: "It has been a big experience for us being with the Cruisers and seeing something of the glamour side of show business. But I am not sorry to be leaving. Frank and me got thoughts about having our own group and playing what we wanted. I have always been a great admirer of Frank. It is great being able to play with him. We both think along the same lines." Away from the big time, the new combo was relegated to working mainly local gigs once again, with their first appearance at Rawmarsh Baths on March 11, 1966.

Frank was always fairly image-conscious. Even in the early days his hair had always been stylishly longer (although painstakingly coiffured) than that of most other youngsters, influenced by musical heroes like Elvis and Don Everly, and he also had his suits made to his own specifications. He also wore horn-rimmed glasses similar to Buddy Holly's. In the mid-Sixties Frank exchanged his horn-rims for one of the first pair of contact lenses that followers can recall seeing anyone wear in Sheffield. He continued to be a snappy dresser with his self-designed Italian-style suits, bright dog-tooth bolero-style jackets, not to mention bright red guardsmen-style jackets!

As the "Big Four": Alan Wood, John Riley, Mal Hooley and that's Frank in guardsman's tunic

Frank's band went on to go through a succession of line-ups utilising people like bass players Nick Farrelly and Mal Hooley, guitarists Alec Shaw, Alan Wood and George Gill, and drummers Gerry Wigley, Fred Guite, Rick Elson and Gary Fletcher. There was also a variety of names, from the Frank White Combo to Frank White's Katters and Frank White's Kommotion. As Frank White's Katters the band recorded four tracks at the short-lived Studio 19 in 1966 on Eyre Street. These were Frank's own versions of a couple of obscure numbers, Little Lonely Summer Girl, originally recorded by one-time Cricket David Box, and Still As the Night, recorded by Phoenix rocker Sanford Clark, plus country-rock adaptions of Buddy Holly songs Take Your Time and Listen To Me. Frank: "We took them to John Ross at Philips in Amsterdam and the first person he mentioned was Reg Presley. I couldn't get a deal with the material I did my own way. You had to sing like Reg Presley or whoever was successful in those days." The original tapes, complete with the studio's original track by track documentation, later turned up in a car boot sale in the early Nineties and were bought for a pittance by another Sheffield guitarist Nick Robinson.

Dave Hopper experienced the frustration of being second guitarist in the band, relegated to playing rhythm. Hopper: "The only time I got any lead work was at the Sun Sound Club when he lost his contact lens and he left me playing!" Alan Wood was another: "Frank came and said, 'I want you to join the band,' and I said, 'Why me?' And he said, 'You're doing exactly what we want.' He wanted a strong under-current type of rhythm without any lead breaks which suited me fine. I was quite happy to go back to being a second guitar player. And John Riley was the best rock'n'roll drummer I ever worked with, a real out-and-out powerhouse." Frank had also switched from a staple diet of vintage rock'n'roll to take in more commercial material, mixing songs like Little Richard's Send Me Some Lovin' and Lucille with stuff such as the Lovin' Spoonful's Daydream. Dave Hopper: "He moved on to an almost progressive vein in one move." Alan Wood: "I helped to shape it a bit. We wanted a rock'n'roll drummer but the Beatles had become big and pop was becoming big and Frank was becoming more commercial. I said, 'The best drummer in Sheffield who's out of work at the moment is without a doubt Fred Guite,' an absolutely awesome drummer. He was very much into the style, at that time, of Bob Henrit, the drummer with Adam Faith's Roulettes, hitting the cymbals on the top, etc." There was also a marked change in Frank's singing, going from a pretty straight rock'n'roll style to a more aggressive and soulful approach. Explaining his new direction in the May '68 edition of Top Stars Special, Frank said: "We changed over to pop because it meant more money and more work, but we still include rock'n'roll numbers in our repertoire." Gaspin Gus, on the other hand, commented in October '68 Top Stars: "Frank too features some pop music these days but he can never project the same sort of atmosphere playing pop as he does when playing rock and country music." Despite the move, Frank's heart wasn't in it: "I used to wear beads and a flowered shirt. I just nodded in that direction. My love of blues and rockabilly were too strong. It would have been stupid to do pop music."

Further progression brought about another change in the band's sound as Alan Wood recalls: "Frank just decided he wanted an organist in the band and that was the way to go. Second guitar players or rhythm guitars were out and organs were in. I'd had no option, and I was replaced by Tommy Eyre. I finished with Frank as it became the Frank White Kommotion." Frank could, of course, outshine anybody when it came to fluent fretwork and his reputation began to spread far and wide. There were rumours of Herman's Hermits making Frank an offer to join them and there was another that even the Rolling Stones had considered him as a replacement for Brian Jones. Also, when Dave Berry appeared on the same bill as the Who, four years after Frank had left the Cruisers, Townshend and co asked about him. "That's one of the things about Frank that speaks for itself," said Berry. "Wherever I'm doing shows and meet people afterwards, they ask about

Frank. It could be the Who, the Trems, anyone. He's still one of the best guitarists around."

As the Seventies dawned Frank's music got louder, playing what was essentially R&B. Black Swan landlord Terry Steeples recalls the amount of volume: "Frank White and I could never see eye-to-eye because he was always too loud. The more I said to him to cut the noise down, the more he used to turn it up." Stu Moseley: "I had problems with a bit of deafness in those days and Frank was unbelievably loud. He used to love it, purr, if somebody said 'a bit louder'. I had cotton wool in my ears." Mal Hooley: "We did quite a few of Frank's own numbers that he'd started writing. Some of the obscure titles we did were things like Wild Billy Smoke Men

TWO TURN THE TAX TABLES!

USUALLY it's the income tax man who supplies the shocks.

But the "tax tables" were turned neatly in Sheffield yesterday when two members of a pop group decided to put in a personal appearance and dressed for the occasion.

Frock-coated Frank White (at right in the picture), aged 23, of Abbeyfield Road, Pitsmoor, Sheffield, leader of the Frank White band, explained: "We usually let our account-

ant deal with income tax matters, but we decided to save him a job today."

The only difficulty was that Frank and his colleague, 22-year-old George Gill, of Wesley Avenue, Aston, had to ask the way to the tax office.

They saw nothing unusual in their "gear." "People do look at us," said Frank, "but when they do we usually give them a cheery wave."

From The Star, August '69

and Good King Wenceslas. He was very strong on Hendrix stuff at the time. A lot of our following came because of that and Frank played it just as well as Hendrix did. He played out of his skin." With manic drummer Kenny Slade and bassist Adrian Jewel now in tow, Frank's music evolved into a high-powered combination of rock-'n'roll, blues and contemporary sounds. His guitar playing sounded better than ever and on stage, as he and Kenny tried to outplay each other, the results were truly awesome. "Frank won most of those battles," recalls Stu Moseley. "Kenny fell off the stool one day at the Swan. On another occasion Frank did Matchbox and did a 20 minute intro and Kenny's dying. Frank's going on and on." Kenny Slade: "They were my favourite gigs and I wish some of them had been recorded." One recording from the Seventies, taped at a gig in Brimington, features Frank and band in full flow as numbers such as Matchbox, Whiter Shade of Pale and Bonie Moronie become frenzied work-outs between Frank's guitar, drums and bass.

With the advent of psychedelia and bands such as Jethro Tull and Spooky Tooth, Frank went that little bit further. He would now be seen wearing torn shirts and ripped jeans (all regularly washed of course) and long hair with his trademark mutton-chop sideburns eventually growing to nearly a foot long! He could often be seen walking round town or hanging out in the Stone House wearing a long-tail coat, crushed top hat, replete with red feather, and a Hawaiian guitar slung over his shoulder. Also accompanying Frank would be fellow guitarist George Gill dressed in a white robe and sandals and bearing a strong resemblance to Jesus! Mal Hooley: "Frank had a lot of fire then. He's mellowed a bit over the years, but then he was a wild man, eccentric." Ray Higgins of McCloskey's Apocalypse: "I have to say that it was Frank White who almost certainly got me started with music. He looked and sounded the part. He had that great bluesy voice, the music was real rock-'n'roll and he looked rebellious. He fired me up to have a go myself."

Frank also played regularly at the Sunday concerts in Weston Park in the early Seventies. Graham Oliver of Sob, who appeared on the same bill as Frank's band in 1970, recalls organiser Glynn Senior's announcement: "He introduced Frank as the old man of pop. I think it was because his son Joel had just been born, he was there and must have been about a month old." Graham also remembers a rare gig when Frank didn't go down too well: "It was at Wickersley Comprehensive school in

Rotherham. Some people didn't like the band and something was said at the interval. There was a fight after. We went out outside to load the van and it was like Wagon Train, hills and all these Indians on the horizon, a gang appeared, 50 or 60 of them, and it ended up in a big scrap. We managed to get out alive."

In 1973 Frank's talent as a guitarist, singer and emerging songwriter was recognised when he signed up by Fantasy Records, the first British act to record for the label that was associated with multi-million selling US band Creedence Clearwater Revival. At the time Frank had joined Sheffield progressive rock club/cabaret band Hollywood along with bass player Alan Wood: "He was fed up with being Frank White. He was in a bit of a void. He needed money and he wanted to be just the guitar player in a band. He was going through one of those phases and Frank had everything we wanted. We did a few interesting gigs, including one at Bernard Manning's club when Bernard was not quite as well known. He made reference to Frank's double-necked Gibson as, 'Dirty bastard guitar, goes on stage and has sex and comes off with two of them!' And when we came off he said: 'Well you're a good band but you're the scruffiest bastards I've ever seen!' We were there for three nights and he gave us money and made us go and buy suits for the gigs. He smartened us up." When Hollywood eventually fizzled out through diminishing bookings Frank decided once again to form a band of his own. He asked former Cruiser Roy Barber: "I was knocking about with Frank Miles and Tommy Rattigan, playing on their songwriting demos, and Frank had heard about it and we went over to Frank Miles' place and did some recording. Prior to that I hadn't had much to do with him. It didn't help he had replaced us in the Cruisers. Frank phoned me up to play bass and I'd never played bass in my life. He must have been really desperate. He must have rung everybody else said so he started ringing rhythm guitarists up!

Loud and hairy: Frank White Band, '69, with George Gill, Mal Hooley, Gary Fletcher and Frank

I said, 'I don't play bass but I wouldn't mind sitting in on guitar.' I think what we did in the end was I played guitar and we managed without a bass. And it worked. Eventually he got a bass player, but playing guitar with Frank is hell of a challenge. On stage, if you're a guitarist, he doesn't do you any favours."

Frank and Roy, temporarily living in London, teamed up with former Chesterfield drummer John Pearson whose girlfriend set up gigs. The band was seen by people from Fantasy who were impressed by both Frank's playing and singing. He went on to cut the album Nice To Be On Your Show, the title being derived from Frank's somewhat sarcastic view of 'show-biz'. Frank was accompanied on the sessions by an old friend from Sheffield, keyboard player Tommy Eyre together with ace sessioneers, drummer Gerry Conway and bassist Pat Donaldson. Roy Barber also provided some excellent guitar work on the album. "That was the best guitar I've ever played really. Frank improved my playing so much. He took me out of the realms of being a good rhythm guitarist and I could compete with him on lead guitar, differently. I could cover all the areas that he didn't do." Roy had a big input on the album, playing on and arranging the songs, so much so that at one time the producer wanted to call it 'Frank White Meets Roy Barber'. Now a collector's item, it mixed classics like Chuck Willis's What Am I Living For and Chuck Berry's Gonna Find My Baby and No Money Down with Frank's developing talent as a songwriter. One of his own songs was Wild Billy Smoke Men about some of Sheffield's infamous characters such as Pond Street Nora and the Duke Of Darnall. Other orig-

inal songs were Punk, Kingdom Hall and Darnall Dog Track, a song that recalled some of Frank's childhood places. A single was issued coupling Frank's version of Buddy Holly's Not Fade Away with an original, Movin' On, which strongly featured Roy Barber's guitar: "Them choppy chords, that's all, mine. That's what holds the song together."

The album received good reviews and Frank put a band together with Barber and London musicians Steve Ash and Alan Coulter to promote the record. What this amounted to was a rather soul-destroying trip across Europe, which left Frank and the band demoralised. Roy Barber: "We toured Yugoslavia and got stuck in Sarajevo and it snowed. We were there a week so we never got to play anymore. We were stuck in this hotel with the band East of Eden and a load of dope, so all was not lost. We were supporting East Of Eden but the whole thing fell apart after that. There's always chaos and disorganisation surrounding Frank, always is. But the music was good, it was exciting, I was having the time of my life, it was the best thing that ever happened to me musically." Frank: "It was a good band, it just fizzled out. Maybe I just wasn't pushy enough."

Back in Sheffield Frank and Roy, together with drummer John Roberts and bass player Dave Green, once again resumed playing around the local scene with regular gigs at the Black Swan and Barrow Hill Hotel. Frank continued to be very much his own man. "In those days, being a band leader, not that I ever thought of it in those terms, I had this direction I wanted to go in. Inevitably there were differences of opinion about the direction. Eventually it became me

Frank's album for Fantasy

employing other people so I bought a van and got my own PA. In retrospect it was the right thing to do. It was a lot to cope with but somebody had to do it."

Since 1969 Frank has been married to Jean, ex-singer with the Whirlwinds and Dave Hawley Combo. Shortly after the birth of son Joel, they moved from Pitsmoor to the Sharrow/Nether Edge area. In 1973 they had a daughter Jody, and Frank's playing took a back seat in favour of spending more time at home with his family. He supplemented his income with an assortment of jobs, including bar work in a couple of city pubs, painting and decorating and record shop manager. By the mid-Seventies Frank's outlook on life underwent a profound change when he became a Jehovah's Witness. At first this was looked on as something of a joke by some of Frank's musician colleagues as religion wasn't something any self-respecting rocker thought about much. But Frank's new found beliefs proved to be genuine. "I had always been interested, always questioning what life is about, since I was a kid. But nobody satisfied my questions until the Jehovah's Witnesses. I was enlightened with not only a sense of urgency, but a sense of certainty of where I was going, my life was directed from then on." Frank also had a deeply moral stance and perhaps sometimes didn't see the funny side of life. Ray Higgins of McCloskey's relates the story of seeing the Frank White Band playing at Cannon Hall, Firvale. Halfway through the set a mongrel dog ran in off the street, had a nosey round and ended up on the stage. It then spotted drummer John Riley's bass drum, filled with blankets to deaden the sound, climbed inside and settled down. Meanwhile, Frank and company studiously ignored this invasion. The loyal audience followed suit. "My sides were aching," says Higgins. "But I couldn't burst out laughing because everybody was trying to pretend the dog wasn't there. If it had been McCloskey's we would've used the dog as a prop. I'd probably have cooked it or eaten it, anything but ignore it."

In 1977 Frank was back out on the road playing with the country-rock orientated outfit Jim Crow. Demos that Frank had recorded at Hull's Fairview Studios caught the attention of former Peddler's bassist Tab Martin who then came up to Sheffield to see Frank play. With a hurriedly revamped band, including future ABC man Dave Clayton on keyboards and Jeremy Holroyd on drums, Frank played an impressive set in the upstairs room of the Marples Hotel and Tab helped him to get a new deal with MAM

Records, the label owned by Tom Jones' manager Gordon Mills. The result was single Shelley, written by Mark Middler. It received extensive local radio airplay and looked like becoming a hit. Some other tracks were recorded in London, including a great song by Frank, Nightbird featuring backing vocalists Sue and Sunny and Chesterfield steel guitar supremo Pete Haywood. "It looked very rosy, but as we were preparing for an album there was some internal struggle that eventually ended with MAM disintegrating," said Frank.

In a 1995 Sheffield Telegraph article he described himself as a maverick: "I've always had a wild streak, a maverick streak. If people want to call me a rock'n'roll musician I have to do something else. If they want to put me in a bag I'd have to tear a hole in it and do something else." Gerry Scanlon: "I remember the first time I saw Frank's name in the Star in Roy Shepherd's Teenage Page, saying that Frank refused to wear a tie in Jimmy Crawford's Ravens." Roy Barber: "It's just Frank. When something's expected of him, he won't do it. It's almost as if he doesn't want to make it." As Keith Strong wrote in the liner notes for Frank's 1988 album: "Frank White, who has always had a bad case of the blues, is also a sad case of the blues. Refusing to compromise, he has ploughed a lonely furrow, stockpiling material and being feted only by the faithful." Frank's problem with time keeping is legendary, as most musicians who've worked with him can testify. Mal Hooley: "Frank was never ever ready. I don't know what it was. I don't know if it was something he'd got to do, but he was never ever ready. I remember once we were already late setting off for a gig and I went to pick him up when he still lived on Bilton Road in Darnall. I'm stood in their kitchen, pacing about waiting for him, and he said to his mother, 'Mother, are you going to do me a few chips?' So his mum then started peeling spuds and putting the chip pan on and we're already late. And that's just one instance. You'd go to pick him up and he'd say, 'Oh I've just got to wash my hair, old boy,' and then he'd disappear, washing his hair and drying it. Crazy really." Stu Moseley: "He used to fix up recording sessions and then never show. You'd be in London or somewhere waiting for him. You'd get to gigs sometimes at quarter past ten. I didn't dare go in. He'd end up with half money or even quarter money." Steve Dawson who drove Frank to gigs in the early Seventies: "Frank was a typical musician, it happened when it happened. I'd be sat at home at six o'clock and Frank would ring up and ask if I would take the band to the Monsal Head Hotel. In between you getting there he would be phoning up the other musicians, so by seven o'clock there'd be a band. On a good night you'd pick them up at half past seven which was late anyway to go to a gig. You'd get everybody in the van and within 20 minutes of setting off you'd be pulling up at a pub and they'd get out and go for a drink. I couldn't afford to drink. This carries on all the way to the Monsal Head, stopping at five or six pubs on the way, and we get to the Monsal Head at ten o'clock. The landlord's going mad. But Frank was the master of walk in, plug in and you're off, without even tuning up, because they had done it so many times. There wasn't the gear there is now, so it only took ten minutes to set up. We used to do the Dog and Partridge in Attercliffe with Frank on a Thursday and that was a marathon because you'd never get out of there before five or six in the morning, ever. Because I didn't drink I'd be waiting to take them home in the van, it was purgatory." Frank's explanation is typically enigmatic: "I always keep time. It's just I use a different clock from everybody else." So we can presume then that, when it's 1pm. by everybody else's clock, for Frank it's 8am?

He could also be exasperating on stage. Alan Wood: "I remember being on stage at the Staniforth Arms and he stopped the show midway through the first set. He said, 'I can't play in these shoes.' He took his shoes off, put his cowboy boots on with the heels and said, 'That's it, I feel better now'. The whole band had to stop and wait while he changed his shoes." As Alan also recalls, Frank could be a law unto himself: "We'd played at the Cock Inn, Ripley, and all I know was that the next day when we went to Stoke-on-Trent my guitar, my Fender

Frank White's video recorded live at the Pheasant

Strat, was missing. We made a phone call and somebody had found it outside the pub and taken it back in. So I had no guitar for the gig. Well Frank was very efficient and very regimental and I had to go on stage and stand at the front and appear to sing and play tambourine even though Frank was singing the majority of the set. I had to look like I was part of the band. And I got a monster telling off... if I ever did this again, and how unprofessional I was with my guitar, it was unforgivable, and whatever. Soon after Mal Hooley was reduced to tears of laughter in the band room because Frank had left his guitar at the Arbourthorne Hotel. Frank's response was, 'But that was just one of those things, old boy.' It was somebody else's fault for not packing his guitar. But I got on as well as you could with Frank. You had to tolerate him, you had to wait for him everywhere, every day. When you went round to pick him up he was never ready, ever, but he was so polite, 'Have a cup of tea old boy?' And you'd wait for an hour. He tested your patience all the time, he was never on stage on time, never ready to come away at the end of the night. But on stage he captured everyone's attention. He'd walk on with a bright red Strat or the double-neck white Gibson and you could hear the apprehension of people thinking, 'I hope he can play that,' and of course he could. He just blew people away. So his 30 to 45 minutes on stage, in his mind, was

Frank enthralls the crowd at the Royal Victoria Hotel

enough to carry him through the rest of his career. But that's rock'n'roll."

As the band continued to change throughout the Eighties and Nineties, having included almost every Sheffield musician of any worth at some time or another, he recorded a couple more albums. One More Lonely Night was recorded in 1987 with Tommy Eyre, his old mate from the Sixties, producing, and backing from George Michael's regular band. It was less guitar-orientated with more emphasis on Frank's song writing but failed to, "reach out for deserved acceptance by a wider audience who have been denied for too many years," as predicted by Star journalist Keith Strong in the album's sleevenotes. He was voted Best British Vocalist at the 1992 British Blues Connection Awards. A new album, Dog It! followed in 1994 and was more the kind of thing that Frank's followers expected consisting of mainly originals mixed with one or two bluesy covers and, of course, laced with Frank's fiery guitar playing.

Frank established one of the country's longest-running residencies, every Friday night at the Pheasant, Sheffield Lane Top. Beginning in October 1980, it was described by one fan as 'a great Sheffield institution'. "We originally did the Pheasant as a one-off," says Frank. "The audience was dwindling for the band that had been playing Fridays. It was suggested they try me. It was a complete success from the word go. I don't know where those people came from, they were climbing the walls, it was wierd. It just took off and it became a focal point for the band's existence. The band has changed over the years but the Pheasant has been very good for me personally." His residency at the Pheasant finally ended in April 1999, opening up yet another era.

Frank's other musical activities have included teaching guitar to students young and old, some of whom have subsequently turned out to be fine players. Through Kingfish Promotions Frank has also been promoting live gigs for more than a decade. These have featured a wide variety of artists including the late Steve Marriott, the Hamsters, Albert Lee, Steve Gibbons and visiting US names like blues powerhouse Luther Allison, former Byrd Gene Parsons and rock-'n'roll legend Sonny Curtis. His promotions have met with various degrees of success, but Frank has persevered in the belief that he felt obliged to bring quality live music to Sheffield.

Despite his loyal following and the rumours of offers from big name bands, Frank has never made it to the fame and fortune many felt he deserved. Frank says: "Lots of people have made it to the big time, or what they call the big time, and made a mess of themselves. It's true I could have taken more advantage, perhaps, of opportunities, but there are some things that are of greater importance to me." For another answer maybe they should ask some of his ex-band members. Bass player Mal Hooley has probably played with Frank more than most throughout the years. "My last stint with Frank White was from 1985 until 1992. The music's always good with Frank and I've had some good experiences. He's still a good player, I can't knock him. I just don't think he recognised a lot of the chances that he had." Dave Hawley: "Frank White is one of the greatest guitarists this country has produced, he's one of the nicest and kindest persons I've met, but he hasn't made it, frankly, because he doesn't like some of the people in showbusiness."

The most important things to Frank are obviously his family, his beliefs and carrying on making music his own way. When asked in a 1991 Radio Sheffield interview what his aims are as a musician, Frank's answer was simple: "All I want to do is earn a living and be respected." In his home city, at least, he's certainly achieved that.

Sheffield legend: Frank White "Thank you old boy"

4. I'M STILL STANDING: JOE COCKER

A shining example of Sheffield's musical legacy is of course the lad from Crookes, Joe Cocker, now recognised as one of the world's finest white soul singers. Thanks to JP Bean's excellent biography on Joe, With A Little Help From My Friends, his career has been well documented, throughout its various highs and lows.

John Robert Cocker was born on May 20, 1944, at 38 Tasker Road, Crookes. He became Joe when he and his friends took the name of an eccentric window cleaner. He was originally influenced by the skiffle music of Lonnie Donegan. "I was about 13 years of age, I was sat on the carpet in front of the radio and out of nowhere came these simple A chords on the acoustic guitar, 'This is the story of the Rock Island Line' and my ears pricked up. I got so excited by the end of it 'cos my voice hadn't broken and Lonnie had a high voice so I could sing along perfect with him." Joe got his start through his older brother Vic who also had his own skiffle group: "I had a band called the Headlanders and they picked up the fact that Joe had got a good voice. I don't know how they found that out but they did and invited him up to sing with us and I think that's how he got his debut really. He started getting a taste for it." His first public appearance was at the Wesley Hall youth club in Crookes but he still had to pay to get in.

Young Joe would often go down to the Hillsborough Memo to watch the other bands. Roger Harrison remembers seeing him there: "Before Joe started playing himself he used to come down and stand and look at all the equipment, not that there was much of it in them days." Joe's first real musical activities began with the Cavaliers, a skiffle group that he'd formed with neighbourhood friends, guitarists Phil Crookes and John Mitchell, and bass player

Bob Everson. "I was originally a drummer," as Joe recalls, "But we were short of a vocalist, so I was forced into it. It used to be so difficult to play and sing, I used to get so worked up." He became the front-man, with Dave Memmott taking over on drums and the band became Vance Arnold and the Avengers, a name, according to Joe, that had been conjured up by the Sheffield Star for an advertisement. However, in a 1995 TV documentary, Joe finally admitted it was he who had picked the name. "I think that Elvis in one of his films had the name Vance. I took Arnold from Eddy Arnold the country guy. For years I used to deny that I had anything to do with it." Stu Moseley recalls another nickname of Joe's: "This mate of mine said to me, 'Have you seen Bubbles?' 'No, who's that?', 'Joe Cocker'. He was Bubbles because he had this curly hair. Then I saw him advertised as Vance Arnold and the Avengers at the Fleur D'Lys and the Wharncliffe."

The band, originally influenced by Buddy Holly and Gene Vincent, was typical of a lot of other local groups: "I was 16 when we started playing pubs. I even did the leg kicks like Cliff Richard." Joe checked out the local scene with Stu Moseley: "We went as a foursome - me and Monica, Joe and Eileen. He was a bugger, he'd sit with his back to the bands. And the bands were usually just young lads with their mums and dads watching, doing Cliff Richard stuff. Joe would be pulling faces. He made me laugh." Joe's own band's first gig was at the Minerva Tavern (now the Yorkshire Grey) on Charles Street as Joe recalls: "It was pretty rough. I remember a pint flying through the air and our lead guitarist ducked just in time." As the band progressed, their musical tastes started to veer towards rhythm and blues and particularly the music of Chuck Berry. They started to pick up gigs and appeared regularly at the Greengate at High Green and the Fleur De Lys, Totley, where

Vance Arnold and the Avengers with Dave Memmott, Phil Crookes, Rob Everson and Graham Bower

audiences were more receptive. Moving further into blues they introduced material by Muddy Waters, Bo Diddley and John Lee Hooker into their repertoire.

Joe also became a regular performer at the Esquire, first approaching owner Terry Thornton for a gig in late 1962. "This shy, chubby-faced teenager politely interrupted me at the bar and asked for a gig as a singer," recalls Terry. "I looked at him and thought 'never in a million years'. He looked nothing like a singer. Joe said he'd played at some pubs and youth clubs and gone down well. Finally after much persuasion I decided to give him a go. I told him I'd try him out for a fiver. He was delighted. The band were terrific and Joe's performance came as quite a surprise."

As Joe developed his vocal style Ray Charles became a particular influence: "What I loved about Ray was he was the blues-gospel connection." However, Joe's dad Harold wasn't so impressed. Joe: "When my Dad first heard Ray Charles he said he sounded like he'd got a pin stuck up his arse." John Firminger can recall first seeing them at Frecheville R&B Club where he and Roy Barber were bowled over by what they heard. Vance's great bluesy Ray Charles-type singing was superbly counterbalanced by Phil Crookes' excellent Merle Travis-style guitar

Singing drummer Vance Arnold with Rob Everson

playing with solid support from drummer Dave Memmott and rhythm guitarist Graham Bower. Top Stars' writer Carol Newton, in the September '63 issue, described Vance Arnold as one of the most stylish and popular vocalists in Sheffield. Dave Berry also added his praise: "I think Vance and the Avengers are the greatest group in Sheffield today." Stu Moseley first saw him at the Fleur De Lys: "I couldn't believe it. I was gobsmacked. The band started up and Joe wasn't on stage. He just walked in and got up on stage. To this day I say I've seen Ray Charles, Aretha Franklin, a few in my time, but those nights at the Fleur with Joe are still the top for sheer energy and wah-h-h."

Possibly feeling frustrated by the group's slow progress, Neil Bridges recalls Joe auditioning as singer for his band the Whirlwinds: "We had an audition at the 'Horti' [Darnall Horticultral Club] and Vance Arnold came. And we said, 'You don't want to sing with us, it doesn't fit.' It must've been the biggest favour anybody's ever done him. If he'd have come with us he wouldn't have become Joe Cocker and he might have still been singing on the clubs." Persevering, Vance Arnold and the Avengers started to gather a following, especially after an impressive appearance on a big showcase of local talent at Sheffield City Hall in October '63. Then Pete Stringfellow gave Joe a helping hand when he booked the Rolling Stones at Sheffield City Hall in November, 1963, and put Vance Arnold on the bill. The Londoners were in the charts with their second single, I Wanna Be Your Man, but they were already causing scenes of mayhem and fan hysteria only matched by the rise of the Beatles earlier that year. Cocker and co were the second act on and virtually stole the show - "He is surely a star of the future, it is doubtful whether even Liverpool can offer a better singer in his class than Vance Arnold," raved the Sheffield Telegraph the following day.

But as the end of 1963 approached, Joe Cocker, despite a loyal following in the city, still looked no nearer making a name for himself outside the environs of the clubs and pubs in the West Riding (as South Yorkshire was still known then) and north Derbyshire. He had even resorted, while still Vance Arnold and the Avengers, to playing the working men's club circuit, doing two sets, lunchtime and evening, and often getting paid off before the second one. He just loved singing and wasn't that bothered whether he got paid much, as long as he got enough for a few pints. He didn't have the ambition or business sense of a Dave Berry, nor did he have the looks. Not that he was jealous of Berry's suc-

Formerly Vance, now Joe

cess - Joe was there cheering Berry along when the TV cameras were filming him at the Esquire. "Joe wasn't a rival, he was more like a colleague," says Berry. "We were from the same background. He wouldn't steal the glory, he was too busy chasing the girls. And people forget that he didn't have a huge following in Sheffield. He didn't have that pop star image. I can remember seeing him at the Penny Farthing [now Uropa on Eyre Street] and there can't have been more than 18 people there to see him. He didn't follow the same route. Most singers built up a big following in one big town or city and then word gets out. Joe seemed to stay pretty low key."

Tony Smith of the R&B Club at Frecheville: "Cocker was never a big draw for us. We didn't get the full houses we got for Berry. But Cocker played all the pubs where you could see him for nothing. I remember seeing him at the Birley Hotel. He sang two numbers and then stopped completely. He went to the bar, ordered a pint, drank it, then went back on stage. It was almost his party trick." Frank White: "It never occurred to me at the time that he was going to make it big in any way. In those days that sort of thing was just not in the air. You could go out any night of the week and have a choice of two or three bands to see. Joe was just part of the scene. You didn't go out looking to see who was going to make it. We all just played for the fun of it."

What Cocker did have was an amazing, expressive voice, an immaculate taste in songs although he, like everybody else, had to throw in Beatles and Motown songs (his opening number in the mid-Sixties would often be The Four Tops' I Can't Help Myself with its unforgettable opening line 'Sugar pie, honey bunch') and oodles of Sheffield-style charm and humour. But he, like Berry, was not a prolific songwriter and in the aftermath of Merseybeat, the only groups that were to survive, and prosper, were such as the Kinks, Stones, the Who and, of course, the Beatles who all wrote the majority of their own material. And in 1963 Cocker wasn't even off the launch pad.

Motivated by the success of fellow Sheffield star Dave Berry, Joe decided to make a demo recording of Vance Arnold and the Avengers and send it to Decca Records. The band recorded six numbers in Joe's front room, in the Spring of 1963 including his individual interpretations of Tennessee Ernie Ford's 16 Tons, Barrett Strong's Money, Bo Diddley's Ride On Josephine, Hank Williams' You Win Again, Arthur Alexander's You'd Better Move On and Ray Charles' Georgia On My Mind. These recordings were later 'rediscovered' 36 years later in a garden shed and released on CD as Joe Cocker: Vance Arnold and the Avengers, put together by Terry Thornton and journalist Don Hale. Thornton claims that he had recorded the tracks on a reel-to-reel with two microphones tied with string, live in the Esquire. However the presence of a seventh track, I'm Free, which dates from four years later, leaves the whole thing open to conjecture. The recordings are a fine, if rather poorly recorded, illustration of the power and presence that Joe was already developing as a singer.

Six months later Joe and the band were summoned by Decca A&R man Dick Rowe to audition at the Southern Sporting Club in Manchester. Heading across the Woodhead

Pass in freezing conditions the club was just as cold resulting in the audition itself being a somewhat solemn affair. Also performing at the audition were Jimmy Crawford and the Shantells who had already signed with Decca. In these less than perfect conditions Joe and the band ran through 16 Tons, You Better Move On, Got My Mojo Workin' and Georgia. At the audition was Dick Rowe, the A&R man for Dave Berry's label, Decca, and who has gone down in history as the man who rejected The Beatles (then again, he did sign the Rolling Stones, Berry, John Mayall's Bluesbreakers, Tom Jones, Them etc). Rowe had brought along a record producer, Mike Leander, later to become famous himself for being behind the success of Gary Glitter. There was little reaction from the two record executives, except to say that they might call the group to make a recording test for Decca. The recording test followed in London but the band, intimidated by their first time in a proper recording studio, failed to live up to the occasion. After managing to lay down four tracks they returned home to await Decca's decision. A recording contract was offered - but only for Joe as a solo artist.

The band continued to be popular in Sheffield and in January 1964 they played at the City Hall alongside Wayne Fontana, Dave Berry and the Hollies. This was followed by a rare treat for Joe and the band on Thursday, February 13, when they supported blues legend Sonny Boy Williamson at the Esquire. In April the band signed a management deal with Esquire owner Terry Thornton and Cleethorpes agent Martin Yale. Thornton stepped down shortly afterwards due to commitments at the club but continued to help them when necessary. "It appeared to have been for many years as the whole band had a liking for Stones bitter and were a nightmare to manage. I helped them from early 1963 until around 1966 and referred to them as Joe Cocker's Booze Band," said Terry. There was a change in line-up when Phil Crookes left, passing the job on to to ex-Stroller Dave Hopper: "Crookie wanted to leave, then he wanted to stay, he couldn't make his mind up. I just started going about with the band wherever they went so I could learn the show. Just at about the point where Phil was getting ready to go, this recording thing came up. Then Phil didn't want to leave in case they suddenly became 'recording stars'. Once they got the notification that they weren't going to be on the record, Phil wasn't bothered then. He said to me, 'You can have this job'."

In June '64 Joe made the trip to London again

to record his debut single at Decca's West Hampstead studios, this time travelling in style care of Stu Moseley. "I took Joe to London in my big Zephyr. It was a beautiful day, we saw planes and we thought 'this is it, you've made the big time'. We got to this huge recording studio and he did Georgia." One journalist described Cocker's arrival at the studio: "His hair flows behind his ears like a dishevelled Royalist fleeing a Roundhead posse. First impression: good grief a singing sheepdog." Cocker, who was still working for the Gas Board, said: "I've got used to people ribbing me about my hair. I've been growing it for seven months now and I'm attached to it - literally. I get some weird looks when I turn up at people's doors. One woman asked me if I was the Wild Man of Borneo. Strange, I thought people in London wouldn't take any notice, but they stare more than the people at home. And I was walking through the West End when a taxi pulled up and a certain member of the Rolling Stones leaned out, fluffed his hair and said, 'You've got a long way to go yet.'"

Backed by a 22-piece orchestra and the full Ray Charles arrangement, Joe cut Georgia On My Mind. However A&R man Dick Rowe didn't think the track had any commercial value. Joe:

"Mike Leander played it to the board of directors and they hated it. So I drove down to London two days later and did a rush cover version of the Lennon and McCartney song I'll Cry Instead." Backed by ace session guitarists Jimmy Page and Jim Sullivan, with backing vocalists the Ivy League, the result was a solid, almost rockabilly, reading. Sixteen musicians were used to lay down the B-side Precious Words, originally recorded by the American Wallace Brothers.

Decca also announced that Vance Arnold was no more and Joe Cocker would now be known by his real name - "Orrible name, from now on I'm Joe Cocker again," said Joe. He also finally relinquished his Gas Board job, although they gave him six months leave instead just in case he changed his mind. There was also a new name for the band - Joe Cocker's Big Blues and changes in the band. Dave Hopper's proficiency as a guitarist was ideal, being heavily influenced by Americans such as Buddy Guy and James Burton, but a more solid backing was needed which eventually saw the departure of guitarist Graham Bower and bassist Bob Everson. Vernon Nash came in on piano, another excellent musician but quite an extrovert as Dave Hopper discovered: "I'm doing these Chuck Berry things on guitar like Ingo and Blue Feeling and he's rolling

Joe recording in Decca studio with Ken Lewis, Perry Ford and John Carter, soon to become the Ivy League

about on the floor in ecstasy. Not because of me. It was because of what I was playing. Every time we did Ingo, wherever we went, it would be touch and go whether he'd actually play it or collapse on the floor. Joe took to him straight away, 'cos he was doing all his Otis Spann bits." On bass was Dave Green who, as Dave Hopper recalls, had already had his eyes set on the job: "If Greeny was in the audience, he'd be joining the week after, so if he turned up to watch the band, the bass player would start worrying." Green, formerly with the Twin Cities Beat Boys, was perhaps the most versatile bass player around at the time and played a unique upright electric 'stick-bass'. He was also a likeable, friendly and polite chap and is fondly remembered as being a bit old fashioned. Dave Hopper: "We used to call him Steed sometimes, 'cos he acted like Steed from the Avengers." John Crookes: "Dave Green quipped in Wilson Pecks one day, 'Money talks and I've got laryngitis.'" Roy Ledger: "He was like a vicar. If you'd have put a collar on him he would have been a perfect vicar - short hair, straight talker - but what a bass player. We never rehearsed with him. We'd just say to him, 'We're doing so-and-so and it's in G,' and he'd just play it. He was perfect, he could play anything." Dave Hopper found the job musically satisfying, the band's material being primarily R&B, incorporating a little rockabilly, country and standards. "My

Decca publicity picture

favourite used to be Georgia because I had least of all to do in it. I just did chords. The feeling from doing that was better than doing any fast licks." The band would make regular appearances at the Esquire: "We used to live there - just about." Ironically, as Dave recalls, Joe and his band were too authentic: "We were sort of an American sounding rhythm and blues band rather than the British 'semi-rhythm and blues' bands that were around at the time."

September 4 saw the release of I'll Cry Instead which received airplay on Luxembourg and Caroline. The publicity for the disc played on Joe's former job as a gas-fitter with headlines like 'It's A Big Gas Man'. Although it was a decent record, it was untypical of Joe's style and failed to make any impact. "It died a death, I died a death. I'd left the the Gas Board. They told me I could go back and get the job if I wanted but my pride was too hurt. I couldn't. We just didn't have any choice at the studios," said Joe who wanted to make sure he got his way for the follow-up. "We want to look out our own material and go down to London prepared to force it on them, as this first one doesn't fit at all with our stage image. That is all very wild r and b."

In September the band was signed up for a national tour with Manfred Mann and Little Eva (of Locomotion fame). It was a disaster with Manfred Mann not showing for the opening night and Little Eva failing to materialise at all. The Merseybeats were left to top the bill, with Joe Cocker's Big Blues at the bottom. After just four nights the tour was aborted. Joe recalls: "We lost a lot money and we had no replacement bookings." Martin Yale eventually managed to put the band back on the road, playing so-called R&B clubs around Lincolnshire. They also travelled farther afield to places like Chester, Carlisle and Manchester, but the work was pretty gruelling especially as Joe preferred to get back home every night. In December, Yale had managed to get Joe and co an appearance on the ITV variety show Stars And Garters. Hosted by camp comedian Ray Martine, Joe sang Jimmy Reed's Shame, Shame, Shame while the band mimed the recorded backing. The appearance did little for the band although it is memorable for seeing Joe with his long, flowing locks. And then Decca didn't renew the recording contract. It looked like Joe had had his big chance and, like many singers before him, it was just assumed that that was the end of it. Undaunted, Cocker returned to Sheffield and carried on where he had left off, playing the pubs and clubs in and around the city. And, if anything, Cocker was more popular in the area than he had ever been. Jimmy Crawford and Dave Berry had been whisked away once they had been successful and perhaps Sheffield audiences were secretly a little bit glad that the same hadn't happened to Cocker.

Joe had become big friends with pianist Stu Moseley. One of their nights out together, watching the Hillbilly Cats at the Shiregreen Hotel, resulted in Joe and Stu getting beaten up: "It was my fault,although Joe likes to think it was because we were rock'n'rollers'" says Stu. "We were there with Joe and Eileen [Webster, Joe's girlfriend] and I went to the bar and looked round and saw this kid dressed as Dangerman. I said something like, 'Fuckin' hell, it's Dangerman,' I was still watching and laughing at Hillbilly Cat Pete Jackson who used to lark about with the double bass, spinning it about and things. When we got outside 'Dangerman' and his mates came for me and I got punched and kicked to the ground. They had winklepickers on and I got kicked under the chin and on my cheek, you can still see the winklepicker-shaped scar. Joe got kicked in the eye but still came to help, he'd no need to do that, but that was Joe for you. Eileen had a go, so did Monica, and Dave Memmott went and hid behind the van. I think there were about six of them. In the van going back home we were both laughing. We went up to the Centre Spot the following night and we both had black eyes."

By the end of 1964 the music scene was turning more towards R&B with bands like the Rolling Stones, Animals, Yardbirds, etc. Joe Cocker's Big Blues was one of the most committed in this field as their popularity around Sheffield proved. They ended the year in great style as they played a storming set at the Esquire's Boxing Night all-night session, sharing the bill with Dave Berry and the Cruisers, Scott William Combo and Dave Hawley.

The band had turned professional five months earlier but Joe and the band were finding the going tough with bookings few and far between. On the way home from a gig in Louth Joe announced, to everybody's amazement, that he was disbanding the group. Terry Thornton tried desperately to keep the band together. He discovered that a band was needed to play American bases in France for six weeks, but had to leave the next day. Joe, frantically ringing round, managed to get the band organised and off to France they went. On arrival in Calais Joe encountered problems with customs when they demanded a £450 deposit for the musical instruments. In Top Stars Joe explained how he overcame this: "I caught the

Girl singer Marie Woodhouse, aka Billie Rae, who toured France with Joe Cocker's Big Blues

next boat back to Dover and entered via Ostend and this only cost me a packet of cigarettes on the French border." In order to secure the tour the band had to have a girl singer and Thornton came to the rescue again by sending Marie Woodhouse out to France a fortnight later. She was a Diana Dors lookalike and apparently received half-a-dozen proposals of marriage while in France but declined in favour of concentrating on her singing career. "It was a tough time," says Thornton. "Joe was constantly on the phone asking for more money and reversing the charges. It cost me a fortune. Later, I received another call, this time asking for a 'moose or a 'pig' - the US request for a girl singer. They arrived at some base and they insisted on a girl. No girl, no gig. Marie had a broad Sheffield accent. The Yanks loved her and she went down a storm." The tour of American bases was centred on Orleans and at first, with no arranged accommodation, the band had to sleep in the van. But they found an audience - made up mainly of black American airmen. The band's opening number, Jimmy Reed's Baby What Do You Want Me To Do, was received with uproar that the band took to be disapproval. But the audience, fed-up of hearing Beatles' songs, loved it. Cocker had at last found an audience that was into his sort of music, a portent for where his future success was to lie. They even dubbed him 'Le Petit Ray Charles', as he told Top Stars: "We just didn't know how our brand of music would go down. Seventy per cent of the audiences we were getting were coloured people, and we'd heard they liked Ray Charles, James Brown and Marvin Gaye. The coloured airmen followed us to every club. We do one number called I Don't Mind by James Brown, a slow jerky blues, and they go crazy about it. One night this number lasted 25 minutes." Stu Moseley: "When he came back from France all he wanted to do was James Brown. He wanted

his band to sound like that."

Back home on the local scene Joe and the Big Blues became resident R&B group at monthly all-night jazz sessions at the Esquire. Elsewhere though his style was still at odds with the current musical trends as Dave Hopper recalls: "What Joe was doing was like more in front of time, or out of step, it wasn't commercial. At that time it was all Hollies and that stuff, like a speeded-up Liverpool sound, everything twice as fast. We'd gone from making more money than we'd been making in day jobs, which was about ten quid a week. We'd been getting about fifteen quid a week. That lasted about two years. We ran out of work at that particular time. The breaking point came when drummer Dave Memmott had to get rid of his van. We'd struggled on up to that point." Van driver Reg Featherstone: "Joe would pay everybody their money and not have any left for himself."

Following the final disbanding of the Big

The original Grease Band, Vernon Nash, Joe, Chris Stainton and Frank Miles

Blues, Joe decided to take time off from playing and got a job working at WH Smith's warehouse, by the Midland Station. Stu Moseley: "It was a bad time for him. I used to go down to see him at lunchtime in the Globe on Howard Street when he was working for Smith's and say, 'look this isn't going to last forever, come on.'"

One break in the clouds for Joe in 1967 was when his hero Ray Charles played at Manchester City Hall on April 20. Joe wrote a one-off review for the Sun Sound Special and noted: "A capacity second house crowd greeted the orchestra (minus Ray) with mild enthusiasm. A very hip-looking young negro was seated at the piano leading the orchestra through various well rehearsed, if slightly boring, instrumentals." The pianist turned out to be Billy Preston who was later to provide Joe with one of his career-songs You Are So Beautiful. The show got into gear when the Raelettes appeared and Joe was particularly taken by their version of a 3/4 blues titled One Hurt Deserves Another: "It moved me almost to tears with the sheer emotion in their voices. A never to be forgotten spot for me." When Ray appeared Joe observed: "Ray looked a lot calmer than on past performances, yet still had those nervous movements that makes it hard to believe that he's no longer taking drugs." The highlight for Joe was Ray's version of Going Down Slow: "A simple moving blues which he poured his heart into." Following Ray's selection of hits from his Modern Sounds In Country and Western period, Crying Time, Together Again etc, Joe elatedly wrote: "Finally he tore the place apart with his never dying smash What'd I Say and getting everyone out of their seats."

It was to be a year before Joe started making the occasional appearances round the city pubs again and, as reported in Top Stars, he was backed on a casual basis by members of Lizards. Deciding to get back on the scene, albeit this time on a semi-professional basis, Joe formed a new band. Green and Hopper's places were taken by two ex-Cruisers, John Fleet on bass and Frank Miles on guitar. Retained from the previous line-up were Vernon Nash and Dave Memmott. This became the first line-up of the Grease Band. Joe commented in Top Stars: "In future we're going to give a wider scope to our blues repertoire. Our numbers will still have a blues feeling, but we want to do more up to date, suitable material." There was also the intention to do cabaret work but John Fleet, who felt that Joe didn't have what it took for the cabaret scene, left after only a short stay with the band. His replacement was Chris Stainton who had met Joe through his song writing and recording activities with Frank Miles. "It was strange that our paths had never crossed all those years, living in the same town," says Chris. "And by 1967 we both could feel the twilight. If we didn't do something soon we'd get lost." With a new line up and impetus a new name was chosen, the Grease Band. "We wanted to choose a name that would upset everyone and that's what we came up with," Joe later told Disc Weekly. There was also a lot of humour in Joe's act at the time with ad-libbed lyrics and flippant remarks that could often be as entertaining as his soulful singing. The 1967 live recording for the Rag Goes Mad At the Mojo captures this to perfection on a couple of songs, Saved and I've Been Trying. Stu Moseley: "A lot of people went for the humour. He was an incredibly funny man. On stage he'd sometimes just keep a riff going and he'd talk about all sorts. He'd have you in fits. He was a most modest guy, everybody loved him and he didn't have an enemy in the world."

He had residencies at the Arbourthorne on Mondays; the Markham Arms on Thursdays and the Highcliffe at Greystones on Saturdays. He also became synonymous with the Black Swan on Snig Hill. But, as landlord Terry Steeples recalls, Joe was reluctant to play there at first: "It took me ages to get him to come. He said, 'I'm not coming to play for townies.' But I finally got him in the Penny Farthing one night. I said, 'Come on, stop messing about. What about doing a lunchtime?' 'Lunchtime?' he says, 'I don't get up till bloody afternoon.' Anyway I got him for noon and night for 25 pound but I had to send a taxi for him to get him out of bed while the crowd were waiting for him. He was still in bed at one o'clock. I sent a taxi, got him there, and he looked like death warmed up. He went an absolute storm."

Grease Band members Frank Miles and Chris Stainton had been collaborating with fellow musician Tom Rattigan as a song writing team and had come up with an instrumental titled March Of The Mysterons. Joe added some lyrics and it became Marjorine. Frank wrote another song called I'm Free which Joe demoed at the Egg-Box studio. By October 1967 Joe Cocker's Grease Band, despite keeping a low profile, was voted Top Group in the Local Awards in that year's Top Stars Poll. Joe was quoted in Top Stars as saying: "You're joking. That's marvellous, it really is," Most of their votes came from the Chesterfield area where they were more popular than in their home city. Joe added: "In Sheffield you can carry on until you die and not get anywhere. It's hopeless." Cocker's big break was about to happen. It started with Chesterfield DJ David McPhie, who had first seen Joe perform at the Lathkilldale Hotel in Derbyshire in 1963 and had been following Joe's development ever since. The Grease Band had started playing original material during the Wednesday night residency at the Barrow Hill Hotel and it was McPhie who persuaded Cocker and Stainton to record some of it on a loaned tape recorder at McPhie's flat in Chesterfield. "Joe was getting very dispirited playing at places like Barrow Hill for £10 a night and I think I stopped him packing it all in," said McPhie. Cocker was not happy: "Disheartened, I felt a freak and awful. It tore me up. Nobody recognised the style and sound I was trying to achieve." He was also hung up about his appearance. Because he tended to the porky side he thought he would never be able make it, especially when tall, slender, good looking singers such as Robert Plant were becoming all the rage. John Fleet, bass player with the Big Blues, summed him up: "He was superb but I never thought he would be famous, he was slightly portly, beer-swilling, not very sartorially elegant. He looked like an unmade bed."

Publicity shot for Regal Zonophone

When Chris and Joe recorded Marjorine, along with two other songs they had written, Sandpaper Cadillac and New Age Of The Lily, McPhie took the tape to London promotions manager Tony Hall, arriving at his door at 3am. "I was just about getting into bed when there was this terrific banging on the door of my flat. You can imagine I was more than irritated. When I opened the door there was a young man on the step waving this demo disc at me and demanding that I should give it a hearing." Hall listened to the demo and was immediately impressed: "It

was Joe's version of Marjorine. I was so knocked out by his voice that I played it all weekend." Hall then played it to several other music people one of whom was independent producer Denny Cordell who, as Chris Stainton recalls, was one of the hottest names in the recording industry: "He was flying high on Procol Harum at the time. He'd got some number one hits and he was the hot producer of the moment." Cordell was knocked out by what he heard and made arrangements to get Cocker signed to EMI's reactivated Regal Zonophone label. Signed up and in the studio, Joe re-cut Marjorine. Denny Cordell: "We went into the studio and laid down the backing tracks first. We had Jimmy Page, Chris Stainton played piano and bass and I think Clem Cattini played drums. So we finished the little track and that sounded great and the time came for Joe to sing and I thought, 'I hope this guy can cut it, 'cos the track sounded good.' He opened his mouth and we could not believe it. We all immediately thought of Ray Charles. He had this deep, tuneful, beautifully expressive, soulful voice." Marjorine immediately found favour with the weekly pop press such as New Record Mirror's Penny Valentine who said: "Some records are definite hits. This is. I can't really explain why but I feel it in my bones - and my bones are as good as anything. Apart from all that, it's a fantastic record. So there." Disc & Music Echo wrote: "The single is already causing such a furore in pop circles that it seems we shall be seeing Mr Cocker in the crowd and picked out for stardom very shortly."

Back home changes were afoot. Joe Cocker and the Grease Band were to play their last gig together at the Arbourthorne Hotel on Sunday, March 24, 1968. Frank Miles had been in this position before with the Cruisers: "Twice in my lifetime. How many times can you take a knock like that?" As Joe explained in Top Stars: "Denny was not satisfied with most of the group and he suggested we should make some changes. So I was left with Chris and started to audition replacements. Over 200 people applied and one day I listened to 42 drummers playing the same song." A new Grease Band was put together recruiting keyboard player Tommy Eyre from former Fortune Glen Dale's band the Candies. Eyre: "Joe kept Vernon on till he knew what I was gonna do and Vernon didn't get a week's notice." After auditions in London, two ex-members of Tom Jones' band the Squires, guitarist Mickey Gee and drummer Tommy Reilly, were also brought in. Having now moved to London, Joe and Chris rehearsed the new band every day for three weeks before they embarked on bookings their management had arranged. The new Grease Band toured the country's college and club circuit alongside bands such as Spooky Tooth, Family and Traffic. The tightness of these bands highlighted a weakness in the Grease Band's rhythm section and replacements for Reilly and Gee were needed. However, none were immediately lined up as Joe was busy in the studio, with Stevie

Winwood and Jim Capaldi helping out. Back on the road two new members were brought into the Grease Band with Sheffield drummer and former Cruiser Kenny Slade - "I'd played with Cocker earlier on in the Cocker Blues Band, standing in" - and Ulsterman and former Eire Apparent guitarist Henry McCullough.

With the help of Chris Stainton, Joe was able to put into music some of his 'head' arrangements for With A Little Help as Linda Harvey recalled: "Chris'd listen to a tune and say, 'It

ought to be done like this.' He helped to change With A Little Help From My Friends completely." However, as Tommy Eyre explains: "Joe had discovered the waltz time. He wanted to do everything waltz time. Absolutely stupid. He did, 'Pack up all my cares and woe, here I go' (Bye, Bye Blackbird). Joe's thinkin', 'All these terrible old songs, let's do 'em in 3/4'." Joe: "I always loved, again, the Ray Charles influence and waltz 3/4 and I was thinking wouldn't it be good to do a modern kind of song in that kind of treatment. For some odd reason I thought of With A Little Help and I was sat on the outside toilet in Tasker Road y'know with my pants down around my knees [laughs]. I don't know why that should give me any inspiration, but I thought it's such an odd song. It was just a thread of an idea with Tommy Eyre and Chris Stainton. Tommy put that brilliant bit of organ in the front and then I envisaged the vocal part and of course it became quite an epic." In Record Mirror of October 19, Joe recalled his feelings on reviving the song: "I was a little worried about doing such an old Beatles number, but my fears were put to rest by Denny Cordell who records me, and almost everyone else who's heard it." The record soon began to gain ground in the charts, helped by TV appearances on shows like Dee Time, the Tony Blackburn Show, How It Is and, of course, Top Of The Pops. Top Stars reported that John Lennon and Paul McCartney were so pleased with Joe's success with the song they sent him a telegram saying, "Thank you Joe, you're far too much." It was a massive hit, reaching the top of the British charts on November 9, 1968, a pattern which was to be repeated across Europe but not, strangely enough, in the States where it faltered outside the top 40. Cocker was in demand, even more so when people finally saw on their televisions the amazing spectacle of his flailing arms and array of tortured facial expressions. His stage persona betrayed a frustrated guitarist as Stu Moseley remembers: "He always wanted to learn guitar but he hadn't got the temperament." Not since the equally bizarre but more spidery and mysterious movements of another singer from Sheffield, one Dave Berry, had such a physically animated stage performer been seen on British TV. Even at this early stage people outside the city were beginning to think there must be something in the water in Sheffield. Joe became big news with features and interviews in all the major music weeklies showing him dressed in his Rotherham bus driver's jacket, combined with a pink shirt and green velvet trousers.

As the record hit number one, Joe returned to Sheffield for another promised gig at the Black Swan on Wednesday, November 13. As was expected the place was absolutely packed with local fans who had come to see Joe and his powerhouse band riding on the crest of a wave. His set blasted off with Moby Grape's Can't Be So Bad and included Ray Charles' Let's Go Get Stoned, Bob Dylan's Just Like A Woman, Marjorine and closed with With A Little Help From My Friends. Sat at the front was Joe's beloved mother Madge, who presented him with a cake with the inscription "With A Little Help From Your Friends" to celebrate his success. Also marking Joe's success, Top Stars afforded him a special four-page spread charting his career, plus words of praise from his father Harold and brother Vic, as well as Dave Berry, Terry Steeples, Pete Stringfellow and Ray Stuart. The November 23 issue of Melody Maker also featured a piece headed Joe Cocker's Friends that introduced each member of the Grease Band, plus Sue and Sunny the two girl backing singers on Joe's chart-topping record.

The beginning of 1969 saw major changes in the Grease band with the departure of Kenny Slade and Tommy Eyre who seemed musically at odds with the other members. Kenny Slade: "We got the sack for being too jazzy. I was playing what was required but Tommy was playing some really awkward chords that didn't really match with what we were doing. We've always been mates and if he went, I went, we were that close." Tommy Eyre: "Our faces didn't fit... You see Joe had been elevated into that super hip society and me and Sladey weren't hip - we didn't say 'vibe' or 'far out' or smoke a lot of ganja,

which made me throw up," partly blaming Chris Stainton because he wanted to play piano. In their places came Londoners Bruce Rowlands on drums and Alan Spenner on bass, both ex-members of Wynder K Frogg, with Chris Stainton moving to keyboards. Joe and the Grease Band spent most of February and March on a nationwide package tour that included Gene Pitney, the Marmalade and Mike Cotton Sound. Sheffield got its first chance to see the new line-up when the tour reached Sheffield City Hall, Joe greeting the audience with the words: "It's quite different in here. Gone is the aroma of the pints of beer we used to have to down at the old Black Swan." Backstage Joe told Top Stars: "I have tried to keep my repertoire as unchanged as possible. Most of my songs are the ones I sang around the Sheffield clubs not so very long ago." He also expanded on the reasons for Slade and Eyre's departures: "We decided to part company - they agreed their personal leanings were towards jazz and mine to rock'n'roll." With A Little Help From My Friends also began to take off in America. An appearance on the Ed Sullivan Show heralded Joe's arrival in the US followed by gigs at major venues like the New York Fillmore and major rock festivals in Newport, California, Atlantic City and of course the momentous Woodstock Fesival. An album, With A Little Help From My Friends, featuring covers of Just Like A Woman, Do I Still Figure In Your Life and Don't Let Me Be Misunderstood, plus Cocker/Stainton originals A Change In Louise and Sandpaper Cadillac, helped consolidate Joe's US success.

In October, 1969, Joe and the Grease Band were back in England, recuperating at the Berkshire home of Island Records' boss Chris Blackwell, and appearing at the Isle Of Wight Festival. Tracks for the next album were laid down including George Harrison's Something and the Beatles' She Came In Through The Bathroom Window. Joe aired six numbers of his new album when he made a guest appearance back at the Black Swan that month. After refusing to do some of the old numbers which made him famous locally, Joe replied: "We are not living in the past, it's the future." The majority of the new album, Joe Cocker, was recorded with Denny Cordell in the A&M studio in the States and included backing from Clarence White of the Byrds, singer Bonnie Bramlett and steel guitarist Sneaky Pete Kleinow. There was also the first fruits of his meeting, through Denny Cordell, with the so-called 'master of space and time' Leon Russell, when Delta Lady hit the British charts in November. The Oklahoma-born session champ went on to play a major role in Joe's career and the great slab of southern rock that is Delta Lady helped maintain Joe's momentum by providing him with the follow up hit to With A Little Help from My Friends.

A second American tour followed but things were beginning to fall apart in the Grease Band again. Cocker was exhausted but found himself committed to a third tour. Only Chris Stainton remained from the band and it was only when Russell stepped in that the tour could definitely go ahead. He assmbled a ten-piece band, mostly pinched from Delaney and Bonnie's band, of top US musicians and singers. The legendary Mad Dogs and Englishmen tour began in February 1970. Excess, both musically and narcotically, hit Cocker physically and mentally. It was also done in the full glare of the camera. Anybody who has seen the Mad Dogs And Englishmen film will find it hard to forget the sheer exhaustion and despair on Cocker's face the further the tour went. Many pop stars before and since have gone through similar experiences but without a camera to tell the whole world that something was seriously wrong. Joe Cocker's agony became public property. Amazingly the tour also yielded a tremendous double live album which yielded two more hits with a new version of the Box Tops' hit The Letter and a superb reworking of the old Julie London hit Cry Me A River.

Despite the success of the tour, album and subsequent film, Mad Dogs And Englishmen took its toll on Joe, as Stu Moseley recalls: "Joe had to do the Mad Dogs tour, he didn't want to do it and there was this argy-bargy with the guys in America who were a bit handy with, you know... He thought his life was in danger, and it probably was." When the tour ended in May, Cocker went into hibernation in Los Angeles. "When it was over there just seemed no point in going on - my mind was confused and all I wanted to do was get away from everything and everyone." He eventually fled back to Sheffield for the safety and comfort of Tasker Road in Christmas, 1970. His return also marked the final breaking of the links with his native city. "After that Mad Dog tour I'd lost the connections I had with the Sheffield musicians and it was always kind of bitter. The guys who were left behind and my age had never got record deals and they made me feel like hey, what are you back here for?' It's a shame because I loved slinking around the pubs - they were a big part of my life." Stu Moseley: "When he wasn't touring, he virtually had a room at our house in Sharrow." Monica Moseley: "He would just sit on the floor gawping into space for hours on end." Stu: "When Leon Russell played at Sheffield University Denny Cordell came round early in the morning to ask if Joe wanted to go but he wasn't interested."

During his sabbatical Yorkshire Television caught up with a visibly worn-out Joe for a short feature on their Calendar programme. The period, which stretched off and on for almost a

Grisly godfather: Joe and godson Matthew Moseley

decade, has been dubbed Cocker's 'lost week-end'. Stu Moseley: "People used to ring up all the time. It became known as double your money time, people asking for money, saying they would pay back twice as much in a few weeks time." Monica: "He was invaded. And we were invaded. People came out of the woodwork and if there was any sighting of him people would come round to our house to see if he was there." Stu: "I'd go to bed at night and I would get up in the morning and there would be guys in my living room that I didn't know." Monica: "His mum and dad used to get cross with us, thinking it was all our fault, but we were just looking after him." Monica: "There was the time Joe said 'right I'm coming down,' and Stu said he'd send a taxi. Joe thought this bloke Stu sent was a friend of his but he wasn't at all he was just from a taxi firm. So when this taxi driver realised who he had picked up he took Joe home to his house and invited him in, introducing Joe to his wife and family. Joe went along with it because he thought the driver was Stuart's friend. Eventually the taxi driver brought him round to our house, by which time it was about four in the morning, I was in bed, and the taxi driver wouldn't go. He wanted to come in. He must have sat there for hours." Stu: "And at the end of it he said, 'that'll be £40,' because it was Joe. We gave him the £40 and I think I threatened him with a bottle of milk because the milkman had been round by that time."

Joe had already had minor skirmishes with the authorities. In October, 1968, he had been fined a total of £55 for possession of cannabis and illegally attempting to export cannabis, and in December the same year a cannabis possession charge against him was dismissed in London. Cocker occasionally tried to make a foray back into touring, mostly with disastrous results. For instance in 1972, in Adelaide, Australia, after an equally disastrous tour of the States, Cocker, Alan Spenner, Chris Stainton, his wife Ellyn, Neil Hubbard, James Karstein and Felix Falcon were charged with possession of marijuana. Each were fined £140, plus a deportation order. Cocker was also charged with assault and using indecent language in Melbourne, charges that were later dropped. He tried to get away and in 1973 he lived in a remote cottage on Bodmin Moor for nine weeks. In the same year the question was asked in the Sheffield Star - what has happened to Sheffield's wandering star? His publicist, one Max Clifford, said: "Nothing much at all. He's quietly hiding away." In 1978 he was refused entry into the United States when he arrived at

Joe in full flight

San Antonio, Texas, without a visa. When he finally did get in he ended up being sued by a landlord for £7,600 damage to a Hollywood house, as reported in the Sheffield Star.

Joe still managed to retain a creditable recording career, releasing a string of albums in the Seventies - Something To Say (1973), I Can Stand A Little Rain (1974), Jamaica Say You Will (1975), Stingray (1976) and Luxury You Can Afford (1978). But apart from the 1974 single You Are So Beautiful, a poignant ballad written by Billy Preston which showed how much Joe's voice had suffered in the meantime, there was no chart success. Indeed he was virtually written off as another rock casualty. In 1975 Joe returned to the stage and undertook a tour of Hawaii. With him again was Kenny Slade this time on congas: "I begged him, I said, 'Come on Joe, tha' wants a reight conga player, let me come.'" On tour Kenny also acted as MC: "I was what they called the warm-up man. I'm on stage shouting 'Is Everybody Allllriight,' in red silk shirt, hat with feathers and high-heel boots!" Along with Kenny was another set of excellent musicians - Pete Gavin on drums, Richard Tee, keyboards, Gordon Edwards, bass, and Albert Lee and Cornell Dupree on guitars. Afterwards

Joe once again returned home to find sanctuary.

Sightings of Joe in Sheffield were few and far between although he did occasionally get up and sing with Frank White's Band at various venues. One of his more infamous appearances was at the Top Rank in 1976/77 where pick up band Hinkley's Heroes, an outfit which featured ex-Grease Band guitarist Henry McCullough, were playing. Martin Lilleker recalls this Afghan-coated, bearded, greasy-haired, wellington-booted, vagrant-looking bloke accosting him in the car park beneath the Top Rank before the concert. "It was a very out of it Joe Cocker. He wanted to know where the Top Rank was." Also there was student Martin Bedford: "The band had played a few numbers and then there was something going on in the audience. This guy was being shoved forward and it was Joe Cocker. He was plastered and you could see that the band were horrified. He got on stage - luckily it wasn't very high - and he started on a song and it was obvious he was totally bolloxed, he was all over the place. The band struggled on and when the number finished Joe just turned round, stuck his fingers down his throat, and threw up over the speaker stack. He then proceeded to do a storming version of A Little Help From My Friends, which was appropriate." It would seem Joe had got vomiting down to a fine art. Deke Leonard of Welsh band Man bumped into Joe in Los Angeles: "We were booked into the Continental Hyatt House. As we walked through the foyer doors we found our way blocked by a paralytic Joe Cocker coming the other way. He swayed from side to side, much like he does on stage, took a deep breath, and vomited at our feet. Holding our noses we skirted the pile of vomit, wished him a pleasant evening and checked-in. He disappeared into the darkness, obviously going out for the night."

His reputation went before him and continued to dog him even after he had cleaned up his act, reaching a culmination in Austria when a promoter accused him of being too drunk to perform at a May 1, 1984, concert in Vienna. Cocker ended up in jail for 36 hours, accused with accepting money for a show he would not do. The truth was that the promoter was covering his own back, as he had failed to provide the necessary equipment for the show to take place, and a blood test proved Cocker was clear of alcohol. Ray Stuart said at the time: "An undeserved reputation has gone before him. He's been condemned because he has been in trouble before. People have always taken advantage of him in other ways too. He has always been generous. When people have asked for money, Joe has given it. Because he's soft, he's been ripped off. Once he was picked up in New York's Central Park as a suspected vagrant - he had a 6,000 dollar cheque in his pocket."

It wasn't until he teamed up with the

Stu Mosely and Joe, September '82 before homecoming gig at the Lyceum

Up where they belong: Joe Cocker and
Jennifer Warnes

Crusaders in 1981, who asked him to sing I'm
So Glad I'm Standing Here Today, a painfully
appropriate sentiment, that his career began to
become re-established. He performed the song
with them at the 1981 Grammy Awards. Cocker
was well and truly on the mend, physically and
careerwise, Mother Madge revealing that
actress Jane Fonda had persuaded Cocker to
live on her 120-acre farm in California to give up
drinking and take up cycling. It was also around
this time that he met his future wife Pam Baker,
an American child care counsellor, who was to
finally straighten him out after his bouts of drink
and drugs excess.

The renaissance continued a year later with
the fine album, again appropriately titled,
Sheffield Steel. He also played his first official
dates in his home city for 13 years when he
appeared on successive nights in September
1982 at the re-opened Lyceum. It was an emotional occasion with musicians and friends from
the previous 20-plus years turning out in force.
He dedicated You Are So Beautiful to mother
Madge who was watching from the 'Royal' box.
A few months later his comeback was well and
truly consolidated when he duetted with Jennifer
Warnes on Up Where We Belong. The theme
song for the film An Officer And A Gentleman, it
almost seemed to have been written about him.
It was a huge hit on both sides of the Atlantic.
He went on to consolidate that success worldwide, although ironically one of his least successful markets has been the UK, whereas in
Germany, Poland and much of Eastern Europe
he is still a superstar. Cocker secretly married
Pam Baker in California in 1987, the service
being conducted by their local plumber who was
also a spare time vicar. She had become his
constant companion on the road. "She's much
more together than I am," he said.

By now Cocker was a regular on the American
and European tour circuits bit it wasn't until
1989 that he made his first official appearance
in Sheffield for seven years, selling out the City
Hall. "Thanks for coming Joe," shouted out one
punter. Joe replied: "It's all right love." After all
those years he hadn't changed. Father Harold
still didn't show up to see his son perform,
always happier potting plants than listening to
pop music. Indeed one of Harold's few public
statements came in a letter to The Star newspaper in the early Nineties, extolling the virtues
of an ironing board that had been, and still was,
an important part of the Cocker household
since the late Thirties. Brother Vic, now a
wealthy man thanks to his job with one of the
privatised Water Boards, was there however.

His home city finally gave Joe's achievements
some recognition in November, 1994, when
Sheffield Hallam University awarded him an hon-
orary doctorate. It was for service to the arts.
Following the ceremony of planting a comem-
morative tree, he looked resplendent in cap and
gown as he received his doctorate on stage at
the City Hall. His proud dad Harold was there to
watch the ceremony but he still declined to go
and watch Joe perform on stage at Sheffield
Arena that night.

More albums have followed and his market is
now bigger than ever, particularly in Europe, but
the music has become bland. He also made an
appearance at Woodstock II in 1994, 25 years
after the original event. "The crowd were doing
that body surfing and passing up these half
naked girls in front of me - I didn't feel as though
I really had their full attention." His visits back
to Sheffield have become even more infrequent,
especially since mother Madge died in 1984. As
reflected in his disappointing UK record sales of
the nineties, it would also seem likely that a full-
scale UK tour would be uneconomical these
days. Therefore visits to his home city are likely
to be few and far between, despite there still
being many, many loyal fans in Sheffield.

He now lives in a 17-bedroom mansion in the
Rocky Mountains amid the stunning wilderness
of Colorado. Residents of the nearby tiny town
Steamboat Springs dubbed it Cocker's Castle.
Cocker has his own name for it, Mad Dog Ranch,
after the infamous 1970 Mad Dogs and
Englishmen tour. He's never lost his Sheffield
sense of humour.

Of course the Joe Cocker story has been told
in detail via the excellent biography A Little Help
From My Friends. The man responsible is one
time member of folk/ bluegrass duo the
Louisville Burglars and local crime historian JP
Bean. As well as following Joe's subsequent
career, the book is certainly another a fine

Still standing: Joe Cocker now

insight into some of the Sheffield music scene of the Sixties, regardless of what Joe's US fans may think. JP Bean: "The Americans like to believe that Joe only began to sing the day he arrived in America." Bean's biography on Joe certainly proved otherwise.

5. THE KILLAMARSH KILLER: CHUCK FOWLER

One of Sheffield's earliest rock'n'roll performers was the pumpin' piano man Brian 'Chuck' Fowler. Born in Beighton, Chuck was the son of a musician: "My father was an organist and a classical music devotee and naturally the house was full of sheet music and classical records. He played the pipe organ in various churches and cathedrals. I started having piano lessons at around the age of seven. It was just a chore really." The first thing Chuck learned to play was Bewitched, an instrumental hit for Bill Snyder, but his first real musical awakening was around 1948/49 through the jazz and pop stylings of people like Glenn Miller, Count Basie, Dakota Staton, Earl Bostic, Lionel Hampton and Stan Kenton. Chuck also got into the stirring gospel singing of Mahalia Jackson along with the hillbilly bop of Tennessee Ernie Ford and the lonesome country sound of Hank Williams. "Settin' The Woods On Fire, that made me sit up

when I heard it at Beighton fair. I used to go up and ask the bloke playing the records, 'Would you mind telling me what that song was?'" Much of these early sounds pointed the way towards rock'n'roll. "I suppose subconsciously, that's what I was looking for. I've always had a liking for boogie woogie and rhythm and blues so I suppose rock'n'roll was a spin-off from those two forms of music."

Chuck got caught up in skiffle and taught himself to play guitar: "I fancied the guitar, and pianos were for cissies at that time. My first guitar was bought from a cousin in Nottingham but I hadn't got a clue how to play it. It was a scabby old Spanish thing. I used to practise strumming. Then I bought another from Cann's down Dixon Lane - a Martin Coletti with a cutaway." He soon put together his first band with older brother Don on drums and neighbourhood pals Frank Miles on guitar and Pete 'Pop' Taylor on bass. Their first booking was at the Angel, Killamarsh: "They demanded we had a name. We couldn't think of anything and the previous night we'd been watching 6:5 Special with Don Lang and the Frantic Five so we said we'll call ourselves the Frantic Four. Frank Miles lived next door and I used to make him play all the lead bits. He was pretty good and he caught on fast. We went out and bought these 78 rpm records and tried to learn them as best we could. Me and Frank spent hours trying to get Scotty Moore and Chuck Berry stuff something like."

Frank Miles explains the kind of music they were playing: "It was a strange thing because skiffle was in but Chuck had always been in with country and rockabilly and Chuck Berry. So even then we were playing bits of all sorts. I wouldn't say we were advanced musically, but we were in our choice of material, but that was Chuck's choice really, he was the one who was into Chuck Berry before anybody else." Other book-

Frantic Four: Brian Fowler, Frank Miles, Don Fowler, Pete Taylor

ings followed at the Cumberland Head in Beighton, the Squirrel at Dinnington and Crown at Clowne. An occasional trip out of town saw them become a popular attraction at the Cock Inn, Ripley. Chuck and his band also made a successful appearance at a talent contest in Skegness: "My brother had gone for a holiday and we went to visit him. We took our guitars and stuff with us and we just got up on stage to sing."

Eventually Chuck returned to his first instrument: "When rock'n'roll came in, particularly the piano stylists, I thought, 'Mmm, there's nobody playing piano. I'll have a go at the piano, same as Jerry Lee Lewis.' And basically that's where I took off. I just copied him, all by ear." Chuck first saw and heard Jerry Lee in the film High School Confidential but he wasn't impressed: "I thought, 'He looks a bit bloody strange, this bloke.' What people don't realise is that basically I class myself as a singer rather than an instrumentalist so I was really into having a good shout down the mike - and the piano just came in handy. It was the beat and I just loved to sing." Frank Miles: "There was nobody playing piano in the rock'n'roll style then in the country, only possibly Roy Budd, and Chuck was rattlin' away like mad."

However, any plans for the band were forgotten when Chuck volunteered for National Service. His brother Don Fowler: "He never told me he was going to join up, I don't know why he did it. If he hadn't, he would have made it in music because nobody else was doing what he was doing." For the next three years Chuck served in the Royal Air Force, stationed in Singapore and then one of the islands nearby. "It was all right but I got fed up in the end of sharing a billet with a load of other blokes. Six months on the island represented a year so it cut my time down by six months which pleased me." To relieve some of the boredom Chuck got involved in music again: "I had various bands while I was in, playing the guitar mainly because pianos were a bit hard to come by. Whenever there was a piano in the naffis I'd play that. But we didn't have much of a regular band while I was abroad. We had one when I came back to England, stationed near Stamford, and they called us the Apaches."

Upon his demob, Brian returned home to find his successor in the Frantic Four, Dave Berry, was now a big local name and on the verge of national success. Naturally Chuck wanted to get back into music and looked round for an opportunity. It came when he saw an advert for a band called Jess Hunter and the Trekkers. "They

Weddings - Parties - Clubs

FRANTIC FOUR

Skiffle - Rock-n-Roll - Pops

Enquire :
A. TAYLOR.

62, Allan Road,
Beighton,
Sheffield.

advertised for a manager cum promoter, must have a van." Trekkers guitarist Mick Brady: "Chuck became our manager simply because he had a van and we needed transport." Chuck: "I went down and they were rehearsing in this bedroom and everybody was plugged into the bloody light-fitting. I remember they were doing a Chuck Berry thing, Little Queenie I think, and I had to put 'em straight. I said, 'You're playing the wrong chords here, lads.'" Chuck also became rhythm guitarist and occasional vocalist/ pianist. Eventually Hunter left and Chuck took over as leader, with drummer Lol Naylor and Bob

Chuck Fowler Six: Dick Dodd, Dave Jones, John Firminger, Keith Chalmers, Jimmy Spencer and Chuck

Taylor on bass. He started concentrating on piano - where there was one. "I've been to clubs and they've said, 'No we haven't got a piano.' Then they'd ask round, 'Harry, has tha' mother got a piano in her back room?' And they wheeled a bloody piano across the street to the club. Sometimes you'd have to tune the buggers up. Sometimes it would be a full tone out from concert pitch so we'd have to de-tune the guitar and bass and I'd finish up singing like Paul Robeson. If a sax player came with us there'd be nights when they couldn't play because of the piano."

Chuck continued to re-establish himself on the local scene fronting a variety of Chuck Fowler Fours or Combos, hammering out the songs of Jerry Lee Lewis, Fats Domino and Little Richard, etc. Chuck was a particular favourite on the Sheffield pub circuit at places like the Birley Hotel, Centre Spot, Shiregreen Hotel, and the Highcliffe at Greystones. Alan Wood joined Chuck as lead guitarist: "I'd worked with Frank White, Dave Hawley and Dave Rawson and I thought I'd have a go and see how it works out. I knew really that it wasn't my thing. I wasn't as fluent as you should be for a lead guitar player. It was all right at the time because Chuck was the lead instrument and he never really wanted an overpowering guitar player. He wanted a rhythm guitar player who could play the odd solo. We played at a mission hut in Barnsley for our first gig."

In December 1965 Chuck decided to break up the band, apparently fed up with the type of music he'd been playing and pub audience response (or lack of it). Chuck, with John Firminger in tow on drums, started working a Friday and Saturday night residency at the County Borough Hotel, Rotherham, a notoriously rough and sleazy venue. They persevered, playing to waifs and strays as well as the odd music fan, for around three months. "The landlord could see we weren't enjoying it," John recalls. "And he was quite understanding when we told him we were chucking it in." Chuck and John then put together a six-piece with Dick Dodd on bass, Bob Threadgold on guitar and featuring the two saxes of Keith Chalmers and ex-Lynch Mob and Dave Clark Five member Jimmy Spencer. Chuck also planned to introduce some of the soul sounds of Otis Redding and

Rockin' partnership: Dave Hawley/Chuck Fowler Combo

Wilson Pickett but as John Firminger recalls: "We played more rock'n'roll than anything else and it was a good solid band. The saxes sounded great when we did the Little Richard or Larry Williams' numbers." The new line-up made an impressive debut at a special New Year's Eve rock'n'roll bash at the Highcliffe Hotel.

Keeping a six-piece band active eventually got too much and Chuck's next move was to join forces with singer/guitarist Dave Hawley. John Firminger recalls the split: "I was pretty cut up when Chuck went with Dave, especially as I'd stuck by him and endured some of the dross we had to play to at the County Borough." Dave Hawley: "I loved Jerry Lee Lewis and Chuck was the only band I wanted to play with. He impressed me from the very first time I saw him." The Fowler/Hawley band proved to be popular, especially with local rock'n'roll fans, however the amalgamation only lasted a few months. Dave Hawley: "I didn't want to be a front man. I just wanted to back Chuck but he wanted me to get out there and sing. I used to do it under sufferance." At the beginning of 1967 Chuck put together his own trio with ex-Jimmy Crawford drummer John Hunt and bass player Keith Richardson and began concentrating on work in the clubs where the old rock'n'roll was still going down well. Another change in early 1968 brought back two musicians from a previous line-up, bass player Bob Taylor and John Firminger on drums. The trio worked regularly as Chuck commented at the time: "We play

Chuck with Terry Jenkinson and Gerry Wigley

clubs, pubs, dances and cabaret - the lot - and average four or five bookings a week." Still continuing as a trio Chuck was reunited with his original guitarist Frank Miles this time doubling on a self-made twin-necked guitar and bass as Top Stars heralded Old Friends Join Up Again. Another former Cruiser and Hillbilly Cat, Roger Jackson, also came in later on drums.

In 1973 Chuck, now with drummer Gerry Wigley and bass player Terry Jenkinson, landed a summer season at Butlins on Barry Island, South Wales. The band was not only popular with holidaymakers but with other musicians working at the camp and would often get together for informal jams. Jenkinson found it particular hard going as Chuck recalls: "He chucked the towel in after the second season. He got brassed off with it. We all did. It was bloody hard work." In 1974 Chuck made a bid for fame when he appeared on Hughie Green's Opportunity Knocks. "We auditioned at Bellhouse Road Club. We just went through our repertoire of Your Cheatin' Heart and Irene Goodnight and they loved it." On TV Chuck and the band - Steve Smith on bass and Ian Matthews on drums - looked striking dressed in garish long-tail coats. "We'd had these satin tails made. The drummer's was purple with yellow lining - they looked cool." Chuck's rock'n'roll went down well but they were only runners-up. "We thought we'd cracked it there, but nothing happened," said Chuck.

Continuing to play the songs of his hero Jerry Lee Lewis, with one of his bands Chuck recorded a storming version of Jerry Lee's version of Chantilly Lace. It featured some fine steel guitar from Roy Barber. Different musicians came and went including, for a very brief stint, monster drummer Kenny Slade. "His playing didn't really suit me 'cos I'm a basic rock'n'roller and it depends on basic drumming and he was too fancy for me." In 1977 Chuck was reunited briefly once again with guitarist/singer Dave Hawley and, along with John Crookes on sax and harmonica, worked together as Breathless. Another ensemble included John Riley on drums and Roy Barber on steel and lead guitar, leaning more towards country/rock. In the late 70s Chuck joined forces with fellow rocker Steve Denton to form a rock'n'roll showband under the guidance of agent Alan Wood: "Rock'n'roll was back in, Shakin' Stevens was hot and there were the Jets, Matchbox and Flying Saucers and all the rockabilly bands. I was getting calls like, 'Do you know any rock'n'roll bands, we've got X number of pounds to spend.' So I thought, 'Right, there's a little niche for a rock'n'roll

Chuck Fowler Band: Dave Smith, Alan Wood, John Crookes, Steve Denton, Chuck, Dave Hopper

band.' So I got together Dave Cannon on drums, myself on bass, Dave Hopper on guitar, Chuck Fowler on piano and vocals, John Crookes on sax and harmonica and Steve Denton vocals." Chuck: "It was Alan's idea to get a kind of Elvis/Jerry Lee sort of show but unfortunately it didn't work out. He wanted Denton dressed up in a GI suit." The band cut an album and also had a single released which managed to get in the top five of the national rock'n'roll charts. Alan Wood: "The album got picked up by Radio One and we did loads of work for Radio One. We did jingles for Peter Powell and Kid Jensen." This attention led to Alan getting the band a recording deal with Rockburgh Records. A single was issued featuring Steve Denton on one side singing Elvis's Mystery Train and Chuck on the other singing a song he'd first picked up in his Frantic Four days, RockabyeBoogie by the Davis Sisters. Alan Wood: "It made number one in the alternate rock'n'roll charts in the Melody Maker, keeping out Shakin' Stevens and everybody. We worked three nights a week and earned good money. It was a show. I'd start with an Eddie Cochran song, Dave Hopper would do a Chuck Berry song with the duck walk, John Crookes would play Yakkety Sax, Chuck would come on and do a Jerry Lee then we'd feature Steve

doing Elvis. We'd got a good cross-section of stuff. We'd got a nice PA system, very organised for such a dishevelled bunch of apparent musicians and we did well." In the end professional jealousy between Denton and Fowler brought frustration to the outfit. Chuck then turned towards the UK country scene, with yet another new band, and they were runners-up in the finals of a national talent contest at Wembley.

Finding it hard to keep a band together, Chuck eventually went solo utilising a keyboard which featuring backing effects, although the results sometimes sounded like a cross between Jerry Lee Lewis and Mantovani. He continued playing solo right up until his death in 1999. His last two appearances were at a couple of benefit gigs to raise money so that Chuck, now stricken with cancer, could go on a final journey to the States to see Gracelands and other rock 'n' roll landmarks. He died just days after the final concert at the Richmond Club, where he gave an incredible final performance. Throughout the various line-ups and styles, Chuck's music basically never changed. Whatever the mood, the rockin' piano-man Chuck Fowler remained one of Sheffield's most durable and popular musical figures.

6. HIGH NOON: JOHNNY TEMPEST

During the beat group era one of Sheffield's most popular performers was singer Johnny Tempest. He went on to enjoy great success in and around Sheffield fronting the Cadillacs. John Greaves was born and raised in Frecheville and as a schoolboy he joined in the skiffle craze with his own group the Border River Scuffle Combo (which is how it appeared in Top Stars Special, which was prone to getting names wrong, so it was most likely the Border River Skiffle Combo). Moving on to rock'n'roll he became Johnny Tempest with his band the Mariners. Their young lead guitarist was Roy Barber: "The first gigs were at the Greystones Ballroom. They had a dance band on Saturday night and we played in between. We also played five nights at the Dog and Partridge down Attercliffe for 20 quid a week for everybody, and they also expected us to do Saturday lunchtime." Even then Johnny was a commanding figure onstage. Roy Barber: "He was older than us so were slightly in awe of him."

When Roy Barber left to join the Cruisers, the Mariners split up leaving Johnny without a band. Another local group the Cadillacs had also had a recent change in line-up with original guitarist Barry Brumpton teaming up with ex-Mariner Chris Stainton on bass, ex-Cruiser John Hall on drums and Malc Towndrow on rhythm guitar. Tempest was persuaded to become their singer. The combination was a winner and the band became popular around the pubs and dances. They performed the usual fare of rock'n'roll songs, but one song will always be synonymous with the name of Johnny Tempest - High Noon, the theme song from the classic Gary Cooper film. He delivered it in a highly dramatic style and audiences loved it. Linda Harvey recalls with affection: "He used to go red in the face and drop on his knees in his white suit." Mal Hooley: "He was a very good showman, on and off the stage. You'd see him in the Sidewalk cafe on a Saturday afternoon with his coat over his shoulders like a cape and all his stage make-up on, surrounded by young ladies. A real character." Tom Rattigan: "He would get a taxi from the City Hall just down to Chapel Walk." Frank Peach: "I can remember seeing Johnny walking down Chapel Walk with his briefcase with just his sandwiches in and he had all the brown make-up on in the daytime." Malcolm Towndrow: "Before we'd go in the Sidewalk, Tempest would ask us all to lend him some money, so when we went inside he'd shout over, 'Do you want to borrow a fiver?' Then he'd take out five pounds, which we'd all lent him, and would impress everybody as it was a lot then." Tempest was bold as well. He once asked the Everly Brothers, whom he had spotted outside their Sheffield hotel, to sing to him. The brothers looked bemused and walked off.

In April 1962 Johnny and the Cadillacs won the marathon rhythm group contest at the Plaza Cinema, Handsworth. "More than 1,000 people attended the finals night with hundreds turned away," said the Morning Telegraph. This resulted in more work for the band as Johnny told Top Stars: "We are really working hard and are determined to take the chances which our competition win has provided. This is a big opportunity for me and the group and we're not going to let it go."

MAKE A DATE WITH

JOHNNY TEMPEST
AND
THE MARINERS

FOR ROCK-N-ROLL RHYTHM AND BLUES

55 SMALLDALE ROAD
FRECHEVILLE
SHEFFIELD 12

184 ALNWICK ROAD
GLEADLESS
SHEFFIELD 12

Rockin' at the Locarno Ballroom, London Road: Johnny and the Cadillacs with Chris Stainton, Mal Towndrow and Barrie Brumpton

But Johnny was always torn between being in a band or taking a steady job. In May 1963, after a year with the Cadillacs, Johnny left having been lured away with work in Jersey. He rejoined six months later only to announce his retirement from the music scene for a "more settled job," joining the staff at the Locarno Ballroom. Undeterred, the Cadillacs carried on working round Sheffield with female singer Karen Young who had been encouraged to join the band after occasionally getting up onstage with them. Dave Berry's rise to success with Memphis Tennessee gave Johnny second thoughts about music and he made a grand comeback in September '63 with an appearance on the big Top Ten show at the City Hall. Proving just how popular he was locally and how much he'd been missed, the show gave Tempest virtually equal top-billing with that of now hit recording star Berry. Top Stars reported: "It was the most welcome comeback of all time... cheers raised the roof, sighs soared to the ceiling." Obliging fans with their request for High Noon, Top Stars said that the song, "Rocked the rafters". Roy Ledger: "He was more than popular, he was big really. That show at the City Hall proved it." Reunited with the Cadillacs once again, Johnny and the band entered the

Mackeson Rhythm Group Contest held in pub venues across the city in October. After winning the fourth heat at the Sicey Hotel, they went through to the final at the Parson Cross Hotel on October 31. Johnny and the Cadillacs gave an impressive performance and came out winners, receiving 100 guineas and a possible recording contract with Columbia. National pop weekly New Record Mirror covered the event in the November 2 issue with a picture of Johnny and co in action at the Sicey Hotel. A week later the paper announced the results of the finals with pictures of Johnny and the Cadillacs alongside the runners-up the Cherokees saying: "The contest held throughout Sheffield came to an exciting climax on Thursday, October 31. The six finalists fought a close battle and the judging panel had a more than usually difficult job deciding the winners." One of the judges was Columbia boss Norrie Paramor who had been responsible for Jimmy Crawford's recording success two years earlier. In November they made another successful appearance at the City Hall alongside the Rolling Stones and Wayne Fontana. They also made a good impression out of town with bookings around South and West Yorkshire.

With the help of managers Pete and Geoff

Johnny Tempest with Dave Berry

Stringfellow, a recording deal with Columbia was set up and the band cut their debut single Being With You. Johnny was thankful to at last get a deal, commenting in Top Stars: "We have had as much experience as Dave and the Cruisers but we are two records behind. Things were really at a standstill 'til we got this contract, in fact we were seriously thinking of giving up the business for good." Just as the record was about to be released, another record came out by Johnny Carr and the Cadillacs. Although Tempest and co had had the name for five years, Carr's band had got there first on record. Johnny Tempest and the Cadillacs became the Texans, a name chosen for them by Norrie Paramor. Being With You, backed by Wondrous Look Of Love, both written by Malc Towndrow and Chris Stainton, was finally released on March 21, 1964. The raucous A-side was a contrived attempt at the Mersey sound, while the flip was more akin to Tempest's familiar ballad style. It received favourable reviews in NME: "Thudding Yeah-Yeah rocker coupled with appealing rockaballad,"

Texans in Fitzallan Square

while Record Mirror described it as: "Different sort of vocal beater, but with plenty of appeal." Naturally there was strong support from Sheffield fans who voted it a resounding hit in Top Stars. Local publicity included photos of the band outside the City Hall and in Fitzalan Square donning cowboy hats and boots along with toy guns and holsters. However the confusion over the change of name didn't do record sales any good and outside Sheffield the record didn't really mean anything.

A few months later the front page of the June Top Stars issue announced the surprise news that the band had changed it's name yet again, this time to the Knives and Forks. Unhappy with

being called the Texans they had been spotted by Brian Poole's manager Peter Welsh who also thought they needed a better name. Suggesting they needed something typically Sheffield, Knives and Forks was mentioned as a joke by Pete Stringfellow and it stuck, much to the amusement of the band. With a new long-term contract worth £200 a week under their belts, the band went off to play from one end of the country to the other. Alongside Johnny's popular ballad numbers, the band moved more into R&B. With Brian Bruce now on lead guitar and John Hall on drums, Tempest would also be featured on harmonica while Chris Stainton was

Johnny Tempest and the Cruisers

planning on bringing the organ into the line-up. The band also dispensed with their cowboy gear for more fashionable mod clothing.

Knives and Forks toured Germany and Denmark as guitarist Malc Towndrow reported in Top Stars: "The Germans were very discerning. If they liked you there was pandemonium, with them banging their beer bootles on the tables and cheering. But if they didn't there was a stony silence and they just turned their backs." After three months away, and Hall complaining that their Christmas dinner had consisted of sausage, they came back to Sheffield. There was a further tour of Germany but the final straw came when Tempest returned home mid-tour to get married. Knives and Forks continued without him for a short while before Chris Stainton left to join forces with ex-Cruiser Frank Miles and ex-Cadillac Tom Rattigan to write and record their own songs in their own makeshift studio. This, in turn, would lead to Stainton establishing a long-term musical relationship with Joe Cocker. However, nearly three years later, Tempest was still remembered by German fans as reported in October '67 Top Stars.

Tempest settled down to married life and performing round local clubs with the Crestas. In 1968 he teamed up with members of the Hillbilly Cats (Pete Jackson and Dave Jones) and Dave Berry's Cruisers (Roger Jackson and Roy Ledger) to form Johnny Tempest and the Cruisers. As Pete Jackson explains, Berry had stopped using the name: "When Roger and Roy Ledger had jacked in with Berry, me and Dave Jones joined two of the Cruisers and kept the name. We got a lot of work because of that name." Roger Ledger: "We asked Berry if we could use the name and he said, 'Yeah', so we

did." From being a rock'n'roller Tempest soon became a seasoned club performer, as Jackson recalls: "He'd sing anything and do anything to get on the right side of an audience. We were a club band and every club band ends up playing some shite to get work. You do songs and you think, 'Oh no, not this one.' We used to do things like Big Spender and Johnny would get dressed up. He used to come on in all the gear like Shirley Bassey - dress, fishnets, the lot. We'd play it as long as we didn't have to dress up and, if it went down well, it was fair-do's. I don't know how, but one night he ended up in the van with all his gear on - dress, fishnets... and we kicked him out, only for the laugh." In the past Tempest had been known as quite a poseur off-stage but not with this band: "He lost all that showbiz thing, 'cos I think we brought him down-to-earth."

In September, 1969, Top Stars ran the headline John Tempest quits the groups. He had decided his future lay in being a solo performer: "The trouble with groups is that they have to change their style every so often when trends change. With a solo singer you can sing the type of material you really want to. I get a lot more satisfaction from singing ballads than some of the pop numbers I had to sing with a group and I find that club audiences are a lot more appreciative to solo singers." Johnny went out on his own performing in clubs throughout the north and Midlands, while holding down a day job as manager of the furnishing department in a city centre warehouse and later as an insurance agent. He carried on performing throughout the Seventies, but his dream of becoming a pop star

Johnny Tempest shortly before his death

had died. He also teamed up with ex-Cadillacs guitarist Brian Bruce as Tempest and Spencer.

Talk to anybody who was around in the early Sixties and they will almost certainly agree that of all the musicians in Sheffield who didn't make it, Tempest was, along with Frank White, the one who really should have followed in the footsteps of Dave Berry and Joe Cocker. Pete Stringfellow: "Johnny was a true professional, a wonderful charismatic guy and a showstopping performer. In Sheffield in 1963 Johnny Tempest and the Cadillacs were as big in the city as the Beatles were nationally."

On April 1, 1982, the Sheffield Star reported that Johnny Tempest had been found dead, aged 41, slumped by his car in a closed garage at his Ecclesfield home. Hours before, he had returned home from a date at Pleasley WMC near Mansfield. His sudden death was a shock to all those who knew him and had seen him perform over the years. The love and admiration that people still had for Tempest showed at his funeral, with the City Road Crematorium overflowing with family, friends, musicians and fans. In attendance were people such as Dave Berry, Bobby Knutt and John's former manager Pete Stringfellow who commented: "Johnny's still packing them in." For the multitude gathered at his funeral a tape of Johnny singing High Noon was played as a final reminder of this special Sheffield musical hero.

7. FRANKENSTEIN'S MONSTER: RAY STUART

Ray Stuart (real name Frank Raymond Brookes) was another of Sheffield's most memorable performers, often for all the wrong reasons, especially when he became Frankenstein with his band the Monsters. Big Ray had been one of Sheffield's earliest rock'n'roll exponents as Dave Berry remembers: "He was before us all." Ray's first group was the North West Ramblers which he formed while in the RAF in Germany in 1956. Back in Sheffield Ray managed and then sang with the Mainliners. Their guitarist Mick Hallam recalls his managerial techniques: "He was very pushy and he was good at buying the concert secretaries pints of beer but he got us bookings." After The Mainliners, his next group was Ray Stuart and the Drifters before becoming Ray Stuart and the Tremors. But Ray didn't make his mark until after the demise of Sheffield's first monster group Count Lindsay and the Skeletons in April

Frank Brooks aka Ray Stuart

1963. Pete Stringfellow took on Stuart as Keith Linaker of the Skeletons recalls: "When we went to Germany, Stringfellow got Ray Stuart and turned them into Frankenstein and the Monsters, copying our act." Peter Stringfellow: "He was a big ugly sod who wanted to be Elvis Presley, not Frankenstein. So he wore this mask." Terry 'Count Lindsay' Roe: "He took over our bookings at the Cavern and Iron Door Club in Liverpool."

Frankenstein's act, which concentrated more on the visuals rather than the music, was quite bloodcurdling, with gruesome make-up. The climax of the act was when a 'body' was wheeled onstage with Frankenstein stabbing it and pulling out its heart - a sponge dipped in pig's blood. Then he would run round the audience waving the 'heart' and shouting and wailing. As reported in The Star, this was too much for the audience at Dobcroft Road Youth Club. Girls fainted and Frankenstein's second booking was cancelled. 'Monster' Dave Robinson: "The publicity did wonders for him, the diary filled up so much after that."

Ray Stuart and the Mainliners

Over the years Stuart used just about every musician on the local scene. Mal Hooley: "I played with Ray quite a bit and Frank White has as well. I didn't get dressed up as a monster but Frank did." The remnants of the Sheffields, following the departure of John Alexander to re-join Jimmy Crawford, became the Monsters for a while. They had previously been known as the Vampires but had nothing to do with the horror scene. One of them was Roy Ledger: "Ray could pull some right money 'cos it was like two shows really." The three backing musicians were usually unrecognisable behind the monster masks which made the job a little less embarrassing as Dave Hopper explains: "I didn't mind doing it so much because I'd got a mask on, so nobody knew it was me. The bit I didn't like was his normal singing act." Dave Robinson of the Daizies who also had a stint as the Monsters: "We stopped wearing masks for a while and started using make-up. We used to slap a mud-pack on and just as it was going to set, you'd move your face and when it cracked drop theatrical blood into the cracks so it'd look as though it was seeping out. The only trouble was it took so long to do that we gave up after a month. But our complexions were fantastic."

While Frankenstein was trying to frighten the living daylights out of his audience he was usu-

ally being made fun of by his fellow rockers. Dave Berry once followed Ray round the Esquire as he was doing his monster act calling out, 'Ray come here. Ray I want you. Ray,' trying to defuse Ray's act. Dave Hopper: "He was supposed to be scaring everybody and he and Berry finished up arm in arm!" Lizards guitarist Pete Jackson also recalls a City Hall show: "It was one of those Stringfellow jobs with about six or seven Sheffield bands on. We were all rehearsing and tuning backstage. The next thing I knew was Ray Stuart, dressed up as Frankenstein, came in. As I looked up he went 'E-e-a-a-g-g-h'. So I just looked at him and said straight-faced, 'Come on Ray. Better get your make-up on. You're on in ten minutes!' So with that, he had instant face on."

Thanks to various self-inflicted injuries through getting carried away on stage, Stuart's 6ft 4ins frame was beginning to resemble something that had been stuck together by Frankenstein himself. Sliding down the central pole at the Esquire was a speciality. One performance saw him plunge 18 feet from the balcony into the audience below. Dave Hawley witnessed this amazing feat: "He climbs over the balcony and someone had greased the pole. By the time he hit the bottom he was doing about 200 mile per hour, kneecaps coming out of his

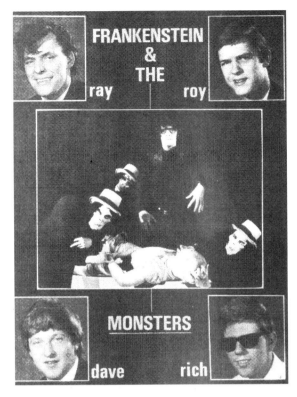

Ray with ex-members of the Sheffields, and below horror on ice: Frankenstein at Silver Blades Ice Rink

cheeks." Ray bit clean through his tongue and ended up in hospital where he caused a bit of a stir by turning up still wearing his monster mask and chains and covered with greasepaint 'blood'. Hawley: "Another time they had painted the pole and he was only one that didn't know, he stuck, he couldn't get up and he daren't let go. There were parts of his uniform stuck to the pole by the time he got down." Dave Hopper: "Ray once picked up that big anchor on the side of the wall at the Esquire in middle of his set, showing off and swinging it round. And he gashed his arm." Steve Saxon: "One night in Mansfield he chased this girl and she shut a glass door on him. He stuck out his arm and the glass just smashed and gashed his arm open. He was losing blood fast and began feeling faint but carried on singing until he fainted. He had to spend the night in Mansfield hospital." On another occasion Ray was attacked by his pet alsatian, Kim, who had been scared by his master's ghastly make-up. Ever hungry for publicity, the story made the Star with the headline "And now a werewolf?" Stu Moseley: "He also set somebody on fire once with this petrol. And in the Stone House he put his false teeth on Phil Crookes' pint pot when Phil went to the toilet. As Phil returned somebody shook the table and the teeth fell into the pot." Roy Ledger: "He was just a big bloke and nothing seemed to bother him. He used to go out into the audience and the kids would be knocking him about and kicking him. He wore big pit boots, and he just used to give them as much as he got. He wasn't frightened of anybody." Dave Robinson: "When these people came into the dressing room to confront him, I don't think they realised how big he was. This geezer came in and he was gonna go for us. Ray shouted at him and made him stand to attention in the end." Stu Moseley: "I saw Ray play at the Magpie with the Daizies when he was doing a Frankenstein set and a straight set. Ray introduces the number and guitarist Dave Robinson has to do the intro but he's fiddling about not quite getting into it and suddenly Ray shouts, 'Come on twat'. Right across the room." Despite various ups and downs Frankenstein and the Monsters were extremely popular and in 1963 found fame of sorts, when a Sunday newspaper splashed the 'horror' story of Frankenstein and his then band the Tremors. In January 1965 Ray recorded two numbers, What You Gonna Do and Going Home, in London with producer Norrie Paramor. However, they were held back in favour of a more original horror number and were never released on record.

Big Ray did go on to get a taste of the big

time, through his friendship with DJ/TV personality Jimmy Savile. In April '65 he had a speaking part in TV documentary The World Of Jimmy Savile. He also appeared on stage at a Monkees' concert in London as a bouncer looking after Savile and lurched about as Frankenstein on Top Of The Pops.

In December 1966 Frankenstein and the Monsters - guitarists Dave Robinson and Spud West, drummer Phil Galley and bass player Paul Jarvis - received the Top Stars Special Award for top group presented to them at the city's Silver Blades Ice Rink after their 'horror on ice' show. Top Stars Special said of them: "They shot suddenly and bewilderingly into prominence. Whereas the trend was mod, the Monsters were often wildly untidy. They went in for all the tricks - bleached hair, speckled jeans and medals. And they aroused fan mania."

By the end of the year they were playing in France, Monaco and Germany but there was still no sign of them making a record. Stuart and co toured and smashed their van up in an accident near Strasbourg. They also came close to being arrested. "We were drinking in a cafe and an armoured car full of gendarmes stopped outside and surrounded us with rifles and escorted us back to the station," said Stuart. "It appeared they had mistaken us for another English group who had not paid their hotel bill the week before," The tour ended when the band quit. In January 1967 the Monsters switched camps to temporarily become the revamped Count Lindsay's backing group. Dave Robinson: "We'd all had enough of Ray 'cos he wasn't paying us, so we thought, 'How can we get out of this?' We all said we were packing it in rather than saying we were leaving." Terry Roe: "The band dumped him, stranded in France, and he had to call Jimmy Savile to send him some money to get back home. Savile knew him through Ray Stuart's wife Val who had a hairdressing salon. Savile used to go and have his hair done there."

Back home, the February '67 issue of Top Stars announced the Monsters official departure from Frankenstein. They had become a popular band in their own right, reflected in the amount of mail Top Stars had received praising them, although most of them were sent in by friends of the group. Ray next teamed up with a psychedelic band from Bury called New Religion. Ray declared that his act would become even more gruesome. "What's the use of having a horror act if you try not to frighten people all the time?" This act didn't last long and by August '67 Ray had found himself yet another new group, this time from Sheffield, known as the Opposition. Then, in an attempt to shed his horror image, his next band, previously known as the Cycle Show Group, was called the Adams Family (as opposed to the Addams Family) and included former Cruiser John Fleet on bass and promising organist Martin Alcock. Frankenstein was once again laid to rest in 1968 when Ray became an agent, setting up office in Snig Hill, just below the Black Swan. Pete Jackson: "He

Ray with the Monsters/Daizies and Coronation Street star Pat Phoenix

started booking bands. He booked himself so he made sure he'd got plenty of work!" This move was typical of Ray as he found a market by capitalising on an already established situation by booking bands into local pubs where they were already working. The idea was to save the landlord the hassle, except that working through Ray meant bands would be playing in the same pubs for less money.

He also took over management of Kalender, an already successful working band. Dave Hopper: "We'd got all the contacts, all the jobs and everything, so all he had to do was answer the phone." Ray's assistant Carl Reid recalls that the job was more than just answering the phone: "We made most of the contacts, getting out on the road and going to clubs and pubs. We also had to send out all the posters and confirm all the bookings, etc, so we didn't get our commission for nothing." But Ray wasn't averse to a bit of fun, as singer Steve Saxon recalls: "He'd got this bird coming to his office who was a big Chris Farlowe fan. So he told me, 'You're Chris Farlowe.' So I gets there and when she arrives Ray introduces me as Chris Farlowe and I'm saying, 'Hello darlin' in a cockney accent although I don't know if she thought I was him." Stu Moseley also remembers Ray's cheek: "He used to do seances, something that Terry Thornton instigated. Ray was pushing the glass, you could see it. It would spell out R-A-Y. Joe Cocker, who was there, thought there was something in it. I was always a bit more cynical than Joe." Ray's next venture was as a DJ with resident spots at the Black Swan and the Crazy Daizy on High Street. This led Ray to comment: "I've been trying to make it as a singer all these years, now I'm earning a steady living just playing records. Maybe somebody's trying to tell me something."

In 1973 and again in 1975 Ray brought Frankenstein back to life, with Frank White's band and Daizie Spud West among his backing musicians. White: "I only did it for a short while. It

was just a laugh really. I'd work with anybody at the time." Dave Robinson: "Spud went back to doing the monster act and his wife also had a white sheet over her head going 'who-o-o-o-h'. It was a disaster."

Ray also tried to muscle in on someone else's patch once again, as DJ Gaspin' Gus recalls: "I used to DJ at the Beehive, Dykes Hall Road, and the landlord told me, 'Ray Stuart's rung up again saying 'I'm better than Gus, Get him out.'" Also following in Gus's footsteps, Ray became a DJ/presenter with BBC Radio Sheffield before moving on to Radio Hallam in 1974. Ray eventually became Hallam's most listened to DJ and was always supportive of local talent as JP Bean can testify: "I remember when Frank White had that single Shelley out, Ray used to play it all the time. If anybody else had played it with anything like the regularity around the country it would've been a big hit, which I thought it deserved to be. He always played Joe Cocker's records. He used to keep Joe's name alive through Radio Hallam, through all the dark days in Sheffield. He also introduced him both nights at the Lyceum in 1982." Ray Stuart must also take some credit for Joe Cocker's biogra-

Ray walks out on Hallam after 13 years with station

By Keith Strong,
Entertainment Reporter

Ray Stuart quits Hallam

PRESENTER Ray Stuart, who once threatened to quit Radio Hallam after being relegated to a late-night slot, has mysteriously parted company with the Sheffield-based commercial station.

A one-time groat Ray, who turned broadcaster after a pop career, jetted off to Spain today amid speculation about a shake-up at Hallam — which has just announced one of the biggest audience increases in the independent network.

The presenter signed off the air at 2 a.m. yesterday without listeners realising that he had made his final broadcast and, before packing his bags, he confirmed: 'I am no longer working for Radio Hallam.'

phy With A Little Help, according to author JP Bean: "Without Ray Stuart I don't think there would ever have been a book on Joe Cocker. Without him I doubt if I would ever have met Joe and got all of his co-operation."

Following a station reshuffle Ray was relegated from his prime daytime slot, appropriately enough considering his Frankenstein days, to the 'graveyard shift' - 10pm till 2am. He was disgruntled with this and, never a man to hold anything back, he made his feelings known on air. But Ray was at least able to play the kind of music he and his friends liked as Roy Barber recalls: "Ray gave me a direct phone number to his show and I'd ring him and ask him to play some Barefoot Jerry tracks which he frequently did." Although a lot of people thought of Ray as being full of himself and at times quite abrasive, Roy Ledger remembers him differently: "A lot of people pull him down but he was a great mate, he'd give you anything."

Ray signed off the air at 2am on March 25, 1987. He left Sheffield and England soon after and moved to Lanzarote where he worked in advertising and local radio. It was there that Ray was admitted to hospital in September 1992 and on October 2 the Sheffield Star carried news of his death due to cancer. It was the end of a varied career and another Sheffield character. He always made quite an impact as Mal Hooley recalls: "What a showman. He could put it over, he'd got a lot of presence." Ray was also never short of confidence as Dave Hopper remembers: "He was talking to Joe [Cocker] in the Stone House and he says, 'Do you think you'll ever make it?' And Joe said, 'No, I'm too fat.' So Ray said, 'Now seriously, who do you think is next in line to make it? There's been Crawford and there's been Berry, so it's got to be me hasn't it?' So Joe said, 'Yeah if you say so.'" Stu Moseley: "Ray wanted to make it and in this town that was a breath of fresh of air."

8. GIRLS, GIRLS, GIRLS: KAREN, CAROL AND LADY LEE

Along with Jimmy Crawford, Dave Berry and Joe Cocker, the only other chart success of any note in the Sixties was for Karen Young from Dronfield who had a top-ten hit with Nobody's Child in 1969.

Karen, who was born Marion Harper in 1945, began her singing career at the Victoria Ballroom in Chesterfield. "I used to sing along to the records, I would to grab the microphone

Karen Young and pet

off the DJ or whoever it was who played the records for the kids to dance to. Dinah Washington's September In The Rain was one of the songs I sang," says Karen. "I can also remember going to see singers like Cliff Richard and Adam Faith at Sheffield City Hall when I was 12 or 13 and I was one of the screaming teenagers in the audience. I think it was the thrill of my life when I eventually played there." And it was at the Victoria Ballroom that she took her first step to being a professional singer. A friend dared her to enter a heat of Lou Preager's Find The Singer contest at the Vic. The 16-year-old ran away from home to take part. "My mother said, 'Right, you aren't going.' I went out through the bedroom window, my first bit of defiance," says Karen. "I just stayed away for a couple of nights with a girl friend before going back." She won the heat, singing the Connie Francis hit Everybody's Somebody's Fool. "When my parents found I'd actually won the heat they were thrilled." She appeared in the TV final - "I came nowhere, I think I had nerves." She went on to work as an assistant at Curtis's record shop on Angel Street in Sheffield city centre.

However, after the TV appearance, word soon got round among Sheffield groups that there was a female singer in Dronfield. "Two of the Cadillacs came round to see me and asked me

Karen Young with The Counterbeats

to join the band which at that time had a Sunday night residency at the Lathkilldale Hotel. Johnny Tempest had a job but worked with the band when he could. Sometimes we used to do duets together but I think there was a bit of rivalry. I don't think he liked it." She ended up combining her job at Curtis's with singing with the Cadillacs and club/ cabaret band the Counterbeats, "as well as trying to do my own gigs." She also found herself up against another singer in the Counterbeats when the then Tony Fitzgerald, later to be Tony Christie, occasionally joined them before taking over from Karen in the mid-Sixties.

She was described as a "red-headed sizzler" in Top Stars Special in 1964, twice won the Top Stars popularity poll for the best local girl singer before she was 18 and was only beaten by Carol Deene the following year. She was a flamboyant performer in more ways than one. "I think I must have been the first punk. I dyed my hair bright orange at one point," says Karen who also made her own stage clothes. "I sang with the Cadillacs at the City Hall on the same bill as the Rolling Stones and I made a dress that completely matched my orange hair. The review in the newspaper the next day said I looked like a ball of fire." Cadillacs' guitarist Malcolm Towndrow: "Karen had these two dresses she'd wear on stage with revealing neck-lines. She always wore quite a bit of make-up and the dresses made her neck and shoulders look quite pale so we'd all take great pleasure in taking turns to rub the make-up into her neck and shoulders, each time getting a bit lower."

In 1965, by which time she was a professional singer, she made her recording debut on Pye Records with Wonderful Summer coupled with We'll Start The Party. The following year she recorded I'm Yours, You're Mine for the Mercury label. She ended up moving - along with toy poo-

dle, Whiskey - to London in 1966 because of cabaret demands in the UK and abroad, only making the occasional home city appearance at the Cavendish Club on Bank Street which opened in 1967. A third single, The Hurt Won't Go Away, this time for Philips, followed in 1967. During a rare visit home in November '68 she accepted her Top Stars award for top local girl singer and announced her new record You Better Sit Down Kids. She recorded for four different labels in as many years - "A lot of people were interested in me. It was a bit like chucking stuff at the wall until something stuck," she said. And it finally worked in 1969 when she recorded Nobody's Child for her managers' label Major Minor, a mournful song about a blind orphan which had originally been recorded by the Scottish Alexander Brothers although her version owed more to country singer Hank Snow's. Dave Hawley has another theory: "We used to do Nobody's Child with the Dave Hawley Combo, it was so popular it became an embarrassment. Karen Young came to see us one night and next thing I know she's in the charts with it."

The record reached number six - and an amazing 21 weeks in the chart. It also put her in the company of fellow Sheffield chart stars Jimmy Crawford and Dave Berry and the three artists were pictured together on the back of the October '69 edition of Top Stars Special.

Chart success was short-lived although she continued to be popular in cabaret and even panto. But she found herself in dispute with another Karen Young, an actress from Beaconsfield, who had registered the name with

Karen with her Top Stars award

actors' union, Equity. Even more confusing was that neither of them was really a Karen Young. While the Dronfield version was born Marion Harper the other was Wendy Schroeder. And despite the former having used the name for more than seven years and releasing six records, the latter had got there first with Equity. And singer Karen needed to get an Equity card to appear on the Bachelors television show. She refused to budge on the name and her Equity application was deferred. "It's never been resolved to this day," says Karen. "People were always getting us confused. Sometimes her picture would appear in the newspapers when it should have been me. I think she ended up working for an estate agent. But she would do anything for publicity - even pretending to be me. People even got me mixed up with the country singer Faron Young and I'm probably the only one who didn't want the publicity."

The follow-ups to Nobody's Child - Allentown Jail, My Elusive Dreams and a double A-side One Tin Soldier and the old Doris Day song Que Sera Sera, with a new arrangement by Paul McCartney - were not successes. She also recorded an album. "None of those songs were really my style," she says. "Allentown Jail was in the wrong key for me anyway. But I had no choice, I was just told that so and so was going to be my next single. Perhaps I never did find my own style. I was very adaptable but I had to be. In cabaret I was having to sing songs by other girl singers such as Dusty, Cilla or even Sandie Shaw, replicating whatever was popular at the time."

Nobody's Child became a bit of a millstone. "Slow sickly songs are not me," she said shortly afterwards. And to this day she wishes she was known for anything other than that song: "Never in a million years would I have chosen a song like that - too bloody miserable. It put a tag on me. But in those days you sort of did what you were told to do. I still cringe when it comes on the radio."

She toured South Africa with the Bachelors, with whom she shared management Dorothy and Phil Solomon, for six weeks in April/ May 1970, only to find that Nobody's Child, which was about a blind orphan, had been banned, objections having been made by the South African Blind Society. She also entertained the forces, along with Dick Emery who was to introduce her to her future husband Peter Elliott, in Gibralter. She moved back to a flat in Dronfield and did a cabaret week at the Fiesta in late 1970, second on the bill to Georgie Fame. Top Stars revealed that, "her stage act is bouncy,

her outfit - a blue see-through trouser suit - revealing." And she was quite happy to be second on the bill: "Once at the Club Fiesta in Stockton I was top of the bill. I had a nerve-racking time." She was at her happiest when she played Prince Charming - "I must have been the most petite principal boy ever," she says - in pantomime at Southsea in 1970, alongside Richard Murdoch and Sam Kydd. "It was the most fun I ever had."

In February, 1971, Karen got married to Peter Elliott who worked in the business side of the entertainment industry, one of his jobs latterly being organising the Royal Variety Show. Various showbiz celebrities were at the wedding including Dick Emery who was best man. Shortly afterwards she gave up her singing career: "I moved on from what I did. You can't look like you did when you were young, it wasn't for me anymore. Peter was involved in the business side of things and I got involved in that, management and production. My last performance on the stage was in 1972 or 73 and I have no desire to go back. I'd rather leave it alone. For some singers it's a lifetime pursuit. At least I managed to get out when I was winning." She and Peter were divorced in the late Nineties and these days Karen runs a successful guest house in West Runton in Norfolk - "I never tell anybody what I used to do, unless I realise they were in

Looking up an old friend: Karen on her wedding day with Dick Emery

the business."

She now calls herself Karen Elliott - "Only my family call me Marion," she says - but the problem with her stage name has never really gone away. In 1978 yet another Karen Young, this time a Canadian disco diva, appeared in the charts with Hot Shot. Twenty-two years later an internet website was advertising The Best Of Karen Young complete with a potted history of the Sheffield singer. Unfortunately the record being advertised was a collection of songs by her Canadian namesake.

The only other local female singer to have success in the Sixties was Carol Deene from Thurnscoe near Doncaster. She started out working in the Co-op at the mining community but went on to have four minor hits, starting with Sad Movies in October, 1961, missing out by just six months from being the first singer in South Yorkshire to make the national charts. But there is some consolation because she was certainly the youngest as she was just 15 when her cover version of Sad Movies by American singer Sue Thompson was recorded. Deene's version made it to number 44, ironically beating the original into the British charts by two months, but Jimmy Crawford had already got there first with Love Or Money. But whereas Crawford was only to get there one more time, Sad Movies was the first of four records to chart for Deene within a year, including top 30 placings for Norman and Some People, in each case her versions beating the originals by American girl singers to the charts. She was also well known for the novelty song, James (Hold The Ladder Steady) and there was also Johnny Get Angry which became the title of a compilation of her records on CD in 1999. There was also the infamous occasion when the panel on Juke Box Jury gave a scathing thumbs down for one of Carol's records, only for the curtain to be opened to reveal the singer sobbing away at the verdict. She also managed to cause a bit of controversy when her 1964 effort to get back into the charts was virtually banned by the BBC. Then again, it was called Who's Been Sleeping In My Bed?

Despite the hits drying up - she went on to record a total of 13 records for her label HMV, notching up more than 500,000 sales - she continued to be a popular name nationally, appearing regularly on television and also in the film, Band of Thieves, which starred Acker Bilk whose acting talents were somewhat secondary to his clarinet playing.

She also became the first female deejay on Radio Luxembourg in 1962, with Carol Deene

Carol Deene

Presents. The twice-weekly show, sponsored by Price McVitie Biscuits, came after a try out with Sam Costa, and it was through that that she met the Beatles. "Their manager - a Mr Brian Epstein - told me thay they desperately needed more radio plugs for their first single," she said at the time. "He said, 'EMI have managed to get us a certain amount of airplay, but we need more - so will you play it on your show as well?' I said, 'Of course,' to which Mr Epstein replied, 'Well if you do, these two lads write songs, and I'll get them to write you a song.' I said, 'OK, fine,' played their record and promptly forgot about them. I was pleased to see Love Me Do in the charts... but I'm still waiting for that song though."

Like many other young singers of that era, she found that success was not all it was trumped up to be, particularly financially. "When the hits came I was green as grass and got taken for a ride. I didn't realise then that people were being nice to me because I was making money for them," said Carol. "I didn't make a penny. You have only got to appear on television and people expect you to come home in a Rolls-Royce. In fact, in the end, I came home with a Mini I hadn't paid for. Even the National Insurance people let me off paying stamps because I hadn't got any money." In 1965 she changed management, started recording her debut album and her picture was on the front of TV Times to coincide with her appearance on magician David Nixon's Comedy Bandbox series. Then in January 1966, having at last acquired some of the trappings of success with the purchase of a new sports car, she was driving home after an engagement in Cardiff when her car collided with a lorry, leaving her with a broken jaw and knee. She recuperated back at her parents' home in Garden Street, Thurnscoe. She recovered sufficiently, with jaw wired up, to manage one appearance with David Nixon. The next week she was replaced by Anita Harris. Her management company, Noel Gay, dropped her shortly afterwards. It signalled the end of her success. The £5,575 she received in damages from the lorry driver seemed hardly any compensation for what the injuries had done to her career.

She tried a couple of comebacks, signing to CBS Records, and releasing When He Wants A Woman: "If the new record does not make it, I'll have to go back to scrubbing floors at Thurnscoe Co-op," she said at the time. In 1973 she tried again, only to have another car crash, breaking her arms on the way from an engagement at RAF Scampton. Her and husband Tony Lindell, also a singer who fronted the original Cruisers after their split with Dave Berry, cut their losses and took over a pub in a village near Barnsley. "It will be nice not to have to live out of a suitcase because I have travelled all over

the world during these last few years. We see it as an extension of what we were both doing before - talking to people, being pleasant and helping to pass the time of day." But the lure of singing would, it seem, never go away. In 1979 she had new management, a new name, Karen Love, and a new record...

Another local girl to make some sort of name for herself (several names for that matter) was Audrey Valentine Middleton. The daughter of a Sheffield fireman, she never did things by halves. She was only 19 when she left her husband and Sheffield for London in 1956, giving up her jobs as a tracer at Jessop's steelworks and an usherette at the Empire Theatre. She went on to become a pop singer, Billy Fury's lover, wife to Kenny Everett and a psychic healer. She changed her name to Lady Lee, then Lee Everett and finally Lee Everett Alkin. She lived the full sex, drugs and rock'n'roll lifestyle.

Born in Popple Street, Page Hall, the slim, leggy blonde had a variety of jobs, from Sunday School teacher at St Thomas's and hairstylist's model to junior at a chemist on Bellhouse Road and typist/ telephonist. She met her first husband Alan Bradshaw at a youth club at 16 and was all ready to call off the subsequent wedding until her mum told her: "You can't do that, I've ordered a hundred trifles." Her first taste of showbusiness was when she became an usherette at the Empire. She met many of the stars, was taken out by Edmund Hockridge and became friends with singer Yana. She also fell for rock'n'roll singer Alex Murray, half of the Most Brothers, whom she followed to London, becoming pregnant and having a miscarriage. "We lived in a haze of drugs, and God knows how we survived," she said. But survive she did, with a job at a revue bar in the West End, moving on to a bit part as a dead prostitute in horror film Flesh and Fiends, singing in clubs and learning various instruments. Eventually, after finally leaving Murray and becoming Billy Fury's lover, she was spotted by agent Larry Parnes and renamed Lady Lee. She signed to Decca Records and released a version of Herman's Hermits' I'm Into Something Good followed by 99 Times Out Of 100 with which she made her television debut on Thank Your Lucky Stars in May, 1965. Animal lover Lee, who was president of the Lady Lee League For The Abolition Of Cruel Sports, was quoted in Top Stars as saying of the single: "If I make a lot of money with this record I'm going to buy an armoured truck so that I can go out every weekend and mess up hunt meetings." A follow-up story claimed she did get the use of a helicopter to follow the hunt

Lady Lee and friend

thanks to a well-wisher. She later signed to Columbia Records and released My Whole World (Seems To Be Tumbling Down). Her eight-year relationship with Fury ended in 1969 when she met Kenny Everett. They were married for 11 years. "I suppose he had much in common with me as he was in permanent emotional pain. What a weird pair we were." The marriage inevitably disintegrated, or took an "unconventional turn" as the newspapers put it, when the DJ confessed he was gay. But their friendship didn't end. When she got married for the third time in 1985, to actor John Alkin who played Cliff Ryan in Crossroads, Kenny was best man and among the guests was Elton John for whom she had done some backing vocals. She had also discovered she had a gift for healing and spiritualism subsequently touring the country with a clairvoyant and Alkin who was also a healer. "I have goofed beautifully in my life but at least I have learned from the things I did wrong," says Lee now. "But I never made the same mistake twice. When I was married to Kenny I went through living hell. He was constantly suicidal and walking around in blackness and despair. The rigorous living took a toll on my body and I was totally asthmatic. I was healed by a medium and have believed in it ever since."

Another singer dating back to the Fifties was Gloria Roma (real name Gloria Wilkinson) who was dubbed Sheffield's answer to Shirley Bassey. But it wasn't until November, 1963, that she finally got her big break when, at 23, she appeared on Granada's Scene At 6.30 programme. Shortly after, with some financial aid from her dad, she recorded a single for Decca. Gloria, who used to sing in a restaurant in the city centre, ended up having elocution lessons and appearing at top night clubs in the north.

Rotherham-born Christina Mitchell, aged 21, released the ballad I Fall In Love With You Every Day on Pye Records in February, 1963, after she won the finals of a nationwide talent contest at the Victoria Palace, London. Her prize was a recording contract with Pye - and a radiogram. She sang with her first band, the Gordonaires, at the age of 16 and three years later was resident singer at the Old Harrow Inn at Gleadless, congregating place for many of the best musicians in and around Sheffield.

9. MOTOR BIKING: CHRIS SPEDDING

As well as the stars that have emerged from Sheffield, there have also been a number of other musicians who have gone on to work with some of the biggest names in the world. None more so than Chris Spedding. But his route from Millhouses, Sheffield, to his present home in Santa Monica, California, has followed a pretty bizarre path. He has been involved with everything from the Wombles and the Sex Pistols to highly-respected jazz outfits as well as having a top 20 solo hit with a throwaway piece of bubblegum pop glorying in the name of Motor Biking. And he has been one of the most in demand session players on both sides of the Atlantic - a true musical chameleon.

Christopher John Spedding was born at Millhouses on June 17, 1944. His father, a retired bank manager, was an amateur keyboard player and part-time music teacher while his mother sang in choirs. Chris went to Abbeydale Grammar School and his first instrument was the violin. He gave that up in his teens and took guitar lessons from local teacher and music shop owner Len Stewart. His first guitar was a DIY model: "For only a few shillings you could send away for a make-your-own-guitar kit. I never got to play it because as soon as I tried to put the first string on and bring it up to tension, the whole sorry thing collapsed. I was very impatient." His first band was the Vulcans in the late Fifties, doing Shadows and Cliff Richard covers. They made their musical debut at Dobcroft Church Hall where he was in the wolf cubs - "We were the young sprogs, we were too young to play in pubs." Although Spedding's involvement in the Sheffield scene was fleeting he did take an interest: "Dave Berry was my local rock hero." Dave Berry: "He saw me at the Gaumont when he was still a teenager. He later said that Crying Game was always one of his all time favourite records, especially the guitar. He went on to record it on one of his albums." Spedding was one of the first local musicians to make the career move to London in 1960 - at 16. "As soon as I left school I left for London and got a job in a shop selling guitar strings and sheet music. London was where it was all happening. There was no great scene in Sheffield in 1960. There was Club 60 but I don't think I played there."

He made his first professional appearance in 1964 entertaining passengers in the orchestra on the P&O liner Himalaya, plying its way to Australia and back. He joined the Nat Temple Band in 1965 - Temple being a dance band star who had his heyday in the 40s and 50s. He also played a tour of US bases with Bill Jordan and the Country Boys. He went on to start a jazz club in Islington with vibes player Frank Ricotti with whom he was to make his first recording as a professional musican on Ricotti's album Our Point Of View in 1968. One of his first rock bands was Smile who played just one gig, at the Isle of Wight Festival in 1967 - and it was televised. He also played bass briefly with Alan Price and Paul Jones before, also in 1967, forming the Battered Ornaments with singer/ lyricist Pete Brown, recording A Meal You Can Shake

Hands With In The Dark in 1969 followed by a Battered Ornaments album without Brown, Mantle Piece, which saw him taking over the vocal role for the first time. Also without Brown, Battered Ornaments were on the bill at the Rolling Stones' concert in Hyde Park in 1969, Spedding playing guitar using two fingers and a bottleneck with his left hand because he had broken his wrist falling off a horse. It was Pete Brown who introduced Spedding to bass player Jack Bruce who had left Cream in 1968. He asked Spedding to join his new band to record the acclaimed Songs For A Tailor album in 1969 followed by Harmony Row two years later. Spedding's first two solo albums, Backwoods Progression and Songs Without Words, appeared in 1970, followed by Only Lick I Know two years later, all on the Harvest label. He also played in various jazz bands, including the Mike Gibbs Orchestra and Ian Carr's Nucleus, holding his own with some of the country's top jazz musicians. He was second to John McLaughlin in the jazz guitarist category in the Melody Maker three years running from 1970 to 72.

Spedding's diverse career continued with sessions for Lulu, Dusty Springfield, Bryan Ferry, Elton John, Nilsson, Gilbert O'Sullivan (he can be heard on hits Nothing Rhymed and Ooh-Wakka-Doo-Wakka Day), David Essex, Roy Harper, John Cale and Donovan for whom he wrote the string arrangements for his 1973 Cosmic Wheels album. He was one of the hottest session players around, fulfilling a similar role to that of Jimmy Page in the Sixties, but he also found time to hook up with former Free bass player Andy Fraser to form Sharks in 1972, one of Island Records' Great White Hopes of the Seventies. Spedding: "It was the only time I committed myself solely to being part of a group." But they were never to reach their potential, despite Spedding's tasteful guitar work. Fraser left after the debut album, First Water, in 1973, leaving Spedding, singer Snips, keyboard player Nick Judd, drummer Marty Simons and new bass player Busta Cherry Jones to record the 1974 follow-up Jab It In Yore Eye. The band disintegrated in November that year in bitter circumstances.It was back to session playing for a while including what was to be his first taste of success on a massive scale in Britain, as guitarist with the Wombles and wearer of the Wellington Womble costume on shows such as Top Of The Pops. "A lot of people have worn that costume. It must be very smelly now," says Spedding who admits to being proud of the Wombles' records. "They were very successful and popular," he says now although he also sounded somewhat relieved when he wasn't called up for a repeat performance when The Wombling Song was back in the charts in 1998.

Perhaps it was that experience with Mike Batt's Wombles that made him even more determined to make it on his own, no matter what, leading to the partnership he established in 1975 with pop svengali/ producer Mickie Most who had already played such a big part in the careers of several Sheffield musicians, including Dave Berry. Most, the man behind Herman's Hermits, Hot Chocolate and Suzie Quatro to name just a few, gave Spedding a distinctive poppy style, with no pretensions to being a guitar hero. "I don't know why people expect flash guitar from me because I've never done it," Spedding said at the time. "I've chosen to play this bubblegum pop style which I quite like. There's no half-baked philosophy that goes with it. It's straight dancing music for pleasure and enjoyment and getting off and dancing around to. I have been through so much in ten years as a professional musician that I can just about play it all now. I have been through all the complicated time changes and technically good guitar playing and I know I can do it if I want to. Now I'm looking forward to getting into something simpler." At the same time he maintained the image of a James Dean-style Fifties rock 'n' roller, leather from head to toe, shades and

Session ace Chris

greased-back jet black hair. "It's reasonably true to life," he said. "I don't dress up specially for the pictures." Indeed in 1975 he was voted best dressed musician in the NME, beating David Bowie. In that same year he was asked to join the Rolling Stones who wanted him to replace Mick Taylor, much like another Sheffield guitarist Frank White who was said to have been in the frame to replace Brian Jones six years earlier. But whereas the Stones never got around to actually asking White, Spedding says he turned them down: "If I was in the Stones I'd only be a back-up man and I want to do my own thing." He went on to have a Top 20 hit with Motor Biking in August 1975. But that was to be his lone solo hit and the subsequent album, Chris Spedding, found him performing a series of brilliantly executed rock pastiches, followed by the 1977 album Hurt.

But perhaps, despite everything he has been involved with, his major achievement was to put the Sex Pistols on the road to infamy and fame. "I was one of the first musicians to take them seriously, when everybody else just thought they were dreadful. I decided the only way to convince people was to record a demo with them. Everybody, of course, just assumed that it was me playing the guitar, but they didn't need me. I just produced the demo, got them their first record deal and put them in touch with the man who was to produce their stuff, Chris Thomas." These days singer John Lydon and guitarist Steve Jones are both near neighbours to Spedding in Los Angeles. The Sex Pistols' anarchic approach obviously had some effect on Spedding's songwriting - his 1979 album, Guitar Graffiti, included classic punk philosophy titles, Bored, Bored, Frontal Lobotomy and More Lobotomy (parts 1 and 2). It was still bubblegum rock 'n' roll however. The solo career lasted for at least another two albums, including the aptly-titled Not Like Everybody Else in 1980, which included his version of The Crying Game.

In the late Seventies he moved to New York - "It wasn't really happening for me in Britain" - to work with rockabilly musician Robert Gordon. "I go where the work takes me. I find New York vital, it's a 24-hour city which suits my lifestyle," he said in 1980. He eventually moved to another 24-hour city, Los Angeles, where he is still in demand for session work, production, and recording for Toronto label, OPM, which, appropriately, for a musician who can play in almost any style, stands for Other People's Music. His most recent call to England came from the man behind the Wombles, Mike Batt, for his latest project, an album of orchestral versions of clas-

A long way from Millhouses: Chris Spedding in California as seen on album sleeve

sic rock songs, including Eve Of Destruction, Whiter Shade of Pale, Born To Run and Paint It Black, recorded in Abbey Road. Spedding can now notch a few more eminent names on to his leather belt, including Shane MacGowan, Marc Almond, Kim Wilde, Roger Daltry, Bonnie Tyler, Midge Ure and Status Quo, all of whom contribute to the album.

Spedding's role in the Sheffield music scene may have been minor but few can match his track record since. Indeed there can be very few musicians in the world who can put their name to such a varied career. The only thing that bugs him is that people still mix him up with the only other eminent Sheffield musician he got to know - Joe Cocker's keyboard player Chris Stainton. "I was once doing a session in New York and the engineer came up to me and said, 'Chris, I love your stuff. I listen to the Mad Dogs and Englishmen album every day.' I put him right but at the end of the project he said, 'I really enjoyed watching you work. Mad Dogs and Englishmen sounds even better now.'"

10. I AM THE MUSIC MAN: CHRIS STAINTON

Woodseats-born Chris Stainton is best known for his work as keyboard player with Joe Cocker and Eric Clapton. However, it was as bass player with Johnny Tempest and the Mariners that Chris began playing around Sheffield in the early 60s. His interest in music began at school, as did that of classmate Roy Barber who recalls Chris's single-mindedness: "He ignored the teachers, he didn't take any notice in class at all. Yet when it came to the end of the year he'd be in the top three - brilliant at everything. He was an oddball at school unless you got to know him, then you'd realise the brilliance in there. We were both in the same physics lesson and he was at the back messin' about, but he remembered and I didn't. He's the closest thing I've ever seen to a genius. He's a phenomenal musician but he could've been a phenomenal anything. He used to hang around with us. I'd joined Tempest and we realised we ought to have a bass player and he said, 'Right I'll play bass.' The fact that he couldn't play bass was irrelevant really. Then he turned up with one

Cadillac Chris Stainton

he'd made out of wood - two pieces of plywood. We put strings on and it all curved because it was just a piece of wood. So I got some files from work and embedded them into the neck to stop it bending and then Chris just started playing it. He was there when we needed a bass player and the die was cast." After Roy and Chris left Rollinson, the school became known as 'Rock'n'Rollinson' because woodwork lessons were given over to making guitars. Looking back at that early beginning and how Chris's career had developed, Roy mused: "I gave Chris a career, as it were, playing bass, now I wished he'd given me one."

Linda Harvey, who was Chris's girlfriend in the early days: "When he left school he was a television engineer. People used to bring televisions in and he would repair them. He'd take all the valves out and make his own sort of amplifier. They sacked him in the end for it as he was too busy doing his own musical things instead of repairing the televisions." After the Mariners, Chris, along with singer Johnny Tempest, joined the Cadillacs which became the Texans and then the Knives and Forks, before teaming up with Joe Cocker in 1967. Malcolm Towndrow recalls when the Cadillacs would go to Chris's house to pick him up: "His mother would shout upstairs, 'Christopher Robin, the band's here.' He'd get in the van and his freshly-ironed shirt would still be steaming." While with the Cadillacs he also started playing piano. He simply sat down and worked it out for himself particularly at impromptu after-hours sessions at the Arbourthorne Hotel. It wasn't long before he was proficient enough to play, as Roy Barber recalls: "I can remember Stainton getting the opportunity to play with Dave Berry when he was doing cabaret. Tommy Eyre had left so he needed a keyboard player and I suggested Chris. He could play some piano. I don't know when and where he started, he just happened to be able to do it one day. But Berry went to see him and he wouldn't have him 'cos he looked scruffy!" Karen Young, who sang with the Cadillacs for a while, remembers Chris as: "A lovely guy, so quiet and talented. He was very nice to me. It can be a bit difficult being the only girl in an all male band, you were always out on your own, but Chris always looked after me."

Chris, along with guitarist Malc Towndrow, wrote a number of songs for the Texans/ Knives and Forks, but he was never really comfortable with the commercial musical outlook. Then there were his musical idiosyncrasies. Linda Harvey: "He used to lock himself away for days if he suddenly had a melody in his mind. He had to write it down. He would say, 'I'll see ya,' and you wouldn't see him for about three or four days and then he'd emerge out of his house with this masterpiece of music and he'd played every instrument on it. Absolutely fantastic. He used to sit at home and then suddenly he'd sit forward and start tapping something out on his

Knives and Forks: Chris, John Hall, Brian Bruce and Mal Towndrow

knees. And he'd go into like a trance. Then he'd disappear and come back and say, 'I've got it,' and pick up an instrument and he'd play this unbelievable piece of music." Malcolm Towndrow: "Chris and I had written a song called Baby Don't Push Me and took a demo of it with Chris's arrangement on bass. The producer, who I think was Alan Freeman(not the DJ), recorded the song with some artist and completely re-did the bass part and it sounded fuckin' horrible." Alan Wood recalls another example of Chris's exceptional musical talent: "We were all invited back to the Barrow Hill Hotel and while everybody was partying downstairs 'cos Joe had hit the charts with Marjorine, I wandered upstairs. I heard this piano playing and Tommy Eyre was sitting in this dimly-lit room playing a concerto or something, a fantastic piece. Chris was stood at the side of him and he said something like, 'No I think that's wrong Tommy. When you played C minor 7th you should've played C augmented.' Tommy said, 'What d'you mean?' and Chris said, 'I'll show you,' and he played it and I'd never heard him play anything other than bass before. I was amazed." Frank Miles: "He'd listen to a record. The first time he heard it he'd tell you all the chords and then he'd play it through three times and he'd tell you what everything was playing. I wish I was like that." Malcolm Towndrow: "We were at Barratts in Manchester, a famous music store at the time, where Chris had seen a vibraphone in the window. He just climbed in among all the instruments and started playing it. The band bought all the equipment so we bought that for him and did a gig with it that night at the Bluebell at Hackenthorpe. The only trouble was we had to detune all the guitars to match that. We didn't keep it very long as its use was limited."

Although a fairly introverted person, Chris's outward appearance was more flamboyant as Linda Harvey recalls: "The Knives and Forks were doing this gig at the Cutlers Hall and they'd said something about being presentably dressed to go there. So he went up town and came back with this flower-power suit. From top to toe, red and pink and orange flowers all mingled in. He said, 'It's not right is it? We've got to do something about it. I've got a great idea. Can you go and find me some orange fur?' And we put orange fur all around the cuffs and round the front of this jacket. And that's how he thought he was well dressed to go to the Cutlers Hall. When Chris lived at my mum's she made him some curtains for his room. He'd chosen the material. Then he decided they'd look even better in a jacket so we took them down and made him a jacket out of these curtains. They were like a green floral pattern. Don't forget, flower-power was at its peak in those days so anything that was flowery or multi-coloured just suited Chris." Then there was his choice of transport. Linda Harvey: "Chris always said, 'If ever I make it, I'm going to have a big pink Cadillac.' Then I heard from his family years later that he was well known for driving round London in a pink Cadillac, which didn't surprise me at all."

Alan Wood recalls when Chris was asked to join Frank White's band: "We went round to Chris's house and told him we needed a bass player and he just looked at us and said, 'I've took the frets off my bass guitar.' That was his idea to make it a fretless bass. He just took the frets off. Frank said, 'Come and see us at the Birley,' but he never came. I suppose that was his way of telling us he didn't want to join the band." Chris was more enthusiastic when it came to Joe Cocker. Linda: "Chris just wouldn't rest until he'd met Joe. He must've obviously seen the guy around. I think all his inhibitions came out when he met Joe. He'd always wanted to be a bluesy type and with Joe he could do all that." Chris Stainton: "Joe was with the Grease Band and I was in a rival band. Joe was doing the blues, funky stuff, a lot of black stuff. I was in a band that was doing pop, Cliff Richard and the Shadows. I didn't like what I'd been doing in

Chris, second left, meets Princess Diana along with Charlie Watts, Steve Winwood and Eric Clapton

the past, the music was a bit lightweight. I loved what Joe was doing, I used to go and see him in the pubs in Sheffield. I loved to play stuff like that."

Another musical co-operation was with musicians turned songwriters Tom Rattigan and Frank Miles at the Egg Box garage studio in Beighton. Roy Barber: "I got involved with Chris again with the recordings. His talent was starting to blossom. He knew the electronics, God knows how, nobody had ever taught him. That phasing effect was coming in and he worked out a way how to do that by swinging the speaker." Linda Harvey: "I used to help him to swing the speakers across the garage to get this daunting sound. Chris could hear all these sounds in his head but could never get them and it used to drive him mad."

Eventually he and Joe Cocker moved to London and got into the rock'n'roll lifestyle. Linda Harvey: "They had a flat in Sloan Square and me and Chris's younger brother Steven went down there. Chris had invited us. When we got there they were all laid out stoned on the floor, hanging over chairs, musicians and stars from the 60s. We had to wait 'til they all came round. I think that's when I realised how far Chris had gone from being the bass player in the Cadillacs. He just seemed a different person."

In 1969 Chris appeared with the Grease Band at the triumphant Woodstock performance and was also part of the Mad Dogs and Englishmen odyssey across the States in 1970. He met his American wife Gail on that tour and afterwards returned to England and bought a house in Buckinghamshire. The Grease Band reformed later that year and Chris took part in an American tour. But that was short-lived and he ended up forming the Chris Stainton Band with steel guitarist Glen Fernando Campbell (formerly of Juicy Lucy), along with Grease Band members Alan Spenner and Neil Hubbard, plus drummer Conrad Isidore. Meanwhile Joe had gone into hibernation, with all sorts of rumours about his health and state of mind. It was Chris who persuaded him to join his new band and in 1971, despite contractual wrangles, Joe became the singer with the Chris Stainton Band for a tour of the States. Inevitably this was seen as Joe's comeback and a 20,000 crowd at Madison Square Gardens was disappointed when Joe didn't perform the favourites, not even With A Little Help From My Friends. Festival dates followed in Britain, then European and more American dates and an ill-fated trip to Australia. Out of all this came the Cocker album Something to Say album in 1972 which featured

Chris today

songs mostly written by Stainton, several with lyrics by Cocker. Then in February, 1973, after six years with Joe, Chris announced he was leaving to concentrate on building and running his own recording studio. It was a devastating blow to Cocker and it was to be another 15 years before they would work together again. Stainton went on to form jazz-rock fusion band, Tundra, making one album in Nashville in 1976 but things didn't work out as planned. By the mid to late Seventies Chris was experiencing lean times after several failed bands and drug problems - leading to bankruptcy and a spell on the dole. Then in September, 1978 or 79, while still drawing unemployment benefit, Chris received a call out of the blue from Eric Clapton. He spent the next six years touring and recording with the guitarist. In 1983 he played in front of Princess Diana for the All Stars Rock Concert. The Sheffield Star carried the headline "Music man from Sheffield is presented to silver-clad Diana," as Chris is seen smiling at the Princess along with colleagues Eric Clapton, Stevie Winwood and Charlie Watts. The Live Aid concert in 1985 saw Chris on stage in the USA with Clapton.

After another period out of work, he ended up playing in the orchestra for Andrew Lloyd-Webber's Starlight Express in London's West End only to get the call from Joe Cocker in 1988. They toured the world together again, including the momentous return to Sheffield at the City Hall in 1991. Eventually Chris rejoined Clapton - for better money - in 1994 but has continued to work whenever he can with Joe Cocker, who says of his musical companion: "Musicians being what they are, soon sense that Chris is extraordinary. I've worked with some marvellous players, but he's something unique."

11. FROM WHAM! TO THE WEST END: TOMMY EYRE

Tommy Eyre is another exemplary Sheffield musician who became a top keyboard player, working with a lot of big names including Joe Cocker, Dobie Gray, Gerry Rafferty, Elaine Paige, Wham!, Gary Moore, Ginger Baker and BB King. Starting out as a guitarist, it seems a few bands credit themselves with discovering Tommy. One of them was Pete Fender's band the Strollers, as bass player Mal Hooley recalls: "Tommy played with Pete Fender for a while in the early days. In fact, to be honest, we discovered him. He was a young spotty-faced lad playing a Fender guitar then." Neil Bridges remembers being taken aback by the talented young guitarist when he stood in with the Whirlwinds: "It was at Alf Pickering's Arbourthorne Hotel, and we hadn't got a guitar player that night. My dad said, 'I've got you this guitar player, he's only 15.' So we said, 'He can't play with us, we're the top group on clubland. Who's going to just get up and play with us with no practice?' Anyway he came, only a young lad covered in zits, and he brought this guitar. He'd got a black Strat and that impressed me and, well, we'd heard nothing like it. He played lead all night and he played everything perfect. He played Yakety Axe, then he got on the piano and God knows what he didn't do. So he joined the band and he stayed with us for quite a long time."

And it was as a pianist that young Tommy, influenced by his pub piano-playing dad, began to get noticed. Frank White: "He was about 15 when his dad brought him to one of my gigs or a rehearsal or something and he sat in and played a few things with us on piano." Tommy's early mentor was drummer Dave 'Cannon' Smith. Alan Wood recalls: "Tommy was at school, City Grammar I think, and Dave Cannon found him and nurtured him and got him into Jimmy Smith and everything. He brought him along." Through Cannon's guidance, Tom started sitting in with Steve Denton's rock'n'roll band. Their guitarist Dave Hopper: "Cannon told us, 'I've got us a piano player. He's only 16 and he's red hot.'" Playing early rock'n'roll gave Tommy an ideal opportunity to show off his talent. Dave Hopper: "He used to be crackers about doing Elvis's One-Sided Love Affair, still is. It's a big boogie shuffle thing. Sometimes he used to do the Warsaw Concerto on his own. We used to show him off doing that."

For a short time Tommy worked with Dave Berry. Roy Ledger: "When Whiter Shade Of Pale and all that came out Berry wanted a keyboard player and I got Tommy in. He was a good player." At the end of 1966 Tommy and Dave Cannon joined forces with singer/guitarist Scott William and German saxophonist Peter Scheerhaut. Working under the name of 007, they went abroad backing singer Marie Woodhouse who had previously worked overseas with Joe Cocker's Big Blues. Tommy recalls the band: "It started off with Phil Crookes and Pete Scheerhaut and Marie who called herself Billie Rae. Peter had been doing a lot of gigs on American bases with whoever he could pick up and he came to Sheffield and fell in love with

Tommy, at right, with 007 Group with Scott William, Dave Smith and Peter Scheerhaut

The Grease Band: Henry McCullough, Chris Stainton, Tommy Eyre and Kenny Slade (at front)

Marie. She could sing a bit and she had big tits, which were essential. I thought I'd got the gig with Cannon 'cos we were such pals but it turned out that because I was only 15 I couldn't get through American customs. So Phil Crookes took the gig and hated it. He left after two months. I got this call and Peter had figured a way to bribe the American guards at the airport." On the continent the group made a series of EP records and appeared regularly on TV in Spain. "We bumped into a guy who was a record producer and we recorded some songs in this studio in Madrid. Then we were in Germany for three months after that. Peter came out of that with a Mercedes car and we came out with twenty quid. And when we found out how much money he'd made and how little we did I said, 'I'm not doing it' and Peter said I'd got to do it because I'd signed a contract. I said, 'Pete, yeah I'm only 16, I'm too young to sign a contract.'" Back in Sheffield Tommy went to work for ex-Fortune Glen Dale playing rhythm guitar in his band the Kandies. They became very popular around the clubs although Tommy was being badgered to join another group. "I'm working with Glen making enough money so I can put a deposit on a Hammond organ. We were working at that club at the bottom of Staniforth Road - Attercliffe Non-Pots - and Cocker came in and said, 'Tom, look, just join our band.' And I said, 'Joe, I can't.' Then my father came back with the

Daily Mirror the next Thursday and said, 'Eh Tom, look at this,' and it said Joe Cocker: Sheffield guy got his own record. I phoned him up and said, 'Joe, about that gig,' and I took it."

It wasn't to last, although Tommy's contribution to the making of Joe Cocker cannot be underestimated, if only for the classical influenced Hammond organ into to With A Little Help. Roy Ledger remembers how Tommy left Joe Cocker: "He always regretted leaving Joe, but Kenny Slade was his mate and when Kenny said, 'Come on, we're off,' he just went with him. He didn't really want to leave but he was knocking about with Kenny and they were buddies. From Cocker Tommy went off to work briefly with original Drifter Clyde McPhatter (or 'Macphalter', as Top Stars renamed him). Tommy and Kenny joined up again in jazz-rock outfit Riff-Raff: "It was bass player Roger Sutton's band, a brilliant writer." But the music proved to be rather complicated, even for Kenny: "We played all clever stuff - 9ths, 13ths, 7ths, 11ths. If you found a 4 you were lucky. It was extremely difficult. It wasn't that I couldn't play it, it was just so complex. I said, 'Give me my bus fare and I'll go.'" During the Seventies Tommy worked with other bands including Aynsley Dunbar's Retaliation with whom he recorded an album produced by John Mayall entitled To Mum With Love. Then there was jazz-rock fusion outfit Mark-Almond and, in a similar

vein, Zzebra, who recorded an album in 1975. He also played for Lenny Henry on the comedian's first tour and apparently saved the day when the PA packed up. Unperturbed, Tommy simply carried on with a selection of pub songs.

In the 80's Tommy got a call from popsters Wham! and became their band leader at the height of their success. This was followed with a spell as Elaine Paige's Musical Director. In 1988 he took time out to produce and play on Frank White's self-titled album, having appeared

Behind The Crimson Veil

Scarlet Rivera & Tommy Eyre

Album recorded with wife Scarlet

on it's predecessor Nice To Be On Your Show, some 15 years earlier. Just as busy in the nineties Tommy worked with Gary Moore, Ginger Baker and B.B. King no less. Living in California he is married to violinist Scarlet Rivera best known for her work with Bob Dylan on his Desire album. Together, Tommy and Scarlet recorded an atmospheric self-composed instrumental album.

Despite the successes of his career, Tommy has returned on several occasions to his roots in Sheffield. He came back to play at a benefit concert at Upper Heeley Club for his mentor Dave Cannon. and attended a family birthday celebration at Sothall Snooker Club, Beighton. However one particular memory that remains with Tom goes back to his first major influence, his dad. "I stood in for him one night at the Wellington in Darnall. He was in hospital, just before he died in 1974, and he just didn't want to let the landlord down so I went and played piano for him at the Wellington, just piano and drums doing all the old songs." Tom's dad certainly had a lasting influence and his enthusiasm and commitment to music shines on through his talented son.

12. HOW LONG: PAUL CARRACK

Another Sheffield musician who has earned recognition as a top session keyboard player and singer/songwriter in his own right, both here and in America, is Sheffield Wednesday fan Paul Carrack. Paul, who was born in 1951, lived at Bole Hill Lane, Crookes, where his parents had a painting and decorating shop, and went to Myers Grove school. He was first bitten by the musical bug as a small child, bashing away at an old 1920s drum kit in his parents' attic, which his Dad had bought him and stuck wallpaper round the sides "to make it look nice". Paul would play along with an old wind-up gramophone - "My dad was great about me practising constantly."

Paul, who has a brother John who is four years older, recalls it being an idyllic life, even if the house only had two bedrooms, one outside loo and a tin bath which was placed in the kitchen. But his life was shattered at the age of 11 when his father fell down the stairs and broke his neck. "I'd had such a happy upbringing that for Dad to die just seemed unfathomable," says Paul. "After my father died, school was a nightmare. Nothing could make me get out of bed in the mornings and I remember my brother John having to force me to get up. I

Savile Row Rhythm Unit: Robert Batty, Paul Carrack and John Whitham

ended up becoming quite rebellious. I think music became my way of getting over his death. The first Christmas after it happened my mum bought me a drum kit on hire purchase, as a way of cheering me up, I suppose. It was the bee's knees and I'd sit there all day playing along to Gerry and the Pacemakers and the Beatles."

School friends recall how he'd display his developing musical tastes by carrying his Aretha Franklin and Otis Redding LPs round with him all the time. But it wasn't until the ripe old age of 14, that he first made his mark as drummer and singer with the Savile Row Rhythm Unit. "That was me and my cousin Rob Batty [bass] and Johnny Whitham [guitar]. We used to get together and practise at my mum's shop at Crookes but we were pretty crap." One reason Paul had got into a band was because it was the only way he could get into some of the city's clubs, "They wouldn't let me in because I was small and young. At the Mojo they would vet you outside and I got turned away in front of some of the girls in my class which was a super embarrassment, so I got into a band so I could get in. I did get into the Mojo once when the Hollies were on, it was something like ten bob to get in, so I paid and got in and they were absolutely brilliant."

Savile Row, with two members aged 14 and one at 15, were one of Sheffield's youngest groups and in a Top Stars article in February, '66, their music was described as a mixture of Tamla Motown and 'pop art'. In January, '66, they had managed to beat off older competition in a contest at the Esquire organised by Unit 19, Sheffield's first independent recording studio. Paul: "It was a fiddle how that happened. We took all our mates along and it was based on audience response. There was this older band on who were a proper good band and they were a bit miffed when we won it." That gave them some free studio time at Unit 19. It was there Paul first had a go on an electronic organ, "I was into that as there were bands like the Animals, Spencer Davis and Small Faces who all had organs in them. In Unit 19 there was a Hammond and this kid who used to do the producing there showed me how to play the chord of C." Savile Row needed a better singer and Clive Morris was enlisted. "They had this singer with them, he had a good voice but he couldn't keep in time so they asked me to join," says Clive. Although Paul's ability was limited, he switched to organ, and a replacement drummer recruited. Shortly afterwards Clive was approached by soul band Reaction to replace vocalist Steve Walker. "Paul was a bit mad 'cos we were just getting the band going," says Clive. Paul: "I was dead jealous, I went to see Reaction at the Silver Blades and I thought they were fantastic." Reaction were also in need of an organist and Clive said to Paul, 'I'll get you in the band.' He said, 'But I can't play very well.' Clive said, 'You'll be all right.'" So he joined on organ in the summer of 1967, "but he couldn't hold a bleedin' note on it," said Clive. "We used to practise down at my dad's big house on Burngreave Road and some of the band went up the wall about his playing. But I said, 'Well if he goes, I go.' And he quickly learned how to play, just sailed. In about a month he was good at holding chords and he was starting to get rhythms going." Paul: "I was teaching myself and Clive knew that I was getting it together." And Steve Walker helped Clive: "They were kicking him out for me and he still came back and we went through songs together, the words and that, to get the band playing quickly, I'll always remember that." Paul was also making headway as Reaction drummer Brian Watson remembers: "He really surprised me when he started playing, he used to have a little Selmer Capri organ, we used to call it 'Plastic 'Un', it sounded like Sooty."

Another member of Reaction was Glyn Owen who recalls the 16-year-old: "Paul was taking his GCEs at the time I'd joined the group. He was the youngest by far and was just at the point of leaving school. He was a very affable lad, very keen, really easy to work with, and for his age seemed very knowledgeable about what he wanted to do. He matured during the time I worked with him. I always remember Paul's little place in the van. He always slept on top of the gear at the back. He was only a short lad so he

C.G. Morris and Reaction, with 16 year old Paul at left

could always stretch out." Clive Morris recalls how Paul would keep his distance from their manager/ driver, "His sexuality was brought into question and he fancied Paul something wicked. I remember once we played this club and the manager brought this guy to see us and he liked the band but he liked Paul more. Paul wasn't having any of that at all and I think we lost the contract."

In October, 1967, the Reaction split into two with some members forming the Big Crowd and the rest CG Morris and the Reaction Soul Band. Glyn Owen recalls the split following a row: "It was purely over petrol money - a few pence. The manager wanted some money for petrol. He said, 'I must have some money off somebody,' and four stayed in and three got out. It was as simple as that." Paul: "Clive argued and did this big bluff with the manager and we ended up getting out and walking home from Leeds. It was pitch black so there was no chance of getting a lift and we got as far as Chapeltown before we got a lift as it got daylight." The remnants of Reaction re-formed briefly with Brian Watson, Glyn Owen, Dick Crews on bass and Paul on Hammond organ and, for the first time, vocals. They got together simply to complete some outstanding bookings, says Glyn: "That's when Paul

got to grips with a lot of the singing and he made it quite clear that he'd got a good soulful voice. He certainly showed his colours by doing all the introductions and doing a show as it should've been and he played great Hammond organ by then." Brian Watson: "He really surprised me when he started singing." Paul was quoted in Top Stars in December, 1967, as saying: "There are too many groups in Sheffield with too little ability," after he and Clive Morris and the other five members of Reaction had gone into the magazine's offices in York Street to demand a write-up. "We want to make a lot of money," said Paul. "We aim big and we reckon we will make it some day." Because the money was poor the band had to drop the brass section. Glyn Owen: "We were at rock bottom, the soul thing was giving way to early Clapton and a bit of psychedelia. All the gear was falling apart and we had to resort to doing our first working men's club, the Tramways at York. The gear was in such a bad state, we'd borrowed Ernie Booth's old 'breadboard' bass, that's how desperate we were. We had no plug-board and Dick Crews got electrocuted in the process of trying to wire all these mains into the wall during bingo. He got the full belt of these two wires and the irony of it was that at this great outburst of pain, all the club could say was, 'Has somebody shouted house?"

With little or no prospects in Sheffield, the band went to Hamburg to play clubs along the Reeperbahn, even though the band's roadie was the only one with a work permit. Paul: "We lived in each other's pockets, were completely skint most of the time, dabbled in a bit of pot and had a great time." On his return to the UK, Paul decided that to further his career he needed to move to London - with a band called Cake. Brian Watson: "We'd seen these two guys in a band called Granny's Attic from Burnley. They were singer Les Walker and bass player Terry 'Tex' Comer. We went up and just said, 'We want to form a band,' so we formed Cake. We hardly did any gigs, just universities, but we got big money." To try to get work abroad the band auditioned at reggae club the Golden Star in London. Paul: "There were literally hundreds of bands all auditioning so we really went for it, we dressed up and moved about, really went for the kill." Brian Watson: "We passed an audition and they came up with these two girl singers, two sisters. They were like Janis Joplin and they couldn't half sing. There was this guy called Tony McCauley who wrote songs for all these daft acts like the Paper Dolls. And they wanted us to be the next Paper Dolls with these two chicks but we weren't having any of that. These girls joined us and that made it a six-piece band and we became the Milwaukee Coasters." They started out living in their van before the four male band members, plus two roadies, moved to a two-room flat above the Golden Star Club. It was far from luxurious. Paul: "You would not believe how

we lived then, there were rats running about but we only paid £5 a week." The band played in Germany and Switzerland but eventually got frustrated and fed-up with the direction the band was heading. The band split up when Brian left, Paul taking a job washing cars. Paul: "I was only 17 and not going anywhere." Eventually Paul, Les and Tex, plus Granny's Attic drummer Dave Pepper, joined forces with sax players Alan Solomon and John Surguy from Jasmine Tea, who were also disillusioned with their band's direction.

The result was psychedelic progressive rock outfit Warm Dust. This would give Paul his first inkling of the big time, although today he hardly acknowledges the band - "absolutely dreadful," is his only comment. Between 1970 and 1972 they released three albums - And It Came To Pass, Peace For Our Time and Third Album on the Trend and BASF labels. Success wasn't forthcoming however and eventually Carrack and Comer jumped ship to form pub-rock outfit Ace. They were joined by guitarists Phil Harris and Alan 'Bam' King, formerly of Mighty Baby and The Action, and drummer Fran Byrne. They recorded three albums between 1974 and '77 - Five A Side, Time For Another and No Strings. It was the insistent melody of How Long, written by Paul, which took them to huge success on both sides of the Atlantic. "I didn't realise at the time how a little ditty like that would endure all this time and make such a difference. It was a complete fluke - Ace were a pub band in '73 and we literally went from playing pubs and colleges straight into a three-month American tour supporting Yes in the Enormodromes. It was fan-

Warm Dust, from left: Les Walker, David Pepper, Alan Solomon, Terry Comer, John Surguy and Paul Carrack

tastic to be in America, but sticking us on stage in front of 20,000 Yes fans was a bit difficult. We got away with it because How Long was such a monster hit while we were there."

By 1976 Paul was living on a ranch outside Los Angeles with the rest of the band. They were unable to emulate the success of How Long and Carrack split the band in 1979. "I'd been getting frustrated musically and I felt I really wanted to play with different types of musicians. I wanted to improve myself. We came back to the UK just when all the punk thing was happening and we just didn't fit in at all. We were the absolute antithesis of everything they stood for, blokes with beards and laidback attitudes who'd just mastered the art of playing on one chord for 20 minutes, and all of a sudden it was high-speed two-minute songs." He returned to Britain and ended up joining Roxy Music as a session player, along with former Grease band members bass player Alan Spenner and guitarist Neil Hubbard - "We were the guys behind the curtains, basically," says Paul. He played on the 1979 album Manifesto and the following year's Flesh and Blood as well as touring with them but was soon on the move again - "I could never have hacked it as a session man, I wasn't that good a player," says Paul. "I always felt I was a singer-songwriter biding my time." He still ended up playing on sessions with Elvis Costello, Carlene Carter, Dr Feelgood and Frankie Miller whom he also toured with.

His debut solo album was Nightbird in 1980. He described it as, "a load of dodgy love songs". Despite his own criticism, the songs reflected his speciality, a soulful blend of melodic pop. It failed to establish him as an artist in his own right and he continued to play sessions, including the Undertones' Positive Touch in 1981, the Pretenders' Learning To Crawl (1984), the Smiths' The Smiths (1984) and five Nick Lowe albums between 1982 and 1990.

He then joined Squeeze, replacing Jools Holland in 1981. "I auditioned at their place overlooking the Thames, and even though they thought I was too old for them - this was 20 years ago - their manager Jake Riviera persuaded them I'd be fine for them." Within a week he found himself playing on what was to become Squeeze's masterwork album, East Side Story, with Elvis Costello producing. It was during those sessions that he sang on a Squeeze song which has become as synonymous with him as with Squeeze. "We'd finished recording and were just messing about one day and we started to play Tempted in a more soulful groove. Elvis Costello said, 'This is more up your street,

you should have a go at this,' so I went in and sang it, and they all said it was great. When I joined them it was all very exciting - we got to America and Tempted was a hit over there - but I knew that at some point I'd have to do my own thing. I stayed with them for about a year and left amicably." He was to rejoin them for a short while in the early Nineties.

He finally had solo success in the American charts with his speciality, the melodic pop of I Need You, which was to be covered by Aaron Neville and Linda Ronstadt. It was taken from his 1982 second solo album Suburban Voodoo. The album was largely ignored in the UK but it was a critical success in the States, being cited as one of Rolling Stone magazine's top 20 albums of the year. Six years later he repeated that success with Don't Shed A Tear from One Good Reason. He also toured the States to promote the latter album with a band that included long-term mates Nick Lowe and Andy Fairweather-Low. He joined Mike and the Mechanics in 1985 and went on to have worldwide success with hits such as Over My Shoulder, The Living Years and Silent Running. He also wrote songs for Diana Ross, Rod Stewart, the Eagles and Aaron Neville and did more session work for John Hiatt, Eric Clapton, Elton John, Madness, Pink Floyd, Roger Waters, Simply Red, Mark Knopfler and BB King. He was also invited by Elton John to play on Something About The Way You Look Tonight which, as the B-side of Candle In The Wind '97, is officially the biggest-selling single ever.

Despite all his high-profile activities, Paul's solo career still failed to take off in his home

Paul in 1989

country until the mid-Nineties. Even in Sheffield it wasn't until 1998 that he played the City Hall for the first time in his own right as part of a 25-date British tour. He was backed this time by a bunch of local musicians, known on the club scene as the Dynamite Brothers, plus Sheffield saxophone player Steve Beighton. He also received acclaim for his solo albums Groove Approved (1989), Blue Views (1996), Beautiful World (1997) and Satisfy My Soul (2000). "I've been lucky," he says. "I've got by with a bit of talent and I got on with people pretty good and I didn't mind that it was hard. I expected it to be hard."

These days he is comfortably settled in a beautiful 16th century mansion in Hertfordshire, with his wife Kath and their four children. With a studio in the garage and easy access to the motorway he can still follow his beloved Sheffield Wednesday round the country. Finally, after 30 years of not being recognised in the street, in 1997 he was impersonated on ITV's Stars In Their Eyes. Paul, as modest as ever, commented: "Now I know I have finally arrived."

13. LOCAL HEROES: PETE FENDER AND SCOTT WILLIAM

One of the coolest of the local rock'n'rollers was Pete Fender, the tall, lanky singer from Swallownest. His real name was Trefor Jones, courtesy of his Welsh father. He dubbed himself Pete Fender when he formed his first band, the Strollers, in 1961. Friendly and mild-mannered, on-stage he was a flamboyant performer. He would wear canary-yellow suits, complimented with startling peroxide blond or pink hair. Moving with the music he would slither across the stage with his arms flailing out, pointing towards something or somebody. Pete is remembered with great affection by all his old band members. Frank White: "Some might say he was over-the-top, I just remember liking him." Strollers' guitarist Roy Ledger: "I always remember coming back and saying to my mother, 'Do you realise who I'm going to join? Pete Fender and the Strollers, they're one of the top bands in Sheffield." Dave Berry: "Yeah, they were a good band, I'd forgotten how good they were." Pete Wardlow: "Pete Fender and Jimmy Crawford were the two most charismatic performers in Sheffield." Although he wasn't a great singer, Fender did have a distinctive if rather subdued vocal delivery. Whether he was singing a ballad

Pete Fender on stage at the Black Cat

or an out-and-out rocker he could build up the tension in a particular song by simply taking the volume down to a low tense climax. "He knew he wasn't the greatest singer," says Roy Ledger. "But he could still sing the song and get away with it."

He would watch both Dave Berry and Jimmy Crawford and then use some of their stage techniques in his own presentation, including one of Crawford's tricks. Roy Ledger: "He'd stuffed a sock down the front of his trousers to make it look like he was well endowed. The trouble was, as he moved round the stage, the sock gradually rolled down his trouser leg and fell out of the bottom on to the stage! I looked at Mal the bass player and we just cracked up. He [Fender] was sound. He'd give you anything, the last penny in his pocket. He'd always got time for everybody as well, people, the fans." Terry Roe: "At one time he'd use the word 'merci', the French for 'thanks', trouble is he went over the top and said it after every song. Nobody really knew what he was on about, especially in Darnall." Another Strollers' lead guitarist was Dave

Hopper whose dad was instrumental in him getting the job: "He [Fender] used to work down the pit and my dad talked me into going down the same pit, Treeton. He said to me one day, 'Pete Fender needs a new guitarist.' So he brought Pete Fender down for tea, to audition me. He just asked me to play one thing, Chuck Berry's Guitar Boogie. He said, 'If you can play Guitar Boogie you've got the job.' So I did and got the job."

After Berry and Crawford, Pete Fender and the Strollers were probably the best rock'n'roll outfit on the circuit and they also had style. Alan Wood: "I came home one day to find a big pink Cadillac on our road. It was Pete Fender and a drummer called Neil Shaw. He had an ambition to own a castle one day, that was his thing. Every time we drove past Conisborough Castle he'd say, 'I want to live there.'" By the time Fender joined the Farinas he was developing into more of a cabaret performer. The Farinas eventually turned into the Pete Fender Show, aiming strictly for clubland as Alan Wood recalls: "Neil Shaw was running things and it was very clubby, things like Crispian St Peters' You Were On My Mind and Bye, Bye Johnny. But it was regular work four, five nights a week." But whatever setting Fender chose to perform in, everyone agrees he was a great showman. Alan Wood: "He'd got so much stage presence, so much

Moving into cabaret: Pete Fender's last band, The Pete Fender Show, with Dave Rawson, Neil Shaw, Pete and Dave Green and, left, news of the inquest on Pete's death

star quality, you couldn't take your eyes off him at all." Of himself, Pete said: "I want to be an entertainer and sing what people want to hear."

Just before Christmas, 1967, Pete decided to disband the Pete Fender Show and get a day job. Just after he had stopped performing, he was killed, at the age of 22, when his van crashed head-on into a lorry at Swallownest in February 1967. He was due to get married a month later. Mal Hooley: "He was a fabulous guy, with a lot of style. Fender was ahead of his time, I thought he was just like how David Bowie is today. I'm sure his career would have gone on for a lot longer." Although Pete Fender never got the chance to record for a proper record label, a recording of him has fortunately survived. Made privately at Regent Sound Studio in London, the single contains Pete and the Strollers' high-powered version of Whole Lotta Shakin' Going On, coupled with an early Cliff Richard-type original piece titled I Guess I Was Wrong. The scratchy acetate is a lasting reminder of one of Sheffield's unsung heroes.

Glaswegian Scott William was already an experienced and well-travelled performer by the time he came to Sheffield in 1962. Real name Bill Goudie, he had started performing at the age of eight with his parents and played most of the variety theatres around Scotland before they began to close down. He decided to move south when he'd heard there was plenty of work around the clubs. He was attracted to Sheffield by its healthy music scene and soon began to impress local musicians with his singing, guitar playing and the fact that he was a bit of a virtuoso on the harmonica. He was steeped in country and western but was also impressive performing rhythm and blues material, which was becoming more popular around the city. "I was no stranger to rhythm and blues," he told Top Stars. "I had a large collection on Jimmy Reed and Muddy Waters records before I ever came to Sheffield. But I never thought I'd sing that way myself. It was a short step from country and western-style singing to the blues. Both need to be sung with great feeling." Scott acquired his own group with guitarist Dave Hawley and drummer Rick Elson and they were soon getting noticed with regular gigs at the Esquire. This line-up can be heard on a rough 1964 demo of an instrumental titled All Night. It features Scott's wailing harmonica and Dave Hawley's somewhat ahead of its time guitar solo. After George Gill replaced Hawley the Scott William Combo continued to build up a steady following and enjoyed a popular weekly residency out at the Greengate Inn, High Green. Almost a per-

Bill Goudie aka Scott William and, below, with microphone fixed to guitar

manent fixture at the Esquire, Scott and his band were booked to back up blues legend Memphis Slim. Although adaptable, when it came to music there was no compromise, as he told Top Stars: "If I couldn't sing what I wanted to sing I'd give up. Unless my heart's in what I'm singing, I don't enjoy my work. This probably sounds ridiculous, but I'm not interested in making a lot of money." The combo went fully pro with Dave Green coming in on bass, Phil Crookes on guitar and Chesterfield drummer Johnny Pearson. They still had to scratch out a living around the city's club, pub and rock venues, as did many of the other bands at the time. But they were one of the most individual bands on the Sheffield group scene, mixing the country music of Hank Williams and Johnny Cash with the soul and blues of James Brown and John Lee Hooker. Top Stars Special described them as: "They follow their own individual way, avoiding the easy pitfalls of chart material or the Cliff Richard moonshine beloved of local groups. Some of the country and western became so cowboy like, you could hardly imagine this music being sung by any other group in the country."

Another special feature of Scott's performance was a microphone that he had fitted to his guitar, giving him freedom to move round without having to worry about leads getting in the way. It was quite a revolutionary concept that hadn't been used before in bands although guitar wizard/inventor Les Paul had come up with the idea in the Fifties. Seemingly tired of the local scene in the late Sixties, Scott joined forces with drummer Dave 'Cannon' Smith, guitarist Tommy Eyre and sax player Peter Scheerhaut in 007 and went off to Spain and Germany. He was last heard of via Tommy Eyre who recalls getting a call from him in 1995 while on tour in Germany where Scott now apparently lives. He is still remembered with great affection by many of Sheffield's musicians.

14. LET THERE BE DRUMS: SLADEY, CANNON AND FRAPPER

Some people believe that all drummers are mad,(or alternatively, as some musicians believe, they are just blokes who hang around with bands). In some cases this may be true - in both assumptions.

One character who certainly made his presence felt with many people was the wild man of

Kenny Slade, top right, with fellow Cruisers Frank Miles, Roy Barber and John Fleet

the drums, KENNY SLADE. Born in Birmingham and real name Ken Bates, he originally wanted to be a jazz drummer. "I'd learnt to play but I'd never got with a band. I got on the stage at the Saxon, Kiveton Park, with the organist. Everyone's saying, 'Get up, and have a play' so I got up and played and just rolled around." However, he emerged on the Sheffield rock scene when he joined Dave Berry's Cruisers in 1962, making his debut at Frecheville Co-op Hall. His brash and abrupt nature was quite a contrast to the quiet demeanour of his predecessor John Hall. Dave Hopper recalls some of the reactions to the new Cruiser: "There was a bit of flack. Some of the fans were playing hell about him because he was so brash." But Kenny was a force to be reckoned with as a drummer, and he didn't mind reminding people: "They'd never seen anything like it. I was playing solos. I took this town apart on the rock'n'roll scene." Roger Harrison: "He was just more technical and much more clever, a very talented guy. It's a shame that he doesn't still play." Linda Harvey: "He was great, a very busy drummer. I used to like his drum solos when he used to go round the tables up and down the club - and never miss a beat." While Berry and the rest of the Cruisers regularly wore stage make-up, the only time John Firminger saw Ken put it on was for a show at the Plaza, Handsworth. When questioned about this he said wryly: "Big show, must make the effort."

Ken went on to join Jimmy Crawford's Messengers. Cruiser Roy Barber: "When they got Kenny they thought they'd just got a really good drummer. Little did they know what was in store!" Jimmy Crawford: "I got on great with Kenny but I once hit him at an American Air Force base, he went through a bloody door. He got drunk in the afternoon. We arrived at this base at Brize Norton and he'd been there all afternoon. He'd set up and the Yanks in the clubhouse had got him on Budweisers or whatever and he was doing a drum solo lasting hours. All the Yanks thought it was marvellous. I arrived at about seven o'clock to do the first set in the officers' club and NCO Club and the agent comes up and says, 'What you trying to do? Fuck my business up? Have you seen your drummer?' I said, 'No, what's the matter?' I peep my head round the door and there's Kenny slowly going crazy. So I had to get a grip on him and I ended up knocking him through this swing door only to find, as I went through, this sergeant, the biggest you've ever seen, who picked us both up and dangled us." But Kenny had the last laugh later that night as he watched Crawford suffering from his own over indulgence - of intoxicating liquor.

Leaving Sheffield in 1967, Ken based himself for a short time in London and toured abroad with the Giants. "There was Harry Kershaw on bass, Tex Cameron on guitar from the Fleerekkers and the sax players from the Fleerekkers, Alby and Allan, Tony Vincent singing and me on drums, it was a good band. The co-manager was Alan 'Fluff' Freeman and we had an album out on Wing that included the William Tell Overture." One of the places Ken turned up was Germany as Keith Linaker of the Citadels recalls: "The first people to come out were English lads, including the Giants. Kenny was superb, he used to do rolls with one stick in Germany. We used to get up in the morning and go and rehearse with Ken for the laugh." Kenny

Kenny with the Messengers, Gran Lawson, Chick Wilson and Johnny Alexander

soon wiped the smiles of their faces though when the Giants' van broke down: "Somebody has a look in the engine and there's some small thing wrong with it so we limped into Hamburg in our van as the Citadels were due to leave." And, as Terry Roe recalls, the Citadels had exactly the same kind of van: "Kenny took the points off our van and put them on theirs so we couldn't move then." Kenny's explanation was simple: "We were a better band than them."

Back in London Kenny played with Paul Jones and Ronnie Jones and the Nightimers and also backed visiting US stars such as Del Shannon and Bobby Hebb: "Del was a right tight-arse, he wouldn't buy anybody a drink and all that, but we sussed him out. We'd just put a bottle of Scotch on his tab. Bobby was brilliant, a gentleman and a scholar. He asked us if we'd mind just backing him with brushes, 'cos it was like an acoustic thing and we said, yeah, whatever. So we went back to this club at night and he came up with a bottle of real quality Scotch and said, 'Thanks very much for backing me, here's a little present for you.'" Relocating to Blackpool Kenny got together with teenage keyboard wizard Tony Ashton: "He was only 15 and he'd never played with a jazz drummer before. He said, 'Come down to Olympic Studios to do some tracking.' I didn't know what it was, just go down and get my 30 quid. And it was the Stones. I weren't bothered who it was really, so I can't say I'm not on a Stones track." Back in South Yorkshire, Kenny worked for nine months with the Chris James Band at Doncaster Top Rank Suite. From there he joined Joe Cocker's Grease Band.

Kenny is still held in awe by his fellow musicians and one of Kenny's great friends was the equally manic drummer Keith Moon. Roy Barber recalled their first meeting: "They just fell in love with each other." Kenny Slade: "He was like a little choir boy when I first met him, you could hardly get a word out of him. Didn't he change?

Kenny the mod? With Martin Allcock, unknown and Roy Ledger

A lovely lad." Stu Moseley recalls another time when the two drummers met: "Frank [White] was doing at gig at Manchester and all the way there Kenny was moaning about how ill he felt and didn't want to play. Shortly after arriving at the gig, and while Frank was checking it out, a big white Roller pulls up, driven by Keith Moon. On seeing this, Kenny makes an instant recovery, saying how great it's going to be with Moony and loads of free whisky about. Frank then appears and says there's been a mix-up and they weren't playing there that night. So back in the van on the way home Kenny's moaning again about how bad he feels and was totally disappointed about not being able to stay with his pal Moony." Kenny was arguably at his most ferocious playing with Frank White. The more Frank put into it Kenny replied with equal power and dexterity. JP Bean often saw them playing together at the Black Swan and recalls the experience: "It was a battle all night long both for volume and for speed, it became faster and louder. At the end of the night you'd come out concussed." Frank White: "At that time Kenny was way in front of all the other drummers, no question about it. But he just lost it through putting too much stuff down his throat." Kenny was renowned for his drinking and would literally drink anything as Dave Hopper recalls: "We're coming back from Hull with Joe [Cocker], and Kenny and Greeny always used to sit together. They'd got all kinds of drinks coming out of their pockets and after a bit they'd run out of drinks altogether. So Kenny says, 'Are tha' sure tha an't got owt left to drink Greeny? Let's have thi pockets aht.' Then he says, 'What's this? Aftershave?' So he whips the top off and takes a swig. A couple of minutes after he dives into the front of van and says 'Stop the van I want to be sick.'."

Although Kenny can sometimes be a handful, especially when under the influence, you couldn't meet a more generous man, as guitarist Roy Ledger recalled: "He'd borrow a tenner off somebody in the pub and then spend most of it on you. I never had any arguments with Kenny." At one time it seemed Kenny Slade was playing with just about every band in Sheffield - Joe Cocker, Bitter Suite, the Typhoons, Pete Fender, Chuck Fowler, Frank White, etc: "If anybody needed a stand-in, they'd always come to our house. The reason being, I'd got a good ear and a good feel for time and I could stand in." Although they might not want to give Kenny their phone number or address, most of the musicians who know him still look back on him with affection. Alan Wood: "He'd always talk music to you, no interest in anything else. He'd always tell you if you were playing fast or slowing down. I loved him, I thought he was a fantastic character, I found him larger than life. He'd help everybody and anybody and always had a laugh and a smile for everyone." Stu Moseley recalls Kenny's musical snobbery: "I was with Frank White along with Kenny and Adrian Jewel. Adrian says, 'Who's Charlie Parker?' And Kenny's in the back of the van going, 'You what, you what, who's Charlie Parker, you don't know Charlie Parker?' And he must have slagged Adrian off for 20 minutes."

Another brief stint saw Kenny with Alan Bown's band before forming his own band around 1972. Kenny Slade's Sea Bird, a progressive jazz-rock outfit, featured a group of exceptional young musicians Kenny had taken under his wing. The line-up included Tommy Eyre's brother Simon on guitar, bass player Jeremy Meek and conga player Danny Cummings. As well as rehearsing the band at his home, Kenny would feed them all and generally act like a father to them. Although short-lived they played a couple of memorable gigs at the Crucible studio and the Drama Studio on Glossop Road. Jeremy Meek "We had to walk Kenny round for about half-an-hour before the gig to straighten him up a bit, but onstage once Kenny was into it, it was incredible to play with him. Kenny was delighted with the band's efforts from a musical point of view concluding: "Money's not always what it's all about." Stu Moseley: "They rehearsed for weeks and then did only a couple of gigs. They were up for big things but it all fell apart. Halfway through the set, Kenny would get up and do his comedian routine."

Another side of Kenny was his thespian leanings as Monica Moseley recalls: "Joe Cocker and his girlfriend Eileen went with me to see Kenny playing in Shakespeare - As You Like It or something - at the Merlin theatre. He was on stage falling about laughing and completely wrecking everything. He was playing a Roman Centurion and he bent over and a packet of Number 6 cigarettes fell out of his top pocket." Stu Moseley: "He's a born actor." In another production Kenny teamed up with the like-minded Ray Higgins and they performed regularly at the Royal on Abbeydale Road, one week playing a fairly conventional set followed by a panto based on Robin Hood or Dick Turpin.

Kenny left Sheffield many times but kept returning. He would always play - and entertain - whether doing his solo Drinking Song or playing at the Mailcoach on West Street with Higgins.

"Still the greatest": Kenny Slade

Kenny's idea for drawing a crowd was to stick his bare bum out of the window and shout into the street, 'You've seen this now come and see us play.' Kenny has experienced life's highs and lows, from living in a beach-house in Malibu to staying in a hostel in Ilfracombe. However, throughout, he has always retained a sense of humour that has probably kept him alive. Now in his mid-sixties, Kenny is still telling everybody he's the best drummer around.

Another drummer with a wild reputation was Fred Guite. His father, also Fred, was for many years resident drummer at Queens Road Social Club. The younger Frederick Kevan Guite became known as Frappin' Freddie because of the way he played. Roger Harrison: "He was a very aggressive player. I've seen him with his hands bleeding many a time, 'cos he used to play so hard and rub the skin off. I remember when he was playing with Frank [White]. I hadn't had this Ludwig drum kit very long and I saw Fred in town and I told him I'd got a new kit. He said, 'Will you bring it down, we're playing at the Cannon Hall at Firvale tonight? Any chance of letting me play it?' So I took it down and during the first spot he bust the bass drum skin and the second spot he bust the snare drum skin and the small tom-tom. I think he did the last spot on just the floor-tom, he didn't bust that one. A very aggressive player but a great style, I used to love his playing." He'd also earned the nickname Frappin', due to the fact that he would often 'frap' anybody whenever he felt like it. Roger Harrison: "You had to be very careful what you said to him sometimes. I remember when I was in the Daizies and we used to go to Bailey's a lot. Fred used to come in there and he went through a period where he used to dress so everybody noticed him. He'd wear shunkly jackets and things like that. You couldn't help but notice him. Sometimes he'd been in a really strange mood and if you said the wrong thing to him he'd just hit you. He never hit me. But I've seen him do it to people." Mal Hooley: "He was wild. I'd call him schizophrenic. He could be frightening at times. I never had any aggravation with him personally but he was prone to violence, he liked a punch-up. I once remember him just kicking my speaker cabinet off the stage as we were packing up at the end of the night for no reason at all. Strange guy but a good drummer." Stu Moseley: "He could do the Jim Capaldi-style spot on. If he ever threw a bit of a wobbler I was able to cool him down a bit." Pete Jackson: "He was all right with us. Me and Stu Moseley and young Glen Turner in Titus Groan. He'd quietened down. I just think if he respected somebody in the band, he was all right. It was only in bands that he thought were shite that he thought, 'What am I doin' here?'" Fred also worked with the Originals, the New Lizards and Frank White: "I got on very well with him because musically there was a respect there. He was a bit of a strange character, definitely schizo. I've seen him turn in a second." Alan Wood: "Fred had that image, with his tooth missing at the front. When you worked with Fred, from getting in the van to getting out of the van, it was like working with a lit stick of dynamite that could go off at any time. It did go off at certain times but he also had a wicked sense of humour. He was a powerhouse drummer and all that really mattered was what he did on stage." Graham Oliver: "We'd go just to see Fred play with whoever and wherever and were always amazed by him." Alan Wood: "He went on later to join Jimmy James and the Vagabonds with

me. We supported the Stylistics at Fairfield Hall in Croydon. Fred had a double bass-drum kit and he was told that because there were people sitting behind you, like at Sheffield City Hall then, there wasn't enough time - and it didn't look good - to be setting up the one drum kit and rigging up another bass drum. All the drummers were supposed to use the same kit. And he said, 'Well I'm not going on then,' and promptly packed his kit up, put it in a taxi and left. So we had no drummer. The Stylistics drummer said, 'I'll play for you man, don't worry." Dave Hopper also played alongside Freddie Guite with Jimmy James and the Vagabonds: "Freddie had got a reputation, you'd got to watch what you said. But after a bit with the Vagabonds I got a little bit closer to him and he wasn't what you'd thought from the outside. He told me, 'I don't like being like this, I hate it being disliked by people.' And he couldn't overcome it."

Sadly, in January 1975 the Sheffield Star carried the news that Fred, aged just 25, had committed suicide by hanging himself, a dramatic end to a dramatic life. Dave Hopper: "Part of me wasn't at all surprised, partly because of that reputation and partly through knowing that little bit more about him wanting to be liked by people. It obviously must have got him down." Freddie Guite could also be a very cheerful and amusing person. I'm sure that all who knew him would want to remember him as that.

Some drummers were more mild-mannered. Dave 'Cannon' Smith was known as the 'gentle giant' and was well liked by most people. He was the mentor for a number of young musicians such as Dave Hopper: "I took this old acoustic guitar up to the youth club at Manor

Freddie Guite, second right, with Lizards Gerry Scanlon, Barry Marshall and Bob Grundy

Cannon with The Citadels Group, Bob Grundy, Pete Fender and Mal Hooley

Park and he said, 'Let's have a look at that then,' and he picked it up and played the beginning to Move It and a bit of the boogie on Twenty Flight Rock and I thought, 'A real guitar player, teach me how to play.' And he said, 'Oh I'm not a guitar player, that's all I know!' but he taught me how to play them parts." Hopper also recalls how Dave earned the 'Cannon' nickname after an incident at school: "He was playing football and he kicked the ball and it knocked this kid out. So they called him Cannonball after that and it got shortened later on to Cannon." He started with the Twilights, going on to play with Pete Fender, the Sharks, Steve Denton, Kalender, and the Chuck Fowler band. Cannon was a solid and adaptable player, as Frank White can testify: "If I didn't have a drummer and I needed one I could ask him to play and he'd cover it." He's also remembered for his humour. Mal Hooley: "Cannon was rock-steady and a fabulous fella, a laugh a minute." He was also mentor to Alan Wood: "He put me right in the early days when I first went on to bass. He'd explain about timings, saying, 'Just play straight fours, stop whizzing round the bass,' and

Dave "Cannon" Smith, left, with Chuck's band

instilled the basic discipline the same as he did with Tommy Eyre. You just looked at him and he'd know when to start, or play a fill or end. Once he'd heard it he knew it instantly. The happiest musician I've ever known, he laughed at everything, a fantastic lad, he lived his life to the full." Instrumental in Tommy's early days, Cannon took him under his wing and helped him to develop his obvious talent by playing along with him and also introducing Tommy to other bands.

After playing with various groups, Cannon spent his final years as resident drummer at Upper Heeley Club. He was a popular figure with both artists and members alike and often helped organise some of the big shows at the club. He was also a big Sheffield Wednesday fan and it was while leaving a match that Cannon died, as Alan Wood recalls: "He went to lots and lots of Sheffield Wednesday matches with me. Wednesday had managed to stay in the Second Division and as he came out he died." A tribute was paid to Cannon in The Star by Keith Strong under the heading 'Goodbye to the big man' and there was also a special tribute concert at Cannon's beloved Upper Heeley club where all his fellow rockers paid their rock'n'roll respects to one of Sheffield's most liked musicians.

15. THE JOKER: NORMAN 'SPUD' WEST

Someone else whose sense of humour will live on in the memory of those who worked with him is the king of the practical jokers, Norman 'Spud' West. Roy Ledger: "I went to school with him so I'd known him since we were five. It was Spud's fault that I started playing guitar, he was the first one to get one on the estate. Spud taught me my first chords but he never learnt any more after that. He only ever knew three!" Spud started out playing with the Cortinas, along with Dave Robinson, but is probably best remembered for his role in comedy/rock band the Daizies. By the end of the Sixties they were established as club favourites with their zany comedy routines. The March, 1969, edition of Top Stars devoted a full page to them including a picture of Spud with a blow-up doll and his familiar crash-helmet complete with light bulbs that lit up. Drummer Roger Harrison also played in the Daizies: "Spud had a gift of seeing comedy in situations that other people didn't see. He used to overstep the mark sometimes and I used to think, God, we're in for it here, we're all

Spud, second left, with Monsters/Daisies Dave Robinson, Phil Galley and Paul Jarvis

gonna get thumped or something. I remember one particular night up in Middlesborough at a working men's club. We was doing the comedy and it was going down really well. But there were four elderly women sat right at the front and they just never stopped talking the whole time, and they were talking loudly. The rest of the club were listening to the band and the comedy and were enjoying it. Spud went off-stage to get changed for the next comedy thing. Next thing he appeared in front of the stage, on the floor, with a fire extinguisher. And he just sprayed these women with that foam stuff and said something like, 'Let's see if that'll keep you quiet.' They were covered in it, the whole table. They just sat there in like a big white dome, four old ladies underneath it. And I can remember thinking, 'God, something's gonna happen here 'cos they'd have relatives, sons, big tough guys in the audience. But, amazingly, there was a silence. And all the people in the club applauded. It'd obviously been bugging them as well."

Spud and Roger Harrison went on to join Dave Berry's backing band, and Dave was often at the brunt of Spud's practical jokes. "He was always doing something with Berry. He used to put things on stage for Berry to fall over when he came on in darkness. He used to put all sorts of daft things on stage like, for instance, a rusty old bike frame. That was at the Poco-Poco Club in Stockport, a massive night club. Spud'd found this old bike frame in the car park and of course Berry came on in the dark and fell over it with a crash. He once found a pair of old shoes, really big, battered shoes. And he used to put them on stage nearly every night at the side of Berry's mic-stand. And when the lights came on there's these battered old shoes there. It used to embarrass Berry, particularly with him having big feet himself. Berry used to try and pinch them off us to throw them away but we always used to get them back somehow. Somebody also taught Spud how to breathe fire and I

remember Berry coming on one night at Blackburn Cavendish with a thousand people sat there. As he came creeping on Spud just blew this ten foot flame at him. No warning. Berry dropped the mic and shouted, 'Fuckin' hell, what's going off?' It really frightened him. It made us all jump. And Spud once sprayed him with a fire-extinguisher as he was coming on. He was dressed in black and Spud covered him in white powder and he couldn't do anything except just carry on covered in white." Dave Berry: "He used to have his pockets full of these wind-up toys and as I was singing a number he'd be putting all these around my feet, and there'd be little dolls making a noise, all sorts of different things going." Roger Harrison: "Berry was top of the bill at Batley Variety Club and the place was packed. In the middle of The Crying Game, all quiet and low lighting, I saw old Spud walk back to his amp, turn the guitar off and the amp up full. He walked back to the front of the stage and then he turned the guitar up full and played this horrible chord - 'praaaang' - then fell off the stage on to a table full of drinks with all the people sat there, knocking all the drinks off. Everybody jumps up, and Berry's still singing and it just killed it. Spud gets back on to the stage and turns his wig round - he wore a long wig in those days - so that the long hair at the back was across his face. Then took his teeth out - he had false teeth. So he's stood next to Berry who's still singing The Crying Game and goes z-z-z-up with the wig, and spun it round so it was dead obvious it was a wig. Then he fished

A light-headed Spud with Dave Robinson and duck

Duck-head Spud West

public eye, Spud was a very genuine guy. A very goodhearted guy, he'd do 'owt for you and was very caring. Totally different from how the general public thought of him, y'know, fooling around. When he got married he was a great father to Christian his lad. He idolised him and used to take him everywhere. He was very good in the house, doing DIY jobs."

In 1992 Spud got back together with Dave Robinson and Roger Harrison as Rock With Laughter. In the summer of '93 he was diagnosed as being terminally ill with cancer. Showing how much they thought of Spud, regardless of all the things he may have done to most of them, many of his old mates from various Sheffield bands, including Dave Berry, took part in a couple of charity shows for Spud but he died in January, 1994.

16. PUNCH AND JUDY: McCLOSKEY'S APOCALYPSE

There were few exceptions in the late Sixties/early Seventies to the domination of covers bands, but one of the most entertaining and theatrical examples were McCloskey's Apocalypse. They had got together in August 1968 with a manifesto to, "bring much needed original material to the local rock scene." They are fondly remembered by the hordes who flocked to see them play in the late Sixties and early Seventies. The rest of Sheffield seems to have forgotten them entirely but then they can't have seen them perform...

The band consisted of Mick Wilson, Ray

in his pocket and put his teeth back in, stood in the spotlight at the side of Berry. Berry was so annoyed, he was really fuming. He used to sack Spud nearly every night." Dave Berry: "I think the band were fed up with him actually. He used to get incredibly drunk, in fact one particular night he came off and Graham the roadie wouldn't let him go back on." Roger: "After all the things Spud had done to him, Berry eventually took it in good part."

Spud's baldness was hereditary, but also partially self-inflicted, thanks to dyeing his hair with bleach. Roger Harrison: "I don't think that helped. Spud's brother Malcolm was the same, bald at an early age, and ol' Spud went the same way. When I first knew him he used to comb his hair forward then kind of part it back and eventually started wearing a wig. His hair was blond naturally, darkish blond, but he bleached it virtually white. I think he just did it with Domestos or something like that!" Dave Robinson: "Comedian Dustin Gee sorted the wig out for him. He was stopping with us and he took a shine to Spud. He knew Spud did comedy and he was very into Viv Stanshall. He said, 'You ought to do something about your hair, y'know. Have you ever thought of wearing a wig? I'll sort you out.' And he came back and he'd got this barnet on him." Roy Barber recalls another side to Spud: "We'd all gone away on holiday together down in Devon, and we'd just sat down for a meal. Spud suddenly began sobbing for no reason. He was a very deep person." Best friend Roger Harrison also knew Spud's quieter side and remembers him with great affection: "Away from all that being on stage and away from the

Dave Seville, Ray Higgins and Mick Wilson

Mick, Dave and Ray

Higgins and former Pharmaseutrical Earth Mover drummer Dave Seville. Wilson started out in 1961 with Dee Curtis and the Diablos and then the Dukes who had Joe Cocker as guest singer on a number of occasions. Band member Stu Moseley recalls Wilson's unusual singing: "He used to make this horrendous noise as a sort of vocal, and this guy at a club in a mining village says, 'If that guy gets up and sings again, we're having your lads.' I ended up singing in some sort of normal way to calm things down. Eventually I got fired from them and Mick threatened to beat me up." Higgins too had a bit of a history, having started out in the mid-Sixties with a band glorying in the name of Dial Diogenes Cynics, named somewhat convolutedly after the Greek philosopher. They were famously billed for one appearance at the Esquire as, 'Come and see the man in a barrel,' Diogenes being reputed to have lived in such a receptacle.

Wilson joined forces with Higgins and Seville to form McCloskey's in 1968. After an uneventful first year slogging round the usual circuit of pit village pubs and clubs it wasn't until they played an impromptu session in the Students Union bar during the 1969 Sheffield Festival that they really made an impression. Seeing how well this had gone down the band decided to add some theatrics to their music. Inspired by the Who's first attempt at a rock opera - the short song cycle A Quick One While He's Away from the 1966 album The Who Sell Out - Wilson followed suit shortly afterwards. Infact The Who, with Tommy, beat them by only a matter of weeks in performing the first rock opera live on stage. The Redemption of Gaylord McCloskey was premiered at Sheffield City Hall's Memorial Hall in 1969. Written by Wilson, the story had McCloskey meeting Robin Hood, getting shot and going to Hell. Developing these ideas over the next three years, the band's finest hour has to be their rock opera version of Punch and Judy. It was an ideal vehicle for the eccentric talents of the extroverts who fronted the band, Higgins and Wilson. Punch and Judy, written by Wilson and starring Higgins, was staged at Sheffield University Drama Studio on Glossop Road in January, 1972. In the audience was the owner of Charisma Records, Tony Stratton-Smith who had been alerted to the band by a mutual friend, Rod Clements of Charisma's biggest band

Lindisfarne.

Higgins takes up the story: "We always carried livestock when we performed and part of the Punch and Judy Show involved me swallowing live goldfish from a bowl which, stupidly, was sat on the main amplifier. Sure enough when it came to the fight scene with the crocodile the bowl was knocked over and fused the amplifier, bringing the whole thing to a halt. We tried to carry on acoustically but it was useless. Perhaps if that incident hadn't happened things would have been different. Stratton-Smith was very nice to us afterwards but couldn't see how to get the thing down on record."

Indeed. How on earth do you encapsulate on record an act which not only played music but incorporated humour, theatre and even circus skills? Higgins would munch his way through the occasional beer glass on stage, making blood-curdling crunching noises down the microphone, while both he and Wilson also indulged in a bit of fire-breathing. Seville had the awesome task of holding the whole thing together while the other two swopped between various instruments, playing what was highly complicated music which still managed to rock. "The time signatures

MC CLOSKEYS APOCALYPSE

AMAZING PUNCH AND JUDY SHOW

were ridiculous but sometimes they had to be," said Higgins. "A song would start in straightforward 4:4 but then go into 2:4 only so that Mick could have time to put the violin down and start playing the bass. But then the chorus would be alternating 7:8s and 9:8s. I can remember spending most of my time at work running through the songs in my head trying to learn the timings. It would keep me at awake at night." Seville: "And that's why we used to do all the original material early in the set because after three pints it just became impossible to get it right."

With McCloskey's, Wilson played bass, elec-

tric violin, viola and whatever else came to hand, while Higgins was on vocals, guitar and organ. Seville also played xylophone and varied percussion. Other instruments included recorder, auto-harp, pixiphone, harmonicas and bells. Wilson: "The thinking behind Punch and Judy was that Ray was such a good front man, performer and comedian that I thought it would be nice to write a show around him." Higgins played Mr Punch. Wilson said at the time: "If you've seen him poncing around the on stage it's not a big step to imagine him wielding a big stick, killing people." Seville, playing Dog Toby and dressed in a white body-stocking with big black spots, had a "stupid" extra drum kit consisting of three oil drums, two washtubs and a dustbin. Augmenting the band was semi-pro actor from Wath, Derek Hewitson, plus a couple of roadies "to hump bodies on and off"

"It took a good few months to put together but none of us were working," says Wilson. "We built the full-size gallows, which had a lever and trapdoor, out of bits of wood which we scavanged from the various bomb sites which were still dotted around Broomhall where we lived. We also built the crocodile out of scavenged wood. It had car headlights for eyes. I found what I thought was an abandoned car in Broomhall and spent ages screwing off the headlights. Then this bloke appeared and said, 'What the fuck do you think you are doing, that's my car.' I spent the next hour carefully putting the headlights back together while he watched over me making various threats." Punch and Judy was a great success and had two runs at the Drama Studio as well as performances at Kingston Poly and in Mexborough. Steve Dawson of Sob: "It was a fantastic show. My most vivid memory was the lighting effects, even the bands at the City Hall didn't have that. They should have made it. If

MC CLOSKEY'S

APOCALYPSE

only they had got out of Sheffield and gone for it."

The band were regulars at the Weston Park open-air concerts and Sheffield University, and besides screaming, fighting and shouting at each other on stage, they also tended to paint themselves green and yellow. They were, along with Shape Of the Rain, virtually the only band around at the time performing original material. "But there was animosity between those two bands," recalls Richard Memmott, bass player with various bands in the Seventies. "I can remember one occasion in Weston Park when McCloskey's wrote an impromptu song about Shape of the Rain. McCloskey's always did something different, going off at a tangent which was great as long as you could ignore the catastrophic bollocks they'd drop every now and then."

From the band's inception in 1968 through to the demise in April, 1973, McCloskey's, as well as being one of the most original bands to come out of the city was one of the most popular. This was particularly evident during a residency at the Broadfield pub on Abbeydale Road which regularly packed in 300 people every Friday night for 18 months. "Places to play were few and far between so we were always looking for residencies," says Wilson. "And I'm pretty sure it was us that found the Broadfield. We were quite cocky little bastards. We thought were by far the best group in Sheffield and, looking back, we did play some highly original stuff. To be honest there were very few bands around at that time so there wasn't that much competition." The Broadfield residency ended when a new landlord decided to charge the band £5 to play there. "The deal had always been that we would charge three shillings on the door and the pub would make money on the beer. He fired us. We ended up moving to the Blue Bell at Hackenthorpe which was too far out and then the Minerva in the city centre but that was too small. We even went to the Dog and Partridge in Attercliffe where the landlord was that pleased to get us that he built a stage specially for us, but that was too far away really. We even ended up hiring church halls for a while."

Trouble was never very far away when McCloskey's performed. On more than one occasion they had the Animal Rights people on their backs. Not least on the occasion at the Broadfield when Higgins managed to anticipate by almost a decade the feat of Black Sabbath's singer Ozzy Osbourne by biting the head off a dead animal. In Osbourne's case it was a bat, something he still has to answer for to this day.

At the Broadfield it was a dead pigeon that Higgins decapitated with his teeth. Steve Dawson of Sob who shared a rehearsal room with them above the Albert pub: "We used to go down and see Ray's antics in the Broadfield. You'd look in the Star on a Thursday night and there was always an advert, McCloskey's Apocalypse at the Broadfield, it was like Frank White at the Pheasant, they were always there. It would also advertise what Ray was going to do. It became like cult reading. It'd say, 'Ray Higgins will drink a bottle of bleach' or 'Ray will eat a pint glass' or a lit cigarette. The thing is he always used to do it. You went to see Ray do something or eat summat." Graham Oliver: "Ray came with us once and we stopped at a chip shop. He went in but because he didn't have any money he asked for a bag of bits and drank some vinegar." Steve: "The drummer was brilliant, one of the first drummers to have a massive proper drum kit. We thought they were like a proper band, we were still learning. They probably don't remember much because they were like a proper rock band where drinking, taking drugs or whatever else it is a rock band is supposed to do, comes first, and the music and performance is like a minor annoyance that goes off in the background. Partying first, music second. Ray should have been a pop star, massive by any standards."

Then there were the infamous goldfish. As part of the Punch and Judy show Higgins would pretend to swallow the said fish, substituting a

At rehearsals, Ray, Dave and Mick

sliver of carrot to give the impression of committing the dirty deed. Inevitably the goldfish copped for it occasionally. Higgins: "I defy anybody to tell a piece of carrot from a goldfish with all the mayhem that was going on stage. I certainly couldn't. The roadie checked the goldfish after the performance and invariably a couple would be missing." The goldfish never did get an easy ride. When the band were due to perform Punch and Judy after being, somewhat bizarrely, booked to play at the Debs' Ball at St John College, Oxford, the band took it in turns to hold the goldfish bowl in the truck which was loaded with gallows et al on the way down. "I had to keep shouting at the driver to slow down because he was going to kill the fish. The water was splashing out of the bowl and we had to keep stopping to fill it back up," said Higgins. Steve Dawson: "McCloskey's really influenced me by taking bits other than music whether it be eating a dead rat or something different like that."

The band's music, written by Wilson, was influenced by everybody from Hendrix and Bartok to Pete Townshend and Ravi Shankar. The lyrics were also not your conventional rock 'n' roll topics. The usual opening number was Sawney Bean, based on the folk tale of a 17th century Scottish cannibal and his family living out in the middle of nowhere who used to waylay lonely travellers and eat them. The chorus started something like: "Eating people every day, Throwing arms and legs away, Chewing hands and chewing feet, Masticating human meat." Then there was Clegg which was about a man in a wheelchair who went around stopping people masturbating; a couple of drinking songs including Last Orders Please which they always played at the appropriate time - 10.20pm; and a smattering of covers including My Generation and Wild Thing, Hendrix-style. The latter was notable for Higgins' party piece, well one of many of his party pieces. The band would drop right down and he would launch into an improvised rhyming monologue. "I remember falling off stage laughing at some of the stuff he would come out with. He was a brilliant showman," says Wilson.

Then there was the fire breathing. Higgins: "It was very much a DIY thing. I would take a mouthful of meths. It was burning my lips and mouth so I wanted to get the stuff out as quickly as possible. We'd bundle matches together to light it. I'd done it loads of times but on one occasion at the Black Swan it went horribly wrong. I lit the meths but I was facing the wrong way. There was a backdraft from the equipment-

loading door behind the stage which had been left open. I ended up with my head on fire. Then I tried again, I faced the other way and it happened again. This time somebody had opened a window because it was hot." Higgins lost his nerve after that and Wilson took up the mantle, with similar results: "There was one occasion at the Minerva when I set this bloke's Afro haircut on fire. His mate had the presence of mind to pour his pint over his head. The guy whose head had been on fire then bought another pint and poured it over me," said Wilson. Years later another Sheffield band, featuring a character as large as life as Higgins, also introduced fire breathing into their act. The man in question, Mick Shedd, managed to set his head on fire but rather than waste his pint putting himself out he did the next best thing - burst into the ladies toilet and shoved his head down the toilet bowl. Henceforth, his band, known until then simply as Shedds, became Shedds On Fire. Fire-breathing also played a part in Punch and Judy. This time Wilson managed to set the baby's cot on fire and the resident jobsworthy revelled in, for probably the first time, the task of using every fire extinguisher in the place to put out the fire. Then there was the occasion at the Minerva when Higgins threatened to turn a fire extinguisher on the audience. He did.

Even the pint pot-eating came in useful on the odd occasion. Higgins had originally discovered he enjoyed a pint pot with his chips when the band played a gig at Louth in Lincolnshire. "The landlord had this helper who was a real big head. Once we had earned our wages we would throw our money at the bar for some afterbird [an expression meaning drinking after time]. Then this twat decided to show off by eating this thin whiskey glass. So I decided to outdo him and had a go at a pint pot. I found I could do it. It became part of the act but it's a horrible thing to do and you do end up with a lacerated arse the next day." This rare talent did come to the band's rescue however when they played in Glasgow. "The audience was just staring at us completely uncomprehending," says Seville. "They scared us. Then finally Ray started doing the glass bit and the crowd went wild. It obviously struck a chord. The next day there were all these Glaswegians walking around with cut mouths." Not that the trip, organised by a Sheffielder mate who was at the university in Glasgow, was a success. "It was the only time in my life I didn't have any money at all. The concerts that were supposed to have been organised for us all fell through. We had hired a van and had a couple of roadies with us. We lived on potatoes for a week," says Higgins.

They even had the honour of giving the final performance at Sheffield Playhouse which held 700 people. McCloskey's sold it out, with queues down the street unable to get in. The band were given a free run at the props and costume room. "It was like being let loose in a magic toy shop, all those things to play with," says Wilson. Higgins, of course, rose to the occasion. His entrance, in full gorilla suit, on to the stage was via a rope swinging from a balcony. One minute he was playing his Hammond organ, disappeared behind the curtain and re-emerged seconds later in full walk-in Queen Victoria costume. It wasn't their first connection with the Playhouse. In 1971 there had been a production of A Midsummer Night's Dream, words by William Shakespeare, music by McCloskey's Apocalypse - 'the best progressive rock group in Sheffield,' as they were billed.

But despite their popularity McCloskey's never really made it much beyond the confines of Sheffield. "Essentially we were a live band. We got stuff on tape but none of it reflected what we were on stage. You always think you deserved better but maybe we should have been braver and gone to London where it was all happening. It was too cosy in Sheffield. I was happy playing at the Broadfield every Friday and trying out new stuff on our audience. Those 18 months there were probably the best time for us," says Wilson. Pity really because their quirky approach was reflected by several other successful acts at the time, notably the Incredible String Band and Frank Zappa's Mothers Of Invention as well as Principal Edwards Magic Theatre and the Bonzo Dog Doo-Dah Band.

Audiences at the time were receptive to most things and Wilson can remember going to see the Who, the Incredible String Band and Indian sitar player Ravi Shankar all in the same week in Sheffield - "It was the same audience for each one, people were deeply interested in whatever was going on." McCloskey's did attempt to go mainstream but it was a failure: "Later on we dropped all the quirky stuff because we thought we'd get more gigs doing cover versions of rock 'n' roll songs. We just ended up another band."

Strangely enough, considering the availability at the time, drugs were not a big part of the McCloskey's inspiration. "We did have one song, Smashed, which was about drugs, but really we were just boozers," says Mick. "I can remember Ray having a smoke once and he proceeded to play this interminable guitar solo. People started throwing halfpennies at him and eventually I had to go over and give him a kick

to get him to stop. We used to invite people back to my house in Hanover Square after a show and one day Joe Cocker and his mates came back. There were 30 people drinking home brew and somebody laid two tabs of acid on me which completely destroyed me. We stuck to drinking after that."

The wheels eventually dropped off in 1973. "We put 18 months work into preparing Punch and Judy and what happened in the end was such a disappointment. I think it was that that finally finished us off," says Seville of the production that they hoped would lead to greater things.

Wilson went on to form a folk duo with his wife Deborah which in 1977 became Acrobats of Desire, reworking some of the McCloskey's material in the process for two violins, viola and cello. There was also Mick Wilson's Scratch Band which included Dave Seville, another outfit to have a Friday night residency at the Broadfield. Wilson eventually left Sheffield to take a BA and then a PhD in Composition at York University, after composing a string quartet - "I realised that I was going to spend the rest of my life writing music so I decided to get educated." He now lives in West Yorkshire and is head of compositional studies at the University of Salford's Music department. He has composed various pieces of orchestral, ensemble, brass band, dance and gamelan pieces since and, yes, occasionally some of those old McCloskey's pieces get in there somewhere.

These days Ray Higgins is a builder by trade, and describes himself as a "frustrated musician, sitting at home with a portastudio." Seville carried on playing in various bands, latterly in Slim and the Big Man Blues Band, before the pressure of work as an English lecturer finally put his musical career on the back-burner. Although their efforts never took them to greater heights, the antics of McCloskey's continue to bring a smile to everyone who witnessed their gigs.

17. LAND OF THE FREE: DEREK BAILEY AND TONY OXLEY

Two Sheffielders who have probably appeared on more records between them than the whole of the lot above and yet remain almost totally without acclaim in their own city are guitarist Derek Bailey and drummer Tony Oxley.

Sheffield's long history of being one of the

A young Derek Bailey

centres of improvised music can be traced back to the early Sixties, when Bailey and Oxley, along with double bass player Gavin Bryars, formed a remarkable trio which played every Saturday lunchtime for almost three years at the Grapes on Trippet Lane between 1963 and '66. All three went on to become major figures in their chosen field. The impact of those sessions at the Grapes was described in Wire magazine in 1999 as: "Now a global phenomenon, a permanent noise fest that laughs in the face of classical and commercial canons." Yet while the last vestiges of beat music continued to dominate the scene in Sheffield and the Mojo and Esquire clubs were having their heyday, the trio's residency went almost unnoticed outside the select few who followed the jazz scene.

Bailey, born in 1930, was brought up in a Victorian terrace house in Tavistock Road, Sharrow, just a stone's throw away from the Abbeydale Cinema, dancehall and billiard hall. His family had musical connections. His grandfather Percy Wing from Grimesthorpe, who died in 1919, played banjo and piano as well as painting pub signs. Indeed he was immortalised on the sleeve of Village Life, an album Bailey recorded with drummer Louis Moholo, which featured a photograph of Percy outside one of the pubs he had painted a sign for. But Bailey's first connections with music in Sheffield was through

his uncle George Wing, who played Hawaiian guitar in the late Thirties/ early Forties.

"I didn't get interested in playing until I got hooked on jazz during the war," says Derek. "I did a lot of listening in the Forties. I can remember a band which used to play at the Cutlers' Hall, led by Jackie Bates, during the big band era. Funnily enough I later worked with him. There was also a band at the Abbeydale dancehall and jazz at the Broadfield and the Royal in the late Forties. I started off playing drums and clarinet before taking up the guitar and ended up playing at dances at the Wagon and Horses on Abbeydale Road in '48/49 before getting called up." He studied music with CHC Biltcliffe and guitar with John Duarte between 1941 and 1952 and went on to play at venues across the country, finally leaving Sheffield in 1957.

Oxley, born at Spital Street, Pitsmoor, on June 15, 1938, started out teaching himself to play piano - at the age of eight. The piano 'mysteriously' disappeared shortly afterwards. He eventually took up drums and at 15 started playing in pubs, some long disappeared, such as the Travellers Rest on the Moor and the Rotherham Arms "on the banks of the River Don" as well as the old Black Swan. He moved on to big bands at 16 while working in a steelworks. His formal music training didn't come until he got called up in 1957. "I signed up for three years with the Black Watch Military Band. We played concert music such as Beethoven and Haydn. I had to learn the full range of the percussion section - glockenspiel, tympani, vibes etc. I had to develop it very quickly. Before that I learned by ear. You were urged to improve your abilities and I used all the facilities available. I started to practise jazz. I had all musical fronts under attack."

Returning to Sheffield in 1960, Oxley again took a job at a steelworks, this time in the office. "I was a pretty qualified musician by this time so I was deciding what to do. I didn't want to go into an orchestra. I had had enough of playing other people's music." Oxley formed a quartet with pianist Fred Boaden, whom he had first played with in the mid-Fifties. He and Boaden got back together as the Jazz Messengers, emulating the hard bop of Art Blakey's Jazz Messengers, and were resident at the Grapes in Dalton, Rotherham, on Sunday nights. "In the two years the group has been together we haven't had one disagreement. We are all agreed on our principles and policy, which is to play good jazz well. We haven't time to disagree," said Oxley at the time.

But it wasn't until 1963 that Oxley and Bailey were to meet. Piano player Brian Pendleton had

Sheffield's Jazz Messengers with Tony Oxley on right

already recruited Oxley to play at his music and gambling Carlton Club in Chesterfield, and put a call in to Bailey, then living in London. It was to be the start of a highly fruitful relationship. Ironically the only reason that Bailey took the job was because his father was ill and wanted to be near him. But it was a move that was to help shape both their careers. "I was amazed. They were a good band and the club had quite a liberal attitude towards music," says Bailey. Also in the Chesterfield line-up were bass player Roly Ashton and vibes man Gerry Rollinson.

Bailey, who lived in Manchester then Blackpool, and Oxley went on to start a jazz club on Saturday lunchtimes upstairs at the Devonshire Arms on Ecclesall Road in Sheffield. It was there that philosophy student and jazz bass player Gavin Bryars came on the scene to complete the classic Joseph Holbrooke line-up, named after an obscure late 19th century composer dubbed the Cockney Wagner. In late 1963, the club moved to the Grapes, renting the small upstairs room still used by local musicians today. "We used to put an advert in The Star each week and the Musicians Union helped us out with the rent for three months," says Oxley. "It was difficult to cover our costs but it was a very profitable time musically for us in the most pitiful of circumstances. It was a tiny room with an oil-cloth floor and a piano that was unplayable. The audience must have come for the music, because it certainly wasn't for the comfort. I don't know why we chose that place because there were plenty of other pubs putting on jazz. But I think most places wouldn't have allowed us to do what we did."

Bailey: "We started out playing contemporary jazz by the likes of Bill Evans and John Coltrane. But we were also interested in playing with no time being stated. We didn't invent it, we pinched the idea from Bill Evans who had been doing it in 1962. I knew nothing of it but the others were into it. There were also a few classical influences in there, with Gavin studying classical music, and I think we had a go at a Messiaen piece on one occasion. We started writing our own stuff and as time went on we started playing totally improvised music. The first half of the set would be tunes, Coltrane modal things, or Round About Midnight. Then we would knock off and have a break and the second half would be free playing. There was never a decision to play free, it wasn't an ideological move, it just happened, perhaps because we were three completely different characters - I was quite a bit older than the others - and it became the best way we could play together."

Oxley: "It came to the point where we felt we should take the free music thing further rather than waiting for the next record by an American exponent. We felt there was more could be done than there was being done with the language. Fortunately we were all in Sheffield and it happened naturally. The audience was mostly from the university. They were very loyal. But when the university term finished the audience would disappear so eventually we would close down for the holidays. We used to practice three or four times a week at Gavin's flat on Crookesmoor Road and I think the audience came to the Grapes to hear what we had done that week, to hear how it had changed."

The audiences may have been small but they were loyal. "It was very very exciting," says one regular John Kapes. "It was like nothing I could listen to at home or anywhere else for that matter - comparable to the excitement I had felt previously on listening to Giant Steps or an Ornette album. Only this time all the normal springboards of melody, chords and regular time were being dispensed with." Not that everyone shared his enthusiasm. The comment from one visitor, George Paxton, a pianist friend of Bailey's from Edinburgh, after listening to the first half of a performance, was, "What the fuck do you think you are doing?" A couple of weeks later Derek received a Get Well Soon card from him.

The Grapes venture finally ended in early '66, after a tour with American alto sax player Lee Konitz. Oxley had been headhunted to join the house band at Ronnie Scott's Club in London.

Tony Oxley

"There was no point in missing the opportunity to play with people like Johnny Griffin. It was back to old ground to play bebop but it was quite an experience. There was nothing there to keep us in Sheffield," says Oxley who now lives in Germany. He remains one of jazz's most respected, and innovative, drummers. At Ronnie Scott's, where he played until the early Seventies, he accompanied visiting Americans such as Stan Getz, Sonny Rollins, Bill Evans and Konitz and contributed to John McLaughlin's 1969 classic album Extrapolation. In that same year he was voted the country's top drummer in the Melody Maker's readers poll. He went on to play with Cecil Taylor as well as leading his own

band, recording several acclaimed solo albums. He has also continued to perform free music with Bailey including the excellent albums Baptised Traveller and 4 Compositions For Sextet for Columbia in 1969 and 1970.

Bryars, the only one of the trio not to be born and bred in Sheffield, having moved to the city from Goole to study at Sheffield University, became an avant-garde composer. He recorded The Sinking Of The Titanic and Jesus' Blood Never Failed Me Yet for Brian Eno's Obscure label in 1975, and wrote operas and composed pieces for guitarist Bill Frisell, the Balanescu Quartet and Julian Lloyd-Webber. He was also founder of the notorious Portsmouth Sinfonia which was basically an orchestra of musical amateurs or musicians playing instruments they were totally unfamiliar with and who, to not put too fine a point on it, good-naturedly destroyed pop and classical standards.

Bailey became a member of the Spontaneous Music Ensemble before leaving to concentrate on solo guitar and duos with the likes of Evan Parker, Tony Coe and a series of percussionists. He has performed solo all over the world, including Europe, the USA and, his biggest market, Japan. He has also pioneered various guitar techniques, particularly prepared guitar: "I used to have an old flat-top Epiphone 12 string. I had loose strings and squeakers and all the usual stuff. See, at one time in the Sixties, there weren't any free players who didn't prepare their guitars. I can remember a piece I played with four other guitar players where you got a bag of paper clips, things that would stick on the strings, and you stuck 'em on the strings and then you got something else out - four guys doing this for as long as you can stand it."

In 1970 he, along with Oxley and Evan Parker, formed Incus Records, the first independent, musician-owned record company which continues to this day. Bailey also wrote a book, Improvisation: Its Nature and Practice In Music, which became the basis for a TV series, On The Edge, on Channel 4. In 1976 he formed Company, an ever changing ensemble of improvising musicians from all over the world, and the next year inaugurated the annual Company week, a five-day event for improvisers worldwide, including some of Bailey's successors in Sheffield such as Martin Archer, John Jasnoch and Mick Beck.

In the book Jazz: The Rough Guide, Bailey is described as: "He has pursued the austere path of total improvisation and abstraction with monolithic integrity, becoming one of the masters in the field. Yet, despite the severity of his

Derek Bailey in later years

approach, his music is often alive with drama, intelligence and anarchic humour." The Wire magazine referred to Bailey as "the Samuel Beckett of improvised music." He has worked with such major figures as fusion jazz guitarist Pat Metheney, sax player John Zorn and pianist Cecil Taylor as well as Japanese art-of-noise avant-rock duo The Ruins and Detroit-born jazz tap dancer Will Gaines. Or as Bailey put it: "I have had the good fortune to work with most of the leading German blasters, American groovers, Dutch acrobats and English kaleido-scopists in this field." Despite his single-minded approach, his 1982 album, View From 6 Windows, was nominated for a Grammy Award. A few jaws dropped when Bailey, at the age of 67 and who has never worked as much as he has since he turned 60, recorded the drum and bass album, Guitars, Drum 'n' Bass, with DJ Ninj but it came together in typical Bailey style. "I live in Hackney and the loudest station I could pick up on my radio was a pirate station which played drum and bass. I used it to practice with and decided I wanted to do an album of it."

Bailey, who was 71 on January 29, 2001, remains a leading figure in the world's free music scene, a pioneer in the exploration of sound and texture.

Between them Bailey, Oxley and Bryars have contributed to hundreds of records - and the roots of it all can be traced back to that coming together of the threesome at the Grapes as the Joseph Holbrooke Trio. But they never made any Holbrooke recordings because of Bryars' deci-sion in 1966 to concentrate on composed music. That was finally put to rights in 1998 when the three of them got back together, 32 years after their last session at the Grapes. The occasion was Oxley's 60th birthday and the radio station in Cologne near Oxley's home devoted a two-day live broadcast to the drum-mer - "An extraordinary experience, it could never happen in Britain," says Bailey. As a result the Cortical Foundation in Malibu asked the trio if they would record for them. The first Joseph Holbrooke Trio album, a two-CD set, was record-ed in two days in November 1998, the first time the band had been heard away from the stage of the Grapes. This prompted Bailey and co to release a recording of a rehearsal at Bryers' flat at 329 Crookesmoor Road from 1965 which they released on CD on Incus in 1999. Incus also released some of the German live perform-ance on the CD Joseph Holbrooke '98. Andrew Shone, who was the doorkeeper at the Grapes, wrote the sleevenotes: "The essence of the trio was there from Bailey's opening acerbic chords, through Bryars' ever attentive basslines, to Oxley's orchestration of time itself. There's no nostalgia here, more the feel of three men resuming a conversation they had begun some time ago, while mindful that their subject matter back then has been widely discussed in many languages since, and that this was a restate-ment through minds enriched with subsequent experiences."

These days Bailey is busier than ever, working with even more musicians, as well as occasion-ally teaming up with Will Gaines - "That's my favourite gig, not least because Will is the only person I work with who is older than me," says Bailey. Gaines himself deserves a footnote in all this, not least because he remains one of the last performers keeping alive the vaudeville tra-dition of tap dancing but also because he was a familiar figure in Sheffield in the Seventies hav-ing moved to Rotherham in 1972. He started out as a street or 'buck' (the American name for the body of a cart) dancer in the States before going on to share the bill with giants such as Count Basie, Duke Ellington and Sarah Vaughan.

Gavin Bryars

As this book started, names like Tony Oxley and Derek Bailey were among the few who really began to shape any kind of popular music scene in Sheffield early on. Although they ended up leaving the city - which has often been the case with Sheffield musicians - to make their mark in music, their subsequent success remains a credit to the city. Their achievements should go alongside those of all the other successful names from Sheffield as well as the many who remained in the city to keep the music alive.

He made his debut in Britain at the London Palladium in 1962.

Bailey came across Gaines shortly afterwards when he played at the Carlton Club. Oxley became Gaines' musical director, playing night clubs and cabaret as well as appearing on TV programmes such as the Arthur Haynes Show. "Will was a real livewire. It was my job to present some musical framework for him to do his thing with," says Oxley. "I would orchestrate show music such as Porgy and Bess and West Side Story for him to dance to." Gaines never went back to the States and ended up performing in working men's clubs before he met Rotherham hotelier Athol Carr at Greasbrough Social Club. He in turn introduced him to British jazz trumpeter Alex Welch who helped resurrect his career. He also settled down in Rotherham - "I was raised in Detroit, a northern working class city, so Rotherham is my kind of town. The North is the same whatever country you're in. It's the province of the working man." Such was his enthusiasm, if he didn't have any money he would walk from Rotherham to Sheffield for jazz gigs, paying his way by dancing on the tables. Now in his early seventies, he lives in Southend.

UPDATES ON CONTRIBUTORS

Derek Bailey - jazz guitarist with various Sheffield ensembles before becoming one of the world's leading musical improvisers.

Roy Barber - Originally guitarist with Johnny Tempest and the Mariners then the Cruisers, and later Frank White before playing steel guitar with Tammy Cline and Southern Comfort. Sadly died in May, 2000.

J. P. Bean - Author of Joe Cocker biography With A Little Help From My Friends, Sheffield Gang Wars and several other books on crime and prison life.

Dave Berry - Sheffield's first singer to enjoy international success with string of hit records. Still highly active today.

Ernie Booth - Guitarist and later bass player with Rotherham band the Thunderbirds with whom he still does the occasional gig.

Neil Bridges - Started out as guitarist with Blue Diamonds skiffle group, later with the Whirlwinds and in recent times with Bobby Knutt's band, the Spare Tyres, before retiring from music.

Phil Brodie - Guitarist with Love Or Confusion, Dave Berry and Bitter Suite. Still playing.

Duggie Brown - One-time member of Imps skiffle group who later became a successful comedian/actor.

Paul Carrack - Former member of Reaction Soul Band before going on to international success with Ace, Squeeze and Mike & The Mechanics and is now well respected musician/songwriter/performer.

Pete Carson - Long-time music fan and organiser of Sheffield Country Music Club.

Jimmy Crawford - Formerly known as Ron Lindsay, singer/front-man with the Ravens and the first Sheffield performer to reach the UK pop charts. Now semi-retired from music business.

John Crookes - Bass-player and later sax player with D.D. Whatson and Big Crowd. Later with club/cabaret band TNT and Chuck Fowler. Now with Blues Brothers Tribute Show.

Phil Crookes - Guitarist with Vance Arnold and the Avengers, Scott William Combo, Chuck Fowler, Reflections. Now occasionally performs as a solo acoustic musician.

Sylvia Dale - 'Garter girl' and singer with the Mainliners, along with her husband Mick, now retired from music.

Steve Dawson - member of Blue Condition, Sob, Son Of A Bitch and Saxon.

Reg Featherstone - Former van-driver for a host of Sheffield groups in the Sixties including Joe Cocker.

Chuck Fowler - Singer-pianist who modelled himself on Jerry Lee Lewis died in August, 1999. Until the end he was still performing solo, mixing rock-'n'roll with country and Fifties pop, sounding somewhere between Jerry Lee Lewis and Dean Martin!

Gaspin Gus - Rock'n'Country DJ who formed the Sun Sound Club in the Sixties and later worked on Radio Sheffield and in and around the city in the Seventies as a pop DJ with 'Gaspin' Gus's Groovy Gramophone Show'.

Jim Greaves - Singer with the Checkers skiffle group and later went on to become one half of top club comedy duo the Barton Brothers, now retired from showbusiness.

Mick Hallam - One time guitarist and founder member of the Mainliners, now retired from music.

Roger Harrison - Longtime Sheffield drummer with bands like the Cherokees, the Daizies and New Jersey Turnpike and still very active today on the local scene.

Linda Harvey - Former girlfriend of Chris Stainton and Sheffield music fan.

Dave Hawley - Guitarist/ singer and former member of Scott William Combo before forming his own Dave Hawley Combo.

Ray Higgins - Madcap frontman with McCloskey's Apocalypse.

John & Anne Holland - Known as John & Anne Ryder, John was the singer with the Whirlwinds, before the two became cabaret entertainers, now retired.

Mal Hooley - Original bass player with Pete Fender and the Strollers and longtime bass player with Frank White, currently retired from music.

Pete Jackson - Formerly guitarist with Deputies, Lizards and bass player and co-founder of the Hillbilly Cats with whom he still plays.

Bobby Knutt - Originally singer with the Questers and Whirlwinds before becoming the Nut in Pea and Nut and then comedian Bobby Knutt.

Roy Ledger - Guitarist with a number of Sheffield/Rotherham bands such as the Chevrons, Strollers, Thunderbirds, Sheffields and Cruisers. Now working as a solo act on the clubs and in pubs.

Pat Leslie - One of Sheffield's first female rock-'n'rollers with Greycats and still active today.

Keith Linaker - Guitarist with the Citadels/Skeletons, now retired from music business.

Barry Marshall - Formerly lead singer with Dean Marshall and the Deputies, Lizards, Jigsaw & Bitter Suite, now works for entertainment agency.

Davy McHarg - Former drummer with O'Hara's Playboys, now resident club musician.

Dave McPhie - drummer with the Blueberries, DJ, record shop owner, Shape of the Rain's manager.

Stu Moseley - Singer with Stu's Blues, Reflections, Titus Groan and Shape Of The Rain and more recently his own band.

John O'Hara - Ex-leader/singer/saxophonist with O'Hara's Playboys, now solo performer

Graham Oliver - Guitarist with Blue Condition, Sob, Son Of A Bitch and Saxon.

Tony Oxley - drummer with various Sheffield jazz bands before going on to world acclaim.

Glynn Owen - Singer/guitarist formerly worked

with CG Morris and Reaction and Delroy and the Good Good Band and still performing today under name of Billy Tudor.

Frank Peach - Formerly singer with Ricky and the Rebels, now runs his own hairdressing salons.

Tom Rattigan - Former guitarist with The Mainliners, Cadillacs and Originals. Also songwriting partnership with Frank Miles and Chris Stainton as Made In Sheffield.

Nev Reaney - Saxophonist with Sheffield Jazz outfit Savoy Quintet, still active today.

John Riley - Drummer with Debonaires, Frank White Combo, The Cruisers and Hillbilly Cats.

Dave Robinson - Singer/guitarist with the Daizies/Monsters, still performing.

Terry Roe - Formerly performed as Count Lindsay III now retired from music but is involved in various local history projects.

Steve Saxon - Former singer with Cutlers Hall house band and currently fronting local band Beer Money.

Gerry Scanlon - Former bass-player with Falcons, Lizards, Four Corners, Jigsaw & Bitter Suite. Now with Blues Brothers Tribute Show.

Dave Seville - drummer with Pharmeseutrical Earth Movers and McCloskey's Apocalypse.

Kenny Slade - Formerly with Dave Berry, Jimmy Crawford, Joe Cocker and Frank White among others, legendary drummer, legendary drinker!

Chris Spedding - Top session guitarist.

Terry Steeples - Fondly remembered ex-landlord of Sheffield's Black Swan.

Pete Stringfellow - Club organiser, promoter, manager, entrepreneur, self proclaimed sex-God.

Ian 'Tag' Waggett - drummer with Shape of the Rain.

Malc Towndrow - Guitarist with Cadillacs/ Texans/ Knives and Forks and co-songwriter with Chris Stainton and still performing.

Pete Wardlow - Drummer with bands Twin Cities Beat Boys, Wolves and CFS before moving into agency and management work.

Brian Watson - Drummer with various bands including the Reaction, Dave Berry, the Works and Hot Property.

Frank White - Legendary singer guitarist/ songwriter and still going strong and a well-respected musician in both Sheffield and on the national rock and blues circuit.

Mick Wilson - Songwriter/bass-play and violinist with McCloskey's Apocalypse.

Alan Wood - Former guitarist and bass player with numerous bands like Kalendar, Chuck Fowler, Jimmy James and the Vagabonds and now runs his own successful entertainment agency in Sheffield.

Brian Wood - bass player with Shape of the Rain, now with Dave Berry's Cruisers

Trevor Woodcock - Originally one-half of duo Mickey and Johnnie who sang with bands like Jimmy Crawford and the Ravens, Cadillacs, Originals and Time. Now runs his own successful

graphic design company in Sheffield.

Alex Wyatt - Jazz pianist and organiser of Club Basie.

Karen Young - Former singer with Cadillacs and Counterbeats who had a chart hit in 1969, now retired from music business.

For their help, grateful thanks go to:
Keith Firminger, JP Bean (Author of Joe Cocker: With A Little Help From My Friends), Stuart Basford, Simon Robinson, Alan Powell, editor of the Sheffield Telegraph at Sheffield Newspapers, and many others. But extra special thanks to Dave Manvell for his much appreciated help.

Sources & Acknowledgments:
DEFINITIVE A-Z OF SHEFFIELD PUBLIC HOUSES, Michael Liversidge, (Pickard Colour Publishing 1999).
SEVENTEEN WATTS, Mo Foster (Sanctuary Publishing, 1997).
PERFECT POP: THE HUMAN LEAGUE, Peter Nash (Star 1982).
SWINGIN' SHEFFIELD The Saga Of Steel City Pop, Alan Clayson (Sheffield City Museums, 1993).
TOP STARS SPECIAL, Sheffield Star 1960 - 1970.
SUN SOUND SPECIAL, 1966 -1969.
LET IT ROCK Magazine, 1973.
BUDDY IN BRITAIN, John Firminger (Pastime Publications, 1988).
SEE FOR MILES RECORDS
SHEFFIELD STAR, Keith Strong
MORNING TELEGRAPH
SHEFFIELD TELEGRAPH
WITH A LITTLE HELP FROM MY FRIENDS, J P Bean (Omnibus, 1990).
500 MILES TO DARNALL, Terrence Roe (Sheffield City Libraries, 1990).
RADIO HALLAM
RADIO SHEFFIELD
NOW DIG THIS, John Stafford January, 2001
COMPLETE DECCA SINGLES CATALOGUE, Paul M Peletier 1984
STONE ALONE, Bill Wyman (Penguin,1990)
HAMMER OF THE GODS, Stephen Davis (Pan, 1985)
KING OF CLUBS, Peter Stringfellow (Little Brown, 1996)
ARE YOU EXPERIENCED, Noel Redding and Carol Appleby (4th Estate, 1990)
POP FROM THE BEGINNING, Nik Cohen (Weidenfeld and Nicholson, 1969)
PAUL CARRACK interview by Lina Das, Mail On Sunday, August 2000.
RHINOS, WINOS AND LUNATICS: THE LEGEND OF MAN A ROCK'N'ROLL BAND, Deke Leonard (Northdown, 1996)
JOE COCKER: VANCE ARNOLD AND THE AVENGERS, Don Hale (Voiceprint, booklet with CD of 1963 recordings).
WIRE magazine, various issues

NOT LIKE A PROPER RECORD
(Rare forgotten demos and live cuts)
Free CD compilation only available with the book Not Like A Proper Job-

1. BLUE DIAMONDS - It Takes A Worried Man (1957). Possibly one of the earliest recordings by a Sheffield group, the 14-year-olds recorded this version of the popular skiffle/ folk tune at a small studio above Curtis's Records on London Road. (two minutes 19 seconds).

2. DAVE BERRY - I'm Coming Home (1962). Live radio recording of Sheffield's recording star of the Sixties and still popular today, this also features the original and equally popular Cruisers on a song recorded by American rockabilly star Carl Mann. (2.12).

3. PETE FENDER - Whole Lotta Shakin' Goin' On (1962). Local favourite and colourful performer who cut this demo of a driving version of the rock'n'roll classic in London with his band the Strollers. (2.32).

4. THE GREYCATS - Just A Fool In Love (1963). One of Sheffield's earliest groups, this line-up features the powerful vocals of singer Patt Leslie on a demo that was recorded in the same London studios as used by the Rolling Stones. (2.41).

5. THE LIZARDS - My Love Goes On (1964). The group that eventually went on to become Bitter Suite, this track was recorded for the Student Union Rag Week and was written by Cadillacs Chris Stainton and Mal Towndrow. (2.16).

6. SCOTT WILLIAM COMBO - All Night (1964). Scott William was equally home with blues and country and western music. This live demo, recorded at the Polish Club on Ecclesall Road, features him on a bluesy harmonica instrumental also featuring guitarist Dave Hawley on an ahead of its time guitar solo. (2.25).

7. JOE COCKER'S BLUES BAND - Saved (1967). A track taken from the live EP Rag Goes Mad At The Mojo, this track captures both the soul and the humour of an early Joe Cocker performance. Recorded at Peter Stringfellow's popular Mojo Club, Joe is backed by what became the original Grease Band. (4.38).

8. GEORGIA AND THE CHEROKEES - What You Gonna Do? (1967). Georgia was possibly Sheffield's greatest female vocalist - and quite a colourful character. This is a demo of a song written by Sheffield singer/ guitarist Pete Jowell and was later re-recorded and released on Columbia. (2.28).

9. DELROY'S GOOD GOOD BAND - Sweet Soul Music (1967). A cover of Arthur Conley's soul classic, it features Delroy Palmer, one of Sheffield's finest soul exponents who was also a highly visual performer. (2.33).

10. O'HARA'S PLAYBOYS - Harry (1967). Scottish soul showgroup who made Sheffield their home and were tremendously popular at pubs and clubs, as well as having a lengthy recording career. This recording was made onstage at a nightclub in Nottingham. (2.49).

11. MADE IN SHEFFIELD - Right Satisfied (1968). The songwriting team of Frank Miles, Tom Rattigan and Chris Stainton, who collaborated with for Joe Cocker to write his first hit Marjorine, recorded this demo of a song later released on Fontana. (2.23).

12. ROY BARBER - Poor Little Rich Boy (1968). Former guitarist with Dave Berry's Cruisers and the Frank White Band on a demo of a song recorded at Made In Sheffield's Eggbox studio. (3.14).

13. FRANK WHITE'S KOMMOTION - Still As The Night (1968). Track taken from an EP recorded at Unit 19, Sheffield's first independent recording studio. This is a version of a song originally done by Phoenix rockabilly star Sanford Clark. (2.29).

14. THE DAIZIES - Time (1969). Another song written by the Made In Sheffield team, this was recorded in Nottingham by popular Sheffield harmony/ comedy band who were also Dave Berry's backing group for a while. (2.46).

15. THE WOLVES - Touch Of Velvet, Sting Of Brass (1969). Another popular Sheffield club and cabaret band, displaying their vocal techniques on a number heard frequently as one of the theme tunes used by pirate station Radio Caroline. (3.01).

16. BITTER SUITE - New York Mining Disaster (1970). This versatile band went from being a showy soul band to a hard-driving rock unit and throughout their changes continued to be popular as ever. This recording, during their Blood Sweat and Tears phase, is a clever arrangement of the Bee Gees' song. (4.28).

17. JIMMY CRAWFORD - Leave Me Alone (1971). This live recording of the Jimmy Crawford Blend during his cabaret period, sees Sheffield's first chart star displaying his great confidence and showmanship. (3.02).

18. SOB - Albert (1971). The band that later evolved into rock heroes Saxon, this live recording was made in their rehearsal room upstairs at the Albert Hotel opposite Sheffield City Hall. (3.12).

19. SHAPE OF THE RAIN - I Don't Need Nobody (1973). Chesterfield band Shape Of The Rain were remembered for their different musical approach, utilising instruments such as pedal steel guitar and percussion. This demo, written by the band, was recorded in London. (2.56).

20. CHUCK FOWLER - Chantilly Lace (1975). The Killamarsh Killer in full flight on a storming version of the Big Bopper/ Jerry Lee Lewis classic backed by a great band with Pete Wright on drums and Mal Hooley, bass, and featuring Roy Barber on steel guitar. (3.30).

TOTAL RUNNING TIME: 59.07.